Law and the Imagination in Medieval Wales

THE MIDDLE AGES SERIES

Ruth Mazo Karras, Series Editor
Edward Peters, Founding Editor

A complete list of books in the series
is available from the publisher.

Law and the Imagination in Medieval Wales

Robin Chapman Stacey

PENN

UNIVERSITY OF PENNSYLVANIA PRESS

PHILADELPHIA

Published by
University of Pennsylvania Press
Philadelphia, Pennsylvania 19104-4112
www.upenn.edu/pennpress

Printed in the United States of America on acid-free paper
1 3 5 7 9 10 8 6 4 2

Library of Congress Cataloging-in-Publication Data
Names: Stacey, Robin Chapman, author.
Title: Law and the imagination in medieval Wales / Robin Chapman Stacey.
Other titles: Middle Ages series.
Description: 1st edition. | Philadelphia : University of Pennsylvania Press, [2018] | Series: Middle Ages series | Includes bibliographical references and index.
Identifiers: LCCN 2018008684 | ISBN 9780812250510 (hardcover : alk. paper)
Subjects: LCSH: Law—Wales—History. | Law, Medieval. | Law and literature—Wales—History. | Culture and law—Wales—History. | Imagination—Political aspects—Wales—History.
Classification: LCC KD9430 .S73 2018 | DDC 349.42909/02—dc23
LC record available at https://lccn.loc.gov/2018008684

For my much-loved son Will (1988–2012),
and all that he was, and for his remarkable sister
Anna and great love Kimmy, who have found
the courage to embrace the world
in all its sharp beauty and sadness

CONTENTS

INTRODUCTION

Reading Law

Some years ago, I found myself teaching a class on medieval law. This was a seminar intended for history majors, many of whom were planning ultimately to enter the legal profession, and the students were both bright and curious. We were discussing a text I knew well, the Welsh Laws of Court, when a student raised her hand to ask about a passage that appeared to limit the sanctuary (*nawdd*) a female baker was allowed to grant an offender to the distance she could throw her baking scraper.[1] I started in with an explanation of how *nawdd* worked and why persons of greater status would have been able to extend more protection had they been approached. She looked confused, so I dramatized the event for her, imagining a scenario in which a wild-eyed offender with pursuers hot on his heels bursts into a prince's kitchen searching for someone to help him. He rushes over to the baker, who is there scraping flour into a bowl, and hurls himself at her feet begging for sanctuary. Taking pity on him, she throws her baking tool into the air, and he then becomes safe from arrest as long as he stays within the space defined by her throw, remaining amid the pots and pans for several days while the terms for his release are negotiated. The questions that ensued were completely predictable. Even to me, the scene I was imagining sounded perfectly ridiculous. Would a person in trouble really seek out a kitchen servant for protection? What if she had hit someone with her scraper? And above all, why would something so incredibly silly be written into the law? Law was supposed to be *true*, not funny, and this sounded more like a joke or an excerpt from a story than anything else. Didn't medieval people know the difference?

The discussion that followed was lively, though ultimately inconclusive, not least because several students immediately pointed out that exactly the same privileges were extended to the laundress and her washing dolly, which for various reasons struck them as even more absurd than the baker's scraper.[2] Inconclusive or not, silly or not, our dissection of these passages did lead me to two different realizations that in the end have proven crucial for this book. The first was that, on some level, I too had nourished a largely unexamined belief in law's essential "truthfulness," and that, indeed, so deeply ingrained was this point of view that I had developed the habit as a reader of simply skipping over things that did not make sense. I also had been amused by the bakeress and her kind on my initial reading of the text, but that had been many years earlier, and they had over time become virtually invisible to me. My tendency now when I saw something odd or humorous in my sources was to chalk it up to "archaic ritual, no longer understood," and move on. In effect, the sources had become for me more of a mirror than a lens, reflecting back to me what I had expected to see rather than sharpening my view of what was actually there.

The second was that the questions my students had posed about story, humor, and law were ones that I could not answer myself. In this, I suspect, I was and am not alone. Scholarly perceptions of historical legal systems are almost inevitably shaped by our knowledge of the law as it functions in the modern world. Imagination has long been a quality associated much more with fiction and poetry than with law; law is often presumed to be sober and practical in ways that literature is not. It is one thing for historians to know intellectually that law in the past was not always written, did not always derive from legislation or the state, and is often extant in stylized and artificial forms. However, it is quite another to refrain from investing the texts in which it is preserved with many of the same qualities—and with much the same level of trust—that we accord to our own law, giving special credence to their descriptions of social institutions and personalities. For all their warts and wrinkles, legal texts seem still somehow reliable and objective in ways that works of literature or poetry are not. And yet there are many indications that historical ideas about the law differed significantly from our own, and many aspects of the extant texts that cannot be explained within the parameters of our own experience.

In fact, even at the time I was teaching my seminar, the notion of written law as an objective and factual genre had been under fire in both academic and practitioners' circles for more than thirty years. From the mid-1970s on, works heralding a new "intellectual field or movement"[3]—known variously as the law and literature "enterprise,"[4] "subdiscipline,"[5] "project,"[6] or "trope"[7]—had begun to appear in great numbers. The stances taken in these works varied enormously; however, what they shared was the probing of traditional assumptions about the objectivity of law and, particularly, its relationship to overtly fictional genres. Over time, two approaches emerged that still continue by and large today to demarcate the parameters of the field.[8] The first is the study of "law *in* literature"—in other words, the exploration of the manner in which legal conundrums, processes, and personnel are depicted in fiction or poetry. Medievalists have been in the forefront of these studies, in part because of the "peculiar linguistic, rhetorical, and generic affinities between medieval law and literature."[9] Howard Bloch's oft-cited 1977 work on medieval France, for example, heralded the advent of a series of works using fictional sources to give added depth to the (relatively) bloodless proclamations of the lawbooks.[10] William Ian Miller, in his study of Icelandic blood-feud, argued on the basis of the saga literature that what was written in the lawbooks did not always correspond with what would probably have happened in real life.[11] Similarly, Stephen White's examination of the chansons de geste and romances not only revealed a multitude of competing ideas about treason in twelfth- and thirteenth-century France, but underscored the need for scholars to proceed with caution in using them, given the textual relationships often obtaining among the texts themselves.[12] Other scholars since have used tales and poetry to explore still more areas of the law, such as wardship and hunting.[13]

The second, and more controversial, category of law and literature studies is that of "law *as* literature"—the idea that law itself ought to be regarded as a form of literature, and that the legal and literary genres, whatever their differences, would thus profit in being read in similar ways.[14] Behind this argument lies the belief that these two genres share common goals and are similarly grounded in the manipulation of words and images. As Paul Gewirtz observed, both law and literature attempt "to shape reality through language, use distinctive methods and forms to do so, and require interpretation."[15] Peter Goodrich was even more explicit:

> Law is a literature which denies its literary qualities. It is a play of words which asserts an absolute seriousness; it is a genre of rhetoric which represses its moments of invention or of fiction; it is a language which hides its indeterminacy in the justificatory discourse of judgment; it is procedure based upon analogy, metaphor and repetition and yet it lays claim to being a cold or disembodied prose, a science without either poetry or desire; it is a narrative which

> assumes the epic proportions of truth; it is, in short, a speech or writing which forgets the violence of the word and the terror or jurisdiction of the text. Law, conceived as a genre of literature and as a practice of poetics, can thus only be understood through the very act of forgetting, through the denial, the negation or the repression by means of which it institutes its identity, its life, its fictive forms.[16]

To put matters more simply: "Law is an institution that has tended to imagine its language as univocal and authoritative"[17] (implication: even when it is not). Of course, as several scholars then and since have been at pains to point out, the consequences of creatively reinterpreting a modern statute can be considerably more serious than those for misinterpreting a poem.[18] Subsequent studies have broadened the notion of law as literature still further to include the importation of literary critical theoretical movements into the study of law, which also has the potential to dramatically reshape judicial practice;[19] law as or in performance;[20] the cross-fertilization of genres;[21] and the "legal storytelling movement," which examines the manner in which storytelling and narrativity themselves form part of the practice and thus also the study of law.[22]

There are obvious differences among these approaches, and in truth many would question the extent to which these authors are actually engaged in a common enterprise.[23] Kieran Dolin very deliberately speaks of law *and* literature (emphasis his) in order to underscore the very wide range of viewpoints at play here.[24] In general, the law as literature approach has seemed to speak more to modern law and jurisprudence than to the study of the Middle Ages. Dolin, for example, chooses not to include any substantial discussion of medieval texts or scholarship in his otherwise excellent introduction to the field.[25] And Richard Firth Green devotes only two scant pages of his essay for the *Cambridge History of Medieval English Literature* to the study of "legal texts as literature" because, he argues, so many of the extant legal sources do not lend themselves well to such questions. Moving from the study of law as literature to law in literature was for him like progressing "from famine to feast."[26] On the other hand, some medievalists clearly have found the law-as-literature approach to be productive. Noël Menuge, for example, characterizes law texts in his study of wardship as "related fictions with consciously constructed narratives and ideological agendas."[27] For him, the lawbooks ascribed to Glanvill and Bracton might present themselves as objective, but are in truth "highly ideological, polemical and positioned" as sources.[28] Similarly, Kathryn Gravdal in her work on rape decries "the way in which scholars privilege certain documents by assuming they are more objective than literary works." As she points out, "The authority of a legal text, although different from that of a literary text, is nonetheless established through writing."[29]

One very productive set of questions for medievalists has been the nature of the rhetorical and ideological exchange obtaining between the legal and literary genres, especially in England, where the intersection seems to have been unusual in scope.[30] Instead of treating law and literature as more or less stable categories, each borrowing from the other without being significantly altered in the process, scholars who take this approach emphasize the often transformative give-and-take between what they describe as two "parallel forms of discourse."[31] Thus, Emily Steiner and Candace Barrington highlight the significance of the side-by-side development of these two genres for the "re-formation of a vernacular literary tradition in England."[32] William Perry Marvin examines the commonality of tropes used by authors in both genres to respond to the violence and injustice inherent in the law of the hunt—the idea of the king as a father who loves game more than he loves his subjects, for example, or the notion that political tyranny is fed by the bloodlust of the chase.[33] And Gravdal's study of the "writing of rape" in medieval France shows that sometimes this exchange was quite literal, as with the Régistre Criminel de la Justice de Saint-Martin-des-Champs à Paris, which drew directly on the rhetoric and imagery of the French pastourelle.[34] This may have been a literary borrowing, but it dramatically reshaped the judicial experience of women in real life.[35] One could also point to connections among legal and literary practitioners, especially in England. Chaucer was a justice of the peace, Gower a lawyer, and Usk an undersheriff of London. *Piers Plowman* contains court scenes, legal maxims, and even charters that reveal its author to have been someone highly conversant in the law.[36] And the Inns of Court were frequently the site of law-themed theatrical productions into the early modern period.[37]

It is these two latter points—the sense of connection (dialogic, literal, transformative) between the legal and literary genres and, most particularly, the idea that law constitutes a form of literature, a purposeful, "consciously constructed narrative"[38]—that have, in the end, most directly informed my approach in this book. It is certainly the case that one does not want to reify the nature or purposes of either genre. Even within the scholarship surveyed above, there is no one exclusively "legal" genre. Some scholars are focused on Glanvill or Bracton, and others on case narratives; some are using court records and others legal treatises. Gravdal and Menuge are working primarily from ecclesiastical records, while Marvin concerns himself largely with forest law and eyre records. Moreover, law can take many forms, including penitential texts, *gesta*, homilies, and the like, and even when medieval law texts look like law as we understand the term, their larger purposes can vary considerably, from positioning peoples with regard to biblical or Roman ancestors, to evoking Carolingian precedents or advancing the claims of a particular king or dynasty.[39] The popularity of the twelfth-century *Leges Edwardi*, for example, was likely due as much to its "literary" vision of the past and its presentation of the Norman Conquest as an agreed-upon "accommodation between peoples" as to any peculiarly legal virtue.[40] As Patrick Wormald has argued, in medieval England—but surely, we are invited to believe, not merely there—"law books . . . were always primarily about something else."[41]

Moreover, "literature" itself is also a less than transparent term, encompassing as it does a wide variety of narratives, venues, and genres, some of which are quite evidently as political, historical, or spiritual as they are artistic or entertainment-driven in nature. Robin Hood's forest can be approached as a real-life wood. However, it can also be read as a reflection of the ethics of the life posited for its outlaw inhabitants: a realm of perennially soft, warm air and fallow deer that is, in its very essence, natural, free, and uncorrupted by injustice. No matter that in reality the forest of the fourteenth and fifteenth centuries was highly developed, meticulously managed, and even in some places verging on urban.[42] No matter either that life as an outlaw was likely one of hardship and privation rather than good-natured comfort, or that the chief audience for the Robin Hood ballads may have been yeoman fraternities dissatisfied with their exclusion from the governance structures of late medieval towns rather than hardy, ale-swigging foresters.[43] In Robin's greenwood, all is eternally spring, a sign—wistful, nostalgic, or pointedly political—that things might be other than how they currently are.[44] And then there are texts in which the literary and the historical are so admixed that it is impossible even to label them in terms of genre. Such, for example, are the works of Gerald of Wales, in which the physical and political geography of twelfth-century Wales is presented side by side with episodes from early British history, dubious animal lore, and a report on the prognosticative habits of Flemings.[45] Another is the Bible: to my mind, one of the most intriguing and imaginative works in the law and literature field is Mary Douglas's exploration of Leviticus.[46]

Partly as a result of this blurring of genres, scholars addressing the relationship between the legal and literary have often tended either to dissolve the boundaries between categories altogether (as Goodrich arguably does[47]) or, more commonly, to adopt a sort of common sense, "know it when you see it" type of approach. The latter almost always involves appeal to adjectives of a particular type. The Welsh lawbooks, for example, have been characterized as "functional literature," more akin to bardic grammars and medical texts than to poetry,[48] and as a "technical"[49] and "practical" form of prose intended primarily to preserve and explain as opposed to literature, which aims mainly to please and amuse.[50] Even specialists in law and literature studies often speak of the sources in this way.[51] Another constant in the scholarship—one that has had a significant impact on my own thinking—is the use of the term "imaginative" in implied (or directly articulated) opposition to whatever qualities law is perceived to possess. Thus, Firth Green contrasts the "comparatively more formal analysis of the lawyer" with the more allusive technique of the "imaginative writer."[52] Marvin defines his main body of sources as "imaginative literature (and other kinds of texts),"[53] while Wormald explicitly distances himself from the idea that legal texts might constitute "exercises in creative imagination."[54] Even Steiner and Barrington, whose excellent work on the literary aspects of medieval English law has done so much to open our eyes to the dangers of positing a stark divide between these two genres, speak in terms of a contrast between "the legal," on the one hand, and "the imaginative," on the other.[55]

What characterizations like these have in common is an implicit, and often unarticulated, belief that law is utilitarian and pragmatic while literature is free-spirited and inherently less factual. It has proven difficult to find a way to characterize the differences between the legal and the literary that does not end up reifying the very stereotypes one seeks to question. And in truth, the attempt to draw a stark line between the two genres may not, in the end, repay the time invested. Every text has its own singular story, its own ways of speaking the truth. But the questions posed by my students were nonetheless perceptive. Many historical societies did distinguish between legal and literary narratives, even if we ourselves cannot always find the language to describe how that was done. Our difficulties in this respect are yet one more indication of how challenging it can be to step outside our own preconceptions. Embedded in adjectives like "practical" and "imaginative" is a host of modern assumptions that may not be appropriate for our historical texts. It is, for example, entirely possible that the practical authority of a medieval legal source may once have resided at least partly in its literary qualities."[56] What I hope to demonstrate in this study is that, for at least some medieval jurists, legal writing was an intensely imaginative form of literature, one acutely responsive to practical concerns and capable of reproducing them in sophisticated symbolic form.

A Land of Law

The focus for this study is the legal tradition of medieval Wales, a venue that might at first seem an unusual choice for such a work. Wales in the twelfth and thirteenth centuries was a land of scattered farmsteads, drafty (and relatively small by European standards) native castles, and intensely regional loyalties. To a sophisticated European traveler of the period, it would likely have appeared to be an undeveloped and relatively backward land: sparsely populated, politically fragmented, a society the economy of which, while changing, was nonetheless still centered as much on barter and pillage as on coinage and trade. Ecclesiastical reforms that had, from the late eleventh century on, been radically reshaping other churches in Western Europe in matters such as marriage and divorce, had yet to make much headway in Wales. Political loyalties were centered on kindred and region rather than on anything resembling a state, and there was as yet no centralized kingship, although not for want of trying, as Welsh lords and princes, particularly from the northern kingdom of Gwynedd, warred constantly among themselves in order to deepen their rule over those whose loyalties they commanded, and extend their power over those whose loyalties they did not. As historian Rees Davies has remarked, a worldly-wise Englishman looking at Wales in this period would have seen a land the "barbarous rudeness" of which marked a sharp contrast with the "sweet civility" of his own.[57]

And yet Wales was also a society steeped in law, possessed by the late twelfth century of an extensive written legal tradition. This fact might well have surprised our hypothetical traveler considerably, not least because Wales was also in this period so visibly a land of conflict—between armies, traditions, and even identities.[58] The basic political reality of the period was of course the back-and-forth hostility between the Welsh and the English Crown that was ultimately to result in the final conquest of Wales in 1282–83. Whenever the English monarchs were distracted by problems at home or abroad—the disaster at Bouvines, Magna Carta, the baronial revolt against Henry III—the Welsh rallied and thrived. Whenever English monarchs felt secure on the throne—or, as with Edward I, needed a good war somewhere other than on English soil in order to feel secure on the throne—war became inevitable. Even more destructive for most native Welshmen were hostilities among the Welsh themselves. By 1218, Llywelyn ap Iorwerth, prince of the northern kingdom of Gwynedd, had made himself master of native Wales. However, his supremacy was not easily won, and was constantly having to be reasserted, often by military means, and often in a way that generated rebellion and resentment among his Welsh contemporaries. Violence was endemic, and disunity within the principality a serious threat. As anyone conversant with the chronicle evidence will know, no one seriously in the power game was immune to the constant murders, feuds, mutilations, and imprisonments described in their pages.

Equally divisive were external attacks on Welsh custom and tradition. Outside critics were numerous. John Pecham, archbishop of Canterbury from 1279 to 1282, is perhaps the best known; his intemperate remarks make clear that he saw Hywel's laws on inheritance, marriage, and personal insult as ultimately diabolical in origin.[59] But attitudes were changing rapidly even within Wales in the thirteenth century. The Welsh princes, under pressure from outside, began to turn away from native traditions of rule in their efforts to increase their own power internally and stave off encroachments on their territories by Marcher lords and English kings. For many of them, the prospect of bringing Welsh custom into conformity with European norms in order to enhance their own authority was an enticing one—and they were not the only ones. The sources reveal that many lesser Welshmen were also beginning to have recourse frequently to legal procedures from English Common Law. Inheritance practices were particularly susceptible, but other aspects of Welsh law also began to lose ground in the thirteenth century, as individual Welshmen started making use of English Common Law procedures like the inquest and jury in preference to native procedures in situations where it seemed strategically advantageous to do so.[60] To the Welsh lawyers and judges charged with preserving and protecting native law, defections of this kind were of particular concern: not merely their authority, but the integrity of the tradition of which they were the primary custodians, seemed suddenly to be under fire.

The lawbooks have long posed something of a conundrum for historians of medieval Wales. No other prose genre exists in as many redactions and manuscripts; no fewer than forty manuscripts, ranging in date from the thirteenth to the sixteenth century, remain extant today, both in Welsh and in Latin. The textual complications posed by the legal manuscripts are considerable, and the study of these issues can sometimes seem like a field unto itself.[61]

Moreover, even the most accessible of these could fairly be characterized as stylized and anything but legislative in appearance. To scholars approaching the Welsh corpus from a knowledge of other contemporary legal texts, these laws can seem unusually discursive and old-fashioned. To historians looking to flesh out the brief narratives offered them by the chronicle sources, they often appear so static and idealized as to be unusable. Indeed, despite the centrality of the legal evidence to nineteenth- and early twentieth-century histories of medieval Wales, the lawbooks nowadays are often marginalized by historians in favor of sources better grounded in "reality." At the very least, the question of the extent to which the lawbooks actually do or do not reflect reality—or even which period of reality they might reflect, if any—is now regarded as a topic for exploration rather than something to be taken for granted.[62] As the late professor Sir Rees Davies remarked, the "chronological uncertainty" of the legal texts is "the despair of the historian." The lawbooks are thus, in his view, "best left to the ingenuity of linguistic experts, social anthropologists and antiquarian-minded lawyers. . . . We will never square our conventional historical evidence completely with the legal and textual studies of the law-texts, for they are based on different *genres* of material and often relate to different periods."[63] Davies concludes that such uncertainties ought not to prevent scholars from utilizing both types of sources whenever possible (although he himself showed a marked preference for nonlawbook sources in his own work).

Another challenge posed by these sources is the manner in which they should be read. Early approaches to the Welsh lawbooks tended to use them either as authoritative sources for the early history of Wales, or as potential sources of information on archaic Celtic or even Indo-European customs and institutions. Implicit in the latter approach were the basic premises of Indo-European historical linguistics, by which the descent of a variety of medieval and modern languages can be traced back to a single distant and no-longer-extant mother tongue, Proto-Indo-European. By comparing written and oral data pertaining to historical and modern Indo-European languages, scholars identified rules of linguistic change that allowed them to reconstruct aspects of these languages in their earliest stages. This comparative methodology originated with specific respect to language; soon, however, it began to be applied outside the linguistic sphere to mythology, religion, institutions, and, almost inevitably, to law.[64] Seen from this perspective, the medieval Celtic lawbooks took on special importance. Not only were the professional poets and jurists to whom the laws were ascribed widely believed at the time to be the direct descendants of the ancient Gaulish druids described by Caesar, but portions of the Irish corpus at least seemed also to be written in an archaic form of the language or, in some cases, even in verse.

Priority in such studies has traditionally been given to the early Irish sources rather than to those extant from Wales. The majority of Irish legal texts can be linguistically dated to between the seventh and ninth centuries CE—in other words, to a period significantly earlier than most of the Welsh legal sources—and two of them are found in an early twelfth-century manuscript (the earliest Welsh lawbook manuscripts date to the thirteenth century).[65] However, both traditions seemed consciously to preserve passages pertaining to outmoded or no-longer-contemporary practices. The tendency to retain archaisms, coupled with the many institutional and terminological similarities between the Welsh and significantly earlier Irish sources, suggested to scholars like Rudolf Thurneysen and Daniel Binchy that the lawbooks might offer insight into Common Celtic, and possibly even into Indo-European institutions. Among the practices they singled out as potentially archaic were the importance of honor and face; the shape of the kindred; the designation of the royal heir; practices like distraint, suretyship, witnessing, and the maintenance by children of their aged parents; and the nature and authorship of the lawbooks themselves.[66] Subsequent historians took these techniques of comparative history even further, using Irish law as something of a baseline so as to explore the evolution and development of Welsh custom over time into the thirteenth century and beyond.[67] More recently, however, the comparative method has fallen somewhat out of favor among historians, reflecting, at least in part, concerns that have been voiced of late about the helpfulness of the term "Celtic" in anything other than a linguistic context.[68] Not everyone is happy with the focus on the archaic that the comparative method seems to encourage, nor are scholars uniformly comfortable with the idea of using texts from the eighth century to explicate twelfth- and thirteenth-century materials. As Patrick Sims-Williams has argued, the "linguistic family-tree" is only one of the possible models for the relationships among the various Celtic traditions.[69]

Consequently, most modern studies of the Welsh lawbooks center now less on Common Celtic institutions and comparisons with Irish law than on the nature of the Welsh sources themselves and the context within which they should be read and interpreted. The texts of all the main Welsh lawbook versions trace the beginnings of written law in Wales to a law-making council summoned and presided over by the tenth-century king Hywel Dda.[70] Some historians accept this attribution as quite possibly correct and argue that the lawbooks as we have them today may go back to a now-lost text of the tenth century.[71] Others regard the story of Hywel's involvement as a myth intended to reassert native identity in the face of the growth of English law within the historical borders of Wales in the century and a half before the end of native independence. For the latter, the lawbooks are less a reflection of the early Middle Ages than the Welsh reflex of the general resurgence in law taking place in Western Europe as a whole in the twelfth and thirteenth centuries.[72] At stake in this debate is not just the specific issue of Hywel, but our general understanding of the nature of the extant texts and the extent to which the lawbooks can be drawn on as evidence for early Welsh history.[73] There are good arguments on both sides, and it is unlikely that the question of Hywel's contribution will be definitively resolved anytime soon.

What all scholars do agree on, however, regardless of their views on Hywel, is that there are extant several different versions (also called redactions or traditions)[74] of the lawbook customarily attributed to him, each represented by a number of different manuscripts. (There are other legal texts as well dating to the thirteenth century, such as the *Llyfr y Damweiniau*, "Book of Eventualities," and the *Llyfr Cynghawsedd*, "Book of Pleadings," but the focus in this book, as in most scholarship on Welsh law to date,[75] will be on the principal lawbook versions.) It would be difficult to summarize the nature and divergence of these versions more clearly and succinctly than T. M. Charles-Edwards has done in his recent (2013) discussion:

> The most fundamental division in the textual history of the laws is between one tradition associated with Gwynedd and another associated with Deheubarth. The former is represented by *Llyfr Iorwerth*, attributed to Iorwerth ap Madog ap Rhawd, and there is good reason to think, first, that Iorwerth really was the author of the text in the form we have it, and, secondly, that he himself belonged to a kindred of lawyers and poets in Arfon and that his floruit belongs to the first half of the thirteenth century. The second tradition is represented by several distinct textual families, by *Llyfr Cyfnerth*, the Latin redactions of Welsh law, and by a Welsh offshoot of the Latin tradition, *Llyfr Blegywryd*. (In the cases of *Llyfr Cyfnerth* and *Llyfr Blegywryd* the ascriptions to named persons are found within the texts but have little or no authority, unlike the ascription of the principal northern lawbook to Iorwerth ap Madog: never the less they remain useful titles.)[76]

Scholars generally use the abbreviations Ior, Cyfn, Bleg, and Lat A, B, C, D, and E as shorthand for these various traditions, although they do so realizing that such abbreviations cannot entirely capture the complexity of the situation.[77] Additionally, individual manuscripts of these traditions are usually known by the sigla given them by Aneurin Owen in his 1841 edition of the *Ancient Laws and Institutes of Wales*.[78] Typically, in scholarly discussions, these sigla will be joined to the standard abbreviation for the tradition in question: thus Ior A refers to the National Library of Wales Peniarth MS 29 version of the Iorwerth text, while Cyfn U refers to the National Library of Wales Peniarth MS 37 version of Cyfnerth.[79]

Unfortunately, the textual and geographical difficulties involved in assessing these manuscripts and traditions are even more challenging than the summary above might indicate. Redactors of manuscripts associated with one tradition had little hesitation in borrowing from manuscripts of another; moreover, individual tractates within the legal tradition could circulate independently, so the textual tradition of one tractate might not always be the same as that of its fellows. For example, Daniel Huws (here, following Charles-Edwards) suggests that what we are seeing in the court tractate from Lat B is a substratum of elements deriving from southwest Wales in a manuscript that itself derived from Gwynedd.[80] Lat C is also associated with the north (Gwynedd) rather than the south (Deheubarth) as might be expected for a Latin redaction text;[81] similarly, both MSS X and Z of Cyfn (British Library Cotton Cleopatra B v and National Library of Wales Peniarth 259B respectively) are northern in their orthography and vocabulary.[82] MS Y (National Library of Wales 20143A) is for much of its length a Cyfn version manuscript, but also contains material pertaining to the Bleg tradition.[83] And *Llyfr Blegywryd* itself is regarded largely as a translation of Lat D, although Paul Russell's recent study of the Three Columns tractate has complicated this considerably, at least for this tractate.[84] In short, paradoxes abound: southern redactions are preserved in northern manuscripts, northern redactions are preserved in southern manuscripts, and some manuscript versions defy easy categorization.[85] In fact, so complex are the interrelations between tractates, traditions, and individual passages that one possibility for manuscripts that are unique or unusually intricate is to edit and discuss them individually, as Dafydd Jenkins did with *Llyfr Colan* (in essence a substantially revised version of Ior) and Sara Elin Roberts has recently done with Cyfn Z.[86]

If it is difficult to pin the lawbooks down to one particular region or locale in Wales, then it is even more difficult to localize their content and composition to a particular time and set of circumstances. This is partly because the versions themselves were constantly being revised over time, some more than others (e.g., Cyfn, which is the loosest of the principal versions, more than Ior). Again, paradox is the byword here. Scholars are generally agreed that Cyfn is probably the earliest of the extant versions in terms of when it was initially composed, likely during the reign of Rhys ap Gruffudd of Deheubarth, who died in 1197. However, Cyfn is also the latest in terms of the manuscripts in which it is preserved: none of the Cyfn manuscripts are earlier than the fourteenth century.[87] As just mentioned, Ior dates to the reign of Llywelyn ap Iorwerth, who died in 1240. However, its oldest manuscripts date to the thirteenth century and are therefore earlier than those of Cyfn; moreover, the phrasing of some of its constituent passages seems to reflect a legal situation older than and separate from that reflected in Cyfn.[88] The earliest of the Ior manuscripts is likely Ior C;[89] the earliest of the Latin redactions is Lat C, which is probably also the earliest of all the northern Welsh versions (Latin and vernacular), dating as it does to between 1226 and 1240.[90] Most of the Bleg manuscripts date to the late Middle Ages, and Charles-Edwards has shown that there is a marked shift over time away from Ior toward Cyfn and Bleg and even, within the Ior manuscripts themselves, away from Gwynedd and toward Deheubarth as a place of origin. In the thirteenth century, Ior was probably the most procedurally sophisticated of the versions—not surprisingly, as Gwynedd seems to have been widely acknowledged as the most important center for jurisprudence and legal study in Wales.[91] However, as Charles-Edwards remarks, it was the south, "the old Deheubarth," that "was the last home of Welsh law."[92]

Despite the fact that none of the versions as they exist today are likely to have been compiled before the twelfth century, it is generally agreed—even by those who are skeptical about the ascription to Hywel—that some sort of Model Lawbook underlies our extant texts that probably predates the composition of Cyfn in the late twelfth century.[93] The similarities among the extant principal redactions are too significant and numerous to be explained in any other way. What scholars do not agree on, however, is the probable nature and date of this Model Lawbook. It is certain that some of the individual passages found in the texts as we have them today go back to the early Middle Ages. These include the short passage on the "Seven Bishop-Houses of Dyfed"; excerpts from an early (possibly sixth- or seventh-century) Continental text called the *Excerpta de libris Romanorum et Francorum*; and provisions from an early eighth-century collection of Irish canons, the *Collectio Canonum Hiber-*

nensis.[94] Likely very old as well is the marriage list known as the *Nau Kynywedi Teithiauc*, which Charles-Edwards has argued corresponds to lists in early Hindu sources.[95] Some of the terms for officers discussed in the court tractate represent borrowings from early English law: the *edling*, "heir," from Old English *aetheling*,[96] and the *distain*, "steward," from Old English *disc-ðegn*, "dish-thane."[97] And there are institutions like *dadannudd*, a highly performative method of claiming land, and *briduw*, a form of suretyship in which God was taken as a surety, that are undoubtedly also ancient, although that does not, of course, mean that the sources in which they are described are necessarily pre-Norman in their extant written form.[98]

The existence of these early passages in the extant redactions makes clear that the lawbooks as we have them today do not, as Huw Pryce has noted, "mark the beginning of written law in Wales."[99] However, this fact does not in itself resolve the issue of the dating of the Model Lawbook, not least because none of the above passages can be shown to have actually been included in the Model Lawbook—all of them seem to have been added to the redactions in which they are found at a later date.[100] Charles-Edwards is the most eloquent proponent of the idea that the Model Lawbook derives from the pre-Norman period. Its early origin, he says, is demonstrated not only by the consistent ascription, across all versions, to Hywel, but by the similarity between some of the practices detailed in it to those of early Irish law—similarities which indicate "that the surviving content of that part of the law is the outcome of a long development very probably older than the tenth century."[101] For example, the section on the sharing of the patrimony among male heirs gives one a sense not only of what the original law might have been, but of how much development has occurred in the meantime and thus how remote in time the Model Lawbook and, by extension, some of the practices detailed in it might be.[102] In fact, he suggests, comparing extant versions is a good way to determine what sections might ultimately derive from the Model Lawbook: "if a particular 'tractate' is found both in *Llyfr Iorwerth* and in the southern lawbooks it passes the first test for supposing that an earlier form of the text may go back to a pre-Norman lawbook that might possibly be the outcome of Hywel's reform."[103] Among the tractates he singles out as passing this test (or at least likely to possess a pre-Norman core) are the Prologue, the Laws of Court, The Three Columns of Law, the Nine-Tongued Ones, the *dadannudd* section of the tractate on land, and the tractates on suretyship and women.[104]

Not everyone would agree, however, that the Model Lawbook ought to be dated so early. Pryce raises the possibility of an early twelfth-century origin, situating its composition within the context of changes taking place in that period in native patterns of rule.[105] I have argued similarly that legal professionals may not have even emerged as a specialized intellectual class from within the broader body of custodians of native learning until the twelfth century, and then in the context of and concomitant with the composition and dissemination of the lawbooks.[106] Much depends on how we imagine these early works, and on what we imagine this Model Lawbook as modeling. For even if Hywel had presided over the compiling of a written lawbook, there is no guarantee that it and the Model Lawbook were one and the same. Many early medieval kings initiated lawbooks, and it only stands to reason that Hywel might wish to imitate contemporaneous English example, as has been suggested by Charles-Edwards among others.[107] However, had Hywel issued a book in imitation of what he would have seen around him—the laws of Alfred, Edmund, or Aethelstan, for example, or the capitularies of the late Carolingian kings—it seems unlikely that that work would have looked like the texts as we have them today.[108] The nature, content, and wording of the extant Welsh lawbooks are just too different from what we see in their English and European predecessors for the latter to have served as obvious models. Moreover, to say that the structure of a given tractate or lawbook version is old, possibly even pre-Norman, is not necessarily to say that its contents as extant are equally venerable. To take just one example: the fact that the extant suretyship tractates of Ior and Cyfn share a structural pattern that seems to go back to a common source, and that the type of suretyship they describe closely coincides in nature and terminology with what is known about eighth-century Irish suretyship practices, does not prove that either reproduces some or all of the actual content of their common source or even that the source originally took lawbook form.[109] Indeed, the Cyfn manuscripts vary so widely in their order and basic content that even the notion of a common structural core may be more complicated than it otherwise appears.[110]

Happily, it is not necessary to decide all of these complicated issues here. What matters most for the present work is not the nature and date of the Model Lawbook but, rather, the nature and function of the lawbook redactions as they are extant today. Even if one were to concede both the matter of Hywel's involvement and the idea that behind the existing versions (perhaps at several degrees of removal) lies a now-lost tenth-century original, questions would still remain about why lawbooks patterned in this way were still being produced, revised, and reworked in such great numbers in the high and late Middle Ages.[111] The fact that a given lawbook has a long history does not in itself guarantee that someone centuries later would choose to reproduce or revise it; nor does it tell us what that latter-day scribe or redactor's aspirations might be for that lawbook in his own milieu. Texts can be reused and reworked in support of objectives quite different from those that originally inspired them. Pryce terms the late twelfth century onward "as an important turning-point in Welsh legal writing,"[112] and attributes the flowering of native law in this period to contemporary concerns among the *uchelwyr* (members of the free landholding class) about changes in native practices of kingship.[113] As he points out, native princes, desirous of consolidating their power both within native Wales and outside, were stretching the traditional boundaries of rule to accomplish their goals. Faced with these threats to the legal tradition of which they were the acknowledged guardians, the authors of the lawbooks—themselves likely *uchelwyr*—looked for ways to reaffirm both the authority of their tradition and the prerogatives they had historically enjoyed. The lawbooks they produced were intended to remind innovating rulers of what governing practices had traditionally looked like.[114] One might also point out that lawbooks would have been needed in the Welsh Marches beyond the thirteenth century, and that this too might have been an additional venue for production.[115]

Such ideas bring Welsh traditions of legal writing much more closely into line with those of England and the Continent than is sometimes emphasized.[116] The revival of Roman law in the late eleventh century and the consequent spread of legal thinking all across Europe had a profound impact on political life at every level. The parameters of European rulership generally were very much in flux, and Wales was not the only place where law functioned to define the limits of princely power or recall errant kings to "traditional" norms.[117] Rulers embraced written statements of traditional law when it served their interests to do so, but they were perfectly capable of ignoring or repudiating them outright when they did not. The existence of a lawbook, particularly one ascribed to an authoritative ruler of the past, could function as a visible reminder of the long historical tradition within which those who exercised power claimed to do so. Moreover, implicit in the lawbook genre, especially in texts with claims to have originated in some variety of popular (albeit noble) assembly, was an emphasis on the collaborative and consultative aspects of rule, a hotly contested topic not only in Wales but across Europe as a whole in this era.[118] In Wales, the height of the lawbook tradition was ultimately to correspond with the final century of native independence, but the authors of these texts could not have known this. For them, as for many of their European counterparts, this deliberate evocation of a (putatively) less autocratic past was likely intended more as a summons to a more prosperous and equitable future than a wistful expression of yearning for bygone days.

Equally critical, of course, was the larger cultural and political context within which the production of written law was occurring. English kings and lords were constantly intruding into Welsh political affairs in the twelfth and thirteenth centuries, if they were not actually on the move within Welsh borders, and law seems to have functioned as one of the primary means by which native identity could be reasserted in the face of such ongoing threats to Welsh sovereignty.[119] Nor did legal writing stand alone in this respect. If the lawbooks were evidence of an honored legal tradition stretching back into the distant past (or at least such was the claim implicit in the association with Hywel), they were also part and parcel of an assertive literary culture comprising works in a variety of genres. In many ways, the lawbooks are perhaps most profitably seen against the larger backdrop of the literary renaissance taking place in Wales in this period, an era of intense cultural production that would ultimately encompass saints' lives, triad collections, prose tales, poetry, and historical works.[120] This renaissance was, like most, grounded in tradition, but the impetus behind it belonged very much to the present. As Pryce notes, the fact that "the content of the Welsh texts was archaic in some respects does not weaken the case for their having been intended as contemporary statements of native law in the late twelfth and thirteenth centuries, indeed . . . it was precisely their emphasis on the archaic and traditional which made them so relevant at the time of redaction."[121]

The Legal and the Literary in Medieval Wales

One of the most visible causes and consequences of the proliferation of law as an intellectual discipline and object of study across medieval Europe was the development of a professional legal class—in most regions, for the first time since Late Antiquity. James Brundage and Paul Brand have traced the development of the legal profession in various European venues, secular and ecclesiastical, beginning in the twelfth century with what Brundage calls "pre-professional lawyers" and evolving to a more fully professionalized status from the 1230s on.[122] However, Ireland and Wales are generally viewed as exceptions in this regard. Professional jurists clearly existed in Ireland in the seventh and eighth centuries if not before.[123] Their most visible legacy was the enormous corpus of written law that helps make Ireland the locus of the most extensive vernacular tradition extant from anywhere in Western Europe. Similarly, the traditional biography of the Welsh *ynad*, "judge," identifies him as a figure of the early Middle Ages.[124] I have suggested elsewhere that the emergence of a specialized judicial class might also have occurred later than this in Wales, possibly concomitant with the spread of the written lawbooks themselves.[125] However, judges and jurists are not necessarily the same things, and the more usual scholarly understanding is still that specialists in law existed earlier than in most other European realms in Wales as they did in Ireland.

In any case, there can certainly be no doubt of the increasing professionalization and curial nature of law in the thirteenth century. Cases that might once have been performative affairs resolved in the presence of members of the community, moved into assemblies or courts presided over by lords.[126] In some of the so-called "Anomalous Laws," for example—legal texts like the *Llyfr y Damweiniau*, "Book of Eventualities," and the *Llyfr Cynghawsedd*, "Book of Pleadings," that exist alongside the lawbook tradition attributed to Hywel[127]—one can see clear parallels between Welsh pleading procedures and those in English sources of about the same (or even later) date.[128] There are other aspects also of the growing curialization of justice visible in these texts,[129] including signs of borrowing back and forth among the Welsh and English and other European traditions,[130] and the enhancing of what appear to be in origin early medieval legal procedures with the trappings of a more lord-centered age. Even the lawbooks attributed to Hywel show evidence of such changes, like the pleading procedure outlined in the Ior tractates on suretyship and land claims,[131] and the reimagining of the archaic and highly performative ritual of *dadannudd* as a formal plea in court.[132] Legal personalities closely associated with the precurial age are visibly integrated into an increasingly curialized world—the *mach*, or enforcing surety, for example, who is actually termed a "living pledge" (or even "hostage") in one passage.[133]

Despite this increasing emphasis on the curial, however, the Welsh lawbooks might still not look like law to those familiar with contemporary legislation from the developed world. Indeed, there is nothing legislative about them—scholars largely agree that they were private compositions, instructional texts for jurists who, while professional in the sense of belonging to recognized legal families and acting within the community as jurists and judges, nonetheless did not as a rule work for state or king.[134] As Charles-Edwards has observed, the Welsh texts are clearly more "royalist" in character than the early Irish lawbooks are, not least in their asserted connection with Hywel.[135] However, they were not commissioned by kings, nor do they consist of royal decrees. Rather, these are books authored by experts in the law who themselves could fill a variety of roles depending on the circumstances—educating, advising, and arbitrating (in some cases) or judging (in others) disputes brought to them by litigants. The books they created appear to have been correspondingly broad in nature and focus, functioning both as textbooks and as histories: the writings from which budding lawyers were instructed in the fundamentals of a native legal tradition that claimed to derive from ancient days. Not surprisingly, many of them display distinctly literary qualities. Like the *De legibus et consuetudinibus Angliae* (traditionally attributed to Bracton)[136] and Eike von Repgow's *Sachsenspiegel* (1235),[137] texts with which the most sophisticated of the Welsh redactions, *Llyfr Iorwerth* (c. 1230), is roughly contemporary, there are lengthy passages of description side by side with prescriptive clauses forbidding particular behaviors. Similarly, one can see in the Welsh laws the influence of other narrative forms such as poetry, historical biography, and myth, just as one sees it in contemporary European lawbooks. Indeed, the prologues have a visibly literary quality to them. Lat B's prologue quotes Horace twice, once the *Epistles* and once the *Satires*,[138] and all prologues follow the well-known European literary trope of emendation and reform.[139]

It is this latter intersection between the legal and the literary that is of particular interest in the present work. That there existed close links between these two in Wales cannot seriously be doubted. Jurists and poets often hailed from the same families, and some persons even functioned in both roles, making an overlap in content and modes of expression nearly inevitable. One of the most moving of medieval poems, an elegy for Llywelyn ap Gruffudd, the last prince of independent Wales, killed in 1282, was penned by Gruffudd ab yr Ynad Coch, "Gruffudd, son of the Red Judge."[140] Gruffudd himself may have been a third cousin to Iorwerth ap Madog, perhaps the most famous of Welsh jurists and the person to whom the principal northern lawbook *Llyfr Iorwerth* has plausibly been ascribed.[141] Einion ap Gwalchmai practiced both poetry and law, while Rhydderch ab Ieuan Llwyd, for whom the prose tale collection *Llyfr Gwyn Rhydderch* was likely written, was an expert in native law and deputy-justiciar under the Crown.[142] Law was considered part of the corpus of traditional learning known as *cyfarwyddyd*, a term encompassing a wide variety of types of cultural learning, from history to genealogies, to poetry and prose tales.[143] Persons called *cimarguitheit* (singular *cyfarwydd*), "experts in *cyfarwyddyd*, traditional learning," appear as experts on local legal dues and renders in Chad 3 of the late ninth century.[144] We do not know for certain what import *cimarguitheit* has in this context; Morfydd Owen and Dafydd Jenkins argue that the word is likely being used here in a general sense to refer to persons who are knowledgeable about local conditions rather than to legal experts per se, and that is certainly possible.[145] However, it is at least suggestive that we find here the term for traditional learning associated with persons acting in a legal capacity. If law did develop originally as an independent discipline with a textual corpus and professionals out of this larger body of traditional cultural learning (much as it may have done in Ireland), then a significant degree of overlap would be expected.[146]

As with law and literature studies elsewhere, the links between the legal and literary in Wales have largely been studied in two principal ways. Most common in the scholarship to date has been a focus on law *in* literature: in other words, the manner in which law and legal knowledge figure in contemporary (or near-contemporary) Welsh poetry and prose. As is well known, several episodes in the four medieval stories known collectively as the Four Branches of the Mabinogi (Pedair Cainc y Mabinogi, usually referred to as either the Mabinogi or the Four Branches) display an intricate knowledge of Welsh law, from the hunting scene in *Pwyll Pendeuic Dyuet* with which the Mabinogi begins,[147] to the gold-and-silver regalia of *Branwen uerch Lyr*,[148] to the footholder of *Math uab Mathonwy*.[149] Most famous is the story of the thief disguised as a mouse and captured by Manawydan in *Manawydan uab Llyr*. As Charles-Edwards points out, not only was Manawydan completely within his rights under Welsh law to hang the thief as he threatened to do, it was precisely because he was familiar with these rights that he was able to stave off disaster and avert the threatened vengeance of Llwyd uab Cil Coed.[150] There are other parallels as well. Many of the offices mentioned in the lawbooks are also mentioned in the prose tales,[151] and the social conventions regarding etiquette that feature so prominently in prose tales like *Culhwch ac Olwen*, *Chwedyl Gereint vab Erbin*, and *Historia Peredur* can often best be explained with reference to passages in the laws.[152] Indeed, with respect to certain subjects such as, for example, the hunting scene in *Pwyll*, one may even need both types of text to make sense of what is going on.[153] Sometimes legal terms or concepts are better explained in the nonlawbook literary sources than in the laws themselves.[154]

Serious scholarship on the relationship between the legal and literary genres began with T. P. Ellis's 1928 study of legal terms and practices in the body of prose tales known collectively as the Mabinogion.[155] Ellis began with the Laws of Court, focusing in depth on the king and the various officers of his household. This analysis led him next to consider a variety of social practices and institutions: homage, military organization, the organization of territories, social class, dues and renders, criminal law, contracts and exchanges, marriage and the greater "law of persons," succession and inheritance, fosterage, and judicial procedure. In each case, his methodology remained the same—the gathering together of legal references from the tales and the laws followed by brief historical speculations about the workings of the office or practice in question. The primary value of his work today lies in its encyclopedic nature and value as a reference tool rather than its specific analytical insights. However, Ellis established in his study a scholarly framework that would be followed to some degree by almost everyone who wrote after him. The paradigm he established of placing legal and literary side by side, and of using one body of sources to flesh out the other when details might otherwise be lacking, continues to shape scholarship on both genres to this day. Indeed, it would be difficult to find a study of the dating, nature, or purpose of the Mabinogi that did not in some way make appeal to the laws, or a study of certain topics in the laws such as hunting or theft that did not reference the literature.[156]

The extent of the parallels between legal and literary led Ellis to also raise in his work the issue of authorship, which continues to be a focus for scholars today. At this point, most would agree that either the Mabinogi author was a lawyer himself, or that legal knowledge was so widely disseminated in the culture that both author and audience must be considered, in a sense, to be experts in the field.[157] Glenys Goetinck, in her study of the Four Branches, remarked on the surprising extent of the legal knowledge displayed by the author,[158] while Michael Cichon argued further that "the redactor of the tales actually had specific laws in mind when he set these tales down."[159] Robert Humphries concluded that, "given the close ties between law and literature, the author, or redactor of the *Mabinogi* could easily have come from a legal or a clerical background, familiar with the *cyfarwyddyd* . . . not only well versed in the laws but also a keen observer of the social and political order, quite possibly attached to a royal court."[160] Meinir Elin Harris was even more specific. Noting that there are more legal parallels in the Mabinogi than in other contemporary prose tales and that the testimony of each type of narrative closely parallels the other,[161] she concluded that it may have been Iorwerth ap Madog himself, or one of his poeticolegal family members, who was responsible for the Mabinogi as we have it today. Indeed, she suggested, the Mabinogi might even in this sense be read as an *enghraifft chwedlonol o'r gyfraith*, "a story version of the law,"[162] with episodes acting as legal precedents or leading cases, somewhat as *cwynion*, "plaints," did in the late medieval period.[163]

Agreement was equally uniform on another important point, albeit one more often quietly presumed than directly articulated. For all these scholars, law functioned as a fixed reference point vis-à-vis the prose tales rather than the other way around. That is to say, tale authors were imagined as shaping their stories around the laws as extant in the lawbooks—laws they were presumed to know by virtue of being lawyers themselves or being closely related to a lawyer—rather than lawbook authors shaping their material around the stories. This led Harris to endorse Ellis's conviction regarding the "genuine nature of the Welsh codal survivals"; where the two traditions disagree, such as in the gender of the footholder, she hypothesized that either the Mabinogi author had gotten it wrong, was reflecting the custom of the (presumed to be later) society in which he lived, or had adapted the legal material to his own purposes.[164] Humphries similarly imagined the author of the Mabinogi selecting "the legal material carefully to give the tales a realistic social setting."[165] Indeed, he argued further, the tales provide a "critical commentary" on the system of justice described in the laws: "the author of the *Mabinogi*," he suggested, "recognise[d] the practical limitations of *Cyfraith Hywel*"[166] and responded to them accordingly. Cichon's 2009 monograph on violence and vengeance spoke of scenes from *Peredur* "being derived almost verbatim from the Laws of Court," and referred to the author's "deliberate framing of the narrative material to conform to Welsh law" as "height[ening] the import of the offence" for both author and audience.[167] Cichon acknowledged elsewhere the possibility of the borrowing going the other way, but he was clearly bothered by the "symbolic or mythic sensitivity on the part of the jurist" that such an exchange would seem to presume.[168] Harris similarly dismissed the idea that the laws might have drawn on the literary tradition.[169]

The parallels to which these scholars point are unquestionably real. However, their reluctance to accept that the laws might have borrowed from the tales or, indeed, as seems most likely, that both the legal and literary genres might have been part of a common and constantly evolving narrative tradition[170] is rooted, I would suggest, on unspoken and largely unexamined presumptions about the nature of law. As I have argued earlier, these are presumptions that derive from our own experience with contemporary legal statutes that do not reflect what is known either about medieval law or about the nature of the medieval Welsh narrative tradition, in which the sharing back and forth of ideas, images, genres, and pseudohistorical "realities" was demonstrably quite common. Paul Russell has shown this with respect to the regalia in *Branwen*;[171] other examples might include the idea of the sovereignty of the isle of Britain, which appears in a wide variety of genres, legal and literary,[172] and the story of Dyfnwal Moelmud, who figures in the laws, the genealogies, and Geoffrey of Monmouth's *Historia Regum Britanniae*.[173] Similarly with respect to the Laws of Court: whereas Cichon spoke of the tales drawing directly from the actual legal tractate of this name, Manon Phillips's more nuanced picture imagined the relationship more in terms of "cross-referencing," a "common milieu," and "drawing on the same traditions."[174] A similar interchange between legal and literary traditions is envisaged in the fifteenth-century verse *Canu i Swyddogion Llys y Brenin*,[175] and still other examples will emerge in the course of this study.

That both law and literature might be part of a common narrative tradition should not surprise us, given what we know about the connections between legal and literary families and individuals in medieval Wales. And, of course, not all elements are shared equally across genres and traditions. As far as we know, for example, the story of Hywel himself as lawgiver is found only in the legal sources and works deriving from them.[176] However, this does not mean that *Cyfraith Hywel* ought to be treated as an immutable monolith against which to measure elements of a tale tradition assumed in its very nature to differ from law in being vital, imaginative, and ever changing. Indeed, on some level, we have long been aware of this. The idea that Welsh law constituted a form of political literature (law *as* literature) has in fact been current in legal scholarship for some years now. It would be difficult to improve on Huw Pryce's formulation of this relationship, which is worth quoting at length:

> The lawbooks can themselves be seen as works of literature conveying their own perceptions of the past as well as the present, and thus defy categorization as purely pragmatic texts in implied contrast to literary compositions such as prose tales. While the law-texts undeniably form a distinctive genre of writing, a point underscored by their status as the sole or principal text in nearly all the extant medieval manuscripts, their contents are not reducible simply to what we could consider "law." In common with other medieval compilations of customary law, they also contain traditional lore and pseudo-history. . . . Above all, the Welsh law-texts resemble other

> coutumiers in presenting what Alan Harding has called "mirrors of society," in the Welsh case idealized pictures of a unitary Wales, under a single ruler and a single law, encapsulated in the "myth of political unification" already achieved in the time of Hywel Dda. In other words, irrespective of their purpose as accounts of native law, the lawbooks make powerful ideological statements about Welsh identity, projecting an image of a purely Welsh Wales (the Marcher lordships never come into the picture), as well as about Welsh kings, whose status is emphasized by the precedence given to the section on the royal court.[177]

David Stephenson has similarly remarked on the admixing of legal, literary, and historical in the legal sources, questioning whether the "Laws of Court" should be regarded as reflecting more the past reality of Wales or, rather, its twelfth- and thirteenth-century ideal.[178] Morfydd Owen hailed the lawyers as "propagandists" in the "struggle for Welsh independence," connecting the stories in the lawbooks to the aggrandizing ambitions of the princes."[179] I have also written in a similar vein.[180] In other words, the idea of the Welsh lawbooks as complex sources that push against modern boundaries of genre rather than sitting neatly enclosed within them is one with which many scholars now find themselves quite comfortable.

It is precisely such observations that this book both picks up from and seeks to extend. Law was an important form of political literature in medieval Wales—indeed, along with the narrative prose tales, which recent studies have shown to have an important political component of their own[181]—one of the most influential forms of political writing in the period, which may explain why legal texts are extant in so many manuscripts and forms. Recent scholarship has helped us appreciate the artificiality of a stark divide between the legal and the literary and significantly expanded our understanding of the complex relationship between the two. For the Welsh jurists at least, and perhaps for other European legal specialists as well, legal writing was very much a work of the imagination. That fact must have implications for how we read these texts. If the lawbooks were indeed part of a vital and evolving literary tradition, then we can no longer treat them as inevitably objective and eschewing of the fictional or funny. The old understanding of law as a type of source the "truth value" of which "varies inversely with how much pleasure it gives the reader: no pain, no gain,"[182] no longer obtains. Rather, we must read the laws in the same manner in which we read the tales: with close attention to setting, symbolism, narrative structure, and voice. And should we come across a bakeress throwing her scraper into the air, we should not look away or consign her actions automatically to the bin of quaint and colorful customs of yesteryear. As we will see, even that which seems ridiculous can have meaning if we are willing to look for it.

PART I

Imagined Landscapes

CHAPTER I

Britain and Wales

In literature, places are never presumed to be merely what they appear to be. Landscapes such as those described in the works of authors like Chrétien de Troyes are understood less as physical locales than as perilous testing grounds on which heroic identities are gained or lost and exiled knights readied for reintegration into the chivalric culture of the court. Similarly, it would be impossible to approach texts such as the early Irish sovereignty tales or the Middle English *Sir Gawain and the Green Knight* without reference to the motif of the wasteland, in which the land blossoms during the reign of the rightful king and withers with the demise of his rule.[1] In the medieval Welsh tales also, landscapes function not merely as literal places but as imaginative settings expressing elements of character and plot.[2] Such is still, for example, a common interpretation of the story of Rhiannon and the enchantment that falls over Dyfed in the Four Branches.[3] And most critics simply take for granted the idea that places mentioned in the tales which are still identifiable today—Arberth, the Severn River, England—are susceptible to interpretations that transcend their significance as literal domains.[4] Even those tales in which known places do not feature prominently (*Ystoria Peredur*, *Owein*) often depend on the construction of imagined space for the development of story line and character.[5] Recent criticism has complicated traditional understandings of the deployment of such ideas in the increasingly diverse cultural and political context in which the tales as we have them were authored,[6] but the symbolic significance of place continues to be a critical jumping-off point for literary scholars looking for fresh insights into these texts.[7]

And yet this is not generally how we read the laws, which most would agree are a related—some would argue very closely related—form of narrative.[8] Scholars have certainly not ignored the issue of place in the laws, but they have generally tackled the question in fairly literal terms. Valuable work has been done, for example, on the historical geography of the lawbook prologues and the Laws of Court tractate. Mentions of particular regions (or of figures known to be associated with particular regions, such as Iorwerth ap Madog and Gwynedd), have been taken as indicative either of the provenance of the manuscript or redaction in question, or of the regional politics behind its composition. Thus, the Ior prologue, which highlights the special compensation due the king of Aberffraw, is interpreted as both reflecting and intentionally promoting the preeminence of the princes of Gwynedd in the thirteenth century. The Cyfn prologues, by contrast, are understood to have a southern bias that links their composition to the reign of Rhys ap Gruffudd, who died in 1197; even more specifically, their attribution to Hywel of a particular territory in Rhwng Gwy a Hafren suggests a connection with Maelienydd.[9] In the Laws of Court tractate also, exalted forms of insult payments are accorded to certain regional kings in accordance with the redactor's perspective.[10] The political affiliations of the Latin redactions and various Bleg manuscripts have proven more challenging to trace, but even with respect to those texts, it is possible to say something about the regional affiliations and priorities that lie behind them.[11]

To date, scholarship on the importance of place within the laws has centered primarily on this issue of provenance: the attempt to deduce from the mention of particular locales within a given text the political, geographical, or familial context in which it was composed. Scholars are aware that certain places mentioned in the laws have a symbolic as well as literal or historical significance in the context in which they are named, but this has not been the crux of recent research.[12] It is my contention in these next two chapters that space and movements within designated landscapes matter much more than we have hitherto realized, and that both in fact function as thematic and structuring devices within the lawbooks as a whole.[13] The symbolic construction of place was an essential aspect of the manner in which the lawbooks were intended to communicate and to be read. Indeed, spatial metaphors arguably lie at the heart even of how important parts of the law itself were conceptualized. One of the earliest tractates in the lawbook is that of the *tair colofn cyfraith*, the "Three Columns of Law" (homicide, theft, and fire). The position of this tractate—at the beginning of the Laws of Country in the Model Lawbook believed to lie behind our extant texts—makes clear the centrality of these columns to Welsh law as a whole,[14] as does the fact that they are, along with the "Value of Wild and Tame," explicitly identified in various sections of Ior as the sine qua non for the assumption of judicial office.[15]

The nature of the columns in question is never explicitly identified, and the image is not unique to the law texts, nor even to Wales.[16] However, the reference seems most likely architectural in nature.[17] Columnar imagery evokes the image of a building of some sort, and the hall is a common topos in medieval and later Welsh poetry, where it is used to symbolize any number of desirable "constructions," including the cultivation of heroic virtue, the articulation of support for a particular person or position, and the desired end product of the compositional process.[18] Indeed, it may be that the jurists were intending here to reference the king's hall specifically. All lawbook versions are concerned with the physical layout of the king's hall to some extent, and the Ior version of the Laws of Court contains a detailed description of the building as resting on three cruck columns.[19] Another possibility is suggested by Paul Russell, who has pointed to parallels in the *Collectio Canonum Hibernensis* and in the writings of Archbishop Wulfstan; in the latter, the pillars or columns in question are imagined as supporting the king's throne.[20] An equally apposite parallel might be the book *Tricolumpnis*, a youthful work by Richard Fitz Nigel, later bishop of London and author of the late twelfth-century *Dialogus de Scaccario* ("Dialogue of the Exchequer"),[21] though opinions vary on the nature of the columns envisaged there.[22] In any case, given the manner in which the image is usually employed in contemporary Welsh poetry, the probability is still that the referent is the hall and that the three columns convey both the architectural solidity of the law (as represented by its core provisions) and the law's centrality to the stability of society as a whole.

Perhaps the most striking indication of the symbolic importance of place in the laws, however, is the very obvious fact—so obvious, indeed, that it has never to my knowledge been remarked upon directly as unusual—that the Welsh lawbooks are actually structured around two very particular landscapes: court (*llys*) and country (*gwlad*). In the context of the laws, these are depicted as the landscapes over which the unnamed king of the Laws of Court tractate presides; they thus function as jurisdictional as well as physical and cultural spaces. This manner of conceiving of the written law appears to be ancient. Scholars generally agree that the juxtaposing of the Laws of Court (*cyfreithiau llys*) and the Laws of Country (*cyfreithiau gwlad*) to form the main body of the lawbook is a feature that probably goes back to the Model Lawbook itself. In other words, the use of landscape to conceptualize both divisions within the law, and the layout of the books in which that law was primarily recorded, are among the oldest aspects of the extant written legal tradition.[23] Iorwerth ap Madog's subsequent reorganization of this earlier pattern, which turned what had been a bipartite text (Laws of Court, Laws of Country) into a tripartite entity (Laws of Court, Laws of Country, Judges' Test Book), has obscured this earlier structure to some degree.[24] However, there can be little doubt that what was originally intended was a lawbook that reproduced in its own structure a particular vision of the political landscape to which it was intended to apply.

What makes this point worth highlighting is the fact that this manner of describing and structuring the law of a given region is patently artificial. Court and country are not the only structures through which the political geography of Wales could have been encapsulated. Nor is a focus on landscape an obvious way of structuring a medieval lawbook. No English or Norman lawbook of the period is arranged in this manner. The *Leges Henrici Primi*, for example, believed to date from before 1118,[25] makes reference to the division of England into geographical jurisdictional units, ecclesiastical and secular. However, these divisions are incidental to the primary focus of the section of work in which this reference occurs, and landscape plays no further role in the overall structuring of the text.[26] Nor are such considerations important to the organizational schema of the *Leges Edwardi Confessoris*, composed around the middle of the twelfth century. This text is divided roughly into five parts, none of which deal with any aspect of place, but focus rather on the peace, ecclesiastical and royal.[27] Cultural geography is similarly not an organizing principle in the *Tractatus de legibus et consuetudinibus regni Angliae* (more commonly known as Glanvill), written around 1188. This lawbook begins with a statement regarding the oral nature of English law and proceeds to the subject of pleas in the king's courts. From there, pleas are distinguished according to whether they are civil or criminal; the bulk of the treatise is devoted to the nature and use of royal writs.[28] Very similar is the treatise known as the *De legibus et consuetudinibus Angliae*, long associated with royal justice Henry of Bratton or Bracton but probably principally composed in the 1220s and 1230s by others. There, law is characterized as private, natural, or civil in nature, and as relating to persons, things, or actions.[29] In short, place does not appear to have served as an organizing principle in other contemporary lawbooks in the way it did in Wales, nor was it elsewhere the metaphor through which the law itself was conceptualized.

In fact, as J. Goronwy Edwards pointed out long ago, the closest parallels to what we find in the Welsh lawbooks are Hincmar's *De ordine palatii*, composed in ninth-century Frankia, and the Anglo-Norman *De Constitutione Domus Regis*, probably authored in response to Stephen's accession to the throne in 1135.[30] To this, one would now want to add the *Dialogus de Scaccario* itself, the first part of which details the duties and positioning within the court of the various officers of the Exchequer in a manner very similar to the Laws of Court tractate.[31] What these works have in common is their focus on the king's household and an apparent equation of the physical structures of the household (*palatium*) with the officers who inhabit those buildings (also *palatium*).[32] All these texts appear in some sense to be describing a landscape that has symbolic as well as literal resonance for the lawbook authors. The Anglo-Norman *De Constitutione Domus Regis* is too truncated to allow us to say very much about the motives lying behind its construction; in the *Dialogus*, however, we see the rendering of accounts on the chessboard tally sheet being imagined as a battle fought between contending parties.[33] And Hincmar is clearly using what purports to be a physical description of the court to comment on a variety of contemporaneously controversial topics, such as the idea that secular court officials ought to be subjected to royal law in a manner parallel to the clergy's submission to canon law.[34] Especially noticeable is Hincmar's curious omission of military offices and personnel from his description of the relentlessly bellicose Carolingian court. Dafydd Walters attributes their absence to the fact that the Frankish court had no chief military officer like the Welsh *penteulu*;[35] one might also point to the fact that, at the time this text was written, Hincmar no longer had an interest in highlighting the wars that had for decades torn the empire apart.[36]

In other words, for Hincmar (and for the Welsh jurists, as I will shortly argue), what purports to be merely a description of institutional space functioned as a vehicle through which to comment on the high politics of the Carolingian era. Even if this is true, however, neither *De Ordine Palatii* nor the *Constitutione Domus Regis* nor the *Dialogus* is directly comparable to the Welsh lawbooks. Not only are the resemblances between them by and large limited to the Prologue and Laws of Court tractates, but they also constitute very different types of sources. None of the Latin texts presents itself as an official book of law in the sense of a text that governs personal behavior and the adjudication of disputes.[37] Moreover, their interest in imagined space is not nearly as sustained as it is in the Welsh texts, where the structuring of space is a narrative device that operates on a variety of different levels. All in all, the use made in the Welsh lawbooks of landscape and movement in space stands out as exceptional in a medieval legal context—an aspect of these texts that invites further comment and exploration. In fact, as I will argue, the closest parallels to the treatment of landscape in the Welsh lawbooks are likely to be found in the prose and poetic literature of the period rather than other contemporary books of law. Fiction was not, in this period, a medium reserved for storytellers alone, and Hincmar's work reminds us that a text that represents itself principally as description can "mean" on several different levels simultaneously. A focus on the symbolic use of landscape and the construction of space offers us access to dimensions of the laws of which we have been previously unaware.

Structuring the Landscape

A concern with place—physical and cultural, real and imagined, historical and contemporary—is evident in all the principal versions of the Welsh lawbooks. Both Wales as an entity, and the ancient kingdoms and capitals of Gwynedd/Aberffraw, Deheubarth/Dinefwr, and Powys as its main constituent locales, emerge as central from the very beginning.[38] The island of Britain itself features as the setting for the laws that follow. The Ior redaction incorporates several stories of an (obviously fictional) era in which the island was purportedly a political whole, united under a British (e.g., early Welsh-speaking) king reigning from London.[39] It is presumably also to this idea that the song, said in all three of the principal redactions to be sung by the bard to the court, makes appeal—*Unbeiniaeth Prydain*, "the Sovereignty of Britain."[40] In fact, *unben*, "lord," comes from *un*, "one," combined with *pen*, "head," and hence literally means "single-head" or "single-lord";[41] the notion of rule by a single individual is thus encapsulated in the very title of the song. This idea—inevitably in the context of the twelfth- and thirteenth-century struggles with English rulers a political statement—is found as well in many literary works of the period, including the Second and Third Branches of the Mabinogi, *Cyfranc Lludd a Llefelys*, and the poetry of the *Gogynfeirdd*.[42] Not surprisingly, the manner in which Wales is presented is similarly political. Whatever one wishes to make of the claim made in the prologues that the initiation of the written legal tradition is to be attributed to the tenth-century king Hywel Dda—described in some lawbooks as the *brenhin Kymry*, "king of Wales," or *tywyssavc Kemry oll*, "prince of all Wales"[43]—it functions within the narrative as an assertion of what R. R. Davies calls the "legal and even constitutional unity" of medieval Wales.[44] The attribution of the laws to Hywel is as much an exercise in symbolic construction as it is a reflection on anything the historical king himself might have done.

In other words, for the lawbook redactors, as for poets and storytellers of the period, landscape was central to what they saw themselves as doing. Even more significantly, the places they describe have symbolic as well as literal significance.[45] It is therefore essential to approach these texts in a manner open to readings of both sorts. As we have seen, first and foremost among the landscapes of the lawbooks is the division between court and country, which I will examine in detail in the following chapter. At this point, it is sufficient to note that while the distinction between these two jurisdictional spheres has long been seen as fundamental to the basic structuring of the lawbook, what has not previously been recognized is that the opposition between them forms part of a textual progression of literal and symbolic landscapes throughout the lawbook as a whole. This progression is particularly visible and well developed in Ior, which scholars agree is the most sophisticated version of all the principal redactions.[46] However, there can be little doubt that it also exists at least in incipient form in Cyfn—generally thought to reflect most closely in its aspect and shape the earliest lawbook versions—and in varying degrees as well in the Latin texts and Bleg. All are structured and worded in very different ways, as we will see, but all also use place to comment directly on the political and social controversies of the day. In this respect, they parallel very closely the use of imagined landscape in Welsh poetry and prose of the period.[47]

All manuscripts containing the lawbook prologue[48] begin in a setting that to contemporaries would likely have seemed precisely defined in place and time: Hywel's assembly at Tŷ Gwyn, the "White House," a place associated from at least the late twelfth century on with Whitland Abbey.[49] We cannot today identify with certainty the exact location intended, but since only two manuscripts (Ior A and E) do not name the place of Hywel's assembly, it seems reasonable to regard Tŷ Gwyn as an important feature of the story. Most likely, as Huw Pryce has suggested, the association with Whitland conferred "a religious aura" on the gathering and reminded contemporaries of the links between Hywel and his important descendant, Rhys ap Gruffudd, prince of Deheubarth and patron of the abbey in question.[50] Also significant—and emphasized in all versions—is the idea that Hywel was acting, in summoning this gathering, in his capacity as king of all Wales. The Cyfn redaction shows a keen interest in the precise local geography of Hywel's putative realm; the Bleg and Latin versions are content merely to stress the fact that Hywel drew on men from the major kingdoms of Gwynedd, Deheubarth, and Powys.

Interestingly, the northern redaction of Ior is the least precise—or most all-encompassing, depending on how one wishes to see the matter—referring to his consultants only as the wisest men *yn y kyuoeth*, "in the kingdom."[51]

The fact that the Hywelian lawbook begins with an account of a royal assembly is in no way surprising. Many legal texts start in precisely this way, including the early Irish *Senchas Már*, the Frankish *Pactus Legis Salicae*, the Anglo-Saxon laws of Aethelred and Cnut, the twelfth-century *Leges Henrici Primi*, the *Leges Edwardi Confessoris*, and others.[52] Because the idea of situating the composition of a particular body of written law in a royal legislative assembly was already a narrative trope by the time it found its way into the Welsh lawbooks, there is no way for us currently to know whether a gathering under the historical Hywel ever took place. However, where the Welsh sources do diverge significantly from their medieval counterparts is in the fact that the laws following on from the story of Hywel's assembly at Tŷ Gwyn are grounded in a variety of imagined landscapes that unfold progressively across the spectrum of the lawbook as a whole.[53] Most central of all is the royal court, or *llys*.[54] As used in the Laws of Court tractate, the term *llys* encompasses both the mobile court centered around the person of the king that traveled about the country on circuit supported by dues and renders, and the static "complex of buildings" occupied by the king's household from which royal jurisdiction was exercised.[55] It is not always easy to tell these apart. The tractate is structured as a graduated discussion of the members of the king's household (*llys*); however, the spaces in which these persons are imagined as moving (*llys*) have a definite physicality to them. There are structures such as chambers, halls, and outbuildings, all of which contain corporeal features such as columns and doors. One might be tempted to regard such references as pertaining to the static court only, but no such distinction is made in the text, and the mobile court household also would have required buildings in which to stay while on circuit. More clearly evocative of the static court are the allusions to the tributary settlements known as *maerdrefi*, which seem to be conceptualized as proximate to the nonmobile *llys*. In any case, the principal opposition established in the tractate is not between mobile and static, but between *llys*—in all senses of the word—and *gwlad*, the officers and lands that lie outside the immediate ambit of the king. The court lies always at the center no matter where it travels. In other words, the landscape we are dealing with here is both symbolic and literal, a landscape of power as well as of space.

Within the *llys*, there is a clear demarcation of space. The tractate on the Laws of Court begins with a meticulous description of the officers who constitute it and an account of the *sarhaed* ("insult") payments and privileges due them. The king, queen, and *edling* ("royal heir") come first; next comes the order of seating within the feasting hall and the lodgings assigned to individual officers. The progression of landscapes can be represented in the following way:

As will be evident from Table 1, there are significant differences among the various redactions (and, of course, among the various manuscripts of those redactions, although the latter are not represented here). In the Cyfn, Bleg, and Latin traditions, the discussion of general seating within the hall is partially incorporated into the paragraph on the *edling*, or heir, for example, whereas in Ior it is separate. Indeed, in Cyfn, Bleg, and the Latin texts, the

Table 1. Structural Comparison of the Principal Laws of Court Tractate Versions

Cyfnerth/Latin texts/Blegywryd	*Iorwerth*
Prologue: Hywel's assembly at Tŷ Gwyn List of the 24 court officers Subtractate on the king (insult to queen treated as part of this section)	Prologue: Hywel's assembly at Tŷ Gwyn List of the 24 court officers Subtractate on the king (insult to queen treated as part of this section)
Subtractate on the *edling* (seating in the hall treated as part of this section)	Subtractate on the *edling* (one sentence on his seating in the hall included here)
Subtractate on seating at three principal feasts *in sede sua*[1]	Subtractate on seating in the hall
List of *nawdds*, "protections" afforded by court officers to offenders	
List of *sarhaed* and *galanas* amounts for court officers	
List of *lletyau*, "lodgings" assigned to court officers	
Subtractates on individual officers	Subtractates on individual officers (*nawdd*, *galanas*, lodging treated as part of each description)
↓	↓

[1]Entitled *De dignitate regis* in Latin A, and *De rege* in Lat D: *LTWL* Lat A 111.7; Lat D 318.28.

edling (whose seat is defined opposite the king and across the fire from him) constitutes the point from which other seats are measured; in Ior, by contrast, he is merely one of six men at the king's mess (*yn chuechet gvr ar seyc y brenhyn*) and court positions are measured from the king.[56] By far the most important structural difference among the various redactions, however, occurs after the passage on seating. The Cyfn, Bleg, and Latin redactions communicate the *nawdd* ("protection, sanctuary"), status (as measured by *galanas*, "homicide," and *sarhaed*, "insult," payment amounts), and *llety* ("lodgings") of the various court officers in list form, only then turning to discuss each officer individually. The Ior redactor, by contrast, incorporates this information into his individual discussion of each. Many of these measures—the lodgings most notably, but some instances of protection as well—have a geographical component to them. The protection of the hall doorkeeper, for example, is the length of his arm and rod extended in the direction of the porter.[57] Alex Sigston has commented similarly on the image created in the text of the *penteulu* "moving past the *porthawr* to his chambers."[58] The effect in all redactions is a veritable layering of political spaces, small and large, within the wider ambit of the court.

Following on from the Laws of Court in all manuscripts that contain them are the Laws of Country. Here, we are introduced to another progression, from interior (court) to exterior (country), that will be repeated in various forms throughout the rest of the lawbook. This progression is most clearly visible in the Cyfn and Bleg traditions because of the creation in Ior of a third lawbook section in addition to the Laws of Court and Laws of Country called the *Llyfr Prawf*, or Judges' Test Book, which consists in large part of material that in the other three versions is situated elsewhere, primarily in the Laws of Country. Table 2 shows how Thomas Charles-Edwards maps out the principal divisions within Cyfn and Ior.[59]

The rationale for the composition of the Test Book can be to some extent inferred from the lengthy prologue to the Test Book found today in Ior manuscript C (but once likely found in all Ior manuscripts apart from A and E), which not only attributes the text to Iorwerth ap Madog (a practitioner himself),[60] but links its composition directly to the need for justices to know the contents of the Test Book before taking up judicial office. As such, it likely reflects the growing complexity of justice and concomitant need for educated judges in the first half of the thirteenth century.[61] Most significant for us here, however, is the fact that both the originally bipartite schema of the Model Lawbook and the progression from court to country are clearly still visible.

Table 2. Structural Comparison of the Cyfn and Ior Lawbooks

Cyfnerth (MS Mk)	*Iorwerth (other than MS B)*
Prologue	Prologue
Laws of Court	Book of the Court
Laws of Country	Laws of Country
1 Three Columns, Nine-Tongued Ones	1 Nine-Tongued Ones
2 Land	2 Women
3 Value of Wild and Tame Animals	3 Injury to Animals
4 Corn-Damage; Surety and Contract; Women	4 Suretyship and Contract
5 Value of Houses, Trees, Equipment	5 Church Protection
	6 Land
	7 Children
Triads	
	Judges' Test Book
	1 Three Columns of Law
	2 Value of Wild and Tame Animals
	Appendages to the Test Book
	1 Value of Houses, Equipment
	2 Joint-Ploughing
	3 Corn-Damage

Indeed, as Charles-Edwards has pointed out, it is this very structure that distinguishes Hywel's Book from the other types of legal texts being composed in Wales at the time, such as the *Llyfr Cynghawsedd* and *Llyfr y Damweiniau*.[62]

From the very beginning of Hywel's Book, therefore, the reader is called upon to contemplate a variety of spaces—historical and contemporary, cultural and physical. Moreover, movement from one type of landscape to another, across time and from interior to exterior space, is a feature inherent to the structure of the lawbook itself. From Hywel's royal gathering at Tŷ Gwyn to the princely courts of latter-day Wales, we progress outward into tractates that explore the world outside the court, ultimately encompassing the agricultural and pastoral realms. And while it might appear that there could be no greater contrast than that between the lavish feasts of the princely court with which the narrative begins and the snorts and rootings of the final landscape evoked in the text, the world of *gwyllt a dof*, "wild and tame,"[63] these landscapes are both literally and symbolically conjoined by the fact of royal jurisdiction and its encapsulation in written law. Indeed, even the Test Book, with its focus on judicial practice and the training of practitioners, builds upon rather than disrupts this progression from court to country. Judicial proceedings were imagined as taking place outdoors, regardless of hot sun or hostile weather.[64] Prominent in those proceedings were not only the courtly officials who presided over them, but also figures whose responsibilities marked them as both part of the princely court and apart from it: the dung *maer* (*maer biswail*), a collector of dues and fines from unfree tenants of the king, and the sergeant (*rhingyll*), a local officer of the peace who summoned offenders to court and collected legal fines once those cases had been resolved. It is surely no accident that the main discussions of transitional figures like these—along with the *cynghellor*, another local royal officer involved in enforcement—appear where they do in most redactions, near the very end of the tractate on the court and before the Laws of Country or in the Laws of Country tractate itself.[65] In Latin D, the section in question is actually entitled "On the public servants [standing] between the king and his men" (*De communibus servitoribus inter regem et homines suos*).[66] Both textually and in the imagined landscape of the lawbooks, in other words, these figures stake out a midway point between the interior world of the royal court and the most distant landscapes of field and forest.

What we have here is a progression from culture to nature that is as marked and symbolically significant as any journey ever undertaken by the heroes of medieval Welsh literature. Indeed, certain aspects of the manner in which the lawbooks are structured mimic in important—and perhaps not entirely coincidental—ways the movement from country to court to country (and often back again) that constitutes the framework of many of the prose tales. Just as the lawbooks begin with a prologue in which persons from all over Wales[67] arrive at Tŷ Gwyn to consult on the state of the law, so do the stories of Culhwch and Peredur begin with the protagonists coming to Arthur's court from the world outside—Culhwch via a pig run and the prophecy of a hideous hag, Peredur, via an encounter with animals and knights from the forest. And just as the peruser of the lawbooks passes first into the world of the court—guarded in those texts by the royal porter—so do visitors to Arthur's court confront Glewlwyd Gafaelfawr, the porter and custodian of what are called in *Culhwch ac Olwen* the *kyfreitheu llys*, "laws of the court," before they are allowed to enter.[68] (Glewlwyd plays a similar role in the *Ystoria Ger-*

eint uab Erbin and in *Owein*, where the term used is *moes y llys*, "the custom of the court").[69] It is from that court that all progress then into the world outside: students of the lawbooks into the Laws of Country,[70] and Culhwch, Owein, Gereint, and Peredur to the adventures that await them. This is not merely a narrative quirk, or even a structure of convenience. Rather, as will become clear in what follows, the movement from inside to outside, from culture to nature, and from the civilized life of the court to the relative wildness of fields and forests, is the thematic axis along which the lawbook as a whole is deliberately structured. The symbolic use of landscape in these texts is far more complex, sophisticated, and pointedly political than we have hitherto recognized.

Measuring the Land

It seems useful to preface a detailed exploration of the symbolic geography of the lawbooks with two very basic observations. First, and most crucial, is the fact that the landscapes, as described in the lawbooks, are essentially fictional constructs. Places mentioned in the laws may be real places; they may have names that resonate with readers today or be described in terms recognizable to those who have visited the venue in question themselves. Historical courts as they existed on the ground may even have looked very similar to courts as described in the lawbooks. In other words, there is no question of these descriptions actually being untrue. However, within the context of the legal narrative per se, they are imagined venues, conceptualized in particular ways in order to communicate specific values, priorities, and political perspectives. Wales itself is an obvious example. We are presented in the lawbooks with several different images of Wales and its rulers. However, it is impossible to pinpoint the narrative as a whole to one particular place and time. Within the first few pages of the lawbook, we pass without warning from Wales in the tenth century under Hywel (the Wales of the prologue), to Wales in a carefully unspecified, but to all appearances seemingly contemporaneous, moment when princely power is exercised from contemporary seats such as Aberffraw and Dinefwr (the Wales of the Laws of Court and subsequent tractates). This latter Wales is particularly (and I would suggest deliberately) hard to pin down. As David Stephenson has observed, in some instances the Laws of Court seem most closely to reflect political conditions of the twelfth century or even earlier, while in others, they show themselves to be au courant with political developments of the thirteenth century.[71] The Wales of the lawbooks is everywhere and nowhere, which was surely exactly the point.

Of course, it would be possible to attribute the chronological complexity of the lawbooks more to the retention of provisions of earlier law side by side with contemporary material than to any grand design of the lawbook authors. This was the traditional explanation, and indeed passages such as the "Seven Bishop-Houses of Dyfed" and the *Nau Kynywedi Teithiauc* are unquestionably older than the redactions themselves.[72] In some cases, we can even identify the (ultimate, if not proximate) sources of particular provisions that found their way into the Welsh lawbooks, such as canons from the early eighth-century *Collectio Canonum Hibernensis* or borrowings from the early medieval *Excerpta de libris Romanorum et Francorum*.[73] Clearly, the importation into Welsh law of older passages like these would inevitably complicate any attempt to pinpoint the lawbook narratives to any one point in time. However, none of these demonstrably older passages occur in the Laws of Court, which is where the setting of the lawbooks as a whole is established.[74] Moreover, what matters most to an understanding of the nature and goals of these texts is not the origin of their individual components, but rather the ways they were perceived and used by twelfth- and thirteenth-century persons, when the legal manuscripts we have today were being produced. In such a context, the refusal to pinpoint the lawbooks in time would seem to constitute a deliberate choice—the intentional crafting of a vision of Wales that embraces past and present simultaneously.

In fact, the Wales of the lawbooks arguably reaches back even further in time, to a point long before the medieval period. Written Welsh law is depicted as rooted in the era of Hywel—that, surely, is the point of the prologue. Welsh sovereignty and independence, however, are consciously grounded in an even more distant past. One of the oddest and seemingly most arcane passages in the Laws of Court—especially considering that the extant versions of this tractate date to the twelfth or thirteenth century—stipulates as compensation for insults done to the king the payment of a herd of magically colored cattle complete with bull, a silver or gold rod as long as the king's body, and a golden goblet with a cover as broad as the king's face.[75] This passage occurs near the beginning of the Laws of Court in the subtractate on the king, and is thus one of the earliest in the lawbook proper. Its importance is underscored by the fact that variations of it are included in all the major redactions of the lawbook, despite the fact that—I would argue *because*—the segment looks and feels archaic and even mythological in nature. The golden vessel said to hold the king's draught is fully of a piece with other ancient Celtic sovereignty symbols such as the liquor-bearing goddess familiar to scholars of early Irish tradition. Moreover, as contemporaries would immediately have recognized, precisely this same form of compensation appears in mythological works of the period set in the ancient British past. In *Branwen*, the Second Branch of the Mabinogi, for example, a silver rod and golden plate are paid for the *sarhaed* committed by Efnisien against the Irish king Matholwch.[76]

Even in overtly literary narratives, the presence of such archaic motifs in texts composed in the high or late medieval period requires some explanation. Earlier presumptions were that texts like *Branwen* or the laws likely preserved fragments of ancient traditions no longer extant in the historical record, and that scholars could make use of such passages in their reconstructions of early Celtic rituals and beliefs. More recently, however, studies have focused on the meaning(s) the evocation of such archaic practices had in the high Middle Ages, when the tales as we have them were composed and performed.[77] Catherine McKenna and Helen Fulton have argued that in works such as the Mabinogi, for example, ancient tropes like the sovereignty goddess served as potent vehicles through which to promote contemporary political agendas or points of view. The ubiquity of these cultural symbols and their rootedness in native tradition lent authority to the (highly contemporary and politically pointed) messages being communicated, providing a foundation on the basis of which change, especially radical change, could either be accommodated or resisted.[78] Given the close relationship we know to have obtained between the jurists and other tradition-bearers of the day, it seems only reasonable to imagine that such would also be true of the archaisms appearing in the laws. Regardless of the significance cattle and golden regalia might have had in the historical past, in other words, it seems reasonable to imagine that their meaning in the lawbooks, like their meaning in the tales, was politically charged and highly contemporaneous. Not only did they serve to underscore the existence and longevity of native traditions of rule, they cloaked in the mantle of tradition the many changes in Welsh law and society that were occurring at the time.[79]

The idea that Welsh sovereignty and independence stretched back into the ancient past to a period long before Hywel is found in all the lawbook redactions. However, it is here that we come to the second of our observations. While such themes are implicit even in the most primitive versions of the lawbooks, it is in the Ior redaction that their symbolic potential is usually—though not always—most fully realized. As we will see throughout this book, narrative tropes, particularly those relating to important political topics of the day, are often developed in Ior tradition manuscripts in ways they are not elsewhere. Frequently, this means that they are enlarged upon, although this is not always the case. The Ior redactor's treatment of the regalian objects due the king is, for example, relatively conservative and suggests a man with his eye not only on native tradition, but on contemporary European ideas about kingship. He either preserves an earlier version of these objects or deliberately modulates many of the picturesque details in which the Cyfn and Latin text redactors revel, and the choices he makes suggest a desire to make room for both native and foreign in his characterization of princely regalia.[80] Susan Aronstein and Catherine McKenna have pointed to the importance for medieval Wales of Homi Bhabha's observations on the culturally hybrid discourses produced by colonized peoples in response to a colonizer's attempts to fix upon them an identity alien to the one they would optimally choose for themselves.[81] Walter Map's parody of the Cyfn and Bleg version of the cattle (depicted in those texts as standing head to tail in a line some three and a half miles long!) is a good indication of the patronizing amusement with which contemporary English courtiers would have regarded this particular bit of native tradition.[82] The Ior redactor's relatively muted treatment of them is surely an instance of the hybrid discourse Bhabha describes: an attempt to embrace native tradition in a way that maintains the connection between present-day Welsh rulers and the mythological past without alienating contemporary European sophisticates.

More usually, however, the Ior redactor builds upon rather than downplays ideas that are already implicit in other lawbook redactions. One such instance—also relating to ideas about the historicity of Welsh kingship and traditions of rule—is the incorporation into Ior of the nationalist myth mentioned earlier, in which Welsh sovereignty is taken back in time beyond Hywel to a (mythical) period in which the island of Britain was ruled from London by a Welsh-speaking ruler. This myth, which is also referenced in the Mabinogi and in Welsh prophetic literature of the period,[83] is alluded to three times in *Llyfr Iorwerth*—once in the Laws of Court,[84] once in the Test Book in the context of the insult payment due the king of Aberffraw,[85] and once in the redactor's discussion of land measurement, in the tale of Dyfnwal Moelmud.[86] The story of Dyfnwal is particularly important for understanding the use of this story in Ior. A figure known from elsewhere in Welsh tradition (he appears in the early Welsh genealogies), Dyfnwal is identified in Ior (and also in Geoffrey of Monmouth's *Historia Regum Britanniae*, where Dyfnwal appears as Dunwallo Molmutius) as king of the island of Britain, *kyn no duyn Coron Lundeyn a theyrnwyalen o Saeson*,[87] "before the taking of the crown of London and the scepter by the Saxons." He is thus understood to be a predecessor of Hywel's, and, in his capacity as an early ruler of Britain, is said to have measured the island and to have been the first to formulate laws by which to govern its people. Significantly, the laws made by Dyfnwal are said in Ior (but not in Geoffrey[88]) to have later been abrogated by Hywel in the course of his own legal reform:

> A'r gur hunnu a oed ur audurdodus doeth, a'r gur hunnu a wnaeth keureythyeu da en er enys hon en gyntaf: a'r keureythyeu a wnaeth ef a parhaassant hyt en oes Hewel Da. A Hewel guedy henne a wnaeth keureythyeu newyd, ac a dyuaus rey Dyuenwal.[89]

> And that man (Dyfnwal) was a wise, authoritative man, and that man was the first to make good laws in this island: and the laws he made lasted until the age of Hywel Dda. And Hywel afterward made new laws and abrogated those of Dyfnwal.[90]

While Dyfnwal's laws are said in Ior to have been changed by Hywel, however, his measurements of the island are depicted as having been kept intact *canys goreu messuruur uu ef*, "because he was the best measurer."[91] The point being made here is an important one. It was customary in the medieval period for owners literally to circumambulate the boundaries of their land in order to demonstrate possession: to measure land was implicitly to own and control it. Indeed, Dyfnwal's measurements are explicitly linked in Ior to the tribute (*mal*) that could be exacted from it.[92] Dyfnwal is here being depicted, in other words, as the original and rightful possessor of the island of Britain, his ownership having been vested in and displayed by his act of publicly marking its boundaries. This is why Hywel as Dyfnwal's successor is shown as having retained Dyfnwal's measurements, but not his laws. Not just Hywel, but Hywel's royal successors as kings of Wales had a rightful claim to the territory Dyfnwal had marked out. Distant claims vested in a line of kings later displaced from the kingship (as Dyfnwal's would have to have been) were susceptible to challenge in the twelfth and thirteenth centuries, of course, when the right to land was vested more in conquest and rightful governance than in an ancient act of marking out boundaries. What lay at the heart of Edward I's claim to authority over Wales was, as R. R. Davies remarked, the imposition (by force) of "good order and sound laws."[93] But Ior's vision of the past provides a response to such objections also: the updating by Hywel, a demonstrably historical king whose rule north and south was impervious to challenge, of Dyfnwal's laws. Proper rulers governed as well as possessed; Welsh kings did both.

Equally significant is the placement of the Dyfnwal story in the Ior lawbook. Its position outside the prologue preserves the primacy of the narrative centered on Hywel as the progenitor of a written Welsh legal tradition separate from English Common Law.[94] But the redactor has also situated Dyfnwal's story in a way that links it to the lawbook's main discussion of foreigners and the conditions on which they can remain on native-owned land—an issue of obvious importance in the thirteenth century.[95] Immediately before the story of Dyfnwal—which placement surely cannot be accidental—we find the following passage:[96]

> E keureyth a deweyt e dele meybyon uchelwyr cadu argluydyaeth ar eu halltudyon ual e dele e brenhyn kadu argluydyaeth ar y alltudyon enteu; ac ual yd a alltudyon en pryodoryon en e petwaregur guedy e dotter ar dyffeyth brenhyn uynt, euelly yd a alltudyon e meybyon uchelwyr en petwaregur en pryodoryon o bydant en guarchadu tyr adanadunt en kyhyt a henne. Ac o henne allan ny deleant uynet y urth e meybyon uchelwyr, canys pryodoryon ynt adanadunt ac na deleant huynteu due pryodolder: vn en e wlat yd hanuoent ohoney ac arall yma. . . . O myn er alltudyon mynet y urth eu hargluydy kyn eu bot en pryodoryon, uynt a deleant adau hanner udunt. Ac os o'r enys hon yd hanuydant ny deleant trygyau en un lle e tu hun e Glaud Offa; ac os tra mor yd hanuydant ny deleant trygyau yma namen hyt ar a guynt kentaf e caffoent mynet y eu gulat, ac o thrygant, emchuelent ar eu keythywet ual kynt.[97]
>
> The law says that *uchelwyr* ("free men," "nobles") are entitled to maintain lordship over their foreigners [*alltudyon*] just as the king maintains lordship over his own foreigners; and as foreigners become proprietors in the fourth generation[98] after they have been established on the king's waste, so also do the foreigners of *uchelwyr* become proprietors in the fourth generation if they have custody of land under them for as long as that. And from then on, they are not entitled to go away from the *uchelwyr*, for they are proprietors

> under them, and they are not entitled to two proprietorships: one in the land from which they come and another here. . . . If foreigners wish to leave their lords before they become proprietors, it is right for them to leave half [of their goods] to them. And if they come from this island, they are not entitled to stay in any place on this side of Offa's Duke; and if they come from across the sea, they are not entitled to stay here except up to the first wind they may get to go to their country, and if they stay, let them return to their bondage as before.

In other words, only after the fourth generation may foreigners claim proprietorship of their lands, and even then they must remain under the jurisdiction of their Welsh lords.

As it stands, this passage forms part of a much larger discussion of land and inheritance, the gist of which is to uphold the privileges and prerogatives of the *bonhedyc canuynaul*, the "innate *bonheddig*," a freeman of Welsh descent on both his father's and his mother's side. "Welsh" is explicitly defined in the course of the discussion as including all the major kingdoms of Wales; foreigners (*alltudion*) here are understood to come from outside of Wales, either from within the island of Britain itself (English or Scottish) or from across the sea (Irish or French).[99] The presumption in this passage would thus seem to be that as land in Wales is rightfully held by native Welshmen, foreigners occupying land owned by native freemen are considered to be in bondage (*caethiwed*)[100] under them up to the fourth generation. Those who seek to flee their dependent status must forfeit half of their possessions to their former lords and leave Wales immediately. The relevance of this passage to the story of Dyfnwal (which follows next) is evident. Dyfnwal (and Hywel and other subsequent Welsh kings) are imagined as the rightful owners and rulers of the kingdom of Britain; those who have come into Wales subsequently, whether English, Norman, or French, are foreigners without legitimate claims to the land they occupy. The story may or may not allude to the dream of certain northern patriots that Dafydd ap Llywelyn would ultimately lay claim to the English throne by virtue of his mother Joan, daughter of King John.[101] As conceptualized in Ior, however, the most immediate basis for claims to Welsh sovereignty over the island is not Dafydd's links to Joan but, rather, the legacy of Dyfnwal coupled with native laws on inheritance. Pryce has pointed out that Ior frequently justifies change on the basis of native rather than foreign principles; this would appear to be another example.[102]

Two other aspects of this story as it appears in Ior require comment. The first is that Hywel's tale is situated in the prologue, Dyfnwal's in the Laws of Country, and the subsequent reference to the "crown of London" in the Test Book. To this may be added the reference found in all extant versions of the Laws of Court to the poet of the warband singing "the Sovereignty of Britain" either before war begins (as Cyfn would have it), or afterward during the sharing out of booty (as is said in Ior).[103] Since this song title itself constitutes a reference to the myth of Welsh lordship over Britain, the claims of the Welsh to historical rulership of the island are thus integrated into every section of the Ior lawbook (Prologue, Laws of Court, Laws of Country, Test Book) and are not merely a throwaway feature. Moreover, the placement of Dyfnwal's tale immediately after the provisions on foreigners shows how thoroughly and carefully this process of integration was done. These are not stories cited at random without reference to anything around them. Rather, what we have here is a deliberately crafted narrative in which two very distinct pseudohistorical themes of the period have been consciously joined. The first, centered on Hywel as the progenitor of written law in Wales, appears to be unique to the legal tradition in Wales;[104] the second, centered on Dyfnwal in this text (but encompassing Bendigeidfran and others elsewhere), is a commonplace in contemporary Welsh narrative generally.

The second point to be made is that the standards Dyfnwal is said to have used in measuring (and thereby claiming ownership over) the land are depicted as being rooted in nature rather than in the arbitrary perceptions of men: the barleycorn, the physical lengths of the human body, the boundaries inscribed by the crashing of the sea against the land.[105] Standards set by men can be changed as circumstances are altered—Hywel's revisions of Dyfnwal's laws being a case in point. The land, however, remains the same as ever it was, and so too, by implication, does its fertility and the inherently British kingship it supports. One might do worse than to paraphrase Andrew Welsh's astute remarks about the enchantment that falls over Dyfed in the Third Branch of the Mabinogi. For the Ior redactor, it is "not nature but culture" that is altered under Hywel—in other words, not the identity of the island as the rightful possession of British-speaking rulers but, rather, the regulations by which it is governed at a particular moment in time.[106] Hywel the lawgiver thus becomes a midway figure in an unimaginably ancient cultural tradition—one of a long and distinguished line of native rulers whose kingship was ultimately rooted in the landscape of Britain itself. The message seems clear. Nature retains in its most basic measures the memory of a British sovereignty once encompassing the island as a whole, while culture retains in the written law the legacy of an ancient pattern of governance that long predates the coming of the Normans to Wales.

Of course, British autonomy had long since been compromised by their advent, and it would be interesting to know whether contemporaries would have perceived a certain poignancy in the juxtaposition of Dyfnwal and Hywel—an acknowledgment of change and diminution of the sort that McKenna has suggested pervades the tales of Bendigeidfran and Manawydan in the Second and Third Branches.[107] Usually, the lawbooks seem not to dwell on the sort of cultural vulnerability and fear of outside intrusion that is such a prominent theme in the literature of the period. However, in the context in which the Ior lawbook was written, it would have been difficult to ignore the much-diminished nature of both the physical extent of Hywel's kingdom and the jurisdiction he and his successors could claim to exercise. Hywel comes across in this story as no longer wielding the authority Dyfnwal had once enjoyed, whether over Britain as a political unit, or over nature itself. Like Bendigeidfran, Hywel is "marginalized . . . and yet powerful"[108] within an all-island kingdom once ruled by his predecessors. His legal position is one of a claimant who maintains his rights to the land on which an oppressor now sits.[109] The lawbook attributed to him, like other works of traditional lore, occupies what McKenna has termed "a perpetual prophetic moment, in which past wholeness and hoped for future recovery of that wholeness are brought into contact in a story or a line of verse that speaks hope for the future by drawing upon the past."[110]

Defining Wales

The Wales of the lawbooks is thus less the real Wales of the twelfth and thirteenth centuries than an imagined entity embracing past, present, and—to the extent that prophecy and hopes for eventual restoration are represented in its pages—future as well. Its boundaries are deliberately conceptualized as encompassing all the warring regions of Wales; its unity and sovereignty are depicted as being vested both in landscape and in beliefs about past events. This unity was itself a construction, as is evident from the chronicles. In reality, Wales was both politically and geographically fragmented, and had been for centuries. Personal loyalties were local and familial, regional at best, and national primarily in the songs of poets or in the presence of a unifying outsider.

Individual Welshmen worked both with and against the foreigners in their midst, adopting or rejecting the practices and innovations they brought to Wales as best suited their situations. Natives were as likely to attack one another as they were to resist intrusions by foreigners. The political ambitions of the princes of Gwynedd constituted for many a greater threat to personal freedoms than the scheming of Edward I. This is not to say that the Welsh entertained no common vision for themselves. Indeed, quite the opposite. Even apart from the perceptions of outsiders—who, as so often is the case, worked paradoxically to cement a common identity rather than to undermine it—there existed a shared language, law, mythology, and pseudohistorical past to which appeal could be and was frequently made. The Welsh saw themselves as a people even if, like peoples everywhere, they did not always act in accordance with that perception.[111]

But Welsh identity was constantly in flux, and no more so than in the period of the lawbooks. There were as many ways of conceptualizing Wales and Welsh tradition as there were Welshmen to live it. As Bhabha has argued, the process of colonization produces new discourses of identity among the colonized that are frequently a source of conflict and negotiation.[112] Just what did and did not constitute Welshness in the circumstances of the thirteenth century was a matter for debate, and the lawbooks were part of this process. The existence of a collectivity known as Wales is implied in a variety of ways across the lawbook redactions: in the prologue describing Hywel's assembly; the references in the lawbook proper to *Cymru* (Wales) and its traditionally constituent regions of Gwynedd, Deheubarth, and Powys; and the insistence that inhabitants of one region of Wales enjoyed equal inheritance rights in another.[113] These passages are often drawn upon by historians as proof that Wales in the thirteenth century was regarded as encompassing all regions equally, and this may well be right.[114] They certainly accord with poetic perceptions of the period and sentiments expressed in the courtly literature of the day. However, it is worth remembering that the laws are not impartial records, aloof from contemporary debates and discussions.[115] There might have been widespread agreement on the existence of Wales as a cultural entity; however, cultural cohesion did not necessarily mean political unity. Violence among Welshmen and kingdoms was rife and represented a tremendous threat both to the peace of the realm and to its prospects for long-term survival. The redactors' insistence on the fundamental unity of Wales reflects as much the desires of an *uchelwyr* class seeking stability in a period of unsettling change as it does reality on the ground. What we are seeing in the lawbooks is essentially a point of view rather than an objective record.

Certainly, there were significant divergences of opinion as to how the various polities of Wales ought to be conceptualized. The partiality of the lawbook redactors is most evident in the places where they disagree. One subject on which the legal sources differed was the kingliness—or lack thereof—of particular Welsh rulers. As we have seen, the focus of the Laws of Court tractate is not Wales itself, nor even the specific royal seats of Aberffraw or Dinefwr but, rather, the individual royal court—unnamed, unprovenanced, and chronologically undefined. The redactions vary significantly in how they imagine this court and the polity it represents. Cyfn is the only redaction to accord gold and silver regalia to kings (*brenhinedd*)[116] of all levels of importance; other lawbook versions restrict them to particularly powerful kings such as the ruler of Aberffraw, chief seat of Gwynedd, or of Dinefwr, chief seat of Deheubarth.[117] Even Cyfn discriminates to some degree, in that its redactor depicts the compensation of the ruler of Deheubarth being enhanced by a line of cattle positioned head to tail, stretching from Argoel to Dinefwr.[118] However, despite these visibly southern sympathies—and it is worth noting that the Cyfn prologue was probably redacted during the reign of Rhys ap Gruffudd[119]—the main point of its tractate seems to have been to underscore the kingliness of many different levels of Welsh rulers, regardless of their prominence and stature. The Wales of the Cyfn redaction is a land of small polities, local loyalties, and many kings, even the most minor of whom had some claim to the symbols of royal status.

What does *not* appear in Cyfn, nor indeed in any of the principal lawbook versions of the period, are the Marcher lordships that, by the time the lawbooks were redacted, were certainly a significant and visible presence in the area.[120] The omission of the Marcher lordships from the political geography of the lawbooks is significant—indeed, it is one of our best indications that what we are dealing with here is a polity imagined in particular ways for particular reasons rather than a straightforward description of place. The March was not left out because Welsh law was irrelevant to those who occupied it; indeed, Welsh law was very much a factor in the March, as the work of R. R. Davies on the cultural hybridity of these lands has shown.[121] Rather, the Marcher lordships were omitted because intrusive aristocratic polities of this sort had no place in the imagined Wales of the lawbooks. Indeed, Cyfn's insistence on the regality of all Welsh rulers may well have been intended primarily as a counterweight against the presence of these intruders. Not even the most noble of Marcher lords enjoyed the mythologically sanctioned sovereignty to which all native rulers, regardless of the size of their kingdom or the wealth of their household, are imagined in Cyfn as being entitled to lay claim.[122] As Pryce observed, the priority here is not to portray reality but, rather, to depict "a unitary Wales, under a single ruler and a single law"[123]—and then to ground that vision in an all-embracing past. Of course, the compliment of cultural erasure was returned in spades. One of the closest parallels for the ignoring of the March is what Simon Meecham-Jones has characterized as the nearly complete "erasure of Wales" from medieval English literature.[124]

The Ior redactor also omits the March from his account. However, for him, unlike the Cyfn redactor, kingliness itself is relative, and not to be extended equally to those claiming royal descent.[125] In Ior, the ruler of Gwynedd alone is entitled to the gold regalia which in Cyfn is accorded to all kings. In fact, this point is made twice in the lawbook—once in the Laws of Court tractate on the king, and once in the Test Book's discussion of insult payments to be made to various ranks.[126] Ior does seem to acknowledge in its terminology that Wales had *historically* been a land of many kings. *Brenin* and *brenhines* ("king" and "queen") are the terms used most frequently in the Ior Laws of Court, despite the fact that, by the thirteenth century, *arglwydd*, "lord," and *tywysog*, "prince, *princeps*, over-king," had become the more usual forms of address.[127] Outside of this tractate, however, *brenin* appears less frequently than *arglwydd*.[128] Dafydd Jenkins has suggested that at least some of the passages in which the word *brenin* is used might be earlier in date, and this may well be right.[129] However, the Laws of Court clearly occupy a special role in all lawbooks that contain them, functioning almost as a pseudohistorical introduction to the lawbook as a whole, so it is also possible that the redactor's lexical choices in this text were deliberate. It is at least worth noting that *brenin* is also the word preferred in the Ior version's Test Book discussion of the golden treasure due the king of Aberffraw and in the story of Dyfnwal Moelmud.[130] And even if the redactor's use of the older terminology in these pseudohistorically loaded sections of the lawbooks is an indication that the narrative(s) on which he drew was genuinely old, one also has to consider why he chose to retain it in the context of the era in which he was writing. If nothing else, its use in a thirteenth-century text underscores both the antiquity of native kingship in Wales and the (putative) historical subordination of kingliness in Wales to the princes of Gwynedd.

The principal intention of the lawbook redactors seems to have been to emphasize the antiquity of Welsh rule—and, in some versions, Welsh hierarchies of rule—rather than to discuss any particular king or court. In fact, the redactors seem to go out of their way to avoid linking the courts they are describing to any one particular place and time. Even passages that likely allude to a specific event in the period contemporary with the lawbooks are often couched in a manner that disguises their contemporary relevance. Hence, the veiled nature in Ior of what is almost certainly a reference to Llywelyn the Great's having disinherited his older illegitimate son Gruffudd in favor of his younger legitimate son Dafydd in 1220.[131] Instead of using the names of the parties involved, the issue is presented as a general question of whether kingship ought to be regarded as open to all heirs or only to the person designated specifically by the reigning monarch.[132] Another potentially identifiable historical allusion in the lawbook is couched in Ior B in a way that makes it appear as though the contemporary controversy to which it speaks actually derives from the distant past. One of the most bitterly contested issues of the twelfth and thirteenth centuries was the homage and dues owed by rulers within Wales to the prince of Gwynedd, and by the prince himself to the English king. In its Test Book discussion of the insult payment due the king of Aberffraw, the Ior B redactor acknowledges that the Welsh ruler owes a one-time payment called the *mechdeyrn ddylyed* to the English king when he receives his land from him.[133] However, after that payment has been made, the text asserts, he owes nothing further save the honorific gifts of dogs, hawks, and horses. This is far less than what the English king would have believed himself to be entitled. Moreover, exactly the same gifts are said to be owed by the king's heir and war leader to the king in lieu of death duties (*ebediw*) because "there is no entitlement to *ebediw*" from persons as closely related to him as these persons are assumed to be.[134] In other words, a passage that appears to acknowledge the subordination of the Welsh prince to the English king in fact ends by asserting a virtual identification with him.

But there is more. The origins of the *mechdeyrn ddylyed* are uncertain. J. Beverley Smith has argued that *mechdeyrn ddylyed* as it appears in Ior owes much to contemporary notions of enfeoffment and, possibly, to the specific conditions of King John's reign.[135] However, it seems likely that English claims to this due preceded the thirteenth century and the reign of King John.[136] Both the section on the *mechdeyrn ddylyed* and the pseudohistorical framework into which it has been inserted are included in Latin C, which Russell has shown to be the earliest of all the extant northern texts, likely predating the composition of the Test Book, though drawing on an Ior-type text.[137] The form of the word as it appears in Latin C is likely much earlier than what we find in Ior: *mechteyrnged* contains the archaic word *ced*, "tribute," which is attested also in the memoranda of the Book of Chad.[138] In fact, *mechdeyrn* itself is a very old word—attested for Breton in the ninth-century *Cartulaire de Redon* and found elsewhere in Welsh literature only in the triads and in verse.[139] Regardless of how old this due actually was, however, it is significant that all versions of the passage (Ior, Latin B, and Latin C) refer to the English ruler as the *brenhyn Llundeyn*, the "king of London" (Latin texts: *rex Londonie*)—a style of title clearly intended both to evoke the myth of an ancient island kingdom ruled formerly by a British king, and to leave open the possibility that one day the king on the receiving end of this payment might once again be a Welsh speaker.[140] In other words, regardless of any contemporary resonance *mechdeyrn ddylyed* might have had for thirteenth-century Welsh persons, it is here being deliberately embedded in the pseudohistorical past.[141] Also mentioned in Latin C is the oath of obedience sworn to the *edling*, again a reference to the oath Llywelyn ap Iorwerth required his nobles to swear in 1226 and again in 1238.[142] It is surely not accidental that the text, here, uses the archaic term *gurthreghat* for the heir rather than the more up-to-date *edling*, a usage that again has the impact of embedding innovation in the distant past.

The golden regalia that might strike the casual reader as a picturesque holdover from a long-dead past thus stand revealed as critical to the manner in which the lawbook redactors imagined not only the office of king, but the political landscape of Wales as a whole. By situating the rulers of contemporary Wales within a regal tradition stretching back beyond Hywel into the distant mythological past, the authors of the lawbooks—and of the Ior redaction in particular—evoke a vision of Welsh sovereignty that was both eternal and embedded in the land itself. Traditionally, the antiquated feel of the Welsh lawbooks has been explained by their tendency to preserve ancient or outdated practices.[143] Stephenson takes a different tack with respect specifically to the Laws of Court, arguing convincingly that its seemingly archaic nature reflects the desire of thirteenth-century jurists to recall aggrandizing princes to the traditional dues and practices of yesteryear.[144] To these arguments might now be added the observation that timelessness is an important aspect of Wales as it is imagined in these sources. What we are witnessing here is the construction of a political landscape that, in refusing to be pinpointed to a particular place and time, consciously lays claim to all ages, past, present, and future.

On the narrative level, the regalia also serve to signpost for readers how the Laws of Court tractate—and, by implication, possibly the lawbooks themselves—should be read. In the context of an Arthurian tale, golden objects and lavish attire generally signal the world of civilization and the court. When such treasure is absent, or when symbols of wealth and luxury are juxtaposed with something that does not seem to fit (Peredur's rustic garb, for example), we know that either we have left that world or that something foreign is intruding into it—something that speaks of exile, of a boorish upbringing, or potentially even of danger. In a book of law, by contrast, gold and silver are usually taken quite literally, as anachronisms or textual remnants of an earlier age. Our expectations of the legal genre predispose us either to skip over such passages or find a logical way to explain them, because law and fanciful imagery are presumed not to intersect. What our study of imagined Wales suggests, however, is that in law also treasure and landscape can mean more than themselves: the glittering world of a courtly past, the hope for a brilliant future to come and, most especially, the advent of a narrative with the potential to transcend the strictly literal.

CHAPTER 2

Court and Country

Wales and Britain are not the only imagined landscapes in the lawbooks. Equally constructed—and equally a focus for the expression of political priorities—are the landscapes of court and country. Indeed, of all the narrative progressions implied in the lawbooks, the one from *llys*, "court," to *gwlad*, "country," is the most visible and important: a feature common to all the principal redactions that appears to have been present already in the Model Lawbook. Despite their significance, however, it is not entirely easy to characterize the nature of these two spaces. Courts historically varied considerably in size and prestige; as we have seen, the court of the Laws of Court tractate encompasses both the mobile and the static *llys* and is kept deliberately vague in terms of time. Similarly, the term *gwlad*, which features prominently in contemporary political discourse, can be used in a number of different ways.[1] Its basic meaning is "lordship," by which is meant the territory over which a ruler might exercise jurisdiction. However, the nature and extent of the area implied can vary from text to text. Whereas in some instances *gwlad* (and its Latin equivalent *patria*) are used to denote large kingdoms like Gwynedd or Powys, in others they indicate much smaller units, such as individual commotes (Welsh *cymwd*), cantreds (Welsh *cantref*), or a collection of cantreds. Commote or cantred are in this sense more geographically precise terms than *gwlad*; however, the latter occurs more frequently in the laws, perhaps because it could be used for both the people who occupy a given territory and the territory itself.[2]

What matters most about the terms court and country, however, is that, as used in the lawbooks, they are as much constructs of the political imagination as they are genuine social or geographical entities. One clear indication of this is the fact that they exist within a political landscape which is not imagined in the same way across all versions. In Cyfn, Bleg, and the Latin tradition lawbooks, this landscape is bipartite in nature, comprised of court and country. Indeed, some texts draw explicit textual boundaries between the laws pertaining to these two political spaces so as to mark the transition from one to the other:

> Hyt hyn gan ganhat du6 kyfreitheu llys rytraethassam. Weithon gann borth ygogonedus argl6yd iessu i grist: kyfreitheu g6lat a dangoss6n.[3]
>
> To this point with the permission of God we have treated of the Laws of Court. Now, with the help of the glorious Lord Jesus Christ, we will present the Laws of Country.

Ior also marks the end of the *Lleuer Llys*, "Book of the Court," and the transition to the Laws of Country (*Ior* 43/13, 44/1). However, its notional political landscape is very different from what one finds in the southern texts. In Ior, there are *three* different regions—not merely court and country, *llys* and *gwlad*—but the *gorwlad* as well, the lands that lie outside the *gwlad*. Moreover, while the location of this *gorwlad* is never made precise, it is consistently envisaged as hostile, a place of danger and predation.

The character of the *gorwlad* is most evident in the passages on the booty, *anrhaith*, taken by the bodyguard in their raids. Whereas Cyfn and the Latin and Bleg traditions fail to associate the bodyguard's booty with any particular locale, Ior consistently identifies it as having been seized from a *gorwlad*, rather than from within the *gwlad* itself. *Ior* 6/21, for example, refers to the *anreyth a dyccer o orwlat*, "booty that may be taken from a *gorwlad*";[4] the corresponding passage in Cyfn speaks merely of the *anreith awnel y teulu*, "booty that the *teulu* may take,"[5] and the Latin redactions and Bleg are similarly silent about the origins of the booty in question.[6] *Ior* 8/22 (on the steward) mentions the *anreyth a del o orwlat*, "booty that may come from a *gorwlad*"; the parallel passage in Cyfn (and, here again, the Latin traditions and Bleg read much like Cyfn)[7] refers only to the *anreith y gan y teulu*, "booty [that may be taken] by the *teulu*," without stipulating where the raid in question might have occurred.[8] *Ior* 10/11 grants the court judge the steer of his choice from the *anreyth a wnel e teylu eg gorwlat*,[9] "the booty that the warband may take in a *gorwlad*"; the equivalent text in Cyfn, by contrast, gives him the share of two men *or anreith a wnel y teulu*,[10] "of the booty that the warband may take." The Latin passages and Bleg likewise say nothing about the venue of the raid.[11]

Very similar to these provisions are *Ior* 13/7 on the poet of the warband, and *Ior* 34/9 on the highly unpopular *rhingyll*, "sergeant," both of which link *anrhaith* to *gorwlad* in a way that the equivalent passages in Cyfn, the Latin texts, and Bleg do not.[12]

This characterization is utterly consistent: the *gorwlad* in Ior is a place existing in hostile opposition to the *gwlad* rather than progressing harmoniously from it. Only three times in the Ior Laws of Court tractate does the word *anrhaith* in the sense of "booty" occur without being specifically associated with *gorwlad*;[13] moreover, and more significantly, *gorwlad* never appears except in association with *anrhaith*.[14] Indeed, only once in Ior's Laws of Court tractate is there even a hint that raiding might take place in the lord's own territory—and that occurs in a sentence in a miscellany of passages which is clearly an addition to the original.[15] Even there, the word *anrhaith* never occurs; instead, the passage describes the king being entitled "to go with his host outside the *gwlad*" (*mynet a'e lu o'r wlat*) only once a year, but "to go in his own kingdom" (*menet en e kyuoeth ef ehun*) whenever he wishes.[16] The phrasing is significant. In the versions of this passage that occur in Latin A, Latin D, and Bleg, the warband of the king is referred to as taking booty from the king's own *patria* (*familia regis si ad predam ierit in patria regis*). In fact, Latin A even stipulates the spoil that the king himself is to receive.[17] In Ior, the reference to hosting has been dropped altogether: the king's progress through his own realm with his retinue appears to be peaceful and ceremonial. No mention is made of raids, let alone the prospect that a ruler might despoil his own *gwlad*.

Ior's linking of *anrhaith* and *gorwlad* is, I would argue, deliberate: a means of constructing the political landscape in a particular way and for particular purposes. The contrast with Cyfn, Bleg, and the Latin traditions is too striking and Ior's terminology too consistent for this to have been anything but intentional.[18] For while the *gorwlad* does appear in Cyfn, Bleg, and the Latin traditions, it is depicted in those texts in a considerably more complex—the words "realistic" or "unmediated" might be even more appropriate—manner than it is in Ior. In Cyfn, *gorwlad* is never associated with *anrhaith*, nor *anrhaith* with *gorwlad*—in fact, only twice in the entire Cyfn lawbook is the *gorwlad* mentioned as a venue in which hostilities might even take place.[19] Bleg and the Latin texts do acknowledge that violence might occur in a *gorwlad*, and Lat D and Bleg once use the word *anrhaith* in the context of booty taken from an outside land.[20] More frequently, however, in these texts as in Cyfn, the *gorwlad* appears as a place from which foreign poets or travelers might journey for peaceful purposes, brides might be sought, or witnesses or guarantors be found to help with a legal case.[21] The differences between these redactions and Ior are numerous, significant, and unlikely to be coincidental.

But which lands was the Ior redactor imagining, then, as constituting the *gorwlad*? One might expect, given the political circumstances in which the text was composed, that the *gorwlad* would consist of places such as England, the March, or other lands occupied by *alltudion*, "foreigners" who reside outside of Wales. However, there is no evidence of this. Like the princely court itself, *gwlad* and *gorwlad* seem throughout the Ior redaction to resist precise identification. Rather, these terms seem to embrace a variety of historical realms, large and small, contemporary and historical. When the redactor distinguishes the *gorwlad* in which raids take place from the *gwlad* in which by implication they do not, he seems to have a wide variety of threats and incursions in view, from full-scale foreign conflicts to border skirmishes with neighboring Welsh lords. Raids of all these levels of seriousness are amply evidenced in the historical record, of course. Between 1212 and 1218, for example, Llywelyn ap Iorwerth won back Perfeddwlad, punished the Marcher lord Reginald de Braose for his defection, overran Powys and forced partition on the princes of Deheubarth, and won significant territorial and jurisdictional concessions from the minority government of Henry III.[22] The Ior redactor alludes to none of these encounters directly, however, just as he refers to no specific historical court. This allows him to envisage competing jurisdictions within Wales while not compromising his depiction of Wales and Welsh unity.[23] The opposition between *gwlad* and *gorwlad* is less an expression of hostilities between peoples than a political state of mind: *gwlad* is whatever seems in context native, local, and safe; *gorwlad* is its opposite.

Ior's treatment of *gwlad* and *gorwlad* parallels the prose literature of the period in important ways. As Catherine McKenna and others have pointed out, a prominent theme in works like *Branwen* and *Peredur* is the disjunction between (in Homi Bhabha's terms) "home" and "un-home"—the loss of certainty attendant on the reshaping of a world intimately known and possessed as a result of contact with outside forces.[24] In general, the lawbooks seem less pessimistic about the political future of Wales than the prose tales do. But the prominence in Ior's narrative of the contrast between interior and exterior, native and foreign, must give us pause. In the omnipresent threat posed by the *gorwlad*, as also in the apparent indeterminacy of its boundaries, we may be catching a glimpse of the cultural unease McKenna describes.[25] Another apposite parallel is the twelfth-century Welsh biography of *Historia Gruffudd ap*

Cynan,[26] in which, as Patricia Malone has pointed out, the distinction between "inside" and "outside" the kingdom is crucial to the structuring of the narrative. Here also, there are few set boundaries. Everywhere Gruffudd finds himself is conceptualized as interior to his rightfully appointed realm; movements against him are conceptualized as intrusions from outside regardless of where they originate.[27] When the sons of Merwydd and the men of Lleyn rise up against him, for example, it is his rightful rule (*brenhinyaeth*) they betray and his kingdom (*kyuoeth*) to which they guide other members of the conspiracy.[28] Similarly, in the account of the battle of Mynydd Carn in 1081, Gruffudd is using Danish and Irish troops to try to regain his kingdom, but it is the people of Trahaern of Arwystli who are depicted as being chased back home through forests and over mountains to their own *gwlad* (*patria*).[29] Ior's characterization of *gwlad* and *gorwlad* precisely reproduces this thematic opposition between inside and outside, native and foreign, culture and chaos. As we will see, such oppositions lie very much at the heart of the lawbook as a whole.

Order in the Court

The Ior redactor's construction of the *gorwlad* as an inevitably hostile place out of which warriors sally forth in search of booty is both deliberate and pointed—a way of underscoring the contrast between home and "un-home" that is the essence of his appeal to his perennially divided compatriots. Equally artificial is his depiction of the court to which he imagines these warriors returning. For within its bounds, the energy and violence of the raid disappears. In stark contrast to the inherently chaotic *gorwlad*, the court appears as a peaceful and ordered environment in which everyone knows and maintains his place. Moreover, here too, there is a marked contrast between Ior and the southern redactions. The most important of the court's buildings is the hall (*neuadd*), the nucleus where feasts are held and political business transacted. In Cyfn particularly, and to a lesser extent Bleg and the Latin texts as well, information on seating arrangements within the hall is scattered throughout the redaction in ways that are frankly somewhat confusing. In one passage, only the king, *edling*, court judge, household priest, and chief poet are said to have a set place in the hall; in another, places are implied also for the *penteulu*, chief groom, chief huntsman, footholder, falconer, poet of the warband, and physician. These apparent discrepancies may be due to differing textual traditions; alternatively, they may reflect the difference between those possessing actual seats in the hall and those sitting on the benches at places reserved for them.[30]

Ior, by contrast, gives seating within the hall special prominence by treating it in a separate section near the beginning of the Laws of Court, following the discussion of the royal family and immediately preceding that of the other court officers (*Ior* §5). Unlike Cyfn, Ior situates fourteen chaired officials (*cadeyryavc*) within the space of the court. Charles-Edwards has already outlined some of the most important aspects of its seating arrangements. As he points out, those to whom seats were assigned were not necessarily the highest-ranking officers at court. Some very important officials, such as the *distain*, "steward," and the *gwas ystafell*, "chamberlain," had no set places, presumably because of the expectation that they would be serving elsewhere during the feast.[31] The hall was imagined as being divided into an upper and a lower half; the upper part, where the king and his heir sat, was regarded as more honorable than the lower, where the prince's warband was situated. The Ior redactor's point here was not to denigrate the leader of the warband, himself often depicted in the text as a relative of the king's but, rather, to present the king's household at peace, in its most festive aspects.[32] Festivity and display were important components of twelfth- and thirteenth-century rule; the seating arrangements described in the hall underscore the importance of the performance of royal power to the king's ability ultimately to exercise it.

Charles-Edwards approaches the passage on seating as a historian naturally would, as a source providing information about how royal courts would actually have been ordered in the period. The basic presumption of the text, he argues, is that courts in one area would have been laid out in much the same way as courts in another. No room is left for variation across different regions; the court is presented as being ordered in the same way regardless of locale. Indeed, this very sameness would in his view have constituted an important prop of Welsh rule: "The king's *llys* was expected to live by the same rules whichever particular *llys* it was inhabiting. Moreover, this pattern of royal life, which was a central element in the political culture, was not confined to a particular kingdom. . . . As the itinerant *llys* extended a single royal authority throughout a kingdom, so did the royal *llysoedd* as a whole, living according to the one rhythm, impose a single political culture throughout Wales."[33] Charles-Edwards's suggestions cannot be verified with certainty from this distance on the basis of the available textual or archaeological evidence, but they do accord well with what we know of other monarchies in this period. The performative aspect of sovereignty tends to leave regrettably few traces on the ground. Archaeology can identify in a general way many of the places from which Welsh lords ruled in this period, but finding even principal structures like the *llys* or church of a given settlement can be tricky in the extreme. Archaeologists and historians alike have thus tended to rely on the laws for a sense of what the courtly enclosures they excavate might have looked like.[34] This seems entirely reasonable. Given what we know about courts from elsewhere in Europe at this time, it would be surprising if something very like what is outlined in the lawbooks had *not* obtained historically in Wales.[35]

The likelihood that Ior's account of seating arrangements within the court expresses something real about Welsh practices of feasting and political display does not, however, change the fact that aspects of its description serve narrative purposes within the text. Not the least of these is the building up of the contrast between *gwlad* and *gorwlad*. It is surely significant that in Ior, but markedly less prominently in Cyfn, Bleg, and the Latin texts, each officer's seat is carefully situated with respect to the stable physical features of the hall—its columns (*colofn*), hearth (*tân*), screen (*celfi*),[36] bar (*corf*), and entrance (*drws*)—as well as to the places occupied by other officers. Thus, the king is said to sit next to the screen with the *cynghellor*,[37] host, *edling*, and chief falconer next to him; the priest of the household is described as sitting across the fire next to the other screen with the court justice and chief poet beside him. The *penteulu*, "chief of the war-band," sits with his left hand toward the entrance to the hall; some members of the warband surround him, while others are positioned on the other side of the entrance. Next to him sits the poet of the warband and the chief groom.[38] The insistence on structural details is not accidental; nor is the manner in which each officer is located with respect to a feature or person with others radiating outward according to rank. The effect here—and I would suggest the intent as well—is to define the court as both a physical and social space, the stability of which is vested not only in material structures, but also in the orderly social relationships of the redactor's imagined and timeless Welsh polity.

It is thus significant that the passage on seating is given such a prominent place in the tractate, after the king and his family and before the other officers. Court and kingdom are portrayed here as grounded in structures of rule that are simultaneously personal and physical. Stability, permanence, and order are the main priorities: dominion is vested both in people and in landscape, in culture and in nature. Regardless of what actually took place at any given historical feast, what mattered most was the idea of the court—immutable and immutably on display. This is probably also why the Ior redactor deliberately chose to integrate information on protections and lodgings into his discussions of individual court officers rather than presenting them simply as mnemonic lists, as was done in Cyfn, Bleg, and the Latin tradition. Lists disrupt the narrative flow and obscure rather than highlight order and positioning within the court. The Ior redactor's transformation of these lists into narrative and his relocation of this material into the subtractates serve not only to further define each officer's service, but to locate each within the geographical and social hierarchies of the court.

Movements in Space

The boundaries separating the world of court from the world outside are marked in a variety of ways: in all redactions by the visible presence of porters and doorkeepers guarding entrances and exits, and additionally in Ior by the contrast posited between *gwlad* and *gorwlad.* Within the interior space of the court, however, there were other, smaller areas—stables, kitchens, sleeping quarters, chambers—between which persons and objects might move. As a general rule, movement across the courtly landscape serves in all the principal redactions as a unifying device; however, as we will see, in some versions it functions also to delineate hierarchies of status within court and kingdom. As Charles-Edwards points out, different court officers exercised jurisdiction over different spheres of activity. Some officers acted as heads of groups of subordinate officials, a relationship marked by special privileges, lodging locations, and gifts. Only certain officers and their men traveled with the royal court on its progresses, and only some had close personal access to the king. Even the prerogatives of the royal family were circumscribed in this respect. Movement within and across these various jurisdictional areas was frequent and played an important role in binding members of the court both to one another and to the *gwlad* of which they were each individually a part.[39]

One example of such movement is the gift exchanges made by the king and queen to the officers who served them, and by certain of these officers to their colleagues in the hall. Some of these gifts were intended as payments and some to subordinate; others expressed alliance or otherwise honored those who received them. Some were payments recipients regarded themselves as entitled to by virtue of their employment at court; others were extraordinary rewards paid in response to remarkable achievements.[40] There was unquestionably a symbolic as well as a practical aspect to these gifts, as is evidenced by the gifts of clothing made on the three principal feasts of Christmas, Easter, and Whitsun, when the court was on full display. At these times, certain court officers passed their clothing on to others, who then passed their clothing on in turn. In Cyfn, the sequence of gifts is said to proceed from the *penteulu* to the steward, from the steward to the poet of the warband, and from the poet of the warband to the doorkeeper; in Ior, the sequence was the same except that it seems to have begun with the king.[41] Charles-Edwards is surely right to underscore the manner in which this exchange of gifts "exemplifies hierarchy" and unites the warband to the other officials of the household.[42] Not only did these exchanges take place in the context of the feast, itself an occasion for the display of political and religious unity, but the order in which they were given would also have caused givers and recipients to process back and forth across the upper and lower halves of the hall. What we have here is political performance writ large: important members of the royal household enacting through their movements and gifts both their relationships to one another and their rootedness within the court.[43]

There are no contemporary records to confirm that the gift exchanges described in the laws actually took place, although garments were valuable property and were often given as wages or bequeathed in wills in this period, so there would be nothing surprising about the idea.[44] However, even if what the lawbooks record here reflects actual (if idealized) historical practice, the manner in which these gifts are described serves the important narrative function within these texts of defining the interior space of the royal hall. The key symbols here are the feast, the hall (*neuadd*), and the court (*llys*) itself. Defined horizontally by the movements of officials across it, and vertically by the hierarchies enacted by the exchange of gifts, the hall as depicted in the Laws of Court is a deliberately enclosed political space. It is surely no accident that the gift exchange ends with the doorkeeper.[45] Like the larger court of which it was a part (itself also guarded by a porter), the hall is a place of tangible physical structures, performative rituals, and, in view of the livery that officers are imagined to be wearing,[46] visibly shared identities. Safe and protected from all external dangers, its interior landscape is presented in Ior, and to a large extent also in the other lawbook versions, as defined not only by the physical space itself, but by the movements of those who inhabit it. Moreover, the movement from feast to hall to court directly parallels the progression from interior to exterior landscapes noted earlier as a primary structuring device within the lawbook as a whole.

In using feast, hall, and court as metaphors for social order, the laws again reflect long-standing motifs in medieval Welsh poetry and prose, where the hall functions frequently as both metonym and metaphor for those who inhabit it.[47] In poetry as in the laws, the hall is as much a symbol of the unity and stability of the king's reign as it is a literal structure. Poetic portrayals of the *llys* as a literal and imagined space stress its importance as a performative venue for rulers, much as in the Laws of Court tractate.[48] The late ninth-century *Etmic Dinbych*, for example, weaves feast and fortress together with the community of warriors in a paean of praise;[49] the twelfth-century *Hirlas Owain* imagines the drinking horn passing from hero to hero as great deeds are communally remembered.[50] The feast is a common (if retrospective) topos in post-Conquest Welsh poetry as well.[51] In works like the poems of the fifteenth-century poet Dafydd Nanmor, for example, the community of feasters is a metaphor for the totality of human existence, communion in its broadest social and political aspects.[52] Indeed, a degree of cross-fertilization between genres is evident in the poet's allusion in his praise for his patron to officers named in the Laws of Court tractate. For him, looking wistfully back over two centuries of English rule, like the lawbook redactors before him, court and hall were symbols of unity, not merely within one particular historical court, but within Wales as a whole.[53]

Gendering the Courtly Landscape

As we have seen, it can be challenging to distinguish between those aspects of the lawbooks that can be taken at face value and those that cannot. And of course, one does not automatically cancel out the other: descriptions of procedure might be at once accurate and yet rhetorically strategic in establishing a redactor's principal themes. Landscapes can be real and still occupy a symbolic role within the context of a given narrative—Jerusalem, for example. Similarly, movements across courtly spaces can be accurately described and yet also be crucial to the furtherance of an authorial agenda. Paradoxically, the easiest passages to judge are those that we believe to have been furthest from the truth. It should be clear by this point that redactors could and did tailor their books to their own liking, leaving things out when they wished to and adding others. What was archaic in origin was not necessarily obsolete or antiquarian in context. As with the gold and silver treasure mentioned in the Laws of Court, the past could be put to good (and contemporary) use by enterprising jurists.[54] The earlier scholarly approach whereby historians carefully separated the chronological layers of their sources has given way to a desire to take each text as we find it, to seek the reasons for which it might have taken its extant form.[55]

One instance where thematic imperative seems to have reshaped historical reality is in the movements attributed to certain individuals in the hierarchy of spaces within the court. For even more important than those possessing designated places within the hall are those constructed by the redactor as being properly separate from it.[56] The queen, for example, appears to have been given special prominence within the Ior version of the tractate.[57] All lawbook redactions describe the queen mainly on the basis of the officers assigned to serve her rather than in her own right. However, in Cyfn, Bleg, and the Latin texts, this information is exceptionally thin and scattered throughout their Laws of Court tractates.[58] The Ior redactor, by contrast, creates an entire section devoted to the officers who serve the queen, which it places at the end of the discussions of the king's officers.[59] Whereas only four queen's officers are mentioned in Cyfn, Bleg, and the Latin texts—her steward, priest, chambermaid, and groom[60]—in Ior, that number is raised to eight. These include not only the officers mentioned in the other redactions, but also a queen's cook, candleman, and chamberlain. Additionally, the doorkeeper of the chamber (*drysor ystafell*), who in other redactions is associated with the king, is reconceptualized in Ior as a queen's officer specifically (*dryssavr e urenhynes* in *Ior* 27/1). Even the queen's groom is exalted in Ior by being placed on a par with the king's chief groom (the *pengwastrawd*) and sharing in his privileged status.[61]

And yet what might appear to mark a significant elevation in the queen's power and status within the court is actually nothing of the kind. For despite the increasing visibility of her entourage, the queen's own movements are imagined as being closely restricted within the political space of the court. Already in Cyfn and Latin C, the earliest of the extant northern lawbooks,[62] the queen is linked much more closely to the realm of the chamber than to that of the court. Her officers are explicitly characterized in Cyfn as the *s6ydogyon yr ystauell*, "officers of the chamber,"[63] and her steward is said, both in Cyfn and in Latin C, to exercise his office in the chamber (*ystafell/camera*) as opposed to the court or hall (*llys* or *neuadd*) in which the king's steward operates.[64] The queen's priest is called the *effeirat brenhines*, "priest of the queen," while the king's is the *effeirat teulu*, "priest of the household."[65] Even the clothing she provides the court officers—linen, as opposed to the woolen garb given by the king—speaks to her association with the interior spaces of the household. For linen was usually worn next to the skin, as a shift or similar type of undergarment; woolen clothing, by contrast, was outerwear and functioned in this case as the livery by which the public and political identities of the royal officers were made known to all.[66] But though the queen is associated primarily in these texts with the chamber, the chamber is not associated uniquely with her. Both the chamberlain (*gwas ystafell*) and the doorkeeper of the chamber (*drysor ystafell*) are conceptualized as king's officers; moreover, it is clear—from Cyfn, the Latin texts, and Bleg—that the chamber in question is imagined as being the same for both the king and the queen.[67] More than a domestic space, it is an environment in which the king and queen move freely, people might be shown to places designated for them, and to which guests might come seeking admittance from the doorkeeper appointed for the purpose.

The Ior redactor not only adopts the association between the queen and the chamber, he extends it. *Brenhines*, "queen," is virtually synonymous with *ystafell* in his account. Whereas the prince and other male officers move easily within and among all spaces within the court, public and private (*ystafell*, *neuadd*, and *llys*), the queen's primary link with the outside world is her chamberlain, who is depicted running errands between the chamber where she is, and the hall, where she is not.[68] Officers are categorized as either pertaining to the court (*rey y llys*) or to the queen (*rey y urenhines*)—a characterization that implicitly constructs an opposition between the queen and the court per se.[69] So thoroughgoing is Ior's association between queen and chamber that what in Cyfn and the Latin texts, is an opposition between the doorkeeper of the hall (who serves the hall and all in it) and the doorkeeper of the chamber (who serves the chamber and all in it), becomes in Ior a contrast between a doorkeeper of the queen, who serves uniquely in the chamber, and the doorkeeper proper, who serves "the hall or other place in which the king may be."[70] Moreover, the nature of that chamber itself is different from what it is in the Cyfn and Latin texts. The king and queen are no longer imagined as sharing the same bedroom; rather, the queen occupies a separate room or suite of rooms and is served by her own domestic servants.[71] On nights when the king stays with her, the king's chamberlain stays overnight and is present to serve them both; on nights when the queen sleeps alone, her needs are met by the chambermaid, who stays in her chamber with her.[72]

Even more significantly, the queen's chamber is reconceptualized in Ior as an entirely domestic and apolitical space, a place where she might sleep, receive guests, or listen to music specifically described as being soft and melodious—a distinct and surely intentional contrast to the political songs described as being performed within the court.[73] The provision on music is phrased in Ior, but not in Cyfn, in a manner that seems to take for granted the queen's absence from the hall.[74] Indeed, it may be that we are supposed to imagine her as not even being present in the hall during feasts. She is said to take food and drink in her chamber,[75] and no version of the seating arrangements (including Cyfn) gives her a designated place within the hall. She is depicted as sending horns of drink to certain officers during feasts,[76] but there is no reason why such drink could not have been delivered from the chamber to the hall. In fact, the stipulation in some Cyfn manuscripts that her priest is to sit across from her would work best if we imagine her dining in her chamber.[77] Furthermore, the additional servants accorded the queen in the Ior account—cook, candleman, chamberlain—imply a private world of eating, sleeping, and entertainment that is highly circumscribed and set apart from the normal course of affairs at court. It is true that all these activities had a political aspect to them in the Middle Ages. However, the general impression left by the Ior account is of a primarily domestic world—visited by the king but not occupied by him, and where even close personal male servants were kept strictly segregated from their lady at night.[78]

It is possible that Ior's account reflects to some degree actual practices in the courts of thirteenth-century Gwynedd. Henry III (d. 1272) was the first English king to maintain sleeping quarters separate from his queen; insofar as the maintenance of separate chambers or households seems to have become fashionable in noble circles all across Europe in this period, Ior's changes to the situation visible in Cyfn and the Latin texts may be evidence of the outward-looking nature of the Gwynedd principate.[79] On the other hand, the link between queen and chamber is so static and artificial in Ior that it seems more likely that the redactor's intention was less to reproduce the Venedotian court known to him than to actively comment on it. The circumscribing of her ability to move within the court is surely a deliberate feature in the narrative. Not only is it integrated as an idea into several different sections of the tractate, it encompasses more than just her relegation to the chamber. Whereas in Cyfn, the Latin texts, and Bleg, the queen is said to be able to offer offenders protection (*nawdd*) across the boundary of the country, in Ior, mention of any such geographically defined protection is glaringly absent. The text makes reference to the existence of a queen's *nawdd*, but the extent of that protection is never actually defined, and there is no indication of her being able to move across the space of the *gwlad* in such a manner.[80]

In fact, even the movements of her most important officers are depicted in Ior as being constrained in a manner that clearly subordinates them to the servants of the king. In Cyfn and Latin C, the queen's officers by and large exercise a protection that is equal to or patterned after that offered by the officers of the king. Thus, while the *nawdd* extended by the king's steward lasts from when he first begins to stand in the king's service to when the last man retires from the court to sleep, the *nawdd* of the queen's steward lasts from when he first stands in service to the queen to the time the last man retires from the chamber.[81] In Ior, by contrast, the queen's steward is allowed to accompany an offender only as far as the king's steward; the latter takes over from there.[82] A similar tradition is also reported regarding the queen's chief groom.[83] And as with protection, so also with lodging: several queen's officials, including the priest, the groom, the doorkeeper, the cook, and the candleman, are all imagined as lodging with the corresponding king's officers.[84]

All in all, the association in Ior between chamber and queen represents a gendering of the courtly landscape that is considerably more thoroughgoing than the pattern visible in Cyfn and Latin C. In those texts, the public and private spheres of the court are imagined as already sufficiently separate that queens could be thought of as occupying a portion of the court only (the chamber) instead of the court as a whole. However, in those texts, the chamber is still envisaged as shared and not associated uniquely with the queen. In other words, for the Cyfn and Latin C redactors, the distinction between *llys/curia* and *ystafell/camera* did not yet constitute an opposition between the uniquely political and the uniquely domestic. The perspective of the Ior redactor, by contrast, is very different, in that he constructs the queen as confined not merely to the private sphere, but to a particular portion only of the domestic space. Her movements within the court are sharply curtailed; she is defined as exclusively domestic and entirely isolated from the political realm of the court. The king's chamber retains some degree of political significance by virtue of its connection to the person of the king. The custom whereby the judge of the court had his lodging in the king's bedchamber was probably on its way out in the thirteenth century, if indeed it had ever reflected reality. But it is, in context, testimony to the overlap between public and private believed to obtain in the immediate proximity of the king himself.[85] Similarly, Ior assigns the safekeeping of the king's treasure to his *gwas ystafell*, which suggests that the royal treasure itself was kept in his chamber.[86] There is no indication of a similarly public role for the chamber of the queen. Many a political issue might have been decided in those quiet moments shared by king and queen within the domestic spaces of the household; in Ior, however, any political activity took place within the royal court and hall, in the absence of the queen. She is safe, secure, and contained: both the beneficiary and the prisoner of the oppositional landscapes the redactor has created.

What she is as well, however, is a construction, and a pointedly political one at that. Ior was redacted during the reign of Llywelyn ap Iorwerth, whose controversial queen Joan, illegitimate daughter of the king of England, was regarded by many native Welshmen as being overly involved in Llywelyn's political affairs. Indeed, the composition of the Ior redaction is generally dated to the decade following 1230, the year Joan was formally accused of an adulterous liaison with the Marcher lord William de Braose, an event that would likely have decreased both her credibility at court and native appreciation for her involvement in matters of state.[87] That she did play a significant role in Llywelyn's political affairs is indisputable. Records show her issuing charters together with Llywelyn and negotiating with John on Llywelyn's behalf before her imprisonment in the de Braose affair,[88] and it did not take her long after her release in 1231 to regain her position. By 1232 she was back in business, negotiating at Shrewsbury on behalf of Llywelyn with Henry III.[89] Huw Pryce has suggested that her status even seems to have increased in later years: before her death in 1237, as she is seen making use of the new and more exalted title "Lady of Wales."[90] Nor was Joan the only woman visibly to participate in native political matters. David Stephenson points to evidence of other Welsh women's involvement in political affairs, some of which doubtless seemed similarly controversial to their contemporaries: Senan, who helped secure the release from captivity of her husband, Gruffudd ap Llywelyn; Eleanor de Montfort, who was active in negotiations between her husband, Llywelyn ap Gruffudd, and Edward I; and Hawise, wife of Gruffudd ap Gwenwynwyn of Powys, implicated in the 1274 conspiracy against Llywelyn ap Gruffudd.[91]

What we have in the Ior redactor's complete relegation of the queen to the domestic sphere, I suggest, is not a straightforward, if idealized, description of court life but, rather, a pointed comment on one particular woman's role in politics and, perhaps, on women's involvement in such matters in general.[92] Indeed, given that Joan's affair with de Braose was discovered when William was found with her in the prince's own chamber[93] during an Easter visit to Llywelyn's court, the emphasis on the queen's remaining quietly set apart from the world of men in her own chamber may have been understood in context as pointedly critical, mockingly humorous, or both. In any case, the imagined enclosure of a politically prominent female figure within the domestic spaces of the household has its parallels in romance literature of the period. In Marie de France's "Lay of Guigemar," for example, a queen is kept prisoner by her jealous husband, with only her maiden niece to move between her chamber and the castle proper.[94] Similarly, Jennifer Smith has suggested that courtly love poets often placed powerful landowning women in indeterminate literary landscapes in order to remove them from the actual political landscape of the Aquitaine. Her words are worth quoting at length:

> Poets then work between landscapes, a fictive landscape of love—where the *domna* may or may not exist—and a 'real' landscape, where the lover resides, as do the 'real' men with whom he desires community and in whom are invested the courtly qualities the poet seeks to emulate. The *domna* is located not in the landscape in which the poet resides, a landscape so often associated with real land, which, in the societies of the High Middle Ages was often certainly connected with real power; but in the fictive landscape, distanced from the arena of power, land and politics. . . . The *domna* [is] trapped, as it were, in the landscape of love. She is the possession rather than the possessor of land, denied any agency to alter her position, or to move between landscapes. The construction of the *domna* may well represent a powerful woman who holds land and authority, but it also denies the possibility of such a woman existing within the poet's immediate interest and influence, where land and power remain firmly in the hands of men, and women firmly under their control. This removal of a powerful, landowning woman from the Occitan landscape reveals an anxiety about powerful women . . . which is likewise present in the customs (the legal statutes of Occitan cities).[95]

In *Owein* also the two widowed countesses who pursue the hero in order to protect their realms in the wake of their husbands' deaths exist within landscapes that are more fictive (indeed, otherworldly) than real. Ior's queen is similarly constrained: the occupant of a gendered political landscape reflecting contemporary fears about the undue influence of powerful women.

Indeed, it is also possible that the concerns reflected in Ior relate to more than Joan herself. Practices regarding female inheritance were visibly changing in the period of the lawbooks, often in ways that were unpopular with traditionalists of the sort the jurists are believed to have been. According to native

Welsh law, women could not inherit land. Ior describes this as a practice associated particularly with Gwynedd, but it has generally been thought to have obtained more widely than this.[96] Of the various lawbook redactions, only *Llyfr Blegywryd* allows a daughter to inherit land, and then only in a case where no other male heir exists. The fact that Latin D, of which *Llyfr Blegywryd* is largely a translation, does not include a similar provision in the relevant section of its lawbook may suggest that this exemption from standard practice was both controversial and limited in application.[97] However, while restrictions on female inheritance may have been strictly observed in certain areas of Wales, they were frequently relaxed in others under the influence of English and Marcher custom, which permitted women both to inherit lands and to occupy them as dower after the death of their husbands.[98] Wealthy Welsh landowners who had only daughters found English inheritance practices useful in preventing estates from being broken up and dispersed among distant male heirs (or sometimes out of the paternal kindred altogether). Similarly, claiming to hold land by English tenure allowed one to escape native dues like *amobr* (the payment owed to a woman's lord on the occasion of a sexual relationship), because such matters were largely determined by the law by which one held one's land.[99] Given these advantages, many Welshmen began looking for ways to circumvent native law regarding inheritance and land tenure.[100]

Anxieties about the abandonment of native legal traditions generally ran high among the jurists who composed the lawbooks.[101] Indeed, the prince of Gwynedd himself, Llywelyn ap Iorwerth, was one of the biggest offenders: his elevation of his younger (legitimate) son Dafydd as heir over his older (illegitimate) son Gruffudd contravened long-standing native practices regarding marriage and inheritance. And female inheritance may have been an especially sensitive issue, not least because the relaxation of native inheritance practices seems frequently to have been happening in the principality itself.[102] It appears likely that attempts to let daughters inherit, or to evade long-standing dues like *amobr*, might have generated considerable resentment among those who lost out as a result of the legal maneuverings involved. Concerns of this sort may also be reflected in the literature of the period. C. W. Sullivan has suggested, for example, that embedded in Lleu's ultimately patrilineal succession to the lordship of Gwynedd in the Fourth Branch of the Mabinogi are reservations about female inheritance of lordship and land,[103] and Roberta Valente has argued similarly that the violation of gender norms is linked in this tale to the transgression of native law.[104] In Ior's relegation of the queen to the private sphere and stern insistence on women's inability to inherit land—possibly also in the silence of the lawbooks generally on the changes taking place in inheritance practices—it may be that we have a reflection of precisely these concerns.

Splitting Heirs

A similar use of landscape to address contemporary anxieties about status and inheritance also features in the discussion of the *edling* and *penteulu*, the heir and the leader of the prince's household troops respectively.[105] As relatives of the prince, they were also potentially his most significant male rivals.[106] Both are situated by the Ior redactor within the space of the court in a manner designed to downplay the threat they represent, but they are treated in very different ways. Already in Cyfn, Bleg, and the Latin texts (including the early northern text Latin C), the *penteulu* is depicted as fully integrated into the rituals, structure, and physical spaces of court and *gwlad*. He gives and receives gifts, occupies the largest and most centrally located house in the *tref*, or "townland"; takes two men's share of the booty, and receives horns of drink from the king and queen.[107] He is not merely present in the hall; he has a special responsibility for the lower part of it, in that he receives a third of the fine paid for offenses committed in his section.[108] The protection he can offer to offenders is said, in Cyfn, to be second only to that of the king and the *edling*, and to embrace an area much larger than court or townland: whereas the *edling* takes an offender *hyt yn diogel*, "to a place of safety," the *penteulu* conveys him safely across the boundary of the commote.[109]

As in its treatment of the queen, Ior enlarges upon these themes, adding details about the *penteulu* designed to underscore his being literally and geographically at the center of court life. Ior is the only redaction to elevate the *penteulu*'s protection to the same level as that exercised by the *edling*—that is, "to a place of safety."[110] The *penteulu* is also said in Ior (but not in Cyfn or Latin C) to receive the garments of the king in the three great feasts and to be able to make use of his horses and dogs—privileges that would visually highlight both his connection to the court and his identity as a close kinsman of the king.[111] Like the *edling*, the *penteulu* is said in Ior to leave his horses and dogs to the king in lieu of *ebediw* (a death duty due to the lord) because both were assumed to be close relatives (conceptualized as physical members of the body) of the king.[112] *Ebediw* and its related due *amobr* (the sum paid to a lord upon a woman's first sexual experience) were obligations arising within relationships of lordship and subordination; gifts of animals associated with hunting and war, by contrast, implied a commonality of background, interests, and exalted status.[113] The redactor's point here is to stress the *penteulu*'s personal identification with king and court. Indeed, so close is the connection as it is depicted in Ior that the *penteulu* is said to preside over the court himself when the king is absent.[114] Only at Christmas, when he goes on circuit, does the *penteulu* leave the prince's side, and even then he seems symbolically to still live within the confines of the court. Officers from the household travel with him and serve him formally in what amounts to a pseudocourt for the duration of his trip.[115]

The *penteulu* thus appears in all redactions, but especially in Ior, as the quintessential inside man: thoroughly integrated into a political landscape that both celebrates and contains him. But Ior's *penteulu* is more than just a paragon of aristocratic fidelity. He is also a perfect foil for the prince's other main rival, the *edling*, the prince's heir, who is imagined in the text as the most powerless of the powerful: an honored guest in a household to which he never fully belongs, but from which he is not allowed to depart. Again, the basic outlines of the *edling*'s position at court are visible in all redactions. In all the principal lawbook versions, the *edling*'s status as successor to the king is emphasized by the seat he is said to occupy in the hall, across the fire from the king. As Charles-Edwards has argued, the fire here is almost certainly a symbol for the kingship to which the *edling* is ultimately expected to fall heir.[116] This is likely the significance also of the lodging assigned to the *edling* in all redactions: the king's hall at night, with all the youths of the court around him and the fueler to kindle the fire and close the doors before retiring.[117] The kindling of a fire on the royal hearth, the heir who sleeps at night in a darkened royal hall surrounded by those who will ultimately constitute his royal retinue—the symbolism here seems so marked as to be inescapable.[118] Of course, it is also worth noting the significance of the doors the fueler is said to close before he departs. This seemingly trivial detail, which appears in all redactions, is unlikely to be coincidental in a narrative in which both movement across the landscape of the court, and its opposite, the relegation of an individual to a particular space only within that court, are used to reflect the political capacity of the individual. The doors to the court over which the *edling* will eventually rule are, for the period of his predecessor's reign, still closed to him.

The idea that the *edling*'s movements and presence at court might be restricted in some way is present in all the redactions. However, it is most fully developed in the Ior account, which significantly enlarges the subtractate on the heir beyond what is found in Cyfn and Latin C. For if the *penteulu* is the ultimate insider in the Ior account, the *edling* is his opposite. Unlike the *penteulu*, whose place within the hall is situated with respect to its permanent interior structures (*tal . . . y'r neuad* and *drws*), the *edling*'s seat is contingent on the physical location of the king's own person. In the court, and yet not of it, the *edling* is described in Ior—but not, significantly, in Cyfn, the Latin texts, or Bleg—as excluded also from all its rituals and reciprocal obligations. Whereas the *penteulu* shares fully in the exchanges of clothing that take place at the three great feasts, giving his clothes to the steward and (in the Ior account) receiving clothes in turn from the king, the *edling* is explicitly said to be exempt from this process unless the king himself wishes otherwise. Even then it is the king, not the heir, who decides on the recipient.[119] Similarly, servants and officers are explicitly forbidden to demand anything from the heir for the service they provide—again, a provision entirely unique to Ior.[120] These exemptions may seem like special privileges granted the *edling* in recognition of his exceptional status at court, and in fact they are. However, they are accorded him not because he stands above the court, but because he is depicted in the text as in some sense standing outside of it: honored as a guest is honored, and simply not a part of the reciprocal obligations and gifts by which court life is defined.[121] The contrast with the king, queen, and *penteulu* is striking.

The *edling* is depicted as isolated in still other ways from the normal run of ritual exchanges marking the social contours of the court. Ceremonial gifts of food, beverages, and in-kind payments form an important part of the compensation of the other court officers, including the *penteulu*, who gets drink, medical care, animal skins, and even a song from the household bard as part of his due.[122] The *edling*, however, is exempt from all these transactions, despite the fact that—or, rather, because—he is supported entirely by the king. Cyfn and the Latin texts make the point that all the *edling*'s expenditures are to be met by the king as a perquisite of his high status: "the king is to provide the *edling* with the whole of his expenditure honorably (*yn enrydedus*)."[123] And Latin C similarly envisages the king providing *omnia necessaria . . . cum honore*, "all his requirements . . . with honor."[124] The main point here would seem to be that, whereas the *penteulu* receives his compensation in return for services he performs, the *edling*'s expenses come to him by virtue of who and what he is rather than what he does.[125] The texts indeed go out of their way to stress the *edling*'s exalted position within the court: *principalis est habendus in curia et honorabilior omnibus post regem,*[126] "he is to be treated as the chief man in the court and with greater honor than everyone after the king."

By contrast, while the Ior redactor also envisages the total provisioning of the *edling* by the king, his treatment of the *edling*'s expenditures is phrased in such a way as to leave the impression of an individual with absolutely no wealth or standing of his own: *a'y holl treul o goffrys y brenhyn, hyt yn oet y offrvm; a'y ueyrch a'y kvn a'y uodrvyeu a'y tlysseu y gan y brenhyn, a'y arueu heuyt,*[127] "and all his expenses come from the king's coffers, even including his offering; and his horses and his dogs and his rings and his trinkets from the king—and his weapons too." Not only is the word "honorably" of the other redactions pointedly left out, but the redactor then adds that the *edling* may not give anything away without the king's permission—a provision not found in any other redaction.[128] The *edling* certainly wants for nothing; anything he requires is to be provided for him out of the king's own stores. And yet he also has nothing he can call his own, not even the offering he makes to the church.[129]

This is not to say that the *edling* is characterized in Ior as unimportant. Rather, the point of the redactor's revisions is not to diminish the honor due the heir, but to safeguard the prerogatives of the reigning king by emphasizing the extent to which the *edling*'s status derives from his. The *edling*'s glory is a reflected glory; it is not he who is served and honored in the court, but the king in him. He has a place in the hall, but strictly on the prince's terms; this is why, in Ior's account (but not in Cyfn, Bleg, or the Latin texts), it is the king, rather than the *edling*, from whom other positions within the court are measured.[130] He can host a banquet, but only at the prince's discretion,[131] and even his gifts are not his own. Eventually, the young men who surround him at night may come to constitute his warband; eventually, the officer who kindles the fire on the hearth for him may come to serve him rather than the prince. For now, however, he is powerful only in name: the prince of a shadow court, an anomaly in a deliberately constructed political landscape.

Nor is this a purely academic distinction. The Ior redactor is here addressing one of the most visible and divisive problems of contemporary European politics—the desire of royal heirs to establish their own courts independent of the ruling king. Disputes over this issue arose frequently in twelfth- and thirteenth-century Europe. Henry the Young King, elder son of Henry II and heir-presumptive to England, Normandy, Anjou, and Touraine, revolted against his father in large part because of the latter's refusal to allow him an independent court. Similar problems plagued the relationship between the

German princes and their nominal overlord, the son of Frederick II; indeed, when push came to shove, the latter sided with his son's opponents. Courts were places where alliances could be forged and rebellions begun; in such environments, princely posturing could come all too quickly to look like royal rule. This is undoubtedly why the Ior redactor depicts *edlings* as being forbidden to leave the royal court without permission. In contemporary European diplomatic parlance, departures of this sort constituted calculated insults and frequently marked the prelude to revolt.[132]

Equally telling is how *edling* and *penteulu* are imagined in Ior as coming to their positions. Both are explicitly identified as king's "members" and as such are linked to the king in ways that other court occupants are not. Ior says explicitly, however, that the *penteulu*'s status comes from the king (*vrth uynet y ureynt ef vrth y brenhyn*): his is an appointed office.[133] By contrast, the manner of the *edling*'s coming to rank is left undecided in Ior, which acknowledges that contemporaries do not agree on whether all the king's members, his sons, nephews, and male first cousins, ought to be considered *edlings*, or whether *nat edlyg nep namyn y nep y rodho y brenhyn gobeyth a gvrthrych ydav*,[134] "no one is an *edling* save him to whom the king gives hope and prospect." This provision may simply reflect a terminological debate taking place among the Welsh juridical class—a quarrel perhaps engendered by the supplanting of the older term *gwrthrych*, "heir," with *edling*.[135] However, it is equally likely (and of course the two explanations are not mutually exclusive) that the Ior redactor has a very specific situation in mind here, one already alluded to: Llywelyn ap Iorwerth's designation in 1220 of his younger, legitimate son Dafydd as heir over his older illegitimate son Gruffudd. Gruffudd did not easily accept his exclusion from the throne. Attempts by Llywelyn to settle Gruffudd on compensatory apanage lands did not resolve the issue, and conflicts between them continued for many years. Llywelyn proclaimed his choice of *edling* several times in many different venues over the course of his reign, which in itself testifies to the difficulty he had in securing uncontested support for his plan.[136] Given the visibility of this struggle at the time Ior was redacted, it is difficult to imagine that this passage could have been penned in isolation from these events.

Indeed, the issue of whether kingship was an elective office or whether reigning kings had the right to designate their own successors was a lively topic generally in twelfth- and thirteenth-century European political circles. The problem was not uniquely Welsh, even though the Ior redactor's portrayal of *edling* and *penteulu* may reflect the struggle between Gruffudd and Dafydd specifically.[137] Significantly, no final opinion is declared in Ior about the matter of succession. The redactor's views on the definition of *edling*, and by extension the manner in which royal heirs ought to be chosen, are left unexpressed, a fact that is strikingly at odds with the usual practice elsewhere in the lawbook.[138] Perhaps succession mechanisms were still too much in dispute; perhaps it was still possible that Gruffudd might win. Most likely the redactor wanted to phrase his categories broadly so as to be able to argue that, whatever Gruffudd's rightful status was, he was bound by it to show obedience and loyalty to the reigning prince. To anyone familiar with events in contemporary Powys, Deheubarth, or Gwynedd, Gruffudd's actions in contesting the succession could have appeared a threat both to the stability of the throne and to the integrity of the principality as a whole.[139] The redactor's reluctance to excise Gruffudd altogether from all possibility of succession is therefore very striking—and perhaps a reflection of the diversity of views on this issue to be found among the *uchelwyr* class by and for whom the laws are believed to have been composed.[140]

Considerably less ambiguity obtains in the Ior passage on the possibility of an *edling* taking lands in apanage. As J. Beverley Smith has shown, one of the ways kings tried to ensure the succession of their own candidate was to settle other potential heirs on apanage lands designed to compensate them for their exclusion from the throne. Once an heir had taken possession of such lands, he was deemed to have given up his royal aspirations; his status would no longer be that of *edling*, but would instead follow the status of the lands he had received.[141] Ior records this practice, but then implies that an *edling* himself might take lands in apanage, and that his status also might be altered by the lands he received: "the *edling* and those whom we named above will be of that status [what the text has just described for the *edling*] until they take land, and after that their status will follow the status of the land they take."[142] It is possible that *edling*s might expect to take on lands and titles in the course of their growing up that would later be added to their royal title once they succeeded, much as Henry II was duke of Normandy and count of Anjou before he became king of England. However, no hint of this appears in the sources, and such arrangements would run directly contrary to the Ior redactor's remarks about the *edling*'s dependence on the king for his material well-being. Much more likely is that the passage is intended to be read against the historical backdrop of relations between Llywelyn and Gruffudd. Llywelyn granted lands in apanage to Gruffudd several times during his reign in an attempt to get him to accept Dafydd as heir to the principality. Gruffudd accepted these lands, but not the diminution of status that went with them; instead, they became the power base from which he launched his next revolt. He obviously considered himself an *edling* despite Llywelyn's proclamation of Dafydd as heir, and to judge from the difficulties Llywelyn had in squelching him, others must have as well. Indeed, just how much support he still carried became evident shortly after Llywelyn's death in April of 1240, when Dafydd's authority collapsed in very short order and Gruffudd's claim to share in the succession was resurrected by a variety of native rulers.[143]

The redactor's admonition to all would-be princes is thus a simple one, and is deliberately underscored by his use of landscape symbolism within the text. Those who have agreed to their exclusion from the throne by the taking of apanage lands must either accept the lands offered them together with the diminution of status and prospects such a gift entailed, or choose to remain an *edling* with all the restrictions on personal movement and property outlined in the text as attendant on that status. In other words, Gruffudd must decide on the status he wishes to claim. Should he opt for the position of *penteulu* to his brother Dafydd—and it was historically the case that one brother would often assume that position for another[144]—he would be, in the words of the *Cronica de Wallia*, "second to him in reverence and in all other matters,"[145] which is exactly the *penteulu*'s position as described in the laws. Charles-Edwards expresses surprise at the "relatively marginal" place accorded the *penteulu* in the lower and less honorable part of the hall, physically separated from the person of the king, and at the fact that the household troops should be placed under the control of a person (the *penteulu*) who might well be a potential rival for the throne.[146] His placement within the hall was probably intended in large part to underscore his role of defending the court against attacks from outside. However, it may have a symbolic significance as well. A *penteulu* who has accepted his exclusion from the throne is imagined in Ior as a person who *is* to some degree marginalized—but only from the royal succession. Otherwise, he is the most trusted and privileged man in the court apart from the royal family itself and, as such, thoroughly integrated into the physical and social structures of the court of the king he has freely chosen to serve.

The *edling*, by contrast, stands in a different relationship altogether to court and king in Ior. Because of his prestige and expectations, he has greater privileges than the *penteulu* in some respects; his proximity to the royal hearth during feasts and at night publicly advertises what his relationship to the court will be in the future. However, the court is not yet his: his movements within it are constrained, and he is tightly bound to the person of the king. It is not difficult to see in these depictions of *edling* and *penteulu* a commentary on contemporary events. The prospect of an heir—officially designated or not—setting himself up as a rival king was a threat that nobles of the period understood all too well. Gruffudd's refusal to accept his exclusion from the succession was thoroughly justified according to native law,[147] but posed a direct danger to unity and peace. Dafydd seems generally to have supported his father in his political maneuverings and constituted less of a threat. However, the extreme dependence by which the *edling* is characterized in the Ior version of the laws is so marked that one wonders whether the text might also be reflecting to some degree contemporary concerns about his actions. Dafydd's spectacular marriage to the Marcher heiress Isabella de Braose in 1229 elevated Llywelyn's own prestige considerably, as it was he who arranged the marriage in the first place; from that point of view, the alliance represented a real coup for the throne of Gwynedd. However, it also enriched and empowered Dafydd. Is it conceivable that embedded in Ior's provisions on the *edling* is a fear that Dafydd might attempt to use his newfound wealth and connections to set himself up on his own or jump the gun with respect to succession? Helen Fulton has identified a concern with succession as one of the principal themes of the Mabinogi;[148] perhaps the same is true of the law as well. Like barons everywhere, the *uchelwyr* to whom the lawbooks are customarily attributed had a vested interest not merely in the judicious exercise of princely power, but in the predictability of its succession from one generation to the next.

The examples of the queen, *penteulu*, and *edling* inevitably raise questions about whether landscape figures into the way other important officers of the court are depicted. It is notable, for example, that the court priest—called in the lawbooks the *offeiriad teulu*, "priest of the warband"—is associated in the first instance with warband, hall, and court rather than with bishop and diocese.[149] This may reflect an older state of affairs; Cyfn U even locates his sleeping quarters in the lodgings of the *penteulu*,[150] though elsewhere he is said to lodge with other clerics of the court. The tension between these two visions of the priest, as layman and kin-member on the one hand, and ordained cleric on the other, runs through all the principal redactions of the lawbooks. However, as Pryce has argued, Ior tends to uphold the interests of the prince rather than the church when the two come into conflict.[151] It may thus be significant that Ior alone fails to assign a particular *nawdd* to the priest as it does for the other court officials.[152] Like the queen, the priest may be being imagined here as circumscribed in his ability to move freely (and accord movement to others) within the court and *gwlad*. It may also be important that in Ior the priest is depicted not only as one of the king's "indispensables," *anhepgor* (as he is in Cyfn), but also as so closely tied to the king's person that he is imagined as exhausting his horse in the process of keeping up with him.[153] The Ior redaction's depiction of the *edling* turns what in other lawbook versions is an entitlement to maintenance by the king into a state of abject dependency upon him. Similarly, the priest's importance to the king is presented in Ior as an inability to move or act independently of him.

For the lawbook redactors, the landscape of the court was thus one of spaces within spaces, much like their vision of Wales itself.[154] A stability of positioning within the court is equated with stability in rule and in the vertical and horizontal relationships constituting that rule. It is surely not accidental that even those without set places in the hall are nonetheless situated within the political space of the court in some way, whether through their lodgings, their service in hall or chamber, or in the protection they provide. Safety consists in remaining not only within the interior landscape of the court itself, but within its smaller spaces as well. Movement within and across these spaces—from chamber to hall, hall to court, court to *gwlad*, *gwlad* to *gorwlad*—implies power and alliance when it is effected in accordance with political expectations, as with the gift exchanges taking place at the three principal feasts, or the departure of the *teulu* from the court to go on a sanctioned raid. However, when done in opposition to convention, or as a prelude to rebellion, movement signals something else altogether. The crossing of boundaries by those who should not cross them is clearly imagined as dangerous in this text. When a queen crosses inappropriately from chamber to hall, the barrier between private and public is breached in a way that poses a threat to the whole. When an heir leaves his father's court in a huff, looking to set himself up independently somewhere else, or a *penteulu* crosses from the lower, nonruling side of the hall to sit himself down by the royal hearth without permission, the hierarchy in which stability is vested is challenged. For the lawbook redactors, keeping to one's designated place was more than just a question of seating.

Moving to the Country

As depicted in the lawbooks, the court is an entity set apart, a place of safety inhabited by persons who move always within particular relationships and social structures. However, it is also the nucleus of the *gwlad*, the territory outside the court over which the prince exercises dominion. A realm of farming, pasturage, and forest, the *gwlad* is also held together by mutual obligations and constraints. These are outlined most clearly in the Laws of Country, which consists of a series of tractates and provisions on suretyship and contract, women, kinship, land division, and other such subjects. Among the most revealing are texts addressing the natural world: laws governing agricultural relationships among neighbors or those engaged in collaborative farming, and laws regulating relations between the human and animal realms. In Ior, three tractates in particular stand out. The tractate on Wild and Tame (animals) must have been an early part of the lawbook, as it occurs in some form or another in all the primary redactions. The antiquity of the tractates on Joint-Ploughing and on Corn-Damage is much less clear, although Daniel Huws and Aled Rhys Wiliam believe it likely that they were also integral to the original book of Ior rather than later additions.[155] The former at least is cited along with the Three Columns of Law in both northern and southern redactions as an absolutely fundamental part of the law. Ior C's Test Book preface even puts a curse on anyone who assumes a judgeship without knowing *teyr kolovyn kyvreyth a gwerth gwyllt a dof ac a perthyn attadvnt*, "the Three Columns of Law and the Value of Wild and Tame and what pertains to them."[156] Other redactions have similar provisions.[157]

That there was a pragmatic, real-life aspect to the regulations on Wild and Tame cannot be doubted. Monetary values are stipulated for many animals that seem to correspond to values in England around the year 1200,[158] and Paul Russell has suggested that amounts cited in the fourth fragment of Latin C's version of the tractate reflect market values on Anglesey specifically.[159] Tractates or other short texts like Wild and Tame may have circulated independently before their inclusion in *Llyfr Iorwerth*[160] and could thus have been used by judges on their rounds. It may be significant that Latin C is easily portable, shows signs of heavy use by practitioners, and contains glossing that suggests that it was used into the late Middle Ages.[161] In other words, the values cited in the Wild and Tame tractate likely had an actual connection to historical reality, and the tractate may have had a practical value in the real world that the Laws of Court, for example, probably never possessed. Be that as it may, even that which is practical can have a symbolic aspect to it when contextualized in a particular way. Whatever its significance in real life, there are several indications that the Wild and Tame tractate, like some of the others we have examined, also served an important narrative function for the Ior redactor.

The first is its placement within the Ior lawbook. Cyfn manuscripts vary considerably in their ordering of the tractates, and regulations on animals that occur together in some manuscripts are scattered throughout the redaction in others.[162] Generally speaking, however, the tractate on Wild and Tame falls roughly in the middle of the Laws of Country in Cyfn rather than at the end; its placement in Bleg and the Latin texts is similarly variable.[163] Ior exhibits a marked contrast in this respect, in that its provisions on animals look to have been deliberately gathered together into a single tractate and placed near the end of the lawbook as a whole.[164] It is not, of course, unusual for individual passages or even entire sections of the laws to float in this manner.[165] What makes Ior's positioning significant, however, is that the effect of its changes is to bookend the redaction as a narrative work with a tractate on the court on the one hand, and a tractate or tractates on the natural world on the other. Like many literary narratives of the period (*Owein*, *Gereint*, *Math*), Ior also begins in the cosmopolitan world of the court and moves outward to the land of farm and forest. Moreover, this progression precisely replicates the other progressions we have traced within the lawbook as a whole. Within the context of Ior's book, we move from culture to nature: from court, to *gwlad*, to *gorwlad*, and from that which is interior, native, and secure to that which is exterior, foreign, and ultimately hostile. Ior's redactor did not invent the bifurcation of the lawbook into the laws of court and country, nor the division of animals into wild and tame. What he does seem to have done, however, was deliberately reposition the material bequeathed to him in a way designed to carry forward the principal themes of the lawbook as a whole.

Equally significant is the nature of the landscape as he describes it. The Ior redactor appears to have reworked the material before him to accord with his vision of the *gwlad* as an interior world into which violence and danger do not intrude. The distinction between wild and tame animals is not unique to Wales; it occurs also in Bracton, which was being written and revised at precisely the same time as Ior. But whereas Bracton is concerned with the issue of ownership and how and under what circumstances wild animals taken in the hunt might recover their "natural liberty" after they have come into someone's possession, the priority of the Welsh texts is altogether different.[166] The immediate referent of wild and tame in the Welsh texts is the nature and temperament of the animals described. However, also implicit in this opposition seems to have been the type of environment they inhabit: forest and uncleared lands on the one hand and settled society on the other. Farm and forest appear as exterior landscapes with respect to the settled world of the court but interior realms with respect to the hostile lands outside the *gwlad*. They are, in other words, part of the *gwlad*, not the *gorwlad*, which remains in Ior an environment defined primarily by the violence of war. In this respect, Ior shows clear parallels with the poetry of the period, in which what are clearly political landscapes are also often imagined as encompassing moors and mountains as well as farms and halls.[167]

The relatively benign nature of the lands interior to the *gwlad* is perhaps most visible in the regulations on animals. Domestic and agricultural animals (such as cats, dogs, geese, pigs, and sheep) are well represented in all redactions; indeed, many of the Latin texts make clear that these are the beasts with which they will be most concerned.[168] Cyfn, Bleg, and the Latin texts also make room in the *gwlad* for wild creatures, such as badgers, wolves, and foxes, whose meat or skins can be useful to humans.[169] In the Ior redactor's vision of the *gwlad*, by contrast, the only wild animals are those that no longer constitute a threat to civilized society: animals found dead on someone's land, or those that have been killed and exist only now as skins.[170] Apart from these, there exist only the deer hunted by the prince's hounds and hawks and those hounds and hawks themselves—which are, quite literally, the exception that proves the rule, in that the landscape with which hunting was most closely identified both in Wales and elsewhere was that of the court. Jenkins has suggested that hunting with falcons was a pastime that actually began at court,[171] and it was certainly associated throughout the medieval world with courtliness and elite behavior. One of the leading courtly monarchs of the thirteenth century, Emperor Frederick II, wrote a treatise on the subject,[172] and hunting and falconry accounted for a significant percentage of total royal expenditures in England in the period from 1234 to 1307.[173] In Wales, the *penhebogydd*, "master falconer," occupied a prominent role in the Welsh court and indeed was even served publicly by the king in certain circumstances.[174] And as with the hawk, so also with the hound: the hunting of deer with dogs was regarded in the medieval world as a noble prerogative.[175] The chief huntsman also occupied a privileged position in Welsh courtly circles; in fact, Cyfn and certain of the Latin texts actually situate the laws pertaining to dogs and deer in the Laws of Court tractate.[176] In other words, deer and hawks form a part of the Ior redactor's vision of the *gwlad* not because they and the forests in which they hunt and are hunted belong to the realm of the wild, but because they are regarded as part of the world of the court.

The opposition between wild and tame in Ior thus resembles the other oppositions we have traced in the lawbooks between interior and exterior landscapes, with the world of farm and forest belonging to the interior realm of the *gwlad* rather than to that of the dangerous and chaotic *gorwlad*. The tractates that follow Wild and Tame in Ior make much the same point. There also, nature is depicted as having been tamed and domesticated by human activity. Plowmen working collaboratively in teams defined by contract and bonds of mutual obligation bring the land to a state of fertility, providing sustenance for all. Cooperation creates peace and prosperity, just as it does in the political realm. It is no accident, I would suggest, that Ior's Joint-Ploughing tractate begins with a section on land measurement that reproduces virtually word for word the passage on the measurements attributed earlier in the lawbook to the pseudohistorical figure Dyfnwal Moelmud. The base text below is taken from the latter, with additions or changes from the Joint-Ploughing tractate marked in parentheses and italics:

> And then they made the measure of the legal acre from the barleycorn (*This is the measure of the acre*). Three lengths of the barleycorn in the inch; three inches in the breadth of the palm; three breadths of the palm in the foot. Four feet in the short yoke, eight (*feet*) in the mid-yoke, twelve (*feet*) in the armpit yoke, sixteen (*feet*) in the long yoke. (*And*) a rod as long as the long-yoke (*that latter*) in the hand of the caller, and (*the caller in front of the oxen, and*) the center peg of that yoke in his other hand (*his hand*), and as far as he can reach and that with the length of his arm (*with the length of his arm and his rod on either side of him*) is two limits (*of the land*), that is the width of a legal acre and thirty times that is its length.[177]

The duplication of this passage at this point in the lawbook serves a variety of purposes. On one level, since the passage occurs first in the Laws of Country and later in the Test Book, it encourages a view of the lawbook as a narrative unto itself, the various sections of which build upon and relate back to one another. On another level, it urges us to reflect on the reasons for which redactors might have chosen to repeat material in this way. Repetition of this sort is rare in the lawbooks and therefore very unlikely to be accidental. As we have seen, the other important duplication in Ior is the golden treasure paid to the king of Aberffraw, which is first outlined at the beginning of the Laws of Court tractate and then reprised in the tractate on *galanas* that occurs near the start of the Test Book.[178] That evocative passage serves not only to connect the Test Book to the Laws of Court—and the lawbook to literary pieces like the Four Branches—but to ground the laws in the mythological past. It stands only to reason that the redactor was attempting something similar in duplicating Dyfnwal's measurements in the Joint-Ploughing tractate. The implicit reference to the mythical kingdom of Britain (which does not occur in this same form in the southern redactions) gives to the domestication of the land a similarly historical dimension, in which past, present, and future are inscribed upon the landscape of field and farm.

Thus, the main images of these final tractates are those of fertility, prosperity, and unity—a land organized and made rich by the collaborative labor of the people who till it. Not all is represented as problem free, of course. Untoward intrusions can occur into planted crops; that is what the tractate on Corn-Damage is all about. However, even these incursions are depicted as internal breaches that are largely domestic in character. Like the court, the agricultural world is also, in Ior (and to a certain extent in the other redactions), a landscape of spaces within spaces. Just as an upstart queen might move from chamber to hall, or a rebellious *edling* leave the hall in which he is set to sleep at night, so also might animals move from one farm or enclosure to another, doing damage as they go from the space in which they belong to one that is not their own. However, none of the intruders pictured here are truly wild. They are, rather, domestic animals such as horses, cattle, sheep, and pigs and, as such, by definition containable: by fences, fines, payments owed in compensation to offended neighbors, and, most significantly, by the local officials of the prince. Even those few creatures that the Ior redactor characterizes as *guyllt*, "wild," are imagined as being animals that one could pen up in an outdoor fold (*em buarth allan*)—in other words, most likely wild pigs or even deer rather than wolves or foxes that one would simply kill.[179]

Moreover, as important as unauthorized movement across the landscapes mentioned in the text is that which is sanctioned and of use to society. The hunt is one such exercise, not merely because the animals killed are eaten, displayed, or ritually celebrated in the court,[180] but because of the prerogative implied by the king and his huntsmen's unhindered movement across the land.[181] The plowing of furrows in a field or the legal driving of stock across the land constitute other examples of the king's power and relationship with his realm, as does the wealth they produce for him. The key figures in this respect are the *maer*, *cynghellor*, and *rhingyll*, royal servants who move between court and country collecting the dues, renders, and fines owed to the king. Their status as transitional figures is marked by their positioning both in the lawbook as physical objects (they occur in both the Laws of Court and the

Laws of Country), and in the boundaries they traverse within the political geography of the realm.[182] The *maer*, for example, banquets in the king's hall, goes on progress (*cylch*) around the king's villeins, and participates with the warband (*teulu*) in raids and the taking of booty; in Ior, he is said to also offer protection to a wrongdoer *tros teruyn tyr e llys*, "across the boundary of the land of the court."[183] The *cynghellor* sits with the king during festivals, presides over legal proceedings, and takes dues from the villeins;[184] the sergeant stands in court sessions or during meals, collects fines from fugitives and death-duties from dependents, and travels on the king's affairs.[185]

It is certainly the case that symbolic readings like these are not the only way to approach the legal sources. Everything we have been talking about, from queens sitting quietly in their chambers to a preference for tame over wild, can be explained in a variety of ways, many of which require no interpretative foray into the symbolic realm. Only animals whose whereabouts are known can be pursued with a mind toward compensation, for example, so it would only make sense that these would be the types of animals that would draw the attention of the jurists. And the authors of the Latin lawbooks declare quite forthrightly that they intend to treat mainly of creatures that are of utility to man in providing clothing or food.[186] The Ior redactor does not consciously circumscribe his legal aspirations in this manner (although a distinction of this sort may lie behind the text's differentiation between clean and unclean animals).[187] On the other hand, the distinction between wild and tame and concern with the niceties of plowing obviously reflect real-life agricultural issues. The fact that something can be interpreted in a symbolic way within a given narrative does not preclude its importance as a real item in a law text that judges might actually have used.

On the other hand, the reverse is true as well. While symbolism does not negate the possibility of a pragmatic reading of a given text, pragmatism does not negate the possibility of a symbolic reading either. Indeed, the complexity of interpretation may well have something to do with the authority commanded by a given text. As Peter Goodrich remarks, "A reading of the legal text which ignores the power of its imagery or the aesthetic of its reception is a reading which is in many senses beside the point in that it ignores precisely that dimension of the text and its context which performs the labour of signification and so gives the text its effect."[188] The *gwlad* as constructed in the Welsh lawbooks—most fully in Ior, but to some degree in the other redactions as well—is by definition both imagined and real. We know from Bracton if from nowhere else that it would certainly be possible for a jurist of the period to include in his lawbook animals that are genuinely wild and undomesticated by man.[189] That is not, however, the lawbook that remains to us today, and we are entitled to ask why. Similarly, the progression from *llys* to *gwlad* to *gorwlad* unquestionably reproduces the actual social experiences of medieval Welsh men and women. On the other hand, it also recapitulates the movement from court to country that lies at the heart of the agenda of the Ior redactor. It is no quirk, nor structure of convenience: it is, rather, the thematic axis along which the texts as we have them today are structured.

These facts in themselves would suggest that we are dealing here with something deeply rooted in the Welsh experience of the twelfth and thirteenth centuries. The contrast between unity and order within, and chaos and anarchy without, is one that speaks both to the needs of the moment and to the priorities of the lawbook authors as persons caught in a perilous and confusing time. The lawbooks are not—or not merely—neutral descriptions of place or articulations of an aspired-to courtly ideal.[190] Rather, they constitute venues through which to reflect on developments in contemporary Welsh politics: innovations occurring in princely government in the twelfth and thirteenth centuries, changes taking place in native practices regarding marriage, inheritance, and the administration of justice. Looming over everything, of course, is the sense of unease generated by the influx of foreign elements into Wales and fears about the impact of English policy and politics on native Welsh lordship. For as we will see in succeeding chapters, it was not merely war that intruders brought with them from the *gorwlad*, but ideas and practices that threatened native traditions in a variety of ways, not least in their efficiency and breadth of appeal. Stephenson has remarked on the silence maintained by the laws on the extensive changes taking place in the machinery of government in this period, a silence he (rightly) interprets as itself a form of critique.[191] To this silence must now be joined the affirmative messages communicated by carefully selected imagery and a frank disregard for the boundaries of genre. What we are seeing in the laws are meditations on contemporary Welsh culture and politics which, if not loudly condemnatory, are at least profoundly uneasy about the perils of change.

PART II

Body and Bawdy

CHAPTER 3

Bodies and Nobodies

The reimagining of natural and cultural space was but one of the ways in which the lawbook authors addressed contemporary concerns over disunity within Wales and changing patterns of princely rule. Another was the deployment of symbols associated with bodies, both animal and human. Few have done more to highlight the importance of this line of inquiry than Caroline Bynum, whose groundbreaking study of body-focused food practices among religious women in the late Middle Ages opened up new ways of thinking about physicality and gender that have continued to inspire scholars ever since.[1] Her book *Holy Feast and Holy Fast* ignited interest in a wide range of related issues, including the meanings and contexts of asceticism and the denial of bodily pleasures,[2] relics and bodily dismemberment,[3] the monstrous, diseased, or transformed body,[4] the construction of gender and of sexual identity,[5] clerical sexuality and repression,[6] and a host of other topics.[7] Appearing almost at the same time were two similarly influential works on the body's relationship to politics. In a pioneering essay still read and cited widely today, Joan Wallach Scott introduced scholars to the notion of gender as a category of political analysis.[8] And Peter Brown's beautifully written *The Body and Society* explored the ways in which bodies could matter to government and citizenship. As he pointed out, it was not the mere fact of having a body, but rather what one did with it that most profoundly shaped the ancient Roman city as a functioning political entity.[9]

Medieval political theorists also used the body as a political symbol, albeit in somewhat different ways. Their speculations often centered on the relationship between the body natural and the body politic, a subject explored most memorably by Ernst Kantorowicz in his now-classic study of the king's two bodies.[10] Perhaps the most important aspect of the political theology outlined by Kantorowicz was the conceptualization of the state itself as a body, a theme occurring already in Plato's *Republic* and Aristotle's *Politics* and subsequently repopularized for the Middle Ages by John of Salisbury in his *Policraticus*, finished around 1159. In his work, John adumbrated his own version of what has come to be called the "organic analogy," in which the state is envisaged as a living organism, with the prince as its head, the priesthood its soul, the senate its heart, and judges and governors as its eyes, ears, and tongues.[11] John himself may have been encouraged in his development of the idea by Marie de France's retelling of a popular fable found originally in Livy and Aesop, entitled "The Man, His Belly, and His Limbs"; he may even have heard her perform this fable at the court of Henry II.[12] Alternatively, John may have found inspiration in William of Conches's *Glosae super Platonem*, or in other texts consulted by him on trips to Italy.[13] In truth, however, the use of the body as a symbol for the corporate polity of the church was so widespread by the time John was writing that he would not have needed either Marie's tale or William's glosses to remind him of the motif. Many biblical, late antique, and early medieval ecclesiastical authors had made similar use of body metaphors in their writings on the community of the faithful, including the authors of Leviticus and Deuteronomy, the Apostle Paul, Gregory the Great, Bede, and Beatus in his *Commentary on the Apocalypse*.[14] Versions of the organic analogy even played a role in the rhetoric surrounding the Gregorian reform.[15]

Encouraged both by the popularity of the *Policraticus*, and by the increasingly widespread availability of Aristotle's works, the organic analogy spread quickly across Europe in the course of the high and late Middle Ages, where it appeared in the work of a number of different writers, including Brunetto Latini;[16] Thomas Aquinas, who in *De regimine principum* characterized the heart, head, and soul as governing powers;[17] John of Paris in his treatise *On Royal and Papal Power*;[18] William of Pagula in *The Mirror of King Edward III*;[19] Marsiglio of Padua in *Defensor Pacis*;[20] John Wyclif in *On the Duty of the King*, and numerous others.[21] The analogy lay similarly at the heart of the treatise *De moneta*, written by Nicole Oresme, a French translator of Aristotle, and it occurred in rare pictorial form in a fourteenth-century illustration contained in a Pierpont Morgan library manuscript of the treatise *Avis au roys*.[22] Perhaps the most famous late medieval exploration of the image was that of Christine de Pisan, who in *Le livre des corps de policie* (c. 1406) equated the king with the head, the knights with the arms and hands, and the common people with the legs and feet.[23]

Several of these texts exemplify yet another common aspect of medieval explorations of the body politic—its frequent association with the princely conduct literature so popular in the period. Often termed "Prince's Mirrors" (or *Fürstenspiegel*), these (frequently vernacular) guides to being and becoming a ruler took a wide variety of forms, including treatises, histories, biographies, letters, and poems.[24] Oresme's treatise, for example, was written for his patron Charles V, while Christine de Pisan's *Le livre des corps de policie* was penned for the French dauphin, Louis de Guyenne. Nor was the use of the organic analogy in works of this type merely a late medieval phenomenon. John of Salisbury dedicated the *Policraticus* to his friend Thomas Becket during Becket's term of service as chancellor of England, while Aquinas's *De regimine principum* was written for the king of Cyprus. In fact, the metaphor of the body politic even played an important role in what might be called the antiroyalist literature of the period. As Robert Yeager has argued, images of the decapitated head of the ruler were frequently used in chronicle accounts of the Peasants' Revolt in 1381, where they clearly evoked (for both sides) the idea of a state that had lost its leader.[25]

Two points in particular are worth highlighting here. First, the organic analogy was clearly already a philosophical and rhetorical commonplace in medieval political theory by the time the Welsh lawbooks were composed. Given its ubiquity in European writings on kingship and rule from the early Christian period onward, it is inconceivable that the jurists who authored the Welsh lawbooks would have been unfamiliar with it. Indeed, in Yeager's words, "the difficulty would be for any literate medieval person to *avoid* it."[26] And in fact the sources leave no doubt but that the notion of the body politic was embedded in the language medieval Welsh persons used to talk about rule in the twelfth and thirteenth centuries. In some Welsh texts, the ruler seems even to function simultaneously as both body and body part—as a symbol, in other words, both of the state itself (body) and of the person who rules it (head). Both the *edling*, "heir," and the *penteulu*, "leader of the king's troops" are, for example, referred to in Ior and the Latin texts as king's "members" or "limbs" because of their familial relationship with him.[27] And Latin B, D, E, and Bleg actually define the king's members as those who *ad regiam dignitatem pertinentes, ea tamen carentes* (Bleg: *y rei a perthyno wrth vrenhinawl vreint, kynys pieiffont*),[28] "pertain to the royal privilege though lacking it themselves," a definition that seems to blur the line between members who belong to the body of the king by virtue of their biological relationship with him on the one hand, and members who belong to the body of the crown by virtue of their proximity to the throne on the other.

The best-known example of the use of political body imagery in Wales is, however, the constant wordplay around the word *pen* that occurs in works of the period. This word literally means "head"; however, like its Irish cognate *cenn*, it was commonly also used from the earliest days to denote "lord, master, ruler," in names and phrases such as Pwyll Pen Annwfn, "Pwyll, lord of Annwfn," in the First Branch of the Mabinogi.[29] Sometimes the metaphor was taken quite literally, as in the Second Branch, in which Bendigeidfran, *urenhin coronawc ar yr ynys hon, ac ardyrchawc o goron Lundein*, "crowned king over this island and invested with the crown of London," is depicted as a ruler (*pen*) who is reduced to nothing more than a head (*pen*) in the course of a disastrous invasion of Ireland.[30] Bendigeidfran's body, which is imagined in the tale as abnormally large, supports his people while he is alive, serving physically as a bridge by which his men are able to cross over the Shannon River. When he is killed, his severed head is brought back on his own instructions to the western edge of the kingdom of Britain, where it continues to feast and entertain the seven of his men who have survived the expedition. After eighty-seven years in a state of enchanted forgetfulness, one of them opens a mysterious door in the hall on the side facing Cornwall, thereby ending the enchantment and opening their eyes to the cruel reality of their ruler's death. The head must now be buried, in London, facing outward toward France as a means of protecting Bendigeidfran's erstwhile kingdom from foreign intrusion; his physical body is already gone, left behind in Ireland. And as with head and body, so also with realm and rule. The kingship of Britain has been taken over by a usurper in his absence, and Bendigeidfran's buried head protects a kingdom that neither he nor his son and heir still possess. The scene, as Catherine McKenna suggests, is one of "diminishment" and "unhomeliness."[31]

This connection between the whole or diminished body of the ruler and the well-being of the state is also found in poetry of the period. Latin eulogies upon the death of the Lord Rhys in 1197 speak of the face and shining hair of the prince, whose hand once touched that of Alexander "in the sun's orbit" (*sensit Alexandri solis in orbe manum*), turning now to ashes with his death.[32] Rhys, alive, was a raging lion, a wild boar, the "unconquered head of all Wales" (*anorchyuygedic benn holl gymry*), who wielded "the arm of prowess, the hand of generosity, the eye and lustre of worthiness" (*breich kedernyt llaw haelyoni llygat ac eglurder adwyndra*)."[33] (Note the use of *pen* here, presumably both in its literal and figurative sense.) With Rhys dead, princely emblems and standards fall to the ground because the hand of a ruler no longer exists to lift them on high; similarly, the "reins of life fall slack full of lamentation," presumably because of the same missing hands.[34] These images of handlessness and bodily fragmentation are anything but accidental, as is the choice to evoke a ruler going into battle on behalf of his people. Lines 13 and 14 of the eulogy underscore this notion of Rhys's disappearance by explicitly contrasting his absence with the proximity of his enemies now that he is gone: *Resus* abest *inimicus* adest *Resus quia* non est (emphasis mine), "Rhys is gone, the enemy is near, for Rhys is no more."[35] Lest one miss the importance of this notion of absence, *Resus abest*—"Rhys is gone"—is repeated in the very next line. Indeed, now that all Wales is widowed (*Wallia iam viduata*), the bodies (*corpora*) of Rhys's bereaved people fall silent.[36]

Perhaps the most moving example of this motif is Gruffudd ab yr Ynad Coch's elegy for the last native Welsh prince, Llywelyn ap Gruffudd, killed in 1282. Gruffudd, whose soubriquet actually means "son of the Red Judge," appears to have come from a legal family and may actually have been a lawyer or judge himself.[37] The imagery of this poem is striking in several respects, but no more so than in its focus on bodies and, particularly, on the body of the prince as a metaphor for the nation over which he had ruled. Both Llywelyn's and his brother Dafydd's severed heads had been sent after their deaths to London and put on display at the Tower, Llywelyn's with "a crown of ivy in mocking fulfilment of a prophecy which said, so the English were led to believe, that one of the Britons would be crowned in London."[38] The image of the prince's decapitated head, impaled on a pike, commands the last several lines of the poem: *pen milwr . . . pen dragon . . . pen f'arglwydd . . . pen f'enaid*,[39] "the head of a soldier . . . the head of a hero . . . the head of my lord . . . the head of my soulmate." As Sarah Higley argues, the staccato-like rhythm of the poem replicates the amputation that lies at the heart of the disaster described in the poem.[40] Llywelyn's body remains implicitly powerful even in its partition:

> Pen tëyrn, hëyrn hëid o'i law,
> Pen teÿrnwalch balch, bwlch edeifnaw,
> Pen teÿrnaidd, flaidd flaengar, ganthaw . . .[41]
>
> Head of a king, iron hurled by his hand.
> Head of a proud princely hawk, he forced a gap.
> Head of a prominent, princely wolf was his.

However, its once-upon-a-time wholeness serves mainly to underscore the extent of the damage done both to it and to the Welsh people as a whole. Playing on the dual meaning of *pen*, the poet here in Higley's words casts "the nation of Wales" into the role of "the grieving and broken body that remains behind, without sense of order, deprived of its 'chief' and 'head' . . . deprived of its will and its virility."[42]

The idea of the king's body as a metaphor for the corporate well-being of the state seems to have been an old one in Wales. The use of *pen* to mean "ruler" in the early medieval poetic compilation *Y Gododdin* and the parallels in etymology and usage between Welsh *pen* and Old Irish *cenn* (also "head" and "lord") are clear indications that the basics of the metaphor were probably known in Wales well before the twelfth century. It seems very likely, however, that the native metaphor remained open to influence from English and Continental models throughout much of the medieval period. Welsh intellectuals were very interested in contemporary European theories on kingship and rule,[43] and Welsh versions of a popular twelfth-century Latin Prince's Mirror, the *Secretum Secretorum*, are known from several different manuscripts of the period. This text, which purported to contain letters written by Aristotle to Alexander, combined advice on statecraft with advice about the body—which is probably why Welsh versions of the *Secretum* (known as the *Cyfrinach y Cyfrinachoedd*) were often preserved in the context of writings on medicine.[44] Their political implications were certainly recognized, however: interest in the Red Book of Hergest version of this text (appended to a medical treatise of the period) was due not only to its value as a medical work, but to its reflections on kingship and on the idealized body of the prince.[45] In other words, a trope found already in native Welsh literature was subsequently reinforced by exposure to contemporary European writings on sovereignty and the nature of rule.

The second point to be made is that animal as well as human bodies played a visible role in medieval European writings on the body politic. As Mary Douglas has shown, there is biblical precedent for this: in the Old Testament, the organs of the animals offered in sacrifice correspond both to precincts within the tabernacle (and those allowed inside them) and to particular areas on Mt. Sinai.[46] In medieval writings also, animals were often used as symbols for different ranks or groups of persons within the kingdom. John of Salisbury alludes frequently to animals in the *Policraticus*, for example, comparing actors, mimes, prostitutes, and other types of persons whose presence in society the prince ought not to encourage to savage beasts and birds of prey.[47] The prince's supporters he likens to bees lifting their king upon their shoulders.[48] A similar image occurs in the late thirteenth-century *Castigos del Rey Don Sancho IV*, produced by the king for his son and heir Fernando IV, in which the realm is compared to a swarm of bees led by a king. Should any bee choose to rebel against the king, the other bees are to slay him with their stingers.[49] Individual animal body parts as well as animals as a group were similarly adduced as symbols. In one passage in the *Policraticus*, John of Salisbury likens the number of feet in the body politic (peasants and others of humble status) to those possessed by the eight-clawed crab or even the centipede; in another, he compares the prince's supporters to the stomach within the body of an animal that dispenses nourishment to the whole.[50]

Animal metaphors were particularly popular in thirteenth- and fourteenth-century European works stressing unity and cooperation among rulers and the ruled. In the treatises mentioned earlier, for example, Aquinas, John of Paris, and Marsiglio of Padua used ants, cranes, and bees to argue that just as social animals instinctively follow a single leader in order not to be torn apart from one another, so also must human societies look to one ruler who can bring together and govern all the disparate parts of the kingdom(s) over which he presides. Their chief inspiration in this comparison was Aristotle, who in his *De motu animalium* ("On the Motion of Animals"), addressed the issue of how the different parts of an animal's body participate when the body as a whole is set in motion. From this, Aristotle was led to consider the soul's role in animating the body and, ultimately, to compare the body of the animal to a justly governed state. Just as a well-functioning commonwealth does not require a series of individual monarchs to preside over every specific task, he argued, but relies instead on a single ruler to control its actions as a whole, so also does an animal's body not require a separate animating force to preside over every particular movement. Rather, he concluded, the individual body parts of the animal work together as nature has designed, each separately fulfilling the task for which it was created.[51]

The organic analogy reached its height in the fourteenth century, well after the initial composition of the extant Welsh lawbook redactions. However, the lawbook redactors were almost certainly aware both of the organic analogy itself, and of metaphors linking bodies (human and animal) generally to the prosperity of the state. What will be argued in the following pages is that reading the Welsh laws against the backdrop of European writings on the body politic significantly changes our understanding of these texts. To be sure, there are differences between the way in which the organic analogy is used in the Welsh sources and the manner in which it functions in European writings on kingship. As we will see, in Wales it is the unity of the court (albeit functioning arguably as a microcosm of the state) rather than of the state or society per se that the analogy is used to express. Moreover, in the Welsh version of the metaphor, politics and the body are imagined as intersecting not only through the construction of human bodies in particular ways, but through the gifts of animal body parts by which officials serving the king are said to have been outfitted and remunerated for their service. Nor is unity the only message. As in many contemporary European formulations, body imagery functions also in the Welsh sources as a form of political commentary, a means by which to remark on the shortcomings of particular officials and, by implication, of the ruler they served. Differences of this sort do not diminish the potency of the organic analogy, however, but rather underscore its remarkable flexibility as an image and its ability to adapt itself to local conditions and needs.

The King's Body

Of all the personalities discussed in the Laws of Court tractate, it is the king whose depiction resonates most closely with body symbolism in medieval tradition generally. The king's body is conceptualized in all the principal redactions as special, set off from other bodies in the court and inviolate in ways that other bodies are not. *Sarhaed* ("insult") for ordinary persons typically entailed physical violence against a person or, if the person suffering the offense was male, causing dishonor to his wife:

> *Ior B*: O teyr ford e serheyr pob den en e byt: o tarau a gossot, a duen treys e arnau, ac os gur uyd, o bedyr gan e wreyc, sarhaed yu ydau.[52]

> In three ways every person in the world suffers *sarhaed*: by (intentional[53]) striking and battery, and by committing violence against him and, if it be a man, lying with his wife is *sarhaed* to him.

The king's *sarhaed*, by contrast, is phrased in such a manner as to admit the possibility only of injury to his dependents rather than to himself:

> Teyr ford y guneyr sarhaet y'r brenhyn: vn yv pan torrer y navd, pan rodo navd y dyn a'y lad; eyl yv pan del deu urenhyn ar eu kyttervyn o achavs ymaruoll, ac yg gvyd y deu urenhyn llad o vr y'r neyll gvr y'r llall; trydyd yv camarueru o'y wreyc.[54]

> In three ways is *sarhaed* done to the king: one is when his protection is broken, when he gives his protection to a person and [that person] is killed; a second is when two kings meet on their common boundary in order to negotiate, and in the presence of the two kings a man of one kills a man of the other; a third is the misuse of his wife.

The first of these triads, on *sarhaed* against ordinary men, is not included in Cyfn and moves around quite a lot in those Latin redactions which contain it. In Ior, Latin D, Latin E, and Bleg, by contrast, it is juxtaposed with the triad on *sarhaed* payments due to the king—I would suggest deliberately in order to underscore the difference between the two. For whereas two of the three stipulations of the triad on ordinary freemen involve physical assault, none of the provisions on the king do. Obviously, an attack on the physical person of a king would have been regarded as an egregious instance of *sarhaed* and punished accordingly; the fact that this is not even mentioned as a possibility underscores the patent artificiality of the triad as phrased. Equally significant is the fact that the king's only vulnerabilities are depicted here as residing not in his own person, but in his relationships with those for whose safety he is responsible: his queen, his officers, and others under his protection.[55] Their bodies are imagined as being vulnerable to assault in a way the king's is not, a fact that again suggests that the phrasing here is intentional.[56]

Such a reading seems particularly persuasive when placed alongside the fact that the theme of the (putative) invulnerability of the royal person also appears in prose works roughly contemporary with the lawbooks. The twelfth-century vita of Gruffudd ap Cynan, for example, contrasts Gruffudd's apparently unscathed escape from the battle of Mynydd Carn with the bloody injuries of his foes, on which the author dwells with considerable relish. Similarly, a favorable description of Gruffudd's physical person, immaculate and whole, follows immediately upon the narration of his lengthy imprisonment in Chester; the contrast between his own lack of injuries and those inflicted on the servants with him when he was captured is surely intentional.[57] A similar characterization of the ruler's body can be found in Cynddelw Brydydd Mawr's "Arwyrain Owain Gwynedd" ("Praise of Owain Gwynedd"), written before Owain's death in 1170. Owain's own body seems to remain impeccable throughout the fiercest fights; he is a *blaidd cyfwyrain*, "wolf rising up for battle," a *gwalch goradain*, "swift falcon," an *eryr huysgwr*, "steadfast eagle."[58] The feasting he provides at his kingly hall (implicit in line 4) marks a sharp contrast with the carrion feasting on the bloodied remains of his foes, which is described in almost grotesque detail:

> Ac eryfoedd trwm rhag tremid angau
> Ac eryfed crau ac eryfain;
> Arwyar ar wŷr, ar wŷr gnofain,
> Ar gnawd y ciglau adnau ednain . . .
>
> Gwelais gadau geirw a rhudd feirw rhain
> Oedd rydd i fleiddiau eu hargyfrain . . .
> Gwelais eu trychni trychant celain,
> Gwelais wedi cad coludd ar ddrain.[59]
>
> And heavy feasting in the wake of death
> And swilling of blood and reveling,
> Blood on warriors, on warriors' bones:
> I heard birds rapacious for flesh . . .
>
> I saw savage troops and stiff red corpses
> It was left to the wolves, their burial . . .
> I saw their ruin, three hundred dead;
> I saw; battle over, bowels on thorns.

His foes are carrion, eaten by wolves, and their bodies mangled and bloodied. Owain, by contrast, is the wolf, the hero who partitions the bodies of his foes while his own remains intact. As in the life of Gruffudd ap Cynan, Owain's body is *digardd*, "unblemished," and remains so throughout his various travails.[60]

Another aspect of the king's body as it is depicted in the laws is the manner in which it directs the movements and fortunes of other bodies within the court. When the king rides out on public business, he is surrounded by the bodies both of his officers and of the horses he has given them to use. The king, moreover, is the only person mentioned whose "indispensables" (*anhepcor*) consist of the bodies of other men. Whereas the "indispensables" of a *gwrda* (freeman) are his harp, his brycan, and his cauldron, and of a villein (*taeauc*) are his trough, his threshold, and his firestone,[61] the king's are the judge, the *penteulu* (or *teulu* in Bleg), and the priest.[62] And while all free persons are said to receive bovine bodies in compensation for insults done to them, high-ranking kings receive the most noble and variegated bodies of all: a literal herd of cattle for every cantred under their rule, each twenty cows with its own bull, each cow and bull of the appropriately exalted color. It is not necessary to believe in the physical reality of this payment to appreciate the symbolic role it plays within the narrative. In Cyfn and Bleg, the king's rule is quite literally inscribed in bodies on the face of the land over which he reigns, in that the cattle paid to the lord of Dinefwr are imagined as stretching in a three-and-a-half-mile line from Argoel to the court of Dinefwr.[63] Nor are the bodies embedded in the king's compensation merely animal in nature: the gold plate (or cover, in some versions) as wide as the king's face, which is also payable in such circumstances to notable kings, is said in all versions to be as thick as the nail of a plowman who has plowed for seven years.[64] Seven years is the period after which a relationship is deemed to have reached full maturity;[65] the king's honor is thus being depicted here as embracing not merely the human and animal bodies under his control, but the labor on which the prosperity of his court and realm depend.

The special status of the king with respect both to his own body and to the bodies of others in the court is also underscored in Ior (though less markedly in the other redactions) by the treatment accorded the *edling* and *penteulu*. Both men are, as we have seen, depicted in that text as usually being biologically related to the king—indeed, they are referred to several times as the king's "members," *aelodau* (defined in Ior as the hands, eyes, lips, feet, and nose[66]). This comparison in itself makes implicit reference to the king as the head of a body that is both personal and political in nature. In the case of the *edling*, the metaphor turns literal, in that he is not allowed to give gifts on his own or even to depart from the king without his permission: he is, in essence, a limb capable of moving only at the command of the head.[67] The *penteulu*'s position is somewhat different; he is both a king's member and (at least in some regions of Wales)[68] an officer of the court; in the latter capacity, he is depicted in Ior as separable from the king in a way that the *edling* is not. Not only does he retain his independent gift-giving prerogatives, but he is also said to go on circuit with the bodyguard during the winter months, thus physically "separating" himself from the person of the king (*gwahanu*, "to separate, detach," is the verb actually used in the text).[69] During that time, the *penteulu* himself commands bodies—a doorkeeper, a cook, and a food officer—who are at his beck and call until he returns to the court.[70]

On the other hand, the *penteulu*'s movements are also imagined in Ior as circumscribed by his relationship with the king. The text says explicitly that once the circuit is over, *ny dely mynet e gantav onyt y'v negesseu ef*, "he is not entitled to go away from him (the king) except on his errands," because he is, like the priest and the judge, one of the "indispensables" of the king and thus cannot be separated from him for very long.[71] Moreover, like the *edling*, the *penteulu* has only delegated authority over bodies. The officers who serve him on circuit almost certainly come from the king; the dogs, hawks, and horses that he and the *edling* receive certainly do.[72] Indeed, insofar as these animals are explicitly said in Ior to be equal in value to the king's own, they ought probably to be regarded as extensions of those with which the king himself is associated.[73] In other words, while the *penteulu* and the *edling* are the only members of the court who receive and control the movement of these high-status animal bodies within the territory, they do this as king's members rather than as individuals who are competent in themselves. This is also why their animals return to the king upon their deaths in lieu of the formal duties (*ebediw*) paid by every other rank of person.[74] Their exemption from having to pay these dues is clearly a mark of special privilege, a sign of their exalted status within the court and kingdom.[75] However, it is also a statement of their extreme dependency upon the ruler. In a very real sense, their bodies have not actually died because they continue in that of the king. Similarly, their control over animal bodies is but an extension of the king's control over all bodies within the court—including theirs, which are, in fact, his own.

Perhaps the most significant aspect of the king's body as it appears in the laws is that he has one at all. The king is the only person in these texts who is depicted as being in possession of an entire human body, at least as symbolized by the payments necessary to compensate for it in case of injury or death. The golden plate (or bowl cover) paid to the king measures the width of his face; the rod of gold or silver that accompanies it is as thick as his finger and spans the fullness of his height, either standing, as in the Ior version, or sitting in his chair, as in Cyfn and Bleg.[76] Because the king also receives cattle, as we have seen, his worth is thus imagined as encompassing bodies that are both human and animal in nature. The king's intimates, by contrast—queen, *edling*, and *penteulu*—are expressly excluded from receiving the plates and rods of precious metal through which the king's body is constructed in the text. Rather, their bodies partake of the royal body in a way that the bodies of other ranks do not, in that their *sarhaed* payments are calculated at a percentage of his own. Thus, the queen's and *penteulu*'s *sarhaed* amounts are a third of the king's, but without gold or silver. The *edling*'s is the same as the king's (again, without the gold) in Cyfn and most of the Latin redactions; in Ior, however, the *edling*'s compensation is reduced to the same level as that of the queen and *penteulu*, which is to say, a third of the compensation awarded to the king.[77] The Ior redaction's diminishing of the *edling* relative to the others is interesting, to say the least. What is most important here, however, is that all redactions agree in privileging the bodies of the king's intimates over all other bodies within the court. Payments made due to injuries done to them might well have been made in cash or animals as they would have been for other ranks; however, the amount of compensation these royals would command is measured in terms of the king's own person.

Other ranks of persons, by contrast, are measured in animal bodies or even, in cases of extreme dependency, reduced to zero. In all lawbook versions, a distinction is drawn between the *sarhaed* and wergild payments made to persons of free or semifree standing on the one hand, and slave status (*caeth*) on the other. As we have seen, persons of noble and freeman status were measured in the bodies of cattle and in currency according to the importance of their office:

> Ior B: Sarhaet e dysteyn a'r penkenedel a'r kyghellaur: nau muu a nau ugeynt o aryant; eu guerth yu nau muu a nau ugeyn muu gan e ardyrchauael. Guerth mab ucheluur a phob den e bo suyd ydau y gan argluyd: chue buu a chue ugeyn muu, gan y ardyrchauael; eu sarhaet yu chue buu a chue ugeynt o aryant. Pob gur ar teylu hep suyd ydau, pedeyr buu a petwar ugeynt o aryant yu e sarhaet. Pob bonhedyc canhuynaul a phob alltut brenhyn, teyr buu a thry ugeynt o aryant yu e sarhaet, a theyr buu a thry ugeyn muu eu guerth.[78]

> The *sarhaed* of the steward and the chief of kindred and the *cynghellor*: nine cows and nine score pence; their worth is nine cows and nine score cows with augmentation. The worth of the son of an *uchelwr* and everyone who holds office from a lord: six cows and six score cows with augmentation. Their *sarhaed* is six cows and six score pence. Every man of the household who does not hold an office, his *sarhaed* is four cows and four score pence. Every innate *bonheddig* and every king's foreigner, his *sarhaed* is three cows and three score pence, and his worth is three cows and three score pence.

In the slave's compensation, by contrast, the body disappears altogether, to be replaced by an empty suit of clothes and the tools with which he performs his labor:

> Ior B: Sarhaet caeth, deudec keynnyauc: chuech er peys a theyr er llauder ac un er raff ac un er gudyf ac un er kuaraneu.[79]
>
> The *sarhaed* of a slave, twelve pence: six for a smock and three for trousers and one for a rope and one for a hedging-bill and one for buskins.

The Cyfn redaction makes it clear that these are clothes in virtue of his work rather than items of apparel actually personal to him:

> Or tereu dyn ryd dyn kaeth, talet ida6 deudec keinha6c. whech dros teir kyfelin ovrethyn g6yn tal pentan ywneuthur peis ida6 6rth lad eithin. Teir dros la6d6r. Vn dros kuaraneu a dyrnu oleu. Vn dros 6dyf neu dros u6ell os koet6r vyd. Vn dros raff deudec kyfelinya6c.[80]
>
> If a freeman should strike a slave, let him pay him twelve pence: six for three ells of homemade white cloth to make him a smock for cutting gorse in, three for trousers, one for buskins and gloves, one for a hedging-bill or for an axe if he be a woodman, one for a rope of twelve ells.

These are clothes that could fit anybody, and any body, and it is only they that warrant replacing if the man wearing them is injured or killed. For all intents and purposes, the slave is, quite literally, a "no-body." The one exception to this serves in fact to prove the rule: in Cyfn, a slave who strikes a freeman is said to forfeit his right hand, presumably the hand with which the blow was struck. In other words, it is only when he comes into contact with a free person that the slave takes on a physical existence at all—and then only in order that he might lose it.[81]

Clothing figures in other ways as a measure of the bodies inhabiting the court. All bodies apart from the king's and queen's are depicted as receiving clothing from the royal couple that will establish their identities within the court and, by extension, within the political arena as a whole. On one level, this speaks to the purely practical issue of provisioning—livery or garments needed for service being one of the tangible benefits that accrue to those who serve the ruler. On another, however, clothing quite clearly has political significance within the laws. Indeed, in that the clothing mentioned is said to include undergarments as well as the outerwear through which allegiance would customarily have been proclaimed, the effect is to construct the bodies of important court officers as politically naked and in need of clothing to define them. The symbolism here parallels that of the prose tales of the period, in which clothing also functions as a way to mark the reshaping of identities and assumption (or reclaiming) of exalted status. Such, for example, is Enid's reclothing in Gwynhwyfar's clothes upon her marriage to Gereint, or Pwyll's resumption of his regal garb after casting off the rags he has worn while attempting to regain possession of Rhiannon.[82]

As usual, most intriguing in this respect are the *edling* and *penteulu*.[83] Neither is said to receive livery from king or queen; on the other hand, as king's members, they have no political identity separate from that of the king. Given that the *edling* was expected to eventually attain royal status himself, the omission of any mention of how he is to be clothed is surely significant. Like the prince he will eventually succeed, his body is not to be clothed by others; indeed, a case could be made that neither he nor his dress can be separated from that of the king. The only accoutrements detailed in the laws for the *edling* are not actually clothes, but adornments and privileged possessions that come from the king originally and go back to him upon the *edling*'s own death. These are of the same value as those used by the king himself; they are clearly intended to display not only his status as aristocrat and royal heir, but the identification of his body with that of the king's: *a'y ueyrch a'y kvn a'y uodrvyeu a'y tlysseu y gan y brenhyn, a'y arueu heuyt*,[84] "and his horses and his dogs and his rings and his ornaments from the king, and his weapons also." Similarly, the only outerwear received by the *penteulu* is the king's own garb on the three special feasts. Intriguingly, however, the *penteulu* (who is depicted in Ior as usually, but not necessarily, a biological relative of the king[85]) is said in that text to receive linen underwear from the queen.[86] The opposition between outerwear and linen undergarments corresponds in this text to the opposition between court and chamber, public and private.[87] The queen's gift thus acknowledges the possibility of the *penteulu*'s having a personal identity that is separate from that of the king—although it is also one that it is in the ruler's interest to reclothe.[88]

Body Parts

As important as the king's own body is the body of the court. Among the most arresting elements of the lawbooks are the rewards of animal body parts by which officers are said to be remunerated for their service. This is a feature of both the Cyfn and Ior versions and, to a lesser extent, of the Latin and Bleg traditions as well—an indication that the Ior redactor was building here on a tradition already in place. Different redactions (and even manuscripts) assign different body parts to these officers. What follows is a summary of how these gifts are assigned in the various redactions:

Distain, "steward"

- skins of cattle slaughtered in the kitchen (Ior; Cyfn; Lat B; Lat C; Lat D; Lat E; Bleg)[89]

Penhebogydd, "chief falconer"

- hearts and lungs of animals slaughtered in the kitchen (Ior; Cyfn)[90]

Ynad llys, "court justice"

- tongue that comes as a gift to honor the king (*anrheg*),[91] and all tongues in the court, and the king is to fill the place of the tongue with the thigh of the animal that the court smith receives (Cyfn manuscript W, and cf. Cyfn V and X)[92]

Pengwastrawd, "chief groom"

- legs of cattle slaughtered in the kitchen (Ior; Cyfn; Lat A; Lat B; Lat C; Lat D; Lat E; Bleg)[93]

Gwyliwr, "watchman"

- eyes of the animals slaughtered in the court (Ior)[94] or the aitch-bone of each steer slaughtered in the kitchen (Cyfn)[95]

Cynutai, "fueler"

- necks of the beasts slaughtered in the court (Ior)[96]

Gof llys, "court smith"

- heads and feet of the cattle slaughtered in the kitchen (Cyfn) or in the court (Lat A; Lat B; Lat D; Lat E; Bleg)[97]

Coc, "cook"

- skins of small animals that come into the kitchen with their skins on such as sheep, lambs, kids, bucks, fawns (Ior)[98]
- skins of sheep and goats, lambs, kids, and calves slaughtered in the kitchen (Cyfn)[99]
- skins of sheep and goats slaughtered in the kitchen (Lat A); from the kitchen (Lat B, and cf. Lat D; Bleg; Lat E)[100]
- entrails, stock and tallow (Ior)[101]
- entrails of cattle slaughtered in the kitchen except for the spleen and rectum that go to porter (Cyfn)[102]
- entrails of all animals slaughtered in the court except the hearts (Lat D; Bleg; and cf. Lat E)[103]

Maer biswail, "dung *maer*"

- stomach (*bloneg*) and fat (*swyf*) from the court and skins of cattle in his care for three nights before being slaughtered in the kitchen (Cyfn)[104]
- skins of slaughtered cattle, and fat and stomach (*sepum et abdomen*)[105] from pigs, if tended them for three days (Lat B)[106]
- skins of cattle in his care for three nights before they are slaughtered (Ior)[107]
- skins of cattle and oxen slaughtered in the kitchen if in his care for three nights beforehand (Lat A; Lat D; Lat E; Bleg)[108]

Porthor, "porter" (keeper of the gate of the court)

- spleen and rectum of cattle slaughtered in the kitchen (Cyfn)[109]
- takes skins off of animals slaughtered in the kitchen and receives a penny for each one (Ior)[110]
- short stick from every cartload of wood that goes through the gate, small pig and docked beast (Ior and Cyfn)[111]

Drysor, "doorkeeper" (keeper of the entrance of the hall or chamber)

- dries the skins of the cattle killed in the kitchen and receives money for each one (Cyfn)[112]
- looks after skins of animals slaughtered in the kitchen until they are divided up and then gets a penny/coin for each one (Lat A; Lat B; Lat D; Lat E; Bleg)[113]
- entitled to a share of the money from the skins (Ior)[114]

There is clearly a pattern here. As several scholars have noted, many of these payments appear to be symbolic of the function filled within the court by the officer in question.[115] Thus, the court judge is said in some Cyfn manuscripts to receive the tongues of animals killed in the kitchen *ar tauodeu oll or llys, kanys ynteu auarn ar y tauodeu oll*, "and all the tongues from the court, because he judges all tongues."[116] The chief groom, whose position it is to care for the horses of the court and keep them in good riding trim, receives the legs in all redactions, and the porter (who guards entrances and exits) gets the rectum, at least according to the Cyfn redaction. The watchman is depicted as taking the eyes in one redaction (Ior) and the two-pronged aitchbone in another (Cyfn), and the fueler is given the necks reminiscent of the one on which he carries his burden of wood.

Not only would I agree with these observations, I would extend them to suggest that *all* references to animals killed in the kitchen or court were intended to allude symbolically to the duties of the officer in question. Thus, the steward (*distain*), who as chief of all the officers holds the court together, is said in all redactions except Latin A to receive the skins of most of the animals killed in the kitchen. Only the skins given to the cook and to the dung *maer* are exempted here, and these exceptions prove the rule, in that both function as steward figures within their respective domains of kitchen and *maerdref* and are explicitly associated with the steward in the Ior account.[117] The smith gets the heads and feet—presumably representing the horseshoes and axe and spearheads on which he would have spent much of his time. The porter, who is said to receive the rectum and spleen in the Cyfn version, is depicted in Ior as the one who actually skins the animals slaughtered in the kitchen, taking a penny in payment for each one. Additionally, all redactions portray the doorkeeper as receiving money for looking after the skins of slaughtered animals in some manner before they are divided up among their respective recipients. The porter and doorkeeper are not the officers one would automatically associate with skins, and while it is possible that it relates to their role in removing the outer wraps of those who visit the court, I would suggest that this is, like the rectum in Cyfn, another reference to control over entrance and egress—the skin being the barrier one must traverse in order to access the heart of the beast. This leaves only the symbolism of the hearts and lungs given to the falconer which, unfortunately, is less obvious to us now than I suspect it would have been to people living at the time.[118] The weight of the other examples is such, however, as to leave little doubt about whether this gift ought to be interpreted in a symbolic manner as well.

If this is true, then we are faced with the question of what to make of these payments and how to interpret them. Historians have generally tended to take them more or less at face value, either noting their potential value as in-kind payments, or seeing them as aspects of the festive nature of the court.[119] Some interpret them as evidence for archaism within the laws. Dafydd Jenkins, for example, compares the Welsh list to two medieval accounts of in-kind renders due to lords from their estates. The origins of these renders appear to be early, a fact that leads him to conclude that the list in the Welsh lawbooks is probably old as well, possibly even predating Hywel in the tenth century.[120] This is certainly plausible. Indeed, it seems not at all unlikely that, at least at some point, payments like these were actually made—possibly, though not necessarily, in a ritual context. The provisions as we have them cannot be exact guidelines, given the differences between the various versions; however, they may well reflect the type of reward regarded as suitable for a given officer within the court. After all, there was certainly a practical side to many of these gifts. Medieval persons placed a high value on making use of as many parts of the animal as possible. Skins and meat were valuable and never to be wasted, as is evident from the elaborate regulations governing the skinning and eating of animals started by another's hound or found dead on another's land.[121] In a few instances, the lawbook texts themselves provide practical rationales for which the animal body part in question was being given to the officer receiving it. Thus, the falconer is said in Ior to use the hearts and lungs of the wild animals slaughtered in the kitchen "to feed his birds."[122] And the fueler's payment of necks is explained as due him *vrth eu eskernegu a'e wyall ef*,[123] "because of their being cut up with his axe."

On the other hand, there are several aspects of these payments which suggest that practicality was not all there was to it. First, while some of the payments are given a practical rationale, the majority are not, and many of the organs involved seem likely to have been of questionable value to the recipient. What was a watchman to do with all those eyes, for example? Or a judge with the tongues of all the animals slaughtered in the court? It is difficult to picture a smith making efficient use of a pile of heads and feet, or a porter dealing with a mass of detached rectums, or a fueler coping with a vast accumulation of necks, regardless of whether they had been cut off with his axe. Similarly, while one can imagine the doorkeeper to the hall being put in charge of watching over a pile of skins waiting to be distributed in the course of the feast, it is difficult to conjure up the circumstances under which it would be the porter who actually skinned these animals. Were the beasts at issue cattle or other domesticated animals, one would expect the kitchen staff to do the butchering; were they deer or other wild creatures, it would surely have been up to the huntsmen or their servants to dress them, as this would need to be done as soon as possible.[124] In short, once one starts probing the practicalities of what the lawbooks report about these payments, a strictly literal reading—one that takes little account of their symbolic aspects, in other words—seems difficult to sustain.

Another aspect of these texts that warrants comment is their insistence on the fact of the animals having been slaughtered in the kitchen or court. This is almost always expressed in precisely the same way. In Welsh, the phrase is either *a ladher en e kegyn* or *a ladher en e llys*. There is more variation in the Latin texts, but again, it is the similarities in phrasing rather than their differences that are most striking: *qui inficiantur in coquina / qui occiduntur in coquina* or *in coquina enectarum / occisorum in coquina / in curia occisorum*. This qualifying clause is consistent across virtually all lawbook redactions. Only once is it omitted entirely, from the Cyfn clause on the tongues awarded to the judge, and this provision occurs only in some Cyfn manuscripts. In all other instances, the animals in question are characterized in this way in at least one redaction or manuscript version and, usually, in all. This consistency in phrasing—from version to version of an individual clause, and from one animal body part gift to another—is highly unusual in a lawbook tradition in which diversity of phrasing and ordering of provisions is the norm rather than the exception. Clearly, the redactors intended for some reason to underscore this particular aspect of these gifts. Nerys Patterson has suggested that it reflects a desire to differentiate the animals given as gifts from the animals taken as booty in the course of a raid by the royal warband.[125] Most of the recipients of the animal body parts would not have accompanied the warband on its raids, and officers who did participate in such excursions received animals taken as part of the booty as their reward.[126] Granting the minor by-products to those in the court who did not participate in the raid may have been a way of sharing the wealth.

This makes good sense. On the other hand, the focus of these qualifying clauses would seem from their wording to be the fact of the animals having been slaughtered in the kitchen or court rather than how they had come into the prince's possession. After all, even animals taken in the course of raiding would likely also ultimately have been killed in the court or kitchen. This raises the possibility—and it is one suggested and supported by the symbolic nature of the animal payments themselves—that court and kitchen are functioning in these clauses as largely symbolic locales. The court we are familiar with already. The meaning of the kitchen may be suggested by symbolism pertaining to the belly in roughly contemporary sources, such as Marie de France's version of Aesop's fable, in which the belly is depicted as that which sustains the political body. Perhaps the main point in the Welsh texts is also to portray the kitchen as feeding and sustaining the court and, by extension therefore, the prince's reign—indeed, this may be why the cook is said to get the entrails in many of the redactions.[127] In any case, the opposition between animals slaughtered for use by the court and animals elsewhere corresponds remarkably well to other oppositions we have seen in the lawbooks: between tame and wild, inside and outside, court and country. Animals that have been butchered and dressed are no longer beasts of the field or forest. Indeed, they are no longer even whole animals but, rather, disjointed bodies made ready for human use and consumption. Once distributed around the court and hall, they become visible symbols not only of the duties of those who receive them, but of the courtly venue whose boundaries and hierarchies they help to mark. It is in chamber, hall, and court that they will be distributed and used, and in chamber, hall, and court that the loyalties they reward will be displayed and exercised. Embedded in the distribution of animal gifts, in other words, is yet another instance of the constructed opposition between spaces that are internal and external to the court.

They also mark its unity. I would suggest that what we have in these animal payments is not (or at least no longer) a quaintly archaic estate render, nor even a practical in-kind form of compensation for the prince's servants. It is, rather, a native and quite contemporary version of the organic analogy. Two political bodies are at issue here: that of the king, and that of the court. The former encompasses both human and animal bodies and is depicted (together with its members) as whole unto itself. The latter, by contrast, is constituted by the king's officials coming together to form the body of the court: its eyes, tongue, legs, neck, skin, head, and feet. There are striking similarities, after all, between what we see in the Welsh lawbooks and the schema outlined by John of Salisbury in his *Policraticus*. The prince constitutes the head in both (the ruler as heart instead of head as becomes common in European political writing only from the late thirteenth century on).[128] Judges, who receive the tongues of the court in Cyfn, are the tongues, eyes, and ears of the state in John of Salisbury's account (V.II). Treasurers and recordkeepers (*quaestors et commentarienses*, defined by A. D. Harvey as "ministers of the private estates")[129] are the stomach and intestines of John's body politic. In the

Welsh texts, the stomachs of animals killed in court and kitchen (V.2) are given to the *maer*, a figure roughly equivalent to the English reeve and thus similar in function to the *quaestors et commentarienses* of John's text. John singles these latter out as susceptible to greed and to taking in so much that they bring disease into the body; similarly, the *maer* in the two Welsh texts is awarded the fat of the animals along with the stomachs. One other possible parallel is the *penteulu*, the head of the warband, who is said in Ior—and this is an odd bit of detail to find in a lawbook text if there is no significance attached to it—to sit in the feasting hall with his left hand toward the entrance to the hall, presumably in order to leave his sword hand free.[130] In the *Policraticus*, John of Salisbury identifies soldiers and those who defend the realm (with and without weapons) as the hands of the body politic (VI.1).

There are, to be sure, significant differences between the two schemas. In John of Salisbury's account, the body in question is human, and the entity it represents the *res publica* as a whole. In the Welsh sources, the body is animal and its symbolic referent is the court—although this may be less of a difference than it appears, in that the timeless court of the lawbooks is surely functioning here as a microcosm of the nation. Those who assist the ruler in John's schema are equated with the sides or flanks of the body politic, whereas the right-hand man of the Welsh ruler, the steward (*distain*), is associated with the skin. Both perform similar functions; they hold the body together, but the images are different. The senate is the heart of the political body in the *Policraticus*, and the peasants the feet; in the Welsh sources, the falconer is linked to the hearts and the smith to the heads and feet. There are elements in the Welsh that are not present in the Latin (the porter, the watchman, the fueler, and the groom), and there are elements in the Latin that are not there in the Welsh (the peasants). The advice element in each text is also different, a point we will return to later. Clearly, the two schemas are not synonymous with one another, and the cultural ubiquity of the organic analogy was such that a first- or even secondhand knowledge of the *Policraticus* would not be necessary to explain how the idea of the body politic might have reached Wales in this period.[131] On the other hand, it is certainly not impossible that a report of the *Policraticus*, or an account of its contents, may have traveled to Wales at some point even if the text itself had not.[132] In any case, what we would appear to have here is an instance in which native perceptions about the political body—perhaps influenced by similar ideas coming into Wales from England and the Continent—have been integrated into what may once have been a list of genuine in-kind payments made to court officials for ritual or practical purposes.

But why then might such ideas have made their way into the lawbooks? As we have seen, the organic analogy featured frequently in instructional literature aimed at princes. This literature took many forms, from the advice genre known as the "Prince's Mirror" to considerably less formal types of works. We know already that lawbooks had something of this aspect to them. Both Huw Pryce and David Stephenson have commented helpfully on their didactic—and occasionally admonitory—aspects. Redactors, themselves members of an *uchelwyr* class made increasingly nervous by what they perceived as encroachments on traditional privileges and patterns of princely rule, used the laws as a vehicle through which to recall contemporary rulers to the practices of an earlier day. Moreover, the Laws of Court were a particularly important text in this regard. Pryce characterizes them as "voicing a conservative reaction to changes in Welsh kingship," while Stephenson speaks of their silence on the many innovations taking place in Welsh government in this period as evidence of their disapproval of these changes.[133] Particularly at issue were the taxes and dues levied by princes and their officials and the perception that their actions were becoming increasingly arbitrary and unpredictable. An additional irritant was the tendency of princes and others to move away from native law in cases where doing so would be financially advantageous or facilitate the transfer of property in nontraditional ways.[134]

To these concerns should now be added what we have seen articulated in the lawbooks about the fractiousness and internecine rivalries that were so much a part of Welsh politics in the period. The redactors expressed their apprehensions in a variety of ways, among them the contrast between internal and external landscapes which, as we have seen, runs as a thematic thread through their work as a warning about the dangers of disunity. This is, I would suggest, precisely the point as well of the provisions regarding the payments of animal body parts to officials within the court. In medieval political writing generally, the organic analogy served most frequently as a reminder of the importance of a ruler and his realm working together in order to achieve a common goal or defeat a common enemy. So also, I would argue, in the Welsh texts. Just as in a physical body, collaboration and unity are envisaged as essential to the political organism of the court. The officers whose duties are symbolized by the parts of the animal they receive must work together, each at their own assigned task, to ensure the security and prosperity of king and country. Absent any one of its constituent parts, the court, like the animal bodies by which it is symbolized, cannot function productively. The redactors' warning could not be more clear, nor their admonitions to the inhabitants of the court more trenchant: body parts must work together, or they will die alone.

In articulating such themes, the laws are once again paralleling themes that were popular in the Welsh literature of the day. Helen Fulton has argued persuasively that French romances of the period differ significantly from their Welsh counterparts in their emphasis on individualism and autonomous political power. Whereas the hero in French tales such as *Yvain* or *Érec et Énide* develops interiorly on his quest, emerging from vassalage by virtue of his own individual prowess to a position of independent lordship, Welsh heroes tend to end where they began. Their quests lead "not to autonomy, but simply to a more responsible kind of leadership which remains within the benign domain of a stable overlord."[135] By contrast with the French tales, in the Welsh romances it is "discourses of co-operation, loyalty and kinship" that are foregrounded rather than individualism, and the collective good that is privileged over the needs or desires of individuals.[136] Counsel is depicted as an essential part of lordship even for powerful princes. A king must listen to the advice of his *uchelwyr*, especially when collective interests are at stake, for it is the interests of the whole, rather than their personal ambitions, that matter most. In turn, the foremost duty of their subjects is the maintenance of the political status quo against external threats.[137] In these tales also, collaboration and cooperative rule are the only means of survival. On this point as well, law and literature stand hand in hand.

Advice to Princes

Up to this point, the gifts to officers have been envisaged as a largely textual conceit, rather than as something that might actually have been enacted within the court as a form of ritual. There are possible hints that such rituals might have taken place. One odd passage, which appears only in a few Cyfn manuscripts, states that the judge is to receive the tongues of all the animals killed in the kitchen, while the smith is to take the heads. Rather than present the smith with a tongueless head, Cyfn V remarks, the king is to fill the place of the tongue with the animal's thigh.[138] This odd bit of detail has a performative aspect to it that may suggest the actual enactment of this particular payment and thus, by extension, of others as well. As has already been mentioned, the exchange of clothing during the three great feasts of the year seems to have been structured in such a way as to cause givers and recipients to cross back and forth across the hall in a manner that dramatized the unity of the space.[139] It is entirely possible that the ritualized presentation of symbolically charged animal body parts might have served a similar purpose. One can imagine the gift of eyes at a feast, for example, serving as a public reminder to all, not only of the importance of the watchman's particular duties, but also of the necessity for vigilance generally. Similarly, the presenting of skins to the steward, or of legs to the chief groom, might easily function in such a context as a celebration of both the officers and the court within which they served.

On the other hand, some of the payments outlined in the lawbooks are difficult to imagine being soberly enacted within the confines of a royal court. The porter receiving the rectum would be a good example of this. Another would be the thigh, just mentioned, which is said in some manuscripts to be given in place of the animal's tongue to the smith, the tongues of the others having already been given to the judge. This thigh—especially if situated as a mock tongue in the gaping mouth of a decapitated animal—is such an obvious sexual symbol that it seems as though its presentation would inevitably constitute a moment of deliberate comedy within the court. Indeed, it was images like these that led Nerys Patterson to suggest that the gifts of animal parts constituted real-life courtly burlesques designed to maintain order and propriety within the court. Casting her argument in terms of the use of "shame as an instrument of social control," Patterson contended that low-status but nonservile persons who committed minor offenses in the course of executing their duties would face ridicule rather than fines as punishment for their transgressions. In her view, status was the key element of such burlesques, in that their primary function was the sanctioning of offenses committed within a relationship of nonservile dependency, such as might have obtained between a king and his servant or a husband and his wife. Slaves had no reputation regardless, and the public shaming of aristocrats was too dangerous. Only those who had honor to lose, but whose subordination was such as to minimize the public impact of their ridiculing, were open to sanctions of this kind. In Patterson's view, the burlesques thus functioned primarily to maintain the status quo. By actively demonstrating the contingency of a dependent's position in a manner designed to bring shame upon that person, they underscored the absurdity of any and all challenges to lordly authority.[140] What we have in the burlesques is a valuable glimpse into the performative sanctions by which order in the court was sustained.

Patterson's is a thoughtful reading of the text and her suggestions are certainly plausible. Smiths are fully of the sort of free but marginal status she identifies as most frequently being the target of such burlesques, and while judges are not, a judge who can be shown to have delivered an incorrect judgment is said in this same text to owe compensation to the king in the amount of his own tongue and to abstain from judging thereafter.[141] However, I would suggest instead that these passages fall more into the genre of pointed political commentary than of the legal sanctioning of individuals. Here, we must return to a textual, rather than a ritual, understanding of these payments. There is no indication in the sources that either the smith or the judge has committed an error for which remonstration is appropriate. Nor, more generally, is it only those who transgress against court decorum who seem to be the target of mocking payments made within the court. Even officials who do not commit offenses are made fun of in this way. The dung *maer* (*maer biswail*), for instance, whose job it was to collect dues and fines from the unfree tenants of the king, is said in Cyfn to receive the fat, lard, and stomach from the court kitchen—a visibly derogatory payment intended presumably to comment negatively on the wealth with which he was perceived to be fattening himself.[142] In fact, precisely this same point is also made with respect to similar figures in John of Salisbury's *Policraticus*. There, too, the greedy accumulations of rapacious managers and stewards are likened to the sort of excessive congestion in the stomach and intestines that damages the organism as a whole.[143]

Even more pointed in the Welsh texts is the portrayal of another official, the *rhingyll* or sergeant, a highly unpopular figure whose job it was to collect legal fines and summon people to court: *gwaet gwlat; a garw gychwedyl gwas y kygkellawr*,[144] "the plaint of a *gwlad*—bad news, the servant of the *cynghellor*," as *Bleg* calls him. Patterson notes the "not quite . . . dignified" nature of the clothing he is described as wearing in the Cyfn and Ior versions of the Laws of Court, but makes little of it.[145] His clothing is significant, however, in that it seems intentionally to construct him as possessing the body not of a man, but of a child, with short little boots and a tunic reaching only to the knot of the cord holding up his trousers. This is visible already in Cyfn, but is clearest in the Ior version:

> Petweryd yv e ryghyll. . . . Ef a dele coesseu er ychen a'r guarthec a kaffer o'y gyhud ef, e wneythur kuaraneu kyuuvch a'e uffarneu; a navuet dyd kalan gayaf peys a chrys a llavder hep tenllyf a dele e gaffael; kyhyt e dele bot e dyllat a chvlem e lavder.[146]

> Fourth is the sergeant. . . . He is entitled to the legs of the oxen and the cattle which are obtained by his accusation, to make buskins as high as his ankles; on the ninth day of the calends of winter he is entitled to receive a tunic and a shirt and trousers without mixed fabric; his clothes ought to be as long as the knot of his trousers.

The Cyfn account omits any direct mention of boots, but short buskins are implied in the stipulation that the length of the leg-hide to which he is entitled should go no further than the ankles (presumably, though not certainly, of the animal from which the leg has been taken). Cyfn then remarks that the linen he receives every year with which to make his trousers should be only three cubits (*kyuelin*) in length (about fifty-four inches in total),[147] reinforcing the idea that, as in Ior, his garments are being deliberately portrayed as unusually short. Indeed, Cyfn further stipulates with Ior that his robe should be "no longer than the knot of his trouser" (*ny byd hyt yny dillat na myn hyt yg cl6m yla6d6r*).[148]

Similarly disconcerting, at least from the likely perspective of your average princely official, is the frankly peculiar nature of some of the other items the sergeant is said to receive. The list of goods said to come to him in escheat from a "dead-house" (defined in Cyfn and Bleg as a man who dies suddenly without leaving a son)[149] is extremely suggestive. This is the Ior version, which is broadly representative of the rest:

> Ef a dele kvbyl o'r kyc bvlch a uo en e marvty, a'r emenyn bvlch, a'r maen yssaf o'r ureuan, a'r llyn glas, a'r wanaf yssaf o'r yt, a'r yeyr a'r katheu, a'r wyall kennut, a'r talar o'r yt en e dayar (ac ony byd talar, y eyryonenneu). . . . Teyr kyuelyn en hyt e waev: dve trach keuyn ac un racdav.[150]

> He is entitled to all of the opened meat that may be in a "dead-house," and to the opened butter, and to the lower stone of the quern, and to the green flax, and to the lowest level of the corn, and to the hens and the cats, and to the fuel axe, and to the headland of the corn (and if there be no headland, to the margins). . . . Three *kyuelin*s [in length] is his spear: two [*kyuelin*s] behind him and one in front.

Cyfn, Latin, and Bleg also list most or all of the same items, although the details on how he is said to carry his spear—with the majority of it behind him rather than in front—are unique to Ior. All the redactions portray his spear as being (or appearing) abnormally short, like his clothing, and the southern texts even attempt an explanation for this, albeit one that does not make a lot of sense: *rac y argan6od*, "lest it be revealed" (Cyfn), or *ut improuise veniat*, "so that he might arrive unseen" (Lat A, Lat B, Lat D, and cf. Bleg).[151]

The list of items received by the sergeant, together with the description of his clothing, has usually been taken by scholars essentially at face value.[152] And there is something to be said for this, as there are some aspects of the description that might make a literal reading plausible. Short garments would allow for greater freedom of movement, for example, a necessity in the sergeant's line of work, and a relatively hidden weapon (or one poised for prodding rather than hurling) might be more effective in the sort of circumstances in which he would likely find himself. Interestingly, the description of his clothes matches more or less the picture of the sergeant preserved in the National Library of Wales manuscript Peniarth 28, a Latin A manuscript famous for its illustrations of figures from the Laws of Court. Since the description of the sergeant's unusually short garments does not occur in Latin A (although the characterization of his spear is the same), this could indicate that what we read in the other redactions about his attire is not very far off the mark (see fig. 1).[153] Similarly, it would make sense that someone in the sergeant's position might be rewarded with the leftover or marginal items remaining in a house in which a death has recently occurred but for which items there is no obvious heir. In other words, the possibility that descriptions of genuine practice might lie behind these passages cannot be discounted.

On the other hand, there are a number of signs in these accounts that warn us against taking them entirely literally, at least in the form(s) in which they are currently extant. The anomalies in the sergeant's clothing and footwear are not limited to their length. It is surely significant that this scanty clothing is imagined as being given to him in winter, when it would be least appropriate and helpful. Moreover, Cyfn and Ior mandate that he receive his heaviest item of clothing, the *mantell*, "mantle, cloak," in February or March, as spring and summer approach, rather than in November and December when he would actually have most need of it. Ior states explicitly that what he receives in winter is the much lighter cape (*cappan*).[154] All redactions (including Latin A) forbid him from having *tenllif*, "mixed fabric" (generally understood to be a form of linsey-woolsey) in his trousers (*yn y lawdyr / llavder / in braccis suis*); according to Cyfn, they are instead to be made of linen.[155] Jenkins remarks on the awkward nature of the phrasing of this provision and is

Figure 1. *Y rhingyll*, "The sergeant."

National Library of Wales manuscript Peniarth 28, fol. 6v.

clearly at a loss as to what to make of it.[156] In fact, its oddity is even more striking than he notes, as linen is firmly associated in this tractate (as many places elsewhere) with underclothing—and not just any underclothing, but the underclothing given to the royal officials by the queen.[157] (Linens are also among the items taken by the wife in a case of divorce.[158]) The main point of explicitly forbidding *tenllif* would seem to be that his trousers are *entirely* made of linen. In other words, not only is the sergeant imagined as wearing childish boots and clothes that are too short, not only is he carrying a short spear and inappropriately dressed for the season, but he is also wearing as outerwear what is typically worn as underwear. One has only to contemplate the likely staining attendant on personal undergarments to get a sense of the sort of picture this description was intended to evoke in the minds of medieval persons.

The items with which the sergeant is rewarded in these texts raise similar possibilities for our understanding of the passage. Again, a literal reading is certainly plausible. It makes sense that a royal official might help himself to the leftover meat and cheese in the circumstances, since they might otherwise spoil before the rightful heir has been located. However, it does not make sense that this same official would receive not only the fuel axe and the hens, but the lower stone of the quern. The latter item would be useless without its mate; from any literal point of view, this is a nonsensical provision. Moreover, parts of the passage on the sergeant are overtly derisive. Most obvious in this regard is the passage on his compensation for *sarhaed*, "insult." The Cyfn and Bleg redactions award him an addled egg and a sieve full of chaff in compensation should *sarhaed* be committed against him while he is sitting during the king's cases (*dadleu y brenhin*); in Ior, that compensation is defined as a sieve full of oats and a single eggshell.[159] Patterson has done an excellent job in clarifying the symbolism here. Because the sergeant is not entitled to sit during the hearing of pleas before the king, she argues, it is permitted to commit *sarhaed* against him should he do this without any meaningful compensation having to be paid. The only compensation due him in such circumstances, the sieve full of oats and the eggshell (the former of which likely incorporates a pun on his name: *rhidyll*, "sieve," is very close to *rhingyll*, "sergeant"), juxtaposes "an image of something that is spoiled because it is too full or solid (the addled or hatching egg) and something that is useless because it is empty."[160]

Patterson's interpretation makes very good sense. However, our foray into the oddities of the sergeant's dress and weaponry encourage us to look for additional ways of understanding what is said in these texts about him. Read symbolically, and in accordance with provisions elsewhere in the lawbook, the passages on the "dead-house" seem designed to diminish the sergeant by intentionally constructing his body as female. The opened meat and butter and lower stone of the quern he receives appear in the laws on women as the woman's portion in the case of divorce; as I will later argue, both are probable sexual references. The hens and cats, like other small domestic animals of the barnyard, were a wife's special charge and intimately associated with her. The green flax is presumably an allusion to the sergeant both as a child—green and immature—and as a woman, since women were normally the ones to work with flax. The small fuel axe constitutes a reference to the size of the person (female or child) typically associated with it.[161] Size and quality are also the issue with respect to grains taken from the margins or headlands of a field, in that these areas are abnormally prone to pests and produce grain notably smaller than that produced elsewhere.

And just in case one has missed the point, the sergeant's spear—surely in context a reference to his physical manhood as well as to a child's toy?—is said to be abnormally short and, in the Ior redaction, to stick out longer behind him than it does in front. It is probably significant that the porter, who is said in Ior to occupy the role of sergeant in the *maerdref* in collecting dues, receives in Ior and Cyfn a short stick, a small pig, and a beast whose tail has been docked (*llvden kvtta*) from the goods that come through the gate.[162] Sticks and tails are common metaphors for the penis in the poetry of the period—indeed, the idea of tails as penises occurs even in the laws themselves.[163] And, of course, these are not ordinary tails and sticks, but ones that are, like the sergeant's clothing and boots, and the axes he wields and the grains he receives, preternaturally short. In fact, this is probably also the point of the derisory compensation afforded the sergeant who sits inappropriately during the king's pleas: the addled (or empty) egg that is the result of his sitting projects him not only into the role of a female, but also into that of a laying, but unproductive and useless, hen. Even as a female, he is not very effective. The fact that these attributes are all being worn or wielded by someone whose visible dress is most closely associated with women—and potentially with excrement and other insalubrious bodily excretions—contextualizes this still further. He is everything a princely official ought not to be: female rather than male, private rather than public in his visible clothing, shivering and silly looking rather than commanding and just.

In fact, the description we get in the lawbooks of the sergeant is so consistently unflattering that it seems almost impossible to imagine that we are dealing with anything other than a deliberately disrespectful caricature of this unpopular figure. Moreover, this set of images resonates across all three redactions. For while only Ior and Cyfn explicitly mention the sergeant's seasonally inappropriate clothing and odd manner of dress, all lawbook versions have the provisions on the dead-house and the passage on his spear, and all forbid the use of *tenllif* in his trousers. In fact, the Latin A manuscript Peniarth 28 illustration seems to capture many of the undesirable attributes of this figure as he is described in other lawbook redactions.[164] It is always difficult to judge such things at a distance, but a comparison of the illustration of the sergeant (fol. 6v) with the figures of the king (fol. 1v), *penteulu* (fol. 3r), steward (fol. 3v), and falconer and judge (fol. 4r) is revealing (see figs. 2–5). These latter officials are depicted as considerably more regal, masculine, and adult looking than is the sergeant; indeed, it would not be too strong to say that the latter looks like a small, truculent child beside them. Whereas the others sport long flowing robes that reach to the ground, and often even a beard (king, judge, chief huntsman, porter), the sergeant is small in size, wears short divided pants, and resembles nothing so much as an angry adolescent. The only

Figure 2. *Y brenin*, "The king."

National Library of Wales manuscript Peniarth 28, fol. 1v.

other figure whose gown appears as short as the sergeant's is the male party of the kissing couple on folio 5r, who is hardly a model for gravitas and proper comportment (see fig. 6 in Chapter 4); the only others wearing visibly divided pants are the porter and doorkeeper who are, as we have seen, subjects of mockery in their own right. Furthermore, his outer garment, in contrast with that worn by almost every other officer in the court, which is either dark green or red, has little or no tint to it—perhaps a portrayal of the linen from which

Figure 3. *Y penteulu*, "The chief of the household troop."

National Library of Wales manuscript Peniarth 28, fol. 3r.

his tunic is said to have been made. Even the groom, the cook, and the smith (fol. 6r) are depicted as possessing a dignity in their work that eludes the sergeant.

Peniarth 28 portrays the sergeant as barking orders with the top part of the spear thrusting out in front of him while the rest of it trails behind. It is difficult not to notice the manner in which he is holding this spear. Not only does it pass directly through his groin at an angle biologically identifiable with his penis—to all appearances in an incomplete rather than full state of erection—but he also appears to be grasping it with both hands, with both thumbs prominently visible.[165] Exactly what he might be doing with his hands on his spear is a question best left up to the viewer—Jan Ziolkowski cautions wisely against simply presuming that something that seems erotic to us would

Figure 4. *Y distain*, "The steward."

National Library of Wales manuscript Peniarth 28, fol. 3v.

inevitably seem so to others as well.[166] However, even without the oddities in how this figure is described in the laws, the sexual and gender implications of this image would be difficult to miss; the fact that those oddities exist must surely make a symbolic reading more likely than not. Certainly, when one compares this illustration to that of the two spearmen in the manuscript known as Liber A or *Littere Wallie* (done in the 1280s; Peniarth 28 dates to the mid-thirteenth century), the difference is obvious. Both spearmen there hold a spear in one hand and a sword in the other; the spear is grasped firmly in the middle, with the tip resting on the ground in front of its bearer.[167] One might argue that the fact that they are also holding swords makes a difference in how the spearmen are standing. However, it is hard to imagine a situation in which holding a spear anywhere other than the middle would make much sense

Figure 5. *Yr hebogydd, yr ynad llys,* "The falconer, the court judge."

National Library of Wales manuscript Peniarth 28, fol. 4r.

from a strategic point of view. Holding it close to the tip, even for the purposes of jabbing, would both unbalance the weapon and bring its holder into perilous proximity to his opponent.

In short, it is difficult to escape the conclusion that what we have here in the lawbooks—both text and image—are not straightforward portrayals of the dung *maer* and the sergeant but, rather, a commentary on the injustices they were perceived as perpetrating in their positions as royal officers. One of the obvious questions raised by these depictions is that of the person to whom these criticisms were thus meant to apply. Both of these officials were unpopular persons of relatively low status and, as such, were subject to mockery, as Patterson has argued. However, both were also agents of the king, and the text makes clear that the mocking payments made to them would arise in the course of the exercise of their duties. Similar critiques of the princely abuse of authority (and of the sergeant in particular) also occur in the literature of the time. Best known are probably the *gravamina* brought by the community of Gwynedd against Llywelyn ap Gruffudd.[168] However, a similar complaint voiced in the *Breintiau Gwŷr Powys*, dated by Charles-Edwards to the period between 1170 and 1195, shows that the misbehavior of the ruler was far from a uniquely Venedotian concern.[169] Also of relevance is the poem *Yr Oianau Myrddin*, preserved in the mid-thirteenth-century Black Book of Carmarthen. The poem itself is heavy with legal language and references—including one to the *ciureithau gulad*, the "laws of country"—and among its dire predictions is one concerning the advent of *meiri mangaled am pen keinhauc*, "*maer*s who are greedy over a single penny."[170] Given the context, it seems probable that the lawbook references to fattened coffers and the unmanly exercise of authority—perhaps even to the gate of the court as a rectum—were intended to apply not merely to the dung *maer* and sergeant, but to the prince on whose behalf they acted.

Potentially significant also in this respect is the provision preserved in all redactions about the bull that the sergeant is entitled to receive from the animals taken in the warband's raids. In some redactions (Cyfn, Lat B), a bull is the only animal mentioned; in the vast majority, however, the sergeant is said to be entitled to a bull, a beast that has never been yoked, or a first-calf heifer (known to be notoriously volatile).[171] The common denominator here is quite clearly the wild and unpredictable nature of the animals in question. In the context of a passage already full of symbolic slights aimed at this unpopular royal official, the comparison to a king trampling arbitrarily over the rights of his people seems almost inevitable. So, too, is the warning implicit in the sergeant's award. Marie de France, in her retelling of Aesop's fable "The Belly and Its Members" (a work that may well have inspired John of Salisbury's own writing), addresses her admonitions as much to the body as a whole as to the belly specifically.[172] For Marie, the travails of the belly offer a warning to lords and their subjects to treat each other honorably and with mutual respect.[173] The importance of respectful reciprocity is a common theme as well both in the *Policraticus* and in the twelfth-century *Leges Edwardi*.[174]

Yeager has argued that by the late Middle Ages at least, the "representations of *bodies*, whether whole or in parts, singly or in numbers, *always* carried a political charge, as d[id] the presence or absence of bodies, or parts of bodies, at junctures crucial for interpretation of any kind, whether aesthetic or ideological."[175] Certainly, the body seems to have been one of the languages through which debates about the nature and boundaries of princely rule were conducted in Wales. The contrast drawn in the lawbooks between the body of the idealized king, inviolate and unblemished, and those of his badly dressed, feminized, and infantilized servants seems both deliberate and pointed. As frequently also in the modern world, the juxtaposition of images of the body as it ought to be with those of how it looks in real life is a powerful way to urge people to particular courses of action or to correct troublesome behavior. The redactors' intent was not merely satirical but also exhortatory: an encouragement to princes to rectify their wrongdoings by returning to the stability of past privileges and exactions. In this sense, the lawbooks can fruitfully be regarded as advice literature—mirrors in which contemporary Welsh rulers might examine and, if appropriate, correct their actions. Dafydd Walters has bemoaned the absence of political theory in the prose works extant from medieval Wales,[176] and perhaps this is true. Perhaps, however, we have simply not known where to look. Scholars of Welsh literature have long argued that the prose tales of the period were constructed in a way that intentionally encouraged audiences to approach them on a variety of interpretative levels.[177] I would suggest here that the same is true of the laws. Like the poets and storytellers alongside whom they worked, the lawbook redactors were not constrained by modern perceptions of genre. For them, law and imagination could go hand in hand.

CHAPTER 4

Humor and the Household

Law is often assumed to be the antithesis of the comic. Indeed, the apparent sobriety of the genre lies very near the heart of its claims to authority. Such pretensions to objectivity may be entirely delusional, as Peter Goodrich contends, however, to most of us, humor would seem entirely out of keeping with the seriousness of the situations to which the law is customarily applied.[1] Hence the challenges of interpreting procedures like the gift exchanges described in the previous chapter. Many seem as though they must have been intended to amuse those who witnessed or read about them. However, our distance from the sources offers us little help in knowing what to make of them. Humor is notoriously difficult to recognize and define, especially when it depends on context, and we cannot even be sure at this point whether these were uniquely textual conceits or rituals physically enacted within the community. Nor can we be there to spot the ways in which physicality and wording intersect. The slightest quirk of the mouth can undermine even the most solemn of oaths, but if it never makes it onto the page, scholars living centuries later can easily misconstrue the nature of the event. We can infer the laughter of the past, but we cannot actually hear it.

An additional complication is that ideas about the comic vary greatly across cultures and periods of time. This is especially true of sexualized or body-oriented humor. As Jan Ziolkowski has remarked, "If ignoring or hiding material because of our own fastidiousness is unfortunate, an equally undesirable tendency is to find obscenity where other people in the past have not seen it or where other modern researchers do not apprehend it."[2] The symbolism implicit in many of the payments we have been examining is unquestionably erotic in referencing sexual acts and organs. Whether it would also have been considered obscene is another matter altogether. The term "obscene" implies the making of a value judgment that is beyond our competency at such a chronological remove; the word "erotic," by contrast, makes no such presumptions.[3] If these events ever did take place in real life, the porter's stick or the addled egg given to the sergeant might have been received with bawdy gesturing and great hilarity. Alternatively, they might have been regarded as making a serious point and enacted in dignified silence—and, of course, there is no reason why a single explanation has to cover all occasions. What inspired solemnity in one instance might have been an occasion for raucous mockery in another. We are simply not in a position to judge. What we can hope to interpret are the messages implied in the textual incarnation of such procedures: the threat posed to the monarchy by improper behavior on the part of the king's officials, the menacing prospect of a divided court weakening itself through internal strife.

It is the argument of this chapter that neither these specific messages about king and court, nor the use of sexualized humor to promote them, are confined to the passages and procedures we have examined so far. Rather, all form part of a larger discourse in the lawbooks linking fertility, sexuality, and orderly relations within the household—courtly and domestic—to Welsh political life. Such a conflation of political and sexual may seem odd to modern eyes. In fact, it is anything but. Exactly the same type of juxtaposition is found in the literature of the period. Prose tales such as the Four Branches frequently draw on ancient traditions of sacralized kingship, reshaped in order to address contemporary political concerns.[4] Equally striking is the court poetry of the twelfth and thirteenth centuries, in which female beauty figures frequently as an aspect of the political landscape. In such works, produced on behalf of (or even by) Welsh princes, patriotism and love for the land meld easily with love for the women who inhabit it. Indeed, in some of these poems, one can scarcely distinguish one love from the other. Hywel ab Owain Gwynedd's "Gorhoffedd" ("Boast"), for example, lovingly details the mountains, valleys, and homesteads of the north, citing particular places by name. The poet—himself a warrior and the son of Owain Gwynedd, one of the greatest Welsh princes of the day—then moves from extolling the land's topographical blessings to praising its virtuous maidens. As many of these maidens are also named, the parallels with the places he has just praised are unmistakable.[5]

Sexual longing and political action are similarly juxtaposed in the roughly contemporaneous "Gorhoffedd" of Gwalchmai ap Meilyr, court poet to Owain Gwynedd:

Ar lles gwledig Môn gwaint ym mhlymnwyd
Ac er bodd llywy lliw eiry ar goed
Pan fu aer rhag Caer, cyforiais waed.[6]

For the ruler of *Môn* (Anglesey) I attacked in battle,
and for the favor of a beauty of the color of snow on trees,
when there was slaughter before Caer, I shed blood.

The contrast between the brilliant white skin of the poet's beloved and the crimson blood shed by him on her behalf is surely intentional. Politics and love are one: he fights for his beloved as he fights for his prince because she, too, is part of the political landscape he is protecting. A recurring image throughout this poem is the poet's sword—the sword of battle, to be sure, but given the extent to which sexual desire and war are intertwined in his verses, perhaps also in this context the sword of love as well.[7] A similar conflation of political and personal manliness is visible in a praise poem written by Prydydd y Moch about Llywelyn ap Iorwerth, prince of Wales until his death in 1240. Llywelyn is lauded first as a warrior, and then as a lover; both aspects of his character are depicted by the poet as being pertinent to his power as prince.[8] What would seem to be the same idea in reverse appears in a love poem written by Prydydd y Moch in praise of Gwenllian, daughter of Hywel. In this work, desire rather than politics is the primary focus, but the nature of the imagery is very much the same, as the poet contrasts his own ferocity in battle against the English with his futile attempts to assail the *caeroedd Gwenllïant*,[9] the "fortresses of Gwenllïan." Conquest is conquest, whether the obstacles to overcome be hostile foreigners or a regrettable (in the poet's view) sense of feminine virtue.

Defining Households

Given the ubiquity of such themes in the literature of the day, it is not at all surprising to find similar ideas and imagery in the lawbooks. The evidence suggests that the household, whether political (the king's court and its inhabitants) or domestic (the freeman's farm and its contents), served many lawbook authors as both a primary metaphor and a basic organizing principle. As we have seen, the main description of the royal household occurs in the Laws of Court and is articulated primarily through the movements and actions of the officers who serve the king. There, one gets a strong sense of the physical landscape of the court and its relationship to the larger political landscapes encompassing it (*gwlad* and *gorwlad*); however, the primary focus of juristic attention remains the manner in which this space is inhabited and traversed by the persons who serve within the court. The most detailed depiction of the freeman's household, by contrast, occurs in texts devoted less to the household than to its dissolution: specifically, the lengthy passages on divorce and sexual transgressions contained in the tractate on the Laws of Women. Here, the physical landscape of the household is less described outright than it is inferred: more negative than photograph, a description of what was and might have continued to be, articulated largely through an inventory of the acts and items by which it had originally been created. Significantly, the focus in these passages is not on the people through which the king's rule is defined but, rather, on the possessions and sexually created relationships through which freemen would exercise their authority. Unity is a primary theme in both; the account of the freeman's household, however, places more emphasis on the consequences of separation than the benefits of remaining together.

That this juxtaposing of political and domestic might have been deliberate for at least some lawbook authors is suggested by the placement of the Laws of Court and Laws of Women tractates in certain versions of the lawbook.[10] This is clearest in Ior B (BM.Cotton MS. Titus Dii), although an argument can be made that it was probably true as well of most Ior manuscripts as currently extant (though likely not of the original Book of Iorwerth, of which those manuscripts represent a reordering). As we have seen, in the Model Lawbook underlying the principal redactions, the Laws of Court were followed immediately by the Laws of Country; a third section known as the Judges' Test Book was added later in Ior.[11] Paul Russell has shown that the Ior Laws of Country originally began with a collection of four "nines" (thematic lists consisting of nine components). Today, only one of these, the short paragraph on *Y Naw Tafodiog* ("The Nine Persons Who Are to Be Believed"), remains in its original position at the beginning of the Laws of Country; the other three nines (known collectively as the "Three Columns of Law") were removed from the Laws of Country in the course of Ior's development to form the beginning of the Judges' Test Book.[12] More than any other characteristic, it is the existence of this Test Book that distinguishes Ior from other redactions.

In most extant Ior manuscripts, *Y Naw Tafodiog* is followed directly by the Laws of Women, which is clearly conceptualized in those texts as part of the Laws of Country.[13] In Ior B, however, the tractate on women has been moved to a position preceding *Y Naw Tafodiog* and has become a body of law entirely separate from both the Laws of Court and the Laws of Country. We know that this reordering was consciously done because the Ior B redactor marks deliberate breaks at the end of each of the major sections of his lawbook. Sentence 43/13 of Ior B indicates the end of the Laws of Court: *ac euelly e teruynha e Lleuer Llys*, "and thus ends the Book of the Court"; sentence 44/1 then picks up immediately with *eman e dechreun ny o kyureythyeu e guraged*, "here we begin the laws of women." Similarly, Ior B 55/16 draws a conscious end to the tractate on women: *ac uelly e teruena keyreyth e guraged*, "and thus ends the law of women," which clause is then followed immediately by the signaling in 56/1 of what is obviously being presented as a new section of the lawbook: *eman e dechreuant keureythyeu e wlat*, "here the laws of country begin."[14] An outline of these developments would look like that shown in Table 3.[15]

Several points emerge from this. First, the schema of the Model Lawbook has been complicated in Ior B in several ways. Two anomalies in particular require attention. The first is the current positioning of the Laws of Women within the Laws of Country in manuscripts other than Ior B. A comparison with Cyfn and the Latin redactions suggests that the tractate on women had originally been situated not near the front, following *Y Naw Tafodiog*, but fairly far back in the Laws of Country. Indeed, in most Cyfn manuscripts the tractate on women comes close to the end, right before the triads.[16] Assuming that this arrangement reflects in a general way that of the Model Lawbook

Table 3. Structural Comparison of the Model Lawbook, Ior, and Ior B

Model Lawbook	*Ior MSS apart from B)*	*Ior (MS B)*
Prologue	Prologue	Prologue
Laws of Court	Book of the Court	Book of the Court
		Laws of Women
Laws of Country 1 Three Columns 2 *Y Naw Tafodiog* 3 Other tractates including Laws of Women	Laws of Country 1 Y *Naw Tafodiog* 2 Laws of Women 3 Other tractates	Laws of Country 1 *Y Naw Tafodiog* 2 Other tractates
	Judges' Test Book 1 Three Columns	Judges' Test Book 1 Three Columns

(as seems likely), then the present position occupied by the Laws of Women in the extant Ior manuscripts—following immediately after either the Laws of Court (Ior B) or *Y Naw Tafodiog* at the beginning of the Laws of Country (other Ior manuscripts)—represents a reordering of the original.[17] The second is the independent status of the Laws of Women and its removal from the Laws of Country in Ior B. Russell suggests that the Laws of Women became independent as a consequence of the removal of three of the four nines to the Test Book.[18] Aled Rhys Wiliam proposes instead that the Laws of Women were misplaced in an early archetype of Ior, implying presumably that the moving of this tractate from its original position was largely accidental.[19] Both of these explanations are certainly plausible. However, each relies on accident to explain the foregrounding of the Laws of Women within the Laws of Country, and neither accounts for the clearly deliberate reconceptualizing of this tractate in Ior B as an independent section of the lawbook.

Another possibility worth exploring is that these reorderings were intentional, done in order to bring the tractates on the royal and domestic households together in a way that called attention to the links between them. The nines were already known as traditionally opening the Laws of Country, so it would make sense that *Y Naw Tafodiog* would retain its position at the head of this section of the lawbook in Ior when the Test Book was created. Subsequently, in most Ior manuscripts, the Laws of Women were repositioned immediately after *Y Naw Tafodiog* because that was as close to the Laws of Court as they could get. (It is worth noting that *Y Naw Tafodiog* is only one paragraph long and thus does not constitute much of a break between tractates.) The redactor of Ior B, by contrast, brought the two tractates together by making the Laws of Women an independent section preceding both the Laws of Country and *Y Naw Tafodiog*. Additionally, the divorce passage through which the agricultural household is primarily imagined was moved in all Ior manuscripts[20] from what appears to have been its position in the Model Lawbook halfway through the Laws of Women (where it is in Cyfn) to the very beginning of the tractate, immediately proximate to the Laws of Court. Thus, what had been in the Model Lawbook a relatively simple progression from court to country became additionally in Ior (and in Ior B particularly) a progression from the nucleus of the royal household (the Laws of Court), to the inner circles of the *gwlad* (as revealed by the domestic households and relationships described in the Laws of Women), to its outermost circles (detailed in the tractates of the Laws of Country on suretyship, land administration and renders, and farming).

There are also thematic parallels among these tractates which suggest that they were meant to be read as conceptually analogous to one another. Not only are the basic metaphors of culture and nature, civilization and wildness, present in all these texts, but they also mirror one another directly in their imagery and contents. It is surely not coincidental that images of articulation (the joining together of body parts) and disarticulation (the separation of items that need to be joined together in order to work, on which see further below) function in all these texts to underscore the virtues of unity and the perils of division. Nor is it accidental that the elements primarily at issue in the Laws of Court are human and bovine bodies, and in the Laws of Women, small domestic animals and household property. As we have seen, the authority of kings is vested in the former, while the authority of freemen is rooted in the latter. There are even internal references and borrowings of images back and forth among these texts. Such, for example, are the quernstones and cut meat and butter assigned in the Laws of Women to the wife in the case of divorce, and in the Laws of Court to the sergeant raiding the household of its goods in cases of death or escheat.[21] Dafydd Jenkins calls attention to the apparent contradiction here, noting the inconsistency of the two passages with respect to who would have claim to the items in question.[22] I would suggest, instead, that these are intended to be read symbolically rather than as literal statements about who got what, and that the parallels between them are quite deliberate.

To this point, we have only considered Ior's development. There is a reason for this: the comparison between these two types of household may have also been implicit in Cyfn and the Latin texts—as that between Court and Country certainly was—but there is little to suggest this in the layout of the texts as they remain to us. In Cyfn and the Latin tradition, the Laws of Court are textually quite separate from the Laws of Women; the juxtaposition of these two tractates was clearly an innovation by redactors working in the Ior tradition. Nor is contiguity of theme nearly as evident in Cyfn, Bleg, and the Latin texts as it is in Ior. To be sure, images of articulation and disarticulation are present in all these texts, as are metaphors of culture vs. nature and civilization vs. wildness. However, many of the most evocative images are either missing from Cyfn and the Latin texts or occur only in part. Thus, while the Latin texts and Bleg mention the cut meat and butter, they say nothing about the separated quernstones.[23] Similarly, Cyfn mentions neither the quernstones nor the cut meat and butter—its division of goods gives almost all the butter to the wife, and disperses the meat and cheese according to whether each has already been hung up to cure.[24] It is thus impossible to be certain whether the Cyfn, Latin, and Bleg redactors also intended parallels to be drawn between the Laws of Court and the Laws of Women and the households they describe.[25] What does seem fairly clear, however, is that whereas Cyfn portrays the court on its own as the central element of the Welsh political landscape, Ior deliberately expands this to embrace both types of household, royal and domestic. The king's hall and the freeman's farm function not only as entities unto themselves, but as microcosms of the greater political whole: the hall as the heart of the court, and the farm as the heart of the *gwlad*.

Such a focus on the household should not surprise us. Joan Scott pointed out long ago that the political and the domestic are often historically interlinked, whether with respect to the actual fashioning of power relations, or to the manner in which historians interpret and view past events.[26] Societies have articulated these connections in many different ways, but the perception that politics begins at home is one that has historically been widely shared.[27] This is why male sexual behavior and proper comportment within marriage were perceived as being so important to the welfare of the Roman state,[28] why the implementation of appropriate marital discipline was promoted by Protestants as a matter of civic policy,[29] and why household governance became such a crucial legal issue in late medieval London.[30] As Shannon McSheffrey has observed, "the properly governed household" has served for many cultures as "the model both of and for the government of the realm." Of course, the cultural presumptions in which such perceptions were grounded differed greatly from those we are dealing with here. Renaissance Augsburg was not medieval Wales. However, the deliberate juxtaposition in Ior of the tractate on women with that on the court, coupled with the seemingly also intentional foregrounding of the passage on the agricultural household within that tractate, suggests that what we have in the Welsh laws is far more than a dispassionate accounting of the structural aspects of native social organization. The focus on the household speaks rather to a concept of native political identity vested in hearth and home, both royal and domestic.

Kings A-Courting

At the heart of the households described in Ior lay the institutions of kingship and marriage. Both are depicted in the lawbooks as collaborative and consultative ventures rather than as institutions experienced uniquely by individuals, a theme that is also visible in Welsh romance literature of the period which, in contrast to its French-language counterpart, emphasizes collective over individual action, and the "counsel of trusted men" over autonomous rule.[31] At least by the time of the composition of the lawbooks, these two types of households were conceptualized as having been created in very different ways. The domestic household was initiated by the lawful sexual union of two individuals, optimally (though not always—the laws are most concerned with instances in which these unions go awry) with the consent and participation of their respective kindreds; we will examine this type of household further in the next chapter. The royal household, by contrast, is depicted in the laws as deriving largely from succession in accordance with traditional norms,[32] and from the fashioning of political bonds through gifts, ritual, and the fulfillment of mutual responsibilities. The king may well be married—indeed, clearly was expected on some level to be (hence the presence of the queen, which is simply taken for granted). However, his sovereignty is not depicted in the laws as deriving either from his own personal sexual relationships, or from his marriage.

On the other hand, literary sources of the period make a clear appeal to earlier sacral kingship beliefs about the king as the spouse of the goddess of the land, and it seems almost certain that on some level at least, the treatment of kingship in the laws was informed by these ideas as well. The idea that sovereignty and fertility are linked is an old one. Fertility and its opposite, the sterility engendered by an unjust rule or the death of a well-loved prince, have long been recognized as major themes both in medieval Celtic literature generally and in Welsh writings specifically.[33] One particularly moving expression of the motif is Gruffudd ab yr Ynad Coch's ("Gruffudd son of the Red Judge") poetic lament for Llywelyn ap Gruffudd, composed in the wake of the latter's death in 1282. In this poem, Llywelyn's death is imagined as wreaking havoc on nature and culture alike. The images here are cataclysmic: driving wind and rain, great oaks beating wildly against one another, waves crashing uncontrollably against the shore, the sun hurtling through the sky while the stars themselves plummet to earth. But nature's suffering is just a herald of the political disasters soon to befall the Welsh. The poet begins by imagining the effects of the catastrophe on the cantreds of Wales before gradually, but inexorably, narrowing his focus to encompass every town (*pob tref*), household (*pob tylwyth*), clan (*pob llwyth*), and infant in his cradle (*pob mab yn y grud*) in the disaster about to unfold. Eventually, we are left only with the drumbeat image of a single, decapitated head (*pen*): the severed head of the prince (*pen*), with all that implies for the future security of the Welsh, and the equally muted head of the poet whose voice cannot adequately encompass the tragedy that has occurred.[34]

The idea that the justice of the king's rule will be reflected in the fecundity of his land is nowhere articulated directly in the laws. But then it does not have to be: for the lawbook authors as for their literary colleagues, this was a trope so basic it had only to be alluded to in order to be understood. The link between kingship and the fertility of the land is a basic presumption in these texts; it is essential both to the conceptualization of the court as a form of home and hearth, and to the image of the *edling* asleep in the royal hall with hearth ablaze, surrounded by his future officers. On some level at least, it must also inform the parallels being drawn in Ior between the royal and domestic households. As T. M. Charles-Edwards has observed, the idea of the king as the *gŵr priod Prydain*, "the husband of Britain," found in the poetry of Prydydd y Moch, clearly embodies within it the ancient concept of a marriage between the king and the sovereignty goddess.[35] This is surely also the conceptual subtext of the lawbook passages allotting bulls as well as cows to kings in compensation for offenses done to them, for example.[36] The bulls are expected to eventually constitute mates for the cows in question: as in early Irish tradition, sovereignty entails jurisdiction not merely over individuals, but over fertile couplings, human and animal.[37] In fact, outside the laws, personal fertility itself appears as a requisite of kingship. The presumption shown by the men of Dyfed in requesting that Pwyll take another wife since Rhiannon had not yet succeeded in giving him an heir—and then in insisting that he separate from her a year later when she was accused of killing their child—speaks to exactly this idea.[38]

Similar ideas are also visible in the notion expressed frequently in the laws that there exists a special connection between the king and the fertility of women under his jurisdiction. Virgins are actually termed the "king's waste" (*diffaith*—his special charge, that from which he stands to profit in the absence of other claimants) in the collection of *damweiniau* found in *Llyfr Colan*.[39] As Nerys Patterson has pointed out, there is a functional equivalency in this text between the lord's responsibility to protect the land of young (male) heirs and his obligation to guard the virginity of young females.[40] In Ior, Col, and Latin E, the royal heir is named as the appropriate tester of maidens who bring a charge of rape claiming that they had previously been virgins. If the *edling* finds the maiden still to be a virgin when he tests her, she does not prevail in her claim of rape. However, she loses nothing of her status as a virgin on account of his involvement; indeed, according to Lat E, she receives a ring from him that will serve as evidence of her (previously, before his testing of her) virginal state.[41] It is impossible to read this provision without being reminded of the prose "Tale of Taliesin," where an *edling* and a ring serve similarly to validate the chastity of an accused wife.[42] The stories are not the same—the issue in the tale is fidelity rather than virginity—but both law and literature appear to be drawing here on well-known story traditions linking kingship, the preservation of sexual virtue, and the giving of a ring.

Another potential expression of this complex of ideas is the gold or silver rods (*gwialen, llathen*) received by important kings as compensation for offenses done to them.[43] It may seem a stretch to read these rods as sexual symbols, but it is worth noting that a gold or silver rod—and in Cyfn only the rod, and not the usually accompanying plate or lidded goblet—is the payment made to a king as compensation for sexual offenses committed against a woman in his realm. A man accused of rape who does not deny his crime must, for example, not only pay compensation to the woman herself, but pay a silver rod (*guyalen aryant*) to the king as well on account of the latter's outraged honor. Significantly, according to some texts, if the offender has not the wherewithal to provide this silver rod, his testicles are taken instead.[44] According to Bleg, castration as a penalty for rape was not a native practice, so the idea here may be that to dishonor the king is symbolically to castrate him and thereby destroy the fertility of his reign.[45] Such a reading would fit well with tales such as the Third and Fourth Branches of the Mabinogi, in which Manawydan and Cigfa are deprived of their respective spouses and must live chastely until the enchantment that is devastating Dyfed is repaired, and in which the rape of Math's virgin footholder recapitulates the shameful assault on his public authority that he has already suffered at the hands of his nephews.[46]

In short, earlier traditions regarding kingship and fertility may inform more of the procedures recorded in the lawbooks than we have hitherto realized. This is not, of course, to say that such beliefs were still taken literally, or that twelfth- and thirteenth-century Welsh princes were actually perceived as sacral figures in the traditional sense. As Helen Fulton points out, there is no solid evidence for such ideas having ever played a role in the kingship of any historical Welsh prince.[47] But as Catherine McKenna and others have argued, traditional matter does not have to be used in traditional ways.[48] It can be rewritten to conform to contemporaneous priorities and conditions or silently reshaped to mask significant cultural change. It can be used to correct or deride those in power, and it can even be parodied—whether for amusement, or as a corrective, or both. We already know that medieval authors engaged in the active manipulation of tradition for political purposes. As Andrew Welsh has remarked, "Any individual tale, it seems, is available for different emphases or different interpretations of its meaning by particular storytellers or authors."[49] Recent scholarship has made clear that precisely this sort of intentional reshaping was a major priority for the author(s) of the Four Branches, for example. *Manawydan uab Llyr*, in its embodying of the shift from the old sovereignty model of kingship to a new kind of rule vested in agriculture, crafts, and law, constitutes in Welsh's view a "radical reinterpretation of an earlier story, one which completely changes the meaning while keeping intact the original structure."[50] Similarly, Fulton terms Math as a "failed king," one who rules "by aura rather than action" and a "parody of the ancient myth of Celtic kingship." Against this outdated mode of rule, she argues, the Four Branches lay out several alternative models for lordship, models that are considerably more reflective of contemporary European norms.[51]

What we have seen so far suggests that the lawbooks mark a similar transition between old and new. In the early Irish law tract *Críth Gablach*, the king's connection to the fecundity of his land is underscored by the fact that his own sexual relations (within marriage, in this Christian text) are portrayed as part of his responsibility to his people, much like the obligation to make war, provide adequate courtly display, and provide justice.[52] As was said earlier, there are no overtly parallel passages to this in the Welsh lawbooks; the king's own marriage does not seem to be portrayed in these texts as a politically constitutive act. However, the idea that the king's personal virility is linked to the fertility of his kingdom certainly appears in Welsh poetry of the period—indeed, is sometimes expressed quite graphically, as in "Mawl Llywelyn ab Iorwerth," where the prince's virility (*gwryd*) is compared to that of Garwy (Hir), "Garwy the Long," famous as a soldier and lover in Welsh tradition.[53] It does not seem too far-fetched to imagine that similar ideas lie behind the *edling*'s testing of virgins or the king's receiving of a rod (or testicles) in cases of rape. Be that as it may, it is nonetheless the case that in these sources as in the Four Branches, the essence of kingship now lies elsewhere: in ancestry, the support of freemen, and the lawbooks themselves.

Courtly Burlesques

Ideas like these return us to the issue of the burlesques discussed earlier. If not merely a textual conceit, procedures like the one concerning the rod paid to the king look very much like sexualized humor being used once again within court and community as a legal or moral corrective.[54] They also imply that the role of humor and the burlesque in the lawbooks was even more expansive than Patterson suggests. As we have seen, she restricts the courtly burlesque to situations where officers of the court were either neglectful in their jobs or where the job they performed, while necessary, had something undignified or dishonorable about it. Bards soliciting low-status individuals are thus penalized by having to sing extra songs for their lack of discrimination,[55] while the king's jester, a sketchy personality by definition, is given his horse with the halter tied around its (or his) testicles.[56] However, while Patterson is undoubtedly correct in many of her arguments here—the addled egg and chaff given to the sergeant as a punishment for sitting, for example[57]—not all the bawdy and performative humor mentioned in the laws is directly punitive or aimed exclusively at persons of marginal status.[58] The way the sergeant's day-to-day clothing is described, and the derisively feminizing awards given to him as death duties, make clear that mockery for him is a constant, regardless of any offense.[59] Similarly, there is no indication that the poor dung *maer*, who according to the Cyfn redaction can be insulted with impunity by the king's servants, has trespassed either against the king or against court etiquette.[60]

Rather, as was argued earlier, the true target of these burlesques was the king himself. The link between kingship and fertility adds still further to our understanding of the breadth of the critique. For the sergeant and dung *maer* are not the only officers made fun of in this way. The Laws of Court passage on the royal chamberlain (*guas ystafell*) links him in all redactions not merely to the chamber, but to the royal bed itself. In Ior, for example, the extent of the protection he can offer (*nawdd*) is linked directly to his making of the bed, and he receives the king's old bedclothes (*hen dyllat guele*) as part of his compensation.[61] In Cyfn, his presumed familiarity with the king's sexual activities is alluded to directly in a passage which stipulates that he receive from the booty taken by the bodyguard in their raids *yg6arthec kyhyt eu kyrn ac eu hyskyfarn*, "cattle whose horns are as long as their ears."[62] Patterson has argued that these cattle constitute "well-recognized sexual symbols," noting that cattle described in this manner are also assigned as a derisive marital due by women who elope.

The parity of their horns and ears reflects, she suggests, the equivalent degree of lust experienced by the two parties; the cattle awarded to the chamberlain thus constitute a burlesque both on his role as a panderer for the king, and on the eagerness with which women coming to the king's room would have accepted his invitation.[63] Her suggestions as to the sexual import of these cattle are surely correct. Indeed, one might even extend her arguments by noting that tails and horns are both common euphemisms in the poetry of the period for the penis, and that the tail actually features as an unequivocal stand-in for the penis in rituals described in both Cyfn and Ior.[64] All in all, given the chamberlain's intimate connection with the king's bedroom affairs, it is difficult to imagine that the sexual inferences here are not intentional.

However, it is also difficult to imagine that the butt of this joke was anyone other than the king himself. Patterson takes the short-horned cattle as a comment less about the chamber servant than about the evils of "female concupiscence."[65] However, there is nothing to this effect in the text, and any chamber servant involving himself in pandering would surely have been acting on the (depicted as married) king's orders anyway. Might not these horns be, along with the docked-tail animal and the short stick scrabbled by the porter from every bundle of wood entering the court, the functional equivalent of the sergeant's embarrassingly abbreviated spear? It may also be significant that the chamberlain's cows are said to come to him not from the kitchen, as is characteristic of the animals assigned to other non-raiding-party members, but from the booty taken by the household troops in the course of their raids. Raids are acts of predation that involve taking things from their rightful owners; if some of the women brought to the king's bed were married or supposed otherwise to be under his protection, then the source of the chamberlain's reward might also constitute a comment on the morals of his royal employer. In any case, it does not seem to be a terribly complimentary characterization of the king's amorous adventures.

That these are not merely modern misreadings is borne out by a glance at the Latin A law manuscript Peniarth 28 (see fig. 6). There, the textual treatments of the king's huntsman and his chamber servant are found side by side; since they are not so located in either the Ior or Cyfn versions, this suggests that the placement was deliberate. In the illustrations that accompany these texts, the former is portrayed in a long tunic holding a hunting horn, whereas the latter is represented by a kissing couple; to all appearances, the huntsman's tunic looks exactly like the gown worn by the woman of the pair. Moreover, he appears to be blowing his horn as the two come together, perhaps as a sign

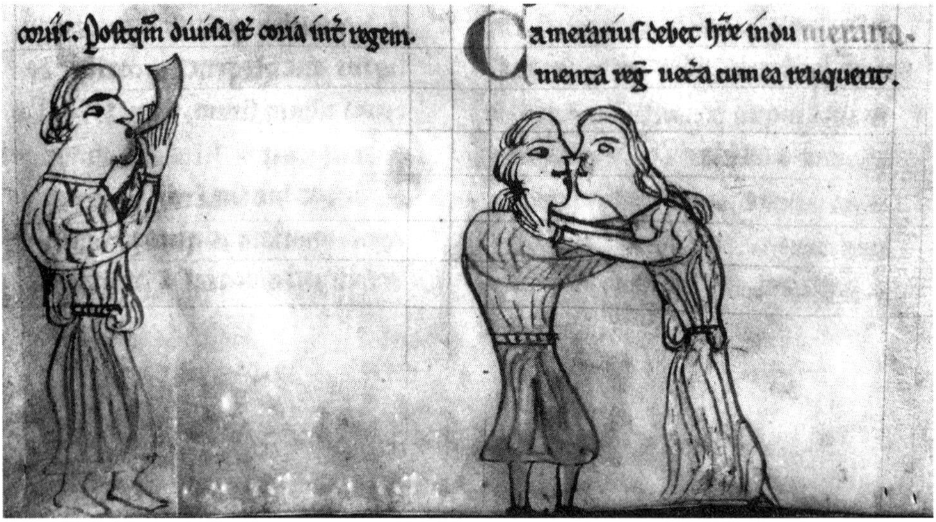

Figure 6. *Y pencynydd*, "chief huntsman," and a kissing couple.

National Library of Wales manuscript Peniarth 28, fol. 5r.

that the prey has been secured.[66] We know that chastity was a virtue urged on kings in the *miroir* genre that became so popular in Wales in the course of the high and late Middle Ages.[67] Could it be that what we have here in the chamberlain's cattle and his pictorial juxtaposition with the huntsman are further instances in which payments to court officers are being used to criticize the rapacious and unchaste demeanor of unjust kings? Another potential example comes from Latin D and Bleg, which portray the chamberlain receiving the heifers and bullocks (Latin: *iuvencula*) taken in raids upon the *gorwlad*. By contrast, animals taken by the king's household troops or by other men from the king's own *gwlad* are said to remain the property of the warriors who took them.[68] Is it possible that also hidden in these passages is a commentary on the inappropriately young nature of the king's nocturnal distractions or, alternatively, an admonition to lecherous kings to seek their sexual partners from a *gwlad* other than the one over which they rule (*gwlad* vs. *gorwlad*)?

Nor are these the only instances of risqué or sexualized humor being used to critique royal patterns of rule. Images of effeminacy and excrement are evoked not only by the sergeant's linen outerwear, for example, but by the animal rectums, docked-tail beasts, and short sticks given to the porter.[69] And surely it is significant that the porter and doorkeeper are the only other figures apart from the sergeant who are wearing linen (and visibly divided, albeit of normal length) pants in the Peniarth 28 illustrations?[70] The judge is said, in all the principal redactions, to sleep at night on the same pillow on which the king sits during the day; if perceived as a reflection on the source of the king's justice, the imagery here does not seem very flattering to either party.[71] As mentioned earlier, Cyfn W stipulates that the thighs of beasts be placed as tongues in the animal heads presented to the smith, the original tongues having already been given to the judge.[72] One has only to visualize either of these public prestations—and for this it is not even necessary to know that the thigh muscle also features in contemporary Welsh poetry as a symbol for the penis[73]—to get a sense of the comic spectacle involved. To these might conceivably also be added the right of the falconer in Ior to have the king hold his stirrup when he gets off his horse to go pee.[74] Even apart from the mention of urination, holding the stirrup was a well-known symbol in this period not merely of service but of actual subordination; a century earlier, Frederick Barbarossa's public refusal to hold the pope's stirrup had caused an angry quarrel that redounded all across Europe. At the very least, the image here involves a visible, and possibly intentionally comic, reversal of hierarchy.[75]

As with the officers we looked at earlier, there is no indication in these texts that any of these royal servants had done anything wrong that would merit a joke at their expense. Perhaps these were onetime events generalized by the lawbook redactors; perhaps they were intended simply to be funny.[76] Or perhaps accounts like these offer us a glimpse of the role played by humorous spectacles and practical jokes in the life of the court. Certainly, there is no shortage of evidence as to the popularity of jokes and bawdy spectacles among noble audiences of the period.[77] What this evidence suggests to me, however, is that these (putative) practices were also gibes aimed primarily at the king and the court over which he presided. We know that at least some jurists were concerned by the rapid Europeanization of princely rule in this period. Relations between the Welsh and the Anglo-Normans settling on their lands were complicated, and by no means entirely hostile.[78] The cultural superiority of the latter was often taken for granted in English and European circles,[79] and Welsh nobles and princes eager to be seen as players on a wider stage began adopting courtly practices and habits of display not previously found in the native tradition. The largest body of Continental loanwords into Welsh in this period relates to fashionable clothing and ornament.[80] Foreign example is also the most likely explanation for other cultural innovations, such as the proliferation of castles and the separation of the king's and queen's households.[81]

Scholars have frequently remarked on the hybrid nature of Welsh cultural self-fashioning in this era: the rejection of native poetic meters and heroic motifs in favor of courtly narratives and themes, the adaptation of myth to circumstances of contemporary rule, the active reimagining of Welsh identity in ways that made sense within the context of both native and European culture.[82] The idea of courtliness itself may not have been a foreign import, and cultural exchange went both ways, as Ceridwen Lloyd-Morgan has argued.[83] However, for many Welsh writers of the period, socializing their compatriots into the proprieties of European kingship ideology and display was a clear priority.[84]

Many native Welshmen actively embraced this process of cultural mimicry, of course.[85] But others rejected it, opting instead for what Susan Aronstein has called "strategic distancing and isolation."[86] Still others may have perceived the manner in which courts were refashioning themselves to be pretentious, inexpertly done, and dangerously reliant on external appearances. David Stephenson has argued that *uchelwyr* attitudes toward innovations in the festive aspects of court life were largely positive, at least as far as can be determined from the tractate on the Laws of Court.[87] Perhaps this is right, but *uchelwyr* attitudes toward anything seem unlikely to have been entirely uniform, let alone on a subject as significant as the importation of foreign practices into the setting of a native court. Perhaps the comic inelegance implicit in these and other burlesques not yet mentioned was deliberate: not only the smith's thigh and the porter's snatching of sticks,[88] but also the candleman's scrounging of bits of broken bread and meat as they fell from the king's plate during dinner,[89] and the alarming number of low-status occupants of the court imagined as throwing their hand tools in the air in order to determine the physical extent of the sanctuary they could offer (including many like the bondman who had no business offering sanctuary at all).[90] So also perhaps the juxtaposition of urination and falconry. Dafydd Jenkins has argued that as a practice imported from England (most likely in pre-Norman times), falconry was still regarded as exotic in the period of the lawbooks.[91] Perhaps this image was also intended to comment on the gap between the realities of Welsh court life and the pretensions of its princely inhabitants to a foreign-based cosmopolitan elegance? Fulton has argued that the primary target of the satirical tale *Breuddwyd Rhonabwy* is a type of rule grounded in external appearances rather than in internal merit.[92] We know that there was hostility among the *uchelwyr* toward some of the legal and jurisdictional practices being adopted by Welsh princes on the basis of foreign example; perhaps the popularity of some of their cultural innovations was also less widespread than has customarily been thought.

Or perhaps the critique is even more trenchant than this. We have seen that the redactors were familiar with cultural tropes associated with sacral kingship—ideas and images that their literary colleagues frequently reworked for political, didactic, or ideological purposes. According to these tropes, kingship properly conducted would result in the fruitful union of king and goddess, the generosity of a fertile land and people, and the wise and discerning judgments of an incorruptible prince. Is it accidental, then, that so many of these burlesque awards—the short sticks, short spears, miniaturized tunics and booties, visible undergarments, docked-tail animals, oddly sized tongues, horns, ears, and thighs, grouped-together tongues, rectums, and dubiously scented pillows—evoke images of flatulence, excrement, gluttony, effeminacy or its opposite, intemperate lust? What we are seeing here is the discomfiture of the many in the *uchelwyr* class with the changing patterns of princely rule.[93] Some of the burlesques we have discussed—the sergeant, the dung *maer*—seem to target officers charged with the collecting of royal dues. But some seem to have other princely failings in mind: the pillow, a comment on the usurpation of traditions of judicial independence; the porter grabbing at bundles brought into the court, a criticism of the grasping nature of the monarchy with respect to even the pettiest of fees. Indeed, if I am right about this, the burlesques may even serve to alert us to issues we had not previously been aware of: the falconer, possibly a comment on the lowering of royal dignity or the unseemly adoption of foreign ways; the chamber servant, a judgment on royal lasciviousness; the indiscriminate bard, an expression of outrage at the prominence of lowborn persons at court. And while I am uncertain as to what the poor smith did to deserve his thigh—given his connection with the king's weapons, and the cultural currency of nicknames like "Softsword" for unpopular war leaders like King John—might this be a comment on the ruler's performance in war?

With such speculations, we have strayed directly onto the perilous ground that awaits those who try to interpret humor—or at least what appears to be humor—across a significant chronological and cultural divide. Clearly, the Welsh were not shy in their use of sexualized humor, and there were elements of Welsh tradition that lent themselves well to symbolic enlargement and adaptation, whether textual (imagined largely on the page) or ritual (performed within court and community). But not all objects that can function as symbols do so in every instance, and it can be deucedly difficult to tell the difference between an actual tradition and a parody of it. The figure of Math in the Fourth Branch of the Mabinogi was long thought to embody qualities associated with sacral kingship, and yet many scholars now read him more as a parody of ancient tradition than an uncomplicated exemplar of it.[94] Similarly, Joan Radner has suggested that while *Culhwch ac Olwen* may seem to embrace native literary conventions, it is actually parodying them as entertainment for the sophisticated courtly audiences of the twelfth and thirteenth centuries.[95] Ned Sturzer also regards *Culhwch* as a "scavenger hunt" of ancient motifs that quite deliberately and ingeniously plays with tradition and pokes fun at itself.[96] The ongoing adaptation of tradition was clearly a common feature of the Welsh storytelling art; indeed, the true challenge (and pleasure) for courtly audiences in this period may have been "to listen in a sophisticated way to literature that was not what it seemed to be on the surface."[97]

Despite such uncertainties, I would suggest that what was true of the literature of the period was likely also true of the laws, not least because of the links that we know to have existed between those writing in the different genres. The lawbook redactors, like their more overtly literary colleagues, not only drew upon but also altered tradition for their own purposes rather than mindlessly replicating it. Recognizably native mythological conceits could be used to bolster the image of kings; however, they could also be employed by redactors who were critical of princely policies to mock and deride, as they certainly did in the case of the dung *maer* and sergeant, and likely also the porter, chamberlain, judge, and falconer. It is striking, in fact, and surely not coincidental, how many of the truly odd or seemingly bawdy passages seem to cluster around issues of princely jurisdiction. And of course, some problems of interpretation may never be solved to everyone's satisfaction. One particularly difficult figure is the king's footholder, the problems with which have already been clearly delineated by McKenna.[98] The footholder of the Fourth Branch of the Mabinogi is a maiden in whose lap Math's feet must be placed at all times except during times of war. The clear implication is that when the tale begins, the sacrality of Math's reign is regarded in some sense as being vested in her and her virginity.[99] By contrast, the royal footholder as depicted in the laws is male and without visible constraints on his sexual behavior. He holds and scratches the king's feet, to be sure; however, there is no indication in these texts that the king's reign would be lost without him.[100]

Traditionally, the female incarnation of this figure has been regarded as the version more proximate to ancient native tradition, part of a constellation of sovereignty goddess motifs linking the king to the fertility of the land.[101]

More recently, however, Ian Hughes has suggested that the female footholder as she appears in the tale is not traditional but, rather, an addition made by the Mabinogi author for narrative purposes, a view toward which McKenna seems at least to some degree sympathetic.[102] Of far greater importance than the origins of this figure in her view, however, is the role played by both footholders, male and female, within the narratives that contain them. Both are, she argues, courtly figures constructed in particular ways to suit the purposes of their creators. For the sluggishly complacent Math, the rape of his footholder, Goewin, provides an opportunity for moral growth. Regardless of whether Goewin would have been recognized as traditional within the courtly milieu in which the tale was performed, her rape serves within the context of the tale as an impetus to jolt Math out of his lethargy and face his responsibilities as lord.[103] The role played by the footholder in the laws is considerably more difficult to pin down. If male footholders were traditional, and female footholders the invention of the Mabinogi author, then the footholder of the laws is probably to be read in a relatively straightforward fashion, as one aspect of the festive display of the court. If, however, female footholders were traditional, and the males the innovation, then what we likely have here in the laws is either a joke or—and the two are not necessarily mutually exclusive—an old mythological trope updated in a manner more suited to contemporary European notions of kingship. It is perhaps worth noting that the redactor of the generally more sophisticated Ior redaction (in contrast to Cyfn), transforms the footholder into something of a personal bodyguard of the king, and that the redactor of Latin C seems confused as to who he might have been in the first place.[104]

In other words, the Ior redactor may be attempting to have it both ways: embracing the fertility and magic associated with this figure in traditional mythology, while finding a way to situate the office within the parameters of contemporary kingship ideology. This is, after all, exactly what he appears to be doing in his version of the Laws of Court, where he retains the mythological symbols of cows, rod, and plate, but in a way that seems intended to minimize and contain them.[105] Alternatively, he may merely be having a good laugh with his male footholder—though in which direction the joke would go is not entirely clear. One can imagine, as McKenna does, that the idea of a female footholder would be received in the courts of the high Middle Ages as a grand joke, a sly dig at an "actual male *troediog* or a lecherous king."[106] But one can also imagine that contemporaries who were accustomed to a female footholder as a linchpin of sacral kingship would have greeted the idea of a male in that office as hilarious and more than a little risqué. It is also entirely possible that the male footholder of the lawbooks ought to be read as yet another example of what has recently been suggested for *Math*—a commentary on the inadequacy of old fertility-based ideas about the lord and his land as a model for effective kingship.[107] C. W. Sullivan has argued that the absence of women at the end of the tale symbolizes the supplanting of the sovereignty goddess by new ideas about the nature of kingship, most particularly the advent of patrilineal lordship.[108] Perhaps what we have in the male footholder of Ior, shorn of any earlier sexual implications and newly imagined as a bodyguard, is the logical extension of the process one sees at work in the Four Branches. There is simply no way to know. One thing surely is clear, however: the footholder's appearance in these two types of narratives is testimony both to the wide-ranging connections between the lawyers and their fellow tradition bearers,[109] and to their willingness to play off of one another in adapting native tradition for their own purposes.

The presumption of a link between sovereignty and fertility thus seems implicit in the laws, but its usage can hardly be counted as straightforward. Indeed, while the redactors appealed to sacral kingship tropes in some instances—the bulls and cows paid to the king, for example, or the idea that virginity forms a special charge of the king—they did so as much to bend these motifs to their own purposes as to confirm their relevance to the Wales of their day. Erotic symbols certainly feature in the laws in a variety of contexts, and aspects of the king's body—and bawdy—were available as images to which appeal could be made when it was helpful. However, they seem often to have been played for humor and used to mock and critique princely policies rather than to further them. From the point of view of the lawbook redactors, the strength of the royal household lay less in the sexual union of king and goddess than in the rights, dues, and reciprocal practices by which *uchelwyr* like themselves were bound to king and court. Sacral kingship was certainly not out of the picture as an ideological support; however, it was traditions of service and rule rather than the mythological imprimatur of the goddess that defined the court and its relationship to the greater political whole. In this, the laws once again parallel the prose literature of the period, in which the virtues of discernment and wise counsel are explicitly promoted over outmoded notions of royal sacrality.[110] Indeed, the overlap between the legal and literary footholder may lie precisely here, in the perceived inadequacy of archaic mythological structures to meet the challenges of a rapidly changing political world.[111]

CHAPTER 5

Sex and Marriage

In moving from the Laws of Court to the Laws of Women, we pass from one type of household to another, from the world of the court to that of the farm. One of the constant criticisms lodged by contemporaries against the Welsh was that of sexual impropriety.[1] Unlike canon law, native practice allowed for divorce and remarriage and made no distinction between legitimate and illegitimate children for inheritance purposes, practices that reform-minded clerics found offensive. An ecclesiastical synod held at Westminster in 1175 pointedly criticized the Welsh custom of "changing wives," for example.[2] And Archbishop of Canterbury John Pecham fulminated loudly against what he regarded as the unique depravity of Welsh sexual mores under Hywel's law, which allowed for the repudiation of "legitimate wives [in a manner] contrary to the Gospels" by appeal to their reputation (or, more accurately in his view, the lack thereof).[3] Indeed, it may have been Pecham himself who made a mark next to the passage on divorcing parties dividing up their bedclothes in MS Peniarth 28, almost certainly as a sign of disapproval.[4] Welsh marriage customs were beginning to move more in the direction of the European norm in the period, but there was still considerable distance between native and ecclesiastical law on this issue as on many others.[5] In response to such criticisms, certain Welsh rulers began to turn away from native practices and adopt canonical teachings regarding marriage and inheritance. In 1222 Llywelyn ap Iorwerth himself asked the pope to approve his younger legitimate son Dafydd as sole heir in preference to his older illegitimate son Gruffudd. That Dafydd was the son of Llywelyn's English wife Joan, daughter of King John of England, must surely have reinforced juristic fears of a native tradition under threat.[6] The choice of which custom to follow was no longer strictly a matter of nationality or language.[7]

Accusations of immorality would inevitably have been on the minds of the redactors to whose efforts we owe the texts that have come down to us. Jurists who were interested in recalling wavering countrymen to the traditions of their ancestors had a vested interest in underscoring in their works the superiority of native law. The tractate on women makes no direct mention of contemporary criticisms lodged against Welsh marriage practices, but so pervasive were these complaints at the time that it is impossible to imagine a text of this sort taking shape without its authors being aware of the potential ramifications of their work. It is thus unlikely to be coincidental that significant attention is paid in all redactions to precisely those areas in which native tradition was most vulnerable to criticism. Separation and divorce are major themes, as is sexual misbehavior on the part of individual men and women, especially sexual relations initiated without the permission of family members or requisite exchanges of gifts and promises. Of course, these are subjects that one might expect to find treated in any contemporary legal text. However, the manner in which they are treated in the Welsh lawbooks reprises ideas and imagery that we have seen already in the context of the court, including the perception that the welfare of the state is linked to individual and domestic propriety, and the use of burlesque to reprove unsanctioned behavior. Indeed, the courtly household was only one of the locales Nerys Patterson identified as a primary venue for the burlesque. The second was the freeman's house and farm, where burlesques were used to mock "dishonourable women" whose families had been shamed by their sexual improprieties.[8]

Divorce, Medieval Welsh Style

One of the most striking passages in the lawbooks is the one that enumerates the domestic and agricultural items taken by members of a divorcing couple in cases where the union had lasted at least seven years.[9] (Marriages that did not last as long as seven years entailed different property arrangements.[10]) This passage is found in all the principal Welsh redactions of the lawbooks and in four of the five Latin versions (the exception being Latin C, where the omission is not significant, as this section of manuscript is missing.)[11] As is so frequently the case, most Ior versions of the list are longer and more detailed than are the Cyfn, Bleg, and Latin versions.[12] The Latin redactions and Bleg have fairly clearly drawn heavily on Ior and cannot really be considered independent of it.[13] Cyfn's testimony, on the other hand, is of considerable interest. Its divorce passage seems to be the earliest and least developed of the major lawbook versions, and yet many of the ideas under discussion here are clearly present in embryonic form in its tractate.[14] Here as elsewhere, rather than departing from the tradition bequeathed to them, the Ior redactors chose instead to build upon that tradition in order to make a point implied, but not fully developed, in earlier lawbook versions.[15] Additionally, while the paragraph on divorce opens the tractate on the Laws of Women in all Ior versions that contain it, all Cyfn manuscripts that include it place it much later in the tractate, perhaps as a way of deliberately juxtaposing the courtly and agricultural households.[16]

The Ior version of the passage in question reads as follows:

> Kyureitheu g6raged
> 2O deruyd y wreic bot rodyeit idi, ydan y hangwedi y dyly bot hyt ym pen y seith mlyned; ac o cheiff teir nos o'r seith[u]et bl6ydyn ac yskar onadunt, rannent yn deu hanher pob peth a uo ar y helo oc a uo udunt. 3Y wreic bieu rannu a'r g6r dewissa6. Y moch y'r g6r, a'r deueit y'r wreic. Ony byd ont y neill, eu rannu yn deu hanher. Ac os deueit a ge[i]uyr a uyd, y deueit y'r g6r, a'r geiuyr y'r wreic. Ony byd ont y neill, eu rannu yn deu hanner. 4O'r meibon y d6y ran y'r tat, yr hynaf a'r ieuhaf, a'r peruedhaf y'r uam. 5Y dotdrefyn ual hyn y rennir: llestri y llaeth oll, eithyr un bayol ac un dysgyl, y'r gwreic yd a, a'r deu hynny y'r g6r. 6Y wreic a dyly karr a ieueu. 5/4Y g6r a dyly holl lestri y llyn. 7*Y g6r a dyly y ridyll a'r wreic y gogyr man.* 8*Y g6r a dyly y maen uchaf o'r vreuan, a'r wreic yr issaf.* 9Y dillat gwely a uo arnadunt y wreic bieiuyd. Y dillat a uo adanunt, y g6r bieu yny wreicaho. Ac g6edy g6reicao, ellynget y dillat y'r wreic. Ac os g6reic arall a g6sc ar y dillat, talct y h6yncbwerth iddi. 10*Y g6r bicu y galla6r a'r bryccan a gobennyd y tra6sdyle a'r k6lltyr a'r v6yall gynnut a'r taradyr a'r pergyg a'r crymaneu oll dyeith[yr] vn cryman, a h6nn6 y'r wreic.* 11*Y wreic bieu y badell a'r trybed a'r u6yell lydan ar a'r g6dyf a'r s6ch a'r llin achlan a'r llinat a'r g6lan a'r trithg6t dyeithyr eur neu aryant, a h6nn6, or byd, y rannu. Ac y sef y6 trithg6t y lla6gyteu ac a vo yndunt odieithyr eur ac aryant.* 12*Or byd g6eeu, eu rannu. Y pelleneu y'r meibyon or bydant; ac ony bydant, eu rannu.* 13*Y g6r a dyly a vo uch daear ac is daear o yt.* 14*Y g6r a dyly yr ieir oll ac vn cath, a'r rei ereill oll y'r wreic.* 15*Y b6yt ual hynn y rennir: y wreic bieu y kic yn heli, a'r g6r bieu g6edy croccer;* 16*y wreic bieu y kic b6lch a'r ka6s b6lch;* 17*y*

wreic bieu kymeint [o ula6t] ac a allo y r6ng nerth y d6y vreich a'e deu lin y d6yn o'r gell hyt y ty. 18*Pob un onadunt bieu y dillat dyeithyr y mentyll; a'r mentyll, eu rannu.* 19*Os y g6r a vyd breinha6l, dangosset y vreint kynn rannu. A g6edy kaffo ef y vreint, ranher mal y dywedassam ni uchot.*

Ior §44. The Laws of Women. 2If it happens that a woman has givers, she is entitled to be under her *egweddi*[17] until the end of seven years. And if she gets three nights from the seventh year and they part, let them divide into two halves everything that is theirs which is in their possession. 3It is for the woman to divide and the man to choose. The pigs go to the man and the sheep to the woman. If they have only one kind, they are to be divided into two halves. And if there be sheep and goats, the sheep go to the man and the goats to the woman. If they have only one kind, they are to be divided. 4Of the children two parts go to the father, the eldest and the youngest, and the middle to the mother. 5The household goods are divided as follows: all the milk vessels, except for one pail and one dish, go to the woman, and those two go to the man. 6The woman is entitled to a car and yokes. 5/4The man is entitled to all the drinking vessels. 7The man is entitled to the riddle and the woman to the fine sieve. 8The man is entitled to the upper stone of the quern and the woman to the lower. 9The bedclothes which are over them shall belong to the woman. The clothes which are under them belong to the man until he marry. And when he marries, let him release the clothes to the woman. And if another woman sleeps upon the clothes, let him pay her face-value to her. 10To the man belong the cauldron and the blanket and the pillows of the bed and the coulter and the wood-axe and the auger and the *pergyng* and all the sickles except one sickle, and the latter goes to the woman. 11To the woman belong the pan and the tripod and the broad axe and the billhook and the ploughshare and all the flax and the linseed and the wool and the *trithgwd* except for gold or silver, and the latter, if there is any, is divided. By the *trithgwd* is meant the handbags and what is in them except for gold and silver. 12If there are webs they are divided. The balls [of wool] go to the sons, if there are any; and if there are none, they are divided. 13The man is entitled to the corn which is above ground and below ground. 14The man is entitled to

> all the hens and one cat, and all the others go to the woman. 15The food is divided as follows: to the woman belongs the meat which is in salt, and after it is hung up it belongs to the man; 16to the woman belongs the cut meat and the partly-used cheese; 17to the woman belongs as much flour as she can carry by the strength of her arms and her knees from the larder to the house. 18To each of them belong their clothes except for the cloaks; and the cloaks are to be divided. 19If the man is privileged, let him reveal his privilege before the division. And when he has received whatever his privilege entitle him to, let the division proceed as we have said above.[18]

Traditional interpretations have taken this passage more or less at face value. As Dafydd Jenkins remarks, "When living partners separate, they share the chattels as instructed by law texts. The rules are no doubt meant to ensure that both parties are reasonably provided for, in default of agreement, though it is not easy to understand why the two stones of the quern, for instance, should be separated."[19] He is undoubtedly right that there is evidence in the text of a concern that parties whose marriage had lasted the statutory seven years start their new lives on a viable and reasonably equal footing. Both Ior and the Latin redactions divide all the gold and silver owned by the two parties evenly between them,[20] and the northern Latin texts B and E follow Ior in stipulating that any debts they may have incurred are also to be divided in this manner.[21] Similarly, while each member of the divorcing couple retains his or her own personal garments, the valuable and unisex cloaks they share between them.[22]

But Jenkins's hesitation about the curious separation of the quernstones is well founded. The deeper one probes into this text, the less sense it appears to make. Certainly, it is difficult to discern the principles governing the division of goods envisaged here. In early Irish law, the apportionment of property in a case of divorce depended on the amount of wealth brought by the parties into the relationship, the status of the marriage entered into, the behavior of the parties, and the amount of labor each put into a particular item.[23] But ideas of this sort are only vaguely visible in the Welsh texts. Nothing is said about the property brought into the marriage determining the amount that could be taken out of it; indeed, we know from other texts that the goods which accompanied the woman into the relationship (*argyfrau*) fell into the common pool after the seven-year period and were, in the case of divorce, divided along with the rest.[24] The natal status of the wife, which was crucial in determining the goods she took with her when the parties divorced before the union had lasted seven years (her *agweddi*), became irrelevant after this period had expired.[25] And while there is certainly evidence in Welsh law of high- and low-status marriages, the passage we are concerned with here speaks only to the dissolution of proper (*priodas*) relationships: the status of the relationship, in other words, cannot explain the peculiarities of the distribution scheme outlined here.[26] Moreover, even women who married without the permission of their kin were entitled to an equal share of the goods if the relationship lasted seven years.[27]

Gender considerations do seem to be a factor in the list. Some items were assigned to the person who would normally have made, consumed, or worked with them. Women are said to receive all the flax and linseed;[28] they also get all the milk vessels apart from a single dish and bowl,[29] and in the Cyfn version all but one container of the butter.[30] The husband, by contrast, receives all but one of the sickles, and all the drinking vessels—the latter an instance of gender consumption rather than of labor, since women were generally the ones who made the ale.[31] The assignment of the pigs to the man and the sheep to the woman is gendered in a variety of ways. Pigs ranged wild and were usually tended by men; sheep ranged widely also, but were closely associated with women by virtue of women's role in milking, cheese manufacture, and cloth production. This division also reflected standard medieval Welsh ideas of hierarchy, in which men took precedence over women and pigs took precedence over sheep.[32] Goats, considered the most ignoble of them all (as they still were in Ireland in the early twentieth century when the goat was characterized as a thief and a sinner in Liam Ó Flaithearta's story "An Chulaith Nua"[33]), were assigned to the wife in the case where the couple owned only sheep and goats.[34] Similarly, the provision stipulating that the woman was to divide the possessions and the man to choose between them is modeled on the procedure used in apportioning land between inheriting sons; as one would expect in a text of this date, the woman is here projected into the role of the younger, and the man into that of the older, son.[35]

However, the matter is not nearly as simple and straightforward as it might appear. For every gender-appropriate item mentioned in the list, there is one that would surely have struck contemporaries as bizarre and inappropriate. In all redactions, it is the woman who receives the huge broad axe used for heavy chopping, for example, even though it is certainly the man who would have used it in daily life. The husband receives instead the much smaller wood axe—and in Cyfn the even smaller handaxe (*b6ell gynnut a'r lla6 u6ell* vs. *b6ell lydan*)—which would have been used by both women and men for cutting kindling and the like.[36] Billhooks were extremely heavy and would normally have been used by men for hedging and related tasks, but, in the text, it is the woman who gets this tool.[37] And although women were the ones responsible for woolen cloth production within the conjugal household, it is the sons of the marriage rather than the wife who receive the balls of wool yarn, which would make no sense at all were things being divided along standard gender lines.[38]

Moreover, the quern is not the only item to be mysteriously partitioned in a way that makes it essentially unusable. The coulter goes with the man and the plowshare with the woman;[39] insofar as both blades would have been needed to break up the ground for planting, this is a division that would have struck contemporaries as nonsensical from any practical point of view. Similarly, the Ior version of the text gives the coarse sieve to the husband and the fine sieve to the wife.[40] Ordinarily, in order to make flour, grain would first have been crushed in the quern, then put through the coarse sieve, and finally have been sifted through the fine sieve. In the division envisaged here, there is no functioning quern, and the two sieves are separated from one another in a way that leaves the husband able to sift the grain coarsely but unable to refine it into usable flour, and the wife with the ability to refine flour but incapable of doing the requisite preliminary sifting. Indeed, since all grain, whether harvested or in seed, went to the man,[41] the wife would have had nothing to sift in the first place—her single quernstone, like her fine sieve, was entirely useless to her. And while her husband might at first appear to have been somewhat better off, in fact he had his own problems. Cats were a necessity around a farmyard to keep mice and other rodents out of the grain, and they also played an important role in keeping down the rats that preyed on the eggs of nesting hens. The man may get all the grain, and all the hens as well. However, he is given only one cat, while his wife, who receives no grain and no hens, gets every one of the remaining cats.[42] One party has everything to protect but little to protect it with; the other has a great deal of protection, but nothing to protect. Whatever lies at the heart of the property division envisaged in the text, it is definitely not agricultural practicality.

What we are seeing here is not a procedure designed to ensure that divorcing parties will be able to support themselves on their own but, rather, a symbolic object lesson in the costliness of divorce. Futility and infertility are the dominant themes of this passage: the earth that cannot be plowed, the grain that cannot be planted or crushed or rendered fit for consumption, the eggs and grain that cannot be protected to maturity. Very similar is the message of the axes—one needs both a large axe for chopping and clearing, and smaller axes to render the resulting pieces usable. Not only are the two separated in this text, the large axe is given to the person who is physically least able to make use of it. Some of the most basic aspects of civilized life become thereby impossible: the clearing of land for cultivation, for example, or the construction of domestic and agricultural buildings, or the provisioning of the hearth with fuel for cooking and warmth. Indeed, the intrusion of nature into what would, in an intact household, be the prosperity of home and farm would seem to be an absolutely central image in the text. Rodents devour the fruits of the farmyard; hedges grow unchecked by a billhook that the wife cannot easily wield; land previously under cultivation retreats back into forest.

Other aspects of this property division underscore the contrast between civilization and wildness, fertility and want. The very social conventions by which humans are distinguished from beasts are put at risk. Men cannot clothe themselves, since apart from such balls of thread and woven fabric as already exist at the time of the divorce, all items necessary to the production of clothing (flax, sheep, the raw wool) go to the wife.[43] Feasting, a crucial element in social and political relations, can no longer take place. The husband has drinking vessels, but in the absence of a quern, he can no longer make ale; he has meat dishes and pigs, but he no longer possesses the axe with which to slaughter the animals in question; he has a cauldron in which large cuts of meat may be cooked, but no smaller pan or tripod with which to cook smaller foods; he receives such cheeses as are already hung for preservation at the time of the separation, but without sheep or milk vessels, he has no way to make more.[44] Indeed, one of the very basic contrasts running through both the Cyfn and Ior versions is that between raw, unprocessed foods, on the one hand, and foods that have been readied for human consumption, on the other: never are they given to the same spouse, or divided between them in any practical manner.[45] Moreover, strange as it may seem to think of military activity as an intrinsic element in civilized life, it was in this period an essential aspect of ensuring the public peace. One of the major uses for the large axe was as a weapon in warfare. The assignment of this implement to the wife thus deprives her of protection and the ability to maintain a civilized life, while undermining the man in the sphere that was most particularly his own.

But it is in the sexual imagery of the text that the themes of the passage are most explicitly articulated. Perhaps the most famous passage in this section of the lawbooks is the one on the separation of the bedclothes. In the division envisaged in all three redactions, the husband receives the bedclothes that have lain beneath the divorcing couple, and the wife those that covered them during their union. The symbolism of this partition is made explicit in Ior and the Latin redactions. If the husband takes another wife, he must send back to his former wife the bedclothes on which they had slept; if he fails to do so, the injured woman is due her honor price as a result.[46] The bottom sheet must thus represent the wife's commitment to sexual exclusivity—a claim presumably rooted not only in the expectation of fidelity associated with the marital vow, but also in the clear presumption of the lawbooks that, in most cases, it would have been to her husband that a wife would first have yielded her virginity.[47] Her sexuality is thus viewed as still belonging to the husband until such time as a second union is consummated, at which point it is returned to her to do with as she wishes. This is consistent with another well-known passage in the lawbooks, which says that if a man who has sent away his wife repents of his action, he can reclaim her even if she has been given to another man as long as he catches her with one foot still outside her new husband's bed—in other words, as long as he intervenes before the second relationship has been consummated.[48] Both of these passages testify to a notable reluctance on the part of the jurists to declare a marriage completely extinct until such time as the establishment of a second union made a reconciliation between the original husband and wife impossible.

The passage on the partitioning of the bedclothes is the most obvious reference to the severing of the couple as a sexual—and therefore as a procreative—unit. However, it is not the only one. It is surely no accident that the provision which immediately precedes the one on the bedclothes in Ior is the one on the separation of the quernstones. Here, the sexual imagery is immediate and explicit: one party lies upon the other, seed is spilled and crushed, and new entities (flour, ale) are created in the process.[49] Moreover, as anyone who has ever used a quern will recognize immediately, over time quernstones become mirror images of one another—rough edge is matched with rough edge, ground-away places on one stone fit naturally into the contours of the other. If the two stones are ever separated, they can never again grind as productively with any other stone, because the fit is never again as perfect.[50] Similar sexual images are at work elsewhere. Certainly the coulter, which makes the initial cut in the earth, and the plowshare, which follows behind readying the earth for the reception of seed, are not difficult items to see in sexual terms. Nor is Ior's revision of what would seem to have been earlier guidelines on the distribution of meat and cheese. In Cyfn, the basic contrast is between the "raised" meat and cheese, which go to the husband, and the meat and cheese that is either fresh or in brine, which go to the wife. This division may originally have reflected the husband's physical labor in lifting these heavy foods to the rafters and the wife's role in salting them for preservation, as well as the contrast between raw and processed foods so central to the ideology of this text. Ior preserves the distinction between meat that is hung up and meat that is in brine; however, it says nothing about cheese, and it goes on to add that meat and cheese which have been "broached"—cut into and partly used—should be given to the wife.[51] This may be an innocent addition to the original; on the other hand, given the context, and the cultural currency of metaphors of wholeness in describing female virginity—*virgo intacta* or *integra*, for example—I strongly suspect it is not.

One could easily go blind looking for symbols of this type in the text, and if one adds a search for phallic symbols into the mix, there is no end to the trouble one can get into. After all, as was observed earlier, with Ior we are in the same century that gave us those last gloriously scandalous lines of the *Romance of the Rose*. It is at least worth noting that among the tools assigned in Ior to the man are not only the coulter, but the auger and the *pergyng*, defined by Aled Rhys Wiliam as a sharp "pointed instrument" or "spear." This latter word came by extension to mean "warrior" or "champion"—in other words, to stand in for the man who wielded it.[52] Similarly, it may not be coincidental that the sentence following directly after the mention of the various long, sharp, pointed instruments taken by the man assigns the pan (*padell*) and the tripod (*trybed*) to the woman. Since both terms occur in a fifteenth-century poem by Gwerful Mechain as metaphors for the vagina,[53] it is not too difficult to imagine sexual symbolism at play here as well. In fact, read in this way, the list seems almost to possess elements of the Welsh poetic technique known as *dyfalu*, by which an object or action is evoked by a series of (often very everyday) images. This device, which often had a satirical or riddling aspect to it, was used frequently in medieval erotic poetry to evoke both sexual intercourse and the genitals.[54]

Now sometimes a *pergyng* is only a *pergyng*, and it is certainly true that not every symbol that is susceptible to such a sexual interpretation should necessarily be read in this manner. However, the constant separating of objects that must be joined together in order to work properly is surely easiest to understand in this fashion. Infertility, futility, the loss of profit and of future generations—these are the results of a broken union, whether the couple in question is a man and a woman, or a coulter and a plowshare, or the upper and lower stones of a quern. Such a reading even offers us insight into why the sons of the marriage might inherit the balls of woolen thread while their parents split the already woven cloth between them. The finished cloth represents what the parents have completed in their years together, the threads the sons for whom a future has yet to be woven. A similar image occurs as well in poetry contemporary with the laws: Prydydd y Moch's "Mawl Gwenllïan" compares the state of a girl who is the "foe of beaux" to a warp that has been readied but has then been left unwoven.[55] Nothing is said in the laws about the division of the equipment used in cloth production—whether spindle, loom, or the whorl go together or apart. However, one has the sense that, barring a reconciliation between the parties, the fabric of this marriage has already been completed.

Indeed, this may be why the passage is structured as it is. It is striking that the objects symbolizing male and female body parts occur all together in Ior (§44/10–11), and that they are bookended by the quernstones and bedclothes on the one hand (§44/8–9), and the wool and cloth on the other (§44/11–12). If the bedclothes and quernstones represent the initial sexual act, the tools the joining together of man and wife during their marriage for the benefit of their farm, and the wool and the cloth the end products of the union, the passage replicates in its structure the duration of their relationship. This might also explain why the man is said in §44/13 to take with him all the corn when he goes—in other words, that which is growing and that which exists only in seed—while the wife gets only such flour as she can carry from the larder to the house (§44/17). Cyfn phrases things somewhat differently, in that the husband is said to take the corn and the wife the prepared flour.[56] However, the fact that in Cyfn the provision on corn follows immediately after the one on bedclothes suggests that sexual symbolism is at play here as well. For while the details and order of the provisions may differ between Cyfn and Ior, the message would appear to be exactly the same. Seed sown during this union has already yielded its crop, and the wife is entitled to what they have produced together. But while the husband may eventually find new ground in which to plant his seed, and the establishment of a new domestic household join separated utensils to new mates, planting and harvest must take place in some other field for the natural order to be restored.

Law or Literature?

It is impossible to know whether the procedure described here ever actually took place in real life. If it did, it must have had a considerable impact on onlookers. And in fact, the lawbooks do suggest that the distribution of marital goods was a highly public occasion. Cyfn states that it was customary for the wife to remain in the house for nine days after the property division was made, and then to leave with her goods traveling immediately in front of her. Only after "the last penny" had gone was she to go herself—in other words, her departure was itself a dramatic enactment of the satisfaction of her claims that would only have accomplished its purpose in the presence of witnesses.[57] But perhaps the most important function of this public division of goods would have been the underscoring for both onlookers and participants of the undesirability of divorce. For those effecting it, it would have marked a moment of public shame—an admission of failure in a relationship that was not only crucial to, but emblematic of, the proper functioning of society. For those witnessing it, the dividing of property in such a manner would have seemed at once humorous, pathetic, wasteful, and even obscene. Patterson did not include the divorce procedure in her account of the burlesque,[58] but that is surely what we are seeing here: not a pragmatic equalizing of accounts between separating spouses but, rather, a legal drama designed to educate the community within which it was performed.

Like the other burlesques discussed so far, the divorce procedure was also humorous and lewd, revolved around mock payments or property transfers effected before witnesses, and constituted an instance of the use of public shaming as an instrument of social control.[59] Equally important for Patterson, however, was the context of nonservile dependency, such as might have obtained between a woman and her kindred or husband. Including the divorce procedure among the burlesques raises interesting questions about her paradigm. Clearly, the husband was regarded in medieval Wales as the superior or lord within the marital relationship.[60] A wife owed her husband the duty of sexual exclusivity, for example, and while we do not know a great deal about the circumstances in which separations would have been permitted in medieval Wales, it is presumed that Welsh husbands, like husbands elsewhere in Europe, generally enjoyed greater latitude in such matters than did their wives. A woman whose husband deserted her for another woman certainly had a just claim for compensation, for example, but she did not appear to be able to prevent herself from being supplanted. By contrast, according to the passage already mentioned from Ior, a husband could reclaim his wife as long as she still had one foot out of the bed of her intended new partner.[61] In many ways, therefore, the situation might seem to parallel very closely the pattern outlined by Patterson.

On the other hand, it is clear that women in medieval Wales also had significant rights within the marriage. Ior §45/4 mentions leprosy and impotence and foul breath as reasons for which a woman might leave her spouse,[62] and other passages imply that a wife who did not leave her husband after he had been unfaithful to her three times herself lapsed into shame.[63] Moreover, the passage on the division of marital goods does not seem to suggest that fault in this instance was imagined as lying more with one party than with the other. The husband in this passage is not a superior injured by the disloyalty or misbehavior of his dependent; rather, he loses and gains in the same public manner as does his wife and seems to be envisaged as an active participant in the failure of the union. Patterson defines her second category of sexual burlesque as being targeted primarily at "dishonorable women."[64] However, one has only to imagine all those phallic objects piling up on the lawn to realize that the occasion would have been as uncomfortable for the man as it was for the woman. Both husband and wife are projected into the role of persons shamed by the failure of their relationship with each other and with the community. Indeed, if anyone stood to gain from the public denunciation of divorce, it was the wife, as she was the more likely ultimately to be damaged by the separation. Women had no claims to land in the case of a separation, only to movables. Moreover, virginity was so prized in wives that women who were no longer virgins could experience difficulties in finding a second husband, something not true of the male member of the pair.[65]

As with the courtly burlesque, then, so also with its domestic equivalent: the purview of this practice appears to have been much broader than the mere rebuking of nonservile dependents for neglecting their duties. The divorce procedure is structurally so similar to the other burlesques in the lawbooks that it cannot be considered in isolation from them. Animal by animal, tool by tool, husband and wife enact through the distribution of their property a parody of their marriage in its most fundamental aspects, from their joint cultivation of land to their activities in bed. Both suffer and are shamed by this performance, and both are reminded item by item of the honorable union they are in the process of surrendering. Still another aspect of the burlesque as social sanction may be applicable here as well. In at least some of the burlesques discussed by

Patterson, the intent of the shaming is to ensure the eventual restoration of quality service by the dependent rather than to sever future relations between the two parties forever. The temporary shaming of the offender aims to restore the balance in the relationship and highlight the importance of the relationship by which they are bound.[66] This may be as well the ultimate goal of the passage on husband and wife. What we have here, I would suggest, is a symbolic homily on divorce. Quernstones can be reunited, and cats can rejoin hens in defense of the common good of the household. Nothing in this procedure forecloses on the possibility of a change of heart by the parties involved.

But in what context, then, might such a procedure have evolved? With this question we return to the issue of whether the divorce passage reflects practices (past or present) actually taking place in the community. This is entirely possible, but it is not a necessary conclusion. It is also possible that the sermonizing in this passage is intellectual rather than literally procedural. Patterson herself seems to vacillate on this issue, being, on the one hand, visibly inclined to discuss the burlesques as genuine practices, and elucidating the role textual conflation has played in their construction, on the other.[67] As with so many other such mysteries in the lawbooks, we may never know the answer. One thing that does seem virtually certain, however, is that what we have in Ior is a deliberate textual expansion of the (presumably earlier) procedure reflected in Cyfn. We know that the basic symbolism of the division of goods is present already in Cyfn, since so many of the crucial objects occur there, including the bedclothes, the coulter and plowshare, and the corn. But it surely is not accidental that among the objects present in Ior but not in Cyfn are those most closely evocative of the perils of divorce, most notably the two sieves, the quernstones, most of the phallic objects and tools, the pan and tripod, the hens and the cats, the balls of wool thread, and the *pergyng*. All speak directly and, I would suggest, deliberately, to the primary themes of the passage: fertility wasted, productivity cut short, civilization on the decline.

The question of origins might thus be most productively rephrased as a textual one—an inquiry into both the context in which the extant versions of the passage might have been penned, and the priorities that lay behind their construction. The period of the lawbooks saw a number of attempts by reform-minded (and often foreign) churchmen to bring Wales into conformity with canon law on subjects pertaining to marriage and divorce. Two native practices were especially irksome to clerical eyes: the relative ease with which married persons were allowed to separate without reference to church law on the subject, and the acceptance of concubinage alongside of marriage to such a degree that the children of such marriages routinely shared in the inheritance. Canonical jurisdiction over marriage was in the process of being established over the course of the twelfth century, and it is possible, as Huw Pryce observes, that some passages in the lawbooks regarding separation predated the widespread dissemination of these new ideas in Wales.[68] (This is also true of some of the literary evidence on the subject: the well-known scene in the Mabinogi in which Pwyll's nobles urge him to separate from Rhiannon may date, for example, to the late eleventh or early twelfth century.[69])

However, Welsh marital customs continued to diverge from ecclesiastical norms into the thirteenth century and beyond, attracting criticism from many high-placed clerics. Nearly twenty years after the Council of Westminster, Gerald of Wales was still complaining that trial marriages were common among the Welsh, with unions frequently not being solemnized until the fertility of the marriage had been proven.[70] And the enthusiasm of even those Welsh rulers who adopted—or professed to adopt—canonical teachings in regard to such matters waxed and waned according to the political advantages of the marriage in question. Llywelyn ap Iorwerth himself was one of the principal offenders in this respect, soliciting papal approval for his on-again, off-again liaison with the daughter of the king of Man before abandoning her entirely for his more advantageous match with Joan.[71] Among the lower classes, trial marriages, separation, and inheritance by illegitimate children seem to have remained common well into the fourteenth century, to judge from court rolls of the period (unfortunately, ecclesiastical court records do not survive from medieval Wales).[72] Customs eventually began to change under the relentless pressure from outside, but divorce remained a live possibility in Wales long after it had disappeared elsewhere in Europe.[73] Only the tiniest hints of the discussions that must have surrounded this clash between native and foreign have been recognized to date in the sources. As Pryce points out, the regulations governing marriage and divorce outlined in the extant lawbooks are fundamentally incompatible with church law as it had evolved by the twelfth and thirteenth centuries, although he suggests that one can see traces of the influence of ecclesiastical teaching in, for example, Ior's preference for serial monogamy over polygyny.[74] Similarly, while foreigners rarely hesitated to indicate their disapproval of Welsh custom—sometimes marking their dissent literally in the manuscripts, as we have seen—native scribes and users of the lawbooks seem to have felt comfortable copying and recopying traditional regulations on marriage despite their contravention of contemporary ecclesiastical mores.

What the paragraph on divorce suggests is that this debate may have been livelier and more urgent among the juristic classes than we have hitherto realized. It is at least worth noting that both of the principal reform objections to Welsh marriage practice emerge as visible concerns in the procedure. As it stands extant today, especially in Ior, the passage constitutes a warning not only against the destructiveness of divorce, but also against concubinage and polygyny in its suggestion that a second union can never be as productive as a first. However, if it is right to see ecclesiastical objections to Welsh marriage law as the backdrop against which the Ior passage was penned, then the images chosen are striking, to say the least. For perhaps the most intriguing aspect of this "homily" is its overwhelmingly secular nature. One might expect a text decrying the evils of divorce to reflect—or even highlight—the concerns of reformers. The Ior passage on the division of goods, however, sidesteps such issues completely. Morality never enters into it, nor does obedience to the church. Rather, what is emphasized most in this passage is the tremendous price to be paid not only by the conjugal unit with respect to its diminished agricultural productivity, but by society as a whole with respect to its enhanced vulnerability to the forces of nature. Even the sexual themes are handled in a manner completely at odds with contemporary church teaching on the subject. A second union is regarded as wasteful, and potentially as an occasion of shame for the parties involved; it is not, however, portrayed as morally wrong.

Pryce's work on the church suggests that the secular tone of the Ior text likely constituted a deliberate choice on the part of the redactor. The jurists of Gwynedd were notoriously zealous in protecting princely prerogatives from appropriation by ecclesiastical officials. Fiscal and jurisdictional rights claimed by the church were carefully scrutinized or curtailed with the aim of subordinating them to princely authority: for example, judicial revenues collected on church estates or ecclesiastical sanctuary rights.[75] Welsh customs on marriage were intimately tied to native tradition regarding inheritance by illegitimate sons, and while this was a matter on which opinions varied even among the legal classes, the Ior redactor explicitly supported the inheritance rights of illegitimate sons on the grounds that, according to the law of Hywel—as opposed to church law, from which it is explicitly distinguished in the passage—a "father's sin and unlawful action" (*pechaut e tat na'e agkeureyth*) ought not to affect the inheritance prospects of his sons.[76] In other words, while the redactor may have agreed with some aspects of the new clerical vision of marriage, he did so without consenting to any implications this might have had for traditional Welsh inheritance practice. It is thus not surprising to find him presenting changes to native custom as having been done for political reasons and not at the direction of the church. In the divorce paragraph's emphasis on the secular, rather than ecclesiastical, consequences of marital dissolution, we are seeing yet another instance of the resistance of Venedotian jurists to the dictation of policy by foreign interests—a resistance paralleled in the secular realm by the wars of the last rulers of Gwynedd against the English Crown.[77]

Alternatively, the reference may be even more pointedly "high politics" than this. The compiler's depiction of marital discord as a source of infertility and danger may have been intended as a comment not (or not merely) on Welsh marriage customs in general, but on one specific union in particular: Llywelyn ap Iorwerth's own marriage to Joan, his wife since 1205.[78] For 1230 was the year in which William de Braose, a powerful Marcher lord with whose family Llywelyn was linked through a series of political marriages, was hanged by Llywelyn *wedy y dala yn ystauell y tywyssawc gyt a merch Jeuan vrenhin, gwreic y tywyssawc*,[79] "after having been found in the chamber of the prince with the daughter of King John, the prince's wife." All indications are that Llywelyn's passions in this matter ran high; however, hanging de Braose was a precarious move, despite the fact that many would have conceded that Llywelyn was within his rights to have acted as he did.[80] In 1230 the de Braose family was still quite powerful: indeed, Llywelyn had only two years earlier forced William de Braose to agree to the prospect of a marriage between his son and heir, Dafydd, and de Braose's daughter, Isabella. And although the de Braose family had had its run-ins with the Crown over the years,[81] no one could predict how the (no longer minority) government of Henry III might react to the events. Ultimately, Llywelyn managed to exploit the death of de Braose to his own advantage, but many must have judged his actions as exceptionally risky at the time.[82]

Many aspects of the Iorwerth version of the passage on the distribution of marital property make a connection with the events of 1230 worth considering. Although we do not know precisely when the Iorwerth redaction was composed, our best current estimate is in the period 1230–1240.[83] As we have already seen, the use of the laws as a vehicle through which to comment not only on contemporary politics but on Joan's activities specifically is known from other places in the lawbooks, most notably Ior's description of the queen. It seems likely that even a redactor who was wary of Joan's political activities would recognize the importance of her remaining on good terms with her husband in the wake of the incident with de Braose: Joan had, after all, played a significant part in restoring some semblance of peace to Wales after the devastating losses of 1211, and she was to reprise her role as negotiator with the government of Henry III in 1232.[84] Moreover, marriage itself as a symbol may have had some resonance with the political culture of Llywelyn's Wales: Susan Aronstein has argued that marriage functions as a symbol for the centralizing policies of the house of Aberffraw in the Middle Welsh romances *Gereint vab Erbin* and *Owein*.[85]

Certainly, the themes of the passage seem consonant with the events of 1230. The fertility of the land is a common motif in mythological treatments of Welsh kingship; it would not be at all surprising to find concerns about that kingship expressed in terms of sterility, decay, and danger.[86] The disruption of husband and wife as a sexual unit is obviously relevant. Similarly, the assigning of only one cat to the husband, with the consequence that he is no longer able to protect his hens and eggs from intrusions from outside (and it must be remembered that this appears to be an addition made by the Ior redactor to the more truncated version reflected in Cyfn), seems to speak directly to the circumstances leading up to de Braose's execution. Indeed, we may have an even more direct—if rather morbid—reference to the manner of his death in the Ior wording of the passage on the division of meat between husband and wife in the event of a separation. As was noted earlier, Cyfn assigns both the *kic drychafedic a'r ka6s drychafedic*, the "raised meat and raised cheese" to the husband. Ior's wording differs significantly here, however. For while it also assigns the raised meat to the husband, it omits all mention of the cheese, and in all manuscripts but one changes *drychafedic*, "raised," to *g6edy croccer*, "after it (the meat) has been hung up."[87] *Crogi*, "to hang," is not used inappropriately in this type of agricultural context. However, its primary associations in legal and political discourse generally are with execution by hanging. Indeed, this is the very verb used in the *Brut y Tywysogion* in reporting William de Braose's fate: *Y ulwydyn honno y croget Gwilym Brewys Jeuanc gann Lywelin ap Ioruerth*, "In that year, William de Braose the Younger was hanged by Llywelyn ap Iorwerth."[88] If the Ior version of the passage on the division of goods was indeed penned around the time of de Braose's death, then the image of hung meat being awarded to the husband in the case of a marital breakup might be a very pointed reference indeed to events in the prince's own household.[89] And while it might be mere coincidence that the provision on the hanging of the meat follows immediately after the mention of the single cat—and the provision of the cat on the assigning of all seed corn to the husband—the ordering of these clauses is, at the very least, suggestive.

Obviously, there is much about this passage that must forever remain uncertain. In the absence of further evidence, we will probably never know whether this procedure was ever actually performed. Even if the framework itself was genuine and old, however, it seems very likely that many of the details described in Ior—and perhaps in early form also in Cyfn—came primarily from the fertile imagination of the jurists. At the very least, the clearly symbolic nature of the additions made by the Ior redactor to the earlier account reflected in Cyfn suggest that his priority lay more in expressing his political views than in accurately describing medieval Welsh marital custom. What those views might have been, and how widespread the presumptions behind them might have been, is difficult to say. Divorce may have been a more controversial topic in native Welsh legal circles than we have realized. Alternatively, the Ior redactor's deliberate expansion and highlighting of this passage may betray a personal perspective: a particular hostility to divorce, or a genuine concern about the state of Llywelyn's union with Joan and the consequent stability of the Welsh state. In the end, all we can really be certain of is that this paragraph cannot be taken as an uncomplicated statement of native custom. These laws must be understood for what they really were: a product of the political imagination rather than an objective record of local practice. Text and subtext must be read together: a *pergyng* on its own can only accomplish so much.

Bush and Brake

The divorce procedure is but one aspect of a broader emphasis in the lawbooks on the formation and preservation of lawful sexual unions. As we have seen, Welsh law diverged from canonical European norms in a number of different ways. In some instances, churchmen and jurists were able to bring native practice (more or less) into conformity with canon law by adapting already existing customs to the new ecclesiastical reality. Church rights to sanctuary in Wales, for example, developed out of the ancient Celtic custom of *nawdd* (early Irish *snádud*), originally a form of protection offered by secular as well as ecclesiastical dignitaries.[90] (Even so, it is worth noting that here as well Ior stands alone among the Welsh legal texts not only in its detailed treatment of the subject, but in its careful protection of secular jurisdiction against inroads by the church.[91]) Not all issues were as tractable, however, and the gap between native and canonical practice with respect to marriage was particularly significant.

Not only did the Welsh (Ior particularly) treat marriage as falling under secular rather than ecclesiastical jurisdiction, but native law also recognized a variety of types of marital unions, some more formal and honorable than others, depending on familial involvement and the consent (or lack thereof) of the woman.[92] This state of being is still reflected in the lawbooks of the thirteenth century—indeed, Charles-Edwards has suggested that polygyny likely remained a possibility in Wales until a date not long before the composition of the lawbooks.[93]

Not surprisingly, the redactors in no way explicitly reject native traditions of serial or polygynous marriage. However, all principal lawbook versions promote the preservation whenever possible of formal *priodas* marital relationships, and all lay great emphasis on the social and economic consequences that can befall those entering into concubinage or other less formal types of union.[94] Many provisions seem actively to discourage divorce by urging parties to established marriages to stay the course to the last moment possible. Thus, as we have seen, a wife abandoned by her husband remains in her home for nine days before departing with the goods she is owed from the marriage—and even so, she is herself the last to leave, almost as though her errant spouse is expected to come hastening up at the last minute to reclaim her.[95] Such a last-minute reprieve for the relationship is surely what is envisaged in the curious passage referred to already, in which a wife who is remarrying can be reclaimed by her first husband if he acts before she puts both feet into what is about to become the marital bed of her second marriage—in other words, before the second union has been consummated.[96] And similar concerns presumably inform the provision requiring a wife to catch her husband being unfaithful to her three times before she can leave him without losing any of her rights or property.[97]

In other words, while the Welsh unquestionably diverged from the European norm in allowing spousal separation at all,[98] the manner in which the issue is presented in the laws makes clear that the redactors were, if not overtly condemnatory of the practice, at least visibly admonitory with respect to its potential impact on the individuals and families involved. Even more telling are the provisions regarding concubinage and other less honorable types of unions. Again, the jurists do not directly repudiate native traditions of informal marriage or openly favor the adoption of European norms. However, they present such liaisons in a manner that clearly seems designed to discourage Welsh men and women from entering into them. Thus, it is acknowledged that an eloping woman may eventually achieve the right to share all property in halves with her husband, as she would have had the union been sanctioned by her family and lasted the standard seven years. However, it is also made clear that if their union lasts less time than that, she will not be entitled to the amount normally accruing to a woman of her status who had, unlike her, married with kindred consent. Rather, the eloping woman receives only three (or six or even nine, according to some lawbook versions) steers with horns as long as their ears.[99] The sexual connotations of cattle of this sort make clear that this award is in fact a derisory payment intended to mock her for her incautious and precipitate lust. Moreover, the procedure is likely even crueler than it first appears, especially given the very public way in which they would likely have been transferred to her. For the animals in question are *eydyon*, a term that frequently (although not always) refers to young castrated males: their sterility reflects the end of any long-term prospects for the union.[100]

Indeed, women who elope or give themselves to men without the consent or involvement of their kindred come in for a great deal of attention in the laws, particularly in Cyfn. Many situations are envisaged in these texts, all of which have different outcomes. Despite their differences, however, all have one thing in common: the public humiliation of one or both parties—always the woman, and sometimes the man as well. This is true even when (as mentioned earlier) the woman's expectation of the union had been that it would ultimately come to constitute a long-term marriage. In one case described in Cyfn, for example, a man is accused by a woman who has given herself to him in "bush and brake" (i.e., not in a fixed habitation, and therefore by implication in a clandestine fashion rather than publicly in the view of others) of subsequently abandoning her for another woman. If he acknowledges her accusation, he need pay her only "a penny as broad as her buttocks" in compensation. If he wishes to deny it, he can clear himself by swearing on a "bell without a clapper" (*rodct y l6 ygloch heb taua6t yndi*).[101] The contemptuous symbolism of the penny is evident, but the bell is more complex. Patterson interprets it as a reference to the woman's voicelessness before the law, since her family had not endorsed the union and would not appear therefore to support her claims in court. Her voice against his is thus "as unresounding as a bell without its clapper."[102] This interpretation makes good sense of the image. However, it is surely pertinent also that the clapper functioned in medieval Welsh erotic poetry as a metaphor for the penis,[103] and that a woman swearing a charge of rape did so by holding (what she claimed to be) the offending penis in one hand and the relic on which she was swearing in the other.[104] Because of her own sullied reputation and failure to take the appropriate securities, the woman in our case does not have the option of prevailing in this way. Advantage in the oath goes to the man, and he is said in the text to have already become involved with another woman. If he chooses to deny his liaison with her, there literally is no penis—no clapper—present in the case by which he can be accused. The man in question has moved on: the clapper in the case is, quite literally, engaged elsewhere.

Even more brutally explicit is another case that is also recounted only in Cyfn, in which a mature woman elopes with a man either to "bush or brake" or to a house and is subsequently abandoned by him:

> G6reic a el yn llathrut gan 6r yn y haeduetr6yd, a'e d6yn o'r g6r hi y l6yn neu y perth neu y ty, a'e hymrein, a'e goll6g o'r g6r trachefyn, a ch6yna6 oheni hitheu 6rth y chenedyl ac yn y dadleu: sef a dyly hi yn y diweirdeb, kymryt tar6 tri gayaf ac eilla6 y losc6rn a'e ira6 a g6er, ac odyna grynya6 y losc6rn tr6y dorgl6yt, ac odnyna mynet y wreic y my6n y ty a dodet y throet 6rth y trotheu, a chymeret losc6rn y tar6 yn y d6y la6, a doet g6r o pop parth y'r tar6 ac erthi yn lla6 pop vn ohonunt y gymhell y tar6; ac or dicha6n hi y attal, kymeret yn y diweirdeb, ac ony dicha6n, kymeret a lynho o'r g6er 6rth y d6y law6.

> A woman who elopes with a man in her maturity and is taken by the man to bush or to brake or to house and copulated with and released by the man again, and who complains to her kindred and in the sessions: this is what she is entitled to for her chastity—let a three-year-old bull be taken and its tail shaved and greased with tallow and then thrust through a door-hurdle; and then let the woman go into the house and set her foot against the threshold and take the tail in her two hands; and let a man come on each side of the bull with a goad in the hand of each to spur the bull; and if she can hold it, let her take it for her chastity; and if she cannot, let her take what sticks to her two hands of the tallow.[105]

Patterson has commented on the "overt sexual symbolism of the bull that was held by the tail," suggesting that the procedure "proclaimed in burlesque that a woman has as much chance of holding on to a man through a sexual bond alone as she had of holding on to a maddened bull in the prime of life by its tail alone."[106] This is surely correct: not only is the bull an obvious symbol of masculinity, the tail is yet another symbol for the penis in the erotic poetry of the period.[107]

However, one can, I think, go further in explicating the symbolism here. This is a remarkably coarse and graphic procedure. The bull's tail is thrust into a hole in the wattle door of the household. Not only is this a clear reenactment of the penis entering the vagina, the seesawing action that ensues as a result of the bull pulling away while the woman tries to pull him back directly mimics the sexual act itself. The tallow that accrues on the shaft of the tail and is transferred to her hands is quite evidently the man's semen; the two men inciting the bull on either side presumably the testicles whence that semen will ultimately come. The abandoned woman will not keep her man, for she has neglected to take the proper securities to ensure that their union will be a lasting one. Rather, she will keep either nothing at all or, symbolically, only what he gave her: the memory of his penis (the bull with its tail) and his seed (the tallow that adheres to her hands). In fact, it is possible that infertility of more than one kind is being enacted here, in that the procedure replicates not only the actual act of sexual intercourse for which the parties are being reproved, but also the manual stimulation of a penis by a woman's hands which, by definition, can result in nothing more than wasted seed.[108]

The humiliation of the woman in this instance is so comprehensive that it is easily overlooked that this procedure, like that described for cases of divorce, reflects negatively on both halves of the couple, and not merely on the woman.[109] The man is turned by this process into a rampaging bull, full of vigor but entirely at the mercy of the genitals by which he was originally ensnared. The woman, by contrast, is positioned by virtue of her situation indoors as the defender of whatever home the two of them might have made together. Regardless of the outcome of her struggle with the bull, however, this is a home that will not endure. Rather, it will be wrecked beyond repair—symbolically and, if one imagines the impact of this sort of tug-of-war on a relatively fragile structure, literally—by the unbridled nature of the sexual act that lay at the heart of their union.[110] Neither party comes away unscathed. The damage done to the woman's reputation is obvious, and even if the man succeeded in playing it in performance as a joke or a tribute to his virility, the young ladies of the neighborhood and their parents would certainly have been adequately warned.

Procedures like these are almost shocking in their harshness and desire to humiliate. If the jurists are describing procedures that actually took place in the community, then bawdy humor and deliberately sexualized mockery must have played a visible role in the judicial process, even if used only occasionally as deterrents. However, the problems here are exactly what they were with respect to divorce: barring the discovery of collaborating documents, it is simply not possible for us to distinguish what is real from what is more likely the product of what R. R. Davies has called "the sophisticated legal casuistry of native Welsh lawyers." As he remarks, passages of this sort have about them "that air of unreality which hardly fosters confidence in the validity of the law-texts as a guide to the central issues of social custom."[111] One might quibble slightly with his formulation, in that even when not straightforward, the law texts actually seem to be an excellent guide to the most pressing social issues of the period; however, his point that these passages are not necessarily proof of the historicity of the events they purport to describe is well taken. But if the problems posed by such passages are the same as those presented by the provisions on divorce, so too is the point that what matters most is less the origins of such provisions than the fact that jurists in the thirteenth century included them in their lawbooks. These are texts put together in a particular way for particular reasons—in this case, to underscore for all the perils of unsanctioned or casual sexual relationships.

It is significant that although the divorce procedure is spelled out in greater detail in Ior than it is in Cyfn (which contains no mention of the quernstones, most of the tools, the cut meat and butter, etc.), the most sensationalist sexual burlesques occur in the Cyfn redaction rather than in Ior. With respect to sexual transgressions, Cyfn not only goes in for the most picturesque punishments, it describes them in the most lurid detail. Thus, while Ior mentions the steer with greased tail as a possible penalty for false virgins, it does not, as Cyfn does, explicate the brutal symbolism of the manner in which that steer is bestowed. Some provisions found in Cyfn—the bell without a clapper, for example—have no parallel in Ior at all. And some of the most visibly arresting or erotic elements of the courtly burlesques—the tongues given to the judge, the thigh replacing the tongue in the animal head given to the smith, the rectums given to the porter, the fat given to the dung *maer*, the cattle with horns as long as their ears given to the chamberlain—also occur in Cyfn but not in Ior.

A divergence in regional custom is one possible explanation for this, but there are others. Cyfn is generally thought to contain the most "old law" of the principal lawbook versions, and the temptation to equate "brutally explicit" with "old" is hard to resist. However, attempting to diagnose the antiquity of passages by what Jenkins called their "fishlike smell" is an inexact science at best.[112] After all, the steer with the greased tail is attested also in Ior, usually accepted as the most up-to-date of the redactions.[113] Moreover, a piscine odor would be easy to fake. One could easily imagine a redactor engaging in intentional archaizing as a way to lend extra validity to his work or indulge his personal fancies about the colorful practices of olden days. Or perhaps the solution is more personal than this: a predilection for the self-consciously erotic or bizarre on the part of the Cyfn redactor. The example of the twelfth-century abbot Guibert of Nogent, renowned among modern scholars for his horrified obsession with sexuality, excrement, and bodily mutilation, comes quickly to mind here.[114] Yet another possibility might be the generalizing as established custom by lawbook authors of what were in fact spectacular, one-time events taking place within the community.

But at least as important as what the Cyfn redactor puts in is what the Ior redactor may be choosing not to include. For if in fact the Ior redactor did have access to the erotic material included in Cyfn, he seems deliberately to be downplaying it. This would be consistent with much of what we have seen elsewhere in Ior, where practices that are especially odd or eccentric are often minimized, presumably in an attempt to make Welsh law appear less barbarous to thirteenth-century eyes. Whereas Cyfn seems intentionally to revel in the archaic-sounding exotica of the king's *sarhaed* (insult) payment, for example, Ior seems by contrast to deemphasize them in the interests of adumbrating a vision of Welsh rule more recognizable to European contemporaries.[115] The main exceptions here are the divorce passage and the burlesques on the king's servants, but if they in fact constitute contemporary satire, as I have argued here, they are exceptions that prove the rule. Lordship and the strengthening of the native legal tradition seem always to have been the Ior redactor's primary concerns; the shockingly brutal burlesques preserved in Cyfn may have struck him as working ultimately against them both.[116]

Men and Women

As we have seen, immorality was a criticism lodged frequently against the Welsh by outsiders, and thus was also a point on which native princes and lawyers likely felt themselves increasingly vulnerable over the course of the twelfth and thirteenth centuries. It is therefore perhaps not entirely coincidental that another theme running throughout the tractate on women is the high degree of importance placed on the honorable sexual behavior of individuals.

To scholars coming to the Welsh lawbooks with some knowledge of contemporary European law, two things in particular will stand out. The first is the extent to which—particularly in Ior and Ior-influenced redactions—men as well as women are depicted as experiencing consequences for their sexual behavior in secular law. We have seen this already in the burlesques, but expectations of this sort are in fact articulated in a variety of ways and venues. In all redactions, for example, women's accusations against men for sexual misbehavior carry significant—and in some cases determinative—weight.[117] Husbands as well as wives owe fidelity to their spouses—in fact, the financial penalties for being caught in flagrante are quite serious, and if repeated over time can result not only in the payment of increasingly high rates of compensation to the offended wife, but in the loss of all the property she brought into or was given during their marriage plus half the couple's communal assets.[118] Wives who are beaten by their husbands are entitled to compensation from them unless the beating was in retaliation for particularly grave offenses.[119] Similarly, financial and legal consequences are stipulated for men who commit adultery with a married woman,[120] have sex with a virgin without her family's involvement,[121] cohabit with a woman without benefit of marriage for more than one night,[122] or make a woman pregnant, even if she is of loose reputation herself.[123] Not surprisingly, provisions governing the woman's behavior are equally stringent.[124]

Wales was not, of course, an egalitarian society. Welsh women may have had unusual rights with respect to remarriage and divorce—as, of course, Welsh men also did by comparison with canon law. But they could not, according to the lawbooks, inherit land, a practice with serious consequences not only for the women in question, but for fathers without sons as well. A. D. M. Barrell and R. R. Davies have suggested that many *uchelwyr* families of the period were the descendants of princely families whose status had been reduced over time through partible inheritance; the inability of women to inherit posed real challenges to families without male heirs, many of whom began attempting to circumvent native tradition by adopting English practices with respect to the inheritance of land.[125] The intent of provisions requiring men as well as women to suffer consequences for irresponsible sexual behavior was less to highlight women's latitude in such matters or make men and women appear equal than to underscore the fact that *everyone*'s rights and responsibilities in sexual matters were circumscribed in native law by notions of honor, family, and sexual propriety. Women as well as men were entitled to compensation for losses inflicted on them; men as well as women were obliged to make good such damage as they might cause. To paraphrase Ior: "The law says that [a woman] ought not to incur expense because of [the actions of] a man when she has not received any benefit from him."[126]

Another constant theme in the lawbooks, particularly in Ior, is the idea that the consequences of sexual behavior, sanctioned or unsanctioned, are experienced by persons of both genders, and are additionally subject to scrutiny by kin and lord. Children are a good example here. Men as well as women are depicted in the laws as being obligated to participate in the rearing of their child, even if (according to Ior) the union in question is clandestine and unsanctioned by anyone other than the parties themselves.[127] The woman must rear the child for the first year and a half, regardless of whether she wishes to do this. After that time, she can refuse to rear the child further herself, although she remains responsible for one-third of the costs. The man is then obligated to shoulder two-thirds of the rearing and, if the child is a boy, to present him to the lord at the age of fourteen in the customary way; at this point he becomes the lord's responsibility.[128] Close supervision by kin and lord of children from the moment of their conception through to adulthood is a prominent theme in Ior's tractate on family law, which constitutes a deliberate addition to that redaction's version of the Laws of Country.[129] Responsibility for the child at every age is carefully delineated, as are the procedures to be followed when a son is affiliated with a given man or kindred. No child is to be without someone exercising authority over him or her during any moment of childhood. In fact, as a new study by Bronagh Ní Chonaill demonstrates, lordship is a central focus of Ior's laws on childhood—which is presumably why its tractate on family law follows immediately after passages dealing with the renders and services owed to lords rather than after the tractate on women.[130]

Another striking aspect of the Laws of Women is the emphasis placed on the preservation of female virginity before marriage. We have already seen in Cyfn the contemptuous treatment of women who give themselves precipitately to men before the appropriate formalities have been observed. Similarly, families are portrayed as responsible should a bride prove to be corrupted on her wedding night. In most of the principal versions, false virgins of this sort can be publicly repudiated with only a derisory compensation. When a bride is discovered by her groom not to be the virgin that he was promised, the wedding guests are called in to witness as her shift is cut off in front and behind her to the height of her genitals. (In Cyfn, candles are brought in and held up to the area in question so that the wedding guests present can judge for themselves). The false virgin can then be dismissed—without any form of compensation, according to Cyfn. Other redactions award her a steer with a greased tail: as in the case of the eloping woman, if she can hold on to it, she can keep it; otherwise, she receives nothing but the tallow that comes off on her hands.[131] Many texts do allow some form of familial response to this charge in cases where the girl denies the accusation and the issue is muddied by the fact that she has reached physical maturity as indicated by the presence of pubic hair, breasts, and signs of menstruation. In these cases, seven of her closest relatives can clear her reputation by oath—a reflection of the fact that girls in Wales were generally brought up in their natal family and not fostered out as they were in Ireland.[132]

Virginity was regarded as important outside of Wales as well, of course, and it may seem as though such an emphasis on virginity in one's bride is common enough as to scarcely warrant mentioning. However, it is rare to find virginity highlighted in such a manner in other secular law narratives of the period. In Bracton's *De legibus*, for example, believed to be roughly contemporary with Iorwerth, virginity is mentioned only in the context of rape.[133] Similarly, Glanvill's classic definition of rape stresses the violence of the crime rather than its impact on the sexual status of the woman involved.[134] Only in the course of the thirteenth century would pleas of rape heard before the king or his justices begin to emphasize the deflowering of the victim rather than the brutality of the act itself.[135] Of course, outside of Wales such matters were regarded as the preserve of ecclesiastical law, and it may not be coincidental that virginity was similarly valued in Germanic law codes written long before canon law had developed to the extent that it had in Europe by the thirteenth century.[136] But virginity was not similarly weighted in all medieval societies. The marriage market value of nonvirgins did not seem to be affected by their compromised sexual status in early Ireland, for example.[137] In other words, the centrality of virginity to Welsh marriage law as it is presented in the lawbooks is not something one can simply take for granted.

One possibility for the emphasis placed by Welsh redactors on female virginity is that it was intended as another refutation of the accusations of immorality levied against the Welsh by European reformers. If so, the primary audience for this message would likely still have been native rather than foreign. There is little about the grounds on which virginity is defended in these texts that would have had much impact on churchmen like Archbishop Pecham and his ilk. Even when Welsh custom was moving into closer alignment with ecclesiastical norms, changes tended to be justified by recourse to native values and customs rather than by appeals to canon law. The rationales offered in the lawbooks for the preservation of virginity—like those offered earlier for the discouraging of multiple or informal unions—have little to do with ecclesiastical concerns. Rather, the emphasis is laid on the rights and responsibilities of both the parties themselves and their lords and families. Even procedures as graphic as the one with the steer's tail, which performatively reduce the union to its lowest and coarsest aspects, speak more to culturally accepted notions of kindred involvement, and (in the case of the false virgin) the security of the union with respect to paternity, than to ecclesiastical sanctions. We hear nothing about the religious reasons for which sex outside of marriage ought to be shunned, and certainly nothing about canon law dictates on the matter. In this respect as in others, the tractate on women parallels what one sees elsewhere. As Pryce has shown with respect to issues like intestacy, in northern traditions particularly, even where ecclesiastical influence seems likely to have helped shape what is recorded in the laws as native tradition, it tends not to be cited as a source.[138]

One reason for highlighting virginity within the laws may have been to provide native Welshmen with a reasoned defense against ecclesiastical slander; another may have been the political implications female virginity was believed to have for medieval Welsh lordship.[139] We have already looked at this subject from the point of view of the court, but the issue has resonance lower down the social ladder as well. As has already been mentioned, one of the dues insisted on in all the principal redactions is a payment called *amobr* (Latin *merces*; occasionally in Welsh also *gobr*),[140] which was paid to every woman's lord upon the initial loss of her virginity—either by the woman herself, or by her kindred, or by the owner of the house to which she was first brought to be slept with. This fee varied according to the status of the woman's father and was claimed even from foreigners (*alltudion*). Lists of these fees and provisions governing their payment occur in every lawbook version; they are clearly one of the things the lawbook compilers cared most about.[141] The origins of this fee are uncertain. One explanation offered in some lawbooks is that the virginity of a female dependent was regarded as the lord's responsibility to protect. One passage in Cyfn U, for example, denies the lord his fee if the woman has been raped because he has clearly failed in his duty to protect her.[142] Jenkins has, however, expressed skepticism about this view, suggesting that protection is a later rationale for what had been in origin a fee paid to compensate the lord for the loss of a valuable asset—which fee had become by the thirteenth century effectively a purchase price for the lord's permission to marry.[143]

This may well be so, but since women could not inherit land in medieval Wales, and since families rather than lords seem (in theory, at least) to have been the primary movers with respect to making marriage arrangements, the idea that a dependent's virginity would be viewed as an asset of her lord's is not something one can simply presume. Additional insight might be gleaned from the fact that the amount of a woman's *amobr* is explicitly equated in the laws with the amount of her father's *ebediw*—by the thirteenth century a death duty, but in origins a heriot returned by a vassal to his lord upon the vassal's death.[144] The implications of this equation would seem to be that the careful preservation of virginity was regarded as in some sense a political duty owed to the lord by the woman and her family—in other words, that a woman's future fertility belonged to her father's lord and could be deployed by him in support of his lordship, much as the arms given by a lord to his man might support that lord's kingdom and rule. However, when a woman's virginity "dies"—is terminated, in other words, by marriage or another type of sexual union—it cannot be returned to the lord in the manner of a heriot, so the lord must therefore be compensated by the payment of the fee of *amobr*. Support for this interpretation comes from the example of the only woman mentioned in the laws as paying *ebediw*, an exception that proves the rule. Because of her chastity, the anchoress—*estauellauc o wreyc*, "woman with a cell"—would never incur the payment of *amobr*.[145] In Ior, however (and only in Ior, a reflection of its constant emphasis on lordship), the anchoress is said instead to owe *ebediw* with respect to the monastic cell she occupies—a recognition of both her anomalous status vis-à-vis her natal and (prospective) marital kin, and the lord's claims to jurisdiction over her fertility, dead to the world because of her decision to deploy it in the interests of the church.

The fact that the deployment of female virginity might be regarded as a prerogative of lordship should not be surprising. In societies where lords directed heiresses into marriage, often collecting fees along the way, virgins were a rich resource available to be tapped. Added to these pragmatic financial considerations, however, is the issue examined in the previous chapter: the fact that virginity and its opposite, the judicious deployment of fertility, were regarded by many contemporaries as symbolically important to governance. Again, the Welsh were not alone in this. In many premodern cultures, the virginity of one or both genders has been viewed as implicitly linked to the fortunes of the state.[146] The Vestal Virgins of ancient Rome are an obvious example, albeit as exceptional presences designed to reinforce the traditional sexual trajectory of Roman women.[147] The various Fortuna cults served similarly to underscore the connection of women's fertility to the welfare of the state.[148] And Protestant leaders decried the preservation of female virginity within the convent not only because they perceived monasticism to be a crucial aspect of the power of the Catholic Church, but because their own systems of rule were centered on what Lyndal Roper has called the "holy household" defined by the marriage of husband and wife.[149] The treatment of virginity and marriage in the Welsh lawbooks makes a similar point: an assertion that, within both the royal and the domestic spheres, the virginity of Welsh women was best deployed in fruitful marriages of benefit to lord and *gwlad*.

PART III

Violence

CHAPTER 6

Dogs in the Nighttime

One of the most famous murderers ever apprehended by Sherlock Holmes was a horse.[1] In fact, the murderer's unmasking was due directly to the actions—or, rather, inactions—of a dog, whose failure to bark on the night of the murder led Holmes to deduce that no stranger had entered the stall in which the killing had occurred. This chapter takes its cue from the central lesson of this tale: that in certain circumstances, a weighty silence can be as revealing as the sound and fury toward which detectives (and historians) naturally incline. We have seen already in this work that silences as well as presences can "mean" in important ways. Written law may purport to reflect what is there, but in fact the reality it conveys has inevitably been refracted through the purposes of those who authored it. Redactors may choose, for example, to neglect or suppress particular practices or, conversely, to include procedures that are later dropped or reshaped in other lawbook versions. Sometimes we can infer what is missing from the shape of what remains; usually, however, we must rely on external sources to tell us what the laws do not. It is when a discrepancy emerges between what we see in the lawbooks and what we learn from elsewhere that we must pay particularly close attention, for it is then that—in Holmesian terms—the game is most likely afoot.

The silence to which I propose to listen in this chapter is a relative one—less an actual absence of sound than a dignified growl in circumstances where a vigorous chorus of barks might be expected. Violence is a subject about which lawyers everywhere tend to write at great length. Homicide, for example, has historically been a particular object of juridical scrutiny. There are several forms of violent death, and most medieval legal systems have found it useful to distinguish among them. Glanvill devotes an entire book to criminal pleas such as homicide, arson, robbery, rape, and counterfeiting, taking care to differentiate murder (*murdrum*, killing done secretly) from ordinary homicide (*simplex homicidium*).[2] Bracton's *De legibus* treats homicide in even greater detail, subdividing it into different types according to its nature and the circumstances behind its commission. Thus, spiritual homicide is distinguished from corporal, and homicide by word (of which there are three divisions, each provided with definitions) from homicide by deed (four divisions with definitions). Bracton also addresses special problems arising out of unlawful killing, such as how homicide is punished and how slayers are to be caught, how homicide is distinguished from killings committed by animals, how issues of intention and negligence figure into homicide prosecutions, how clerical killers are treated relative to their secular counterparts, what coroners do, and how inquests are held, and so on.[3] Similar attention is paid in the text to wounding, assault, castration, rape, arson, robbery, and other violent crimes: each is defined, distinguished from other types of crimes or occurrences, and provided with some sort of remedy.[4]

Vernacular lawbooks of the period such as the French *Établissements de Saint Louis*, Icelandic *Grágás*, and German *Sachsenspiegel* also pay close attention to unlawful killing and other forms of personal violence.[5] Problems addressed in the *Grágás*, for example, include the circumstances under which men are allowed to kill; the age of culpability; the distinction between intentional and (allegedly) accidental killing; assault by the insane; the killing of men of particular statuses; the murder of foreigners; settlements for wounding; plots to disfigure another person; the killing of shipmen; self-inflicted wounds; and the procedures that govern these cases and more.[6] Similarly, the *Établissements de Saint Louis*, roughly contemporaneous with the period of the Welsh lawbooks, addresses crimes such as the murder and rape of a pregnant woman; fights that result in serious injury; the abetting of homicide; threatening or plotting homicide; making war on the king; striking a lord or his officers; making accusations of homicide; and mounting an armed expedition against the property of another.[7] The *Sachsenspiegel*'s discussions of violence of all kinds (including judicial violence) are well known and even illustrated in some manuscripts. Madeline Caviness argues persuasively that in many cases these illustrations complicate both the authority of the text and the meaning violence had for contemporaries, but its frankness on such subjects is still remarkable.[8]

The attention accorded homicide and other forms of personal violence in these sources contrasts sharply with the way matters of this sort are imagined in the medieval Welsh lawbooks, especially in Ior, generally regarded as the most cutting-edge of the principal redactions. In distinguishing between violence per se and violence as imagined, I do not intend to imply that what is said in the Welsh lawbooks is actually wrong. Indeed, with respect to homicide (*galanas*) specifically, R. R. Davies's study of the court rolls suggests that the lawbooks have the basic outlines more or less right, despite the fact that the institution seems to have been on the wane even before 1284.[9] Nor is it my intent to suggest that homicide and other forms of violent crime are completely ignored in the Welsh laws. As we have already seen, rape and its remedies are addressed in the Laws of Women.[10] The Three Columns of Law—a section of the lawbook consisting of subtractates focused on homicide, theft, and arson—occupies a front and center position in all lawbook versions (at the head of the Laws of Country in all redactions apart from Ior, and at the head of the Judges' Test Book in the latter). Indeed, Davies even remarks on "the considerable prominence given in the laws to the section on *galanas*."[11] And one of the governing presumptions of Michael Cichon's work on violence in Middle Welsh narrative is that the laws were regarded as sufficiently authoritative on the subject that many of the violent incidents described in the tales were in fact "derived almost verbatim" from them.[12]

However, whereas studies like these suggest a close congruence between the treatment of violence in the Welsh lawbooks and its treatment in other types of contemporary narrative, there may be more—and, significantly, less—to violence as it is portrayed in the laws than has so far been recognized. Barbarous incivility and a propensity to violence were, of course, among the most common accusations made against the Welsh by outsiders in the twelfth and thirteenth centuries. As Davies remarks, land conveyances in Shropshire could not even be warranted against Welshmen because they, "like acts of God," were regarded as being "beyond any insurance policy."[13] Critics commented regularly on the Welsh fondness for mutilation and murder, most especially of relatives. Gerald of Wales, for example, in a section of his *Descriptio Kambriae* entitled "The Less Good Points," noted wryly that Welshmen love their brothers most passionately once they are dead, and are especially pleased if somebody else happens to have killed them because then they can take revenge on the killers as well.[14] Gerald's exaggerations aside, it is clear from the chronicle sources that violence was endemic in Wales, especially in periods when no strong prince existed to impose peace upon his subjects. Plunder was a significant aspect of the Welsh economy well into the twelfth century, a fact that guaranteed a constant give-and-take of raids and reprisals.[15] Welsh decapitation and mutilation practices have been the focus for more than one full-length scholarly study,[16] and while it is clear that violence was a problem in all European countries at the time, and that some Welsh practices (castration, most notably) were borrowed from or inspired by the Anglo-Normans rather than (as has traditionally been imagined) suppressed by them,[17] there can be little doubt that homicide and mutilation were frequent occurrences.

Moreover, Gerald was right to observe that much of the most spectacularly brutal violence took place among those joined by ties of kinship, lordship or fosterage.[18] One has only to consider for proof of his assertion the numerous assaults and murders occurring within the kindred of, for example, Idwal Foel, five of whose sons and six of whose grandsons were killed, imprisoned, or mutilated in struggles over power within Gwynedd, or Bleddyn ap Cynfyn, killed by a distant cousin in 1075. One of Gruffudd ap Cynan's sons was responsible for the deaths of three of his uncles; Rhys ap Gruffudd was at one point seized and imprisoned by his own sons. Llywelyn ap Iorwerth's family seems to have preferred imprisonment or exile to homicide and castration for their nearest and dearest, but similar charges of interfamilial strife could be made of just about anyone who was seriously in the power game up to and including the last prince of native Wales, Llywelyn ap Gruffudd, who was killed by English forces after having narrowly escaped an earlier assassination plot engineered by his own brother.[19] Without a doubt, the Welsh folded, spindled, and mutilated along with the best of them in this period. The only real question is whether they were, as their critics alleged, worse than their contemporaries in this respect.[20]

Violence is also a prominent theme in the poetry and prose narratives of the era. Catherine McKenna has called attention to the manner in which, for example, the language of the Second Branch intentionally underscores the "appalling violence" of Efnisien's mutilation of Matholwch's horses.[21] Similarly, in the Fourth Branch, the forceful rape (*treis*) of Goewin is graphically reenacted through the symbolic emasculation of the rapists Gilfaethwy and Gwydion with a magic rod that turns them into breeding pairs of animals who beget and bear offspring with one another.[22] And horrific images of slaughter characterize the accounts of the death of Trahaearn at the battle of Mynydd Carn in the Latin and the Welsh prose lives of Gruffudd ap Cynan. Trahaearn is said there to have been "pierced through spilling his entrails," falling so flat on the ground that he appeared to be "eating the grass with his living teeth"; his corpse is then described as being preserved in salt "like pork being turned into bacon."[23] Equally brutal images can be found in the poetic corpus. Cynddelw's song of praise for Owain Gwynedd, for example, implicitly contrasts the feasting of men before the battle with the feasting of carrion in its wake. The poem seems almost to luxuriate in images of gore and dismembered bodies: *gwaedlaw ar ddarwedd*, "blood-shower pouring," *celyrnedd dachwedd*, "massacre's buckets," *coludd ar ddrain*, "bowels on thorns."[24] Very similar are the images evoked in the lament penned by Gruffudd ab yr Ynad Coch upon the death of Llywelyn ap Gruffudd, with its rhythmically relentless insistence on the decapitated head of the fallen prince.[25]

So gripping indeed is the imagery of these texts, and so bloodthirsty the reality of medieval Welsh politics, that returning to the lawbook accounts is a somewhat disorienting experience. Existing scholarship seems almost to take for granted that the level of brutality and constant infighting so prominent in the chronicle and literary evidence is also reflected in the laws. More striking to my mind, however, is the relative *silence* of these texts on such subjects. Lawbook treatments of offenses like homicide are on the whole brief, muted, and peculiar, as we will see. Rape merits only a small amount of attention in comparison to other subjects, especially in Cyfn and Ior;[26] the lawbooks are clearly more concerned with women who elope, marry without the consent of their kin, or take up with a man other than their husband, than with those forced unwillingly into sexual intercourse.[27] And several other types of violent crime—all addressed in Bracton—appear only in passing or not at all in the Welsh redactions, including robbery, forcible imprisonment, and (especially significant, given contemporary evidence on the subject), kin-slaying.[28] Ior is particularly noteworthy in this respect, and it is primarily with its account that this chapter will be concerned. Even if one were to add together everything in that lawbook as exemplified in the standard printed edition (itself based on Ior B) that even remotely pertains to violent crime—including theft and arson, which take up seven pages on their own and do not necessarily entail violence anyway—one would arrive at approximately fifteen pages (out of 103) in the standard edition, only slightly more than the amount of space given over to the value of animals and household goods, and considerably less than that devoted to the officers of the court and to disputes over land. Considering the prominence of killing and violent assault in the tales and chronicle evidence, the relative thinness of the treatment of these subjects in this lawbook is striking.

Perhaps most startling is the treatment of homicide, which in all redactions is primarily addressed in the subtractate on *galanas*, itself part of the Three Columns of Law.[29] This subtractate is the principal locale in the lawbooks for the discussion of unlawful killing, and yet it was constructed around an original core that focuses not on the offense itself, nor even on the offender but, rather, on the *naw affaith galanas*, the "nine accessories of homicide"—in other words, on the nine actions that constitute aiding and abetting a killer in his crime. Included in this group at the lowest level of liability is the person who points out the victim to his attacker, or who consults with the latter about the plan. A second tier of responsibility encompasses persons acting as lookouts or accompanying the killer to the place in which the crime takes place. Most serious of all are those who restrain the victim or otherwise help the killer, or who witness the act but fail to intervene.[30] Over time, this original core—only seven sentences long in the standard edition of *Llyfr Iorwerth*—attracted to itself provisions dealing with other issues arising out of homicidal violence, such as the detailed calculations by which killer and kin pay and receive payments owed by or to them as a result of the crime. These provisions are arranged differently across the various lawbook redactions; however, together they constitute the subtractate on homicide as we have it today.

Easily the most remarkable feature of this subtractate is its focus—consistent across almost all versions of the principal redactions—on accessories (*affaith*, pl. *affeithau*) rather than the principal offense itself. Relatively little is said about the crime of homicide per se. Only in Latin B is there any attempt made to delineate the types and causes of homicide, and it has been argued that this is a secondary and relatively late discussion.[31] Of course, aiding and abetting was indeed a serious crime; many legal texts address this, including Bracton.[32] And many of the categories of accessory outlined in Bracton overlap with those delineated in Welsh law, including holding the victim, advising the killer, or assisting him directly. The discussion in Bracton even transcends the strictly procedural to address some of the subtleties attendant on abetments, such as the issue of intent. Plaintiffs appealing against an accessory are, for example, advised to make sure that they explicitly characterize the accessory's actions as having been committed *nequiter et in felonia*, "wickedly and feloniously," since a person might throw his arms around another out of friendship as well as out of a desire to restrain or injure.[33] In contrast with Welsh law, however, Bracton takes as its starting point the idea that principal offenders must be pursued before accessories and places the onus squarely on the primary offense rather than on the abetment. Nor is Bracton alone in this. Early Irish law also preserves two short tracts on accessories which are interestingly parallel in certain ways to what we see in the Welsh texts.[34] However, there is no sense here of the abetment overtaking the principal crime as the focus for judicial action, and provisions on killing and the various forms of violent death are found elsewhere in the Irish legal corpus.[35] In short, neither of these parallels really diminishes the oddity of what we find in the Welsh lawbooks. Paul Russell terms it "striking that the prominence given to the *naw affaith* has the effect that the subsidiary activities of abetment are given greater prominence than the acts of homicide, arson, and theft themselves."[36]

The modern editors of the *Naw Affaith* offer two principal reasons for the importance accorded accessories relative to the main offense. One has to do with the nature of abetment itself. Whereas the killing was primarily a tort, compensable largely by payment to the kindred, abetment was a crime, and hence something of an anomaly requiring explanation, since most offenses under Welsh law tended to result in payments to both victim and lord.[37] The other explanation is textual. The Laws of Country in the Model Lawbook began with a collection of lists of "nines," to which the nine accessories of *galanas*, fire-setting, and theft all belonged. The list-like nature of this part of the lawbook was, however, "progressively obscured" when these three nines began to attract "to themselves material on the principal offenses of homicide, theft, and arson, material originally to be found in other parts of the lawbooks."[38] A fourth nine, *y naw dyn credadwy*, "the nine persons who are to be believed [on their own unsupported word]," did not evolve in the same way and over time became separated from the other three lists. (It is unclear at what point the lists of abetments came to be known as the Three Columns of Law.) With the creation of the Judges' Test Book in Ior, the three nines of homicide, theft, and arson were removed from the Laws of Country to become the lead tractate in the Test Book. In other words, the prominence of the abetments that is so evident today was essentially a by-product of the manner in which the lawbook itself evolved.[39]

Both of these explanations make good sense, and of course, they are not mutually exclusive.[40] However, neither really explains the *continuing* emphasis in most redactions on abetments rather than on the principal offense. The fact that abetments are anomalies that litigants might need help understanding may explain why abetments receive their own special treatment; however, it does not account for why homicide (a complex area of the law that litigants might require assistance negotiating) itself gets such short shrift.[41] Likewise, the creation of the Test Book, which explains the placement of the Three Columns but not their content. It would still be entirely possible to build a lengthy discussion of homicide and its causes and permutations around a short text focusing originally on abetments, and yet many of our texts do not do this (as will become evident, the Latin/Bleg texts and Col come the closest). What must be explained, in other words, is not merely the importance of the abetments in the Model Lawbook, but their ongoing textual prominence in thirteenth-century accounts, and not merely the subordination of the primary offense of homicide to abetment, but the relatively scant attention paid in those accounts to what is generally regarded as the worst of all crimes.

The Redactions

The textual foregrounding of abetments seems to have been a feature of the Model Lawbook. However, there are marked differences in the manner in which primary and secondary offenses are treated in the redactions as we have them today. Some redactors added material on homicide to their abetment lists in a way that expands their treatment of the subject, while others did not. In part, this reflects a difference in approach visible elsewhere in the lawbooks. Redactors had varied views on whether to add supplementary materials to established tractates. As a general rule, Ior redactors chose to situate new materials in separate legal compilations (*Llyfr y Damweiniau*, "Book of Eventualities"; *Llyfr Cynghawsedd*, "Book of Pleadings") that they often then attached to their lawbooks. Cyfn, Bleg, and Latin redactors, by contrast, preferred to integrate new materials directly into the texts of the lawbook proper.[42] There are many possible explanations for this: redactors may have had different materials available to them, and they certainly had varying intentions for their compositions.[43] Russell has argued, for example, that Latin B as a whole "has the air of an antiquarian collection," which fact might explain both the diversity of materials on which its redactor drew and the relatively disordered nature of its treatment of *galanas*.[44] Latin D, by contrast, developed in an entirely different manner, betraying simultaneously conservative and innovatory tendencies on the part of its redactor.[45] But while such larger differences in approach are well documented, it is also possible that there was something specific about homicide and violence that would help us account for the discrepancies in how individual redactors treated these subjects. One would not wish to argue that every sentence in a given redaction was put there in service to a thematic goal, but it is at least worth considering that certain texts might most profitably be explored as deliberate constructions rather than as haphazard hodgepodges of material.

Of all the *galanas* subtractates, it is probably Cyfn about which it is most difficult to generalize because its contents and ordering are so fluid across the various manuscripts. However, some general points can be made.[46] Cyfn's discussion of *galanas* is both brief and relatively basic. In addition to the nine abetments, the core Cyfn text consists of lists of wergilds and *sarhaed*s (insult payments) sorted according to status from king's representative (*maer*, *cynghellor*) down to slave (*caeth*),[47] and a short passage detailing the payment and denial procedure for *cynllwyn*, "secret killing," and *cyrch cyhoeddog*, "public (homicidal) violence."[48] Other provisions commonly included in Cyfn are material on how homicide payments should be divided and paid among the killer's kin (covered in all manuscripts, although there are more and less extended treatments of this subject);[49] a list of payments due for injuries to various parts of the body (a short text often referred to by scholars as the Value of Limbs);[50] and provisions on bloodshed and scars.[51] Both the wergild/*sarhaed* list and the Value of Limbs were originally located elsewhere in the Laws of Country, but due to the proximity of the subject matter were later attracted into the Three Columns in most (but not all) Cyfn manuscripts.[52] Cyfn X adds to its subtractate an additional few provisions found in other Cyfn texts well outside the Three Columns, including one on dispersed *galanas* (when a killer's kin are scattered among different *gwlad*s),[53] and one on *oergwymp galanas*, the "chill disaster" of *galanas* (when a killer is himself killed by someone not related to the victim after his own kindred have paid compensation on his behalf).[54] All Cyfn manuscripts additionally include passages pertaining to homicide in their triad collections, including provisions on vengeance, fines for fighting and violent assault, and deaths that result from the negligent carrying of weapons.[55] Indeed, what is perhaps most striking is how much of the material most directly pertinent to the subject of homicide is found in many Cyfn manuscripts outside the Three Columns—material that could have been added to the *galanas* subtractate but was not.

This marks a real contrast with the Latin/Bleg versions.[56] There is, to be sure, a significant degree of overlap among them and their Cyfn counterparts: the abetments list, the discussion of how *galanas* is to be divided, paid, and received among kin (though details vary);[57] the clause on *cynllwyn*;[58] and the provisions on *oergwymp galanas*[59] and *cyrch cyhoeddog*.[60] However, the Latin/Bleg subtractates are generally longer and more detailed than their Cyfn counterparts because material found in Cyfn outside the Three Columns has been integrated into the Latin subtractates in a way that greatly expands their treatment of homicide. Examples of this include the *tri dygngoll cenedl*, "three dire losses of the kindred" (often linked in these texts to the *oergwymp galanas*);[61] a provision on how vengeance may be taken when killer, victim, and kindred are located in different *gwlads*;[62] and a triad on how a spear ought to be carried in public sessions in order to prevent its owner from liability.[63] As with Cyfn, further materials pertaining to homicide (triads detailing the three shames and the three insults to a dead body) are found outside the Three Columns in Latin/Bleg,[64] as are provisions on bloodshed and the Value of Limbs (which in Cyfn sometimes occurs within and sometimes outside of that text).[65] Latin B and Latin E also contain (well outside the *galanas* subtractate, in Latin B) provisions on homicide taken from an early Breton legal collection known as the *Excerpta de libris Romanorum et Francorum* (*Canones Wallici*).[66]

Interestingly, Latin/Bleg tractates also seem to reflect judicial developments contemporary with the lawbooks. Some are specific enough that they might reflect decisions arising out of cases that had actually come before the court. This may be the case with the provision on coming armed to a public assembly, for example, which occurs in Latin A (outside the Three Columns tractate), Latin B, and Latin E.[67] All three versions include samples of direct speech by which an armed person entering such a gathering might in full view of all place his weapon in a safe spot and publicly proclaim his intentions not to do harm. As the provision begins with a clause on what happens when one man kills a person with weapons belonging to another, it seems likely that this paragraph might have arisen in response to an actual occurrence.[68] Another passage possibly reflecting a real-life situation is a curious provision on someone wishing to deny that another was killed *in exercitu*, "in an army." It is not entirely clear to what situation this sentence refers—a death that occurred in training, perhaps? However, its oddity suggests that an actual incident may lie behind it.[69]

As will already be evident from this brief survey of Latin/Bleg, much of the material in them actually does speak directly to the issue of homicide. Indeed, these redactions more than most seem consciously to expand their scope in a manner that creates more of a balance between abetments and primary offense.[70] What starts as a list of abetments thus ends up in many Latin/Bleg texts constituting a subtractate on *galanas* itself—one informed (if the speculations just mentioned are correct) by judicial cases taking place at the time. For the Latin D redactor at least, this shift in emphasis was clearly intentional—a deliberate reconceptualizing of the Three Columns. Whereas other lawbook versions begin with a relatively simple introduction speaking entirely to the issue of abetments, Latin D broadens the focus immediately:

(Lat B): Huc usque de curialibus legibus ad regem et reginam pertinentibus, et eorum ministris. Consequenter dicendum est de illis que ad curiam pertinent et ad patriam, sumentes exordium ab hiis que dicuntur tres columne legis, id est, *teir colouyn kyureith*, que sunt: *nau affeith galanas, nau affeith tan, nau affeith lledrat.*[71]

To this point [we have spoken of] the laws of the court pertaining to the king and queen and their ministers. From now on those [laws] pertaining to the court and to the country are to be discussed, beginning with those which are called the three Columns of Law, that is, *the Three Columns of Law*, which are: *the nine abetments of homicide, the nine abetments of arson, the nine abetments of theft.*

(Lat D): Primo autem de columpnis iuris dicemus, que sunt: *galanas a'e na6 affeith; tan a'e na6 affeith; et lledrad a'e na6 affeith. Galanas*, id est, hostilitas, hominem interficere. *Tan*, id est, combustio, est ignem in illud quod comburitur prefigere. Furtum id quod furtim aufertur de loco suo mutare. Quicquid fiat circa hec tria malefacta *affeith* est homicidii uel combustionis uel furti. Ter ix *affeitheu* uero sunt cause quibus fiunt hec tria malefacta per consensum; unde omnes *affeitheu* sunt consensus, quidam per uisus, quidam per uerba, quidam per opera, id est, *llygadruthyaeth*, et *taua6drutyaeth*, et *gweithred.*

But first we shall speak about the columns of law, which are *homicide and its nine abetments*; *arson and its nine abetments*; *theft and its nine abetments. Homicide*, i.e. enmity, is to kill a man. *Arson*, i.e. burning is to set fire to that which is burnt. Theft is to move from its place that which is stolen by stealth. Whatever happens around these three wrong-doings is an *abetment* of homicide or arson or theft. The three nine *abetments* are the reasons for which these three wrong-doings occur through consent; whence all abetments are consents, some through seeing, some through words, some through deeds, i.e. *red-eyedness*, and *red-tonguedness* and *deeds*.[72]

Other Latin texts also highlight the offense as well as the abetments to some degree—to witness, Latin B's paragraph on *negatio homicidii*, "denial of homicide."[73] However, only in Latin D is this shift in focus acknowledged directly—a by-product perhaps, of its redactor's legal sophistication or familiarity with contemporary European law.

Latin D's deliberate change in emphasis forms a stark contrast with most of the versions of Ior, especially Ior B. Indeed, it is in the Ior tradition that we hear the silence of the nonbarking dog most clearly. T. M. Charles-Edwards has identified four principal manuscript versions of the Ior subtractate on *galanas*, all of which differ significantly from one another. Ior E, he argues, is a copy of the original version of Ior, while Ior B and Col—and, to an even greater extent, the highly truncated Ior F—represent independent revisions of a previously revised version of the original text.[74] The basic components of the core Ior subtractate are clear from a comparison of these manuscripts: the *naw affaith*, a paragraph on how *galanas* is to be paid and received, a text on *sarhaed*, and a list of *galanas* and *sarhaed* payments sorted according to status.[75] There are miscellaneous provisions in addition to this core that differ across the various Ior versions. Ior E, for example, addresses the question of whether women could pay or receive *galanas*; its reference to "some judges" who allow this suggests that Ior E is reflecting here a divergence in contemporary judicial opinions.[76] Ior B adds a paragraph on *galanas guasgarauc* (*galanas* payments made when the kindreds involved are living in different regions of Wales), which appears in Ior E's *damweiniau*, but not in its principal tractate.[77] And Col has a number of passages (many paralleled in the Latin texts) that are not present in Ior B, including provisions on borrowed weapons subsequently used against someone;[78] *oergwymp galanas*;[79] offenses that cause one to lose one's patrimony;[80] "public attack" (*cyrch cyhoeddog*);[81] and "secret killing" (*cynllywn*).[82] This latter is particularly revealing of the manner in which priorities differ even among the redactors of the various Ior versions. It is part of the core tractate in Cyfn, but all Ior versions except Col omit any mention of it. If sentences on this subject had indeed been a part of the Model Lawbook, as suggested by Russell,[83] they either dropped out over time or were deliberately removed by the redactors of all Ior manuscripts apart from Col.[84]

Of these various Ior versions, it is Ior B, the one on which Aled Rhys Wiliam based his edition, that stands out as most interesting, in that it appears to have been deliberately structured in a way designed to downplay the problem of violence and showcase the unity and order of Welsh society. One of its most striking departures from the original as reflected in Ior E is the decision to focus on *sarhaed* (insult and insult payments) instead of *galanas* (homicide and homicide payments) in the status list with which the discussion of homicide ends. Ior E's version of this status list starts with the *galanas* of the king of Aberffraw and proceeds from there down to the *caeth*, "slave":

> Galanas brenhyn Aberfrau yu y sarhaet teyrgweyth. Galanas gwreyc y brenhyn a'y uab a'y edlyg a'y ney a'y benteulu trayan galanas y brenhyn, ac eu sarhaet trayan sarhaet y brenhyn. Galanas merch y brenhyn hanner galanas y braut, a'y sarhaet y uelly kynn no'y gura.
>
> The *galanas* of the king of Aberffraw is his *sarhaed* multiplied three times. The *galanas* of the king's wife and his son and his heir apparent and his nephew and his captain of the warband are a third of the king's *galanas*. The *galanas* of the king's daughter is half the *galanas* of her brother, and similarly her *sarhaed* until she marries.[85]

In Ior E, therefore, the status list constitutes merely one paragraph, is list-like in structure and tone, and focuses primarily on *galanas*, with *sarhaed* coming in only secondarily. The only narrative portion of Ior E's list concerns the *sarhaed* of the slave, which details the clothing and tools paid in compensation for insulting him and the penalties imposed on him should he himself insult a freeman (Ior E 110/10–13). Col similarly puts the focus more on *galanas* than *sarhaed*.[86]

In stark contrast to this stands Ior B's account, which shifts both the focus and the rhetorical tone of the text in significant ways:

> Val hyn e traethun ny o'r sarhaedeu: en gyntaf o sarhaet brenhyn Aberfrau. Sef er edrechus e keureyth pa beth esyd sarhaet, ac ydau ef ac y paub; ac esef reweles e keureyth, nat sarhaet e nep namen un o try peth en enwedyc: guneythur guaratwyd ydau am e wreyc, neu lad e gennat, neu torry e naud. Sef mal e dywegyr ydau am e wreyc, klaur eur ydau kyulet a'e vynep a chyn tewet ac ewyn amaeth yryffo amaeth nau mlyned, a llathen eur kehyt ac ef ehun a chyn urasset a'e vys bychan, a chan muu urth pob cantref a uo ydau, a tharu guyn eskyuarllennyc urth pob can muu onadunt. . . . O deruyd y ur o wlat arall e sarhau, teyr a thry ugeyn punt yu y sarhaet (a henny yu e uechteyrn delyet enteu e urenhyn Llundeyn pan gymero y tyr y ganthau; ac amen henne heuyt hy dele dym byth y ganthau namen kun a hebogeu a meyrch).[87]

> Thus we treat of *sarhaeds*: first of the *sarhaed* of the king of Aberffraw. This is what the law looked at: what type of thing constitutes *sarhaed*, both to him and to everyone; and this is what the law saw: that nothing is *sarhaed* to anyone except for three things specifically: causing shame to him concerning his wife, or killing his messenger, or breaking his protection. This is how he is compensated for his wife: a golden plate [is to be paid] to him as broad as his face and as thick as the nail of a plowman who has been a plowman for nine years, and a golden rod as tall as he is and as thick as his little finger, and a hundred cows for every *cantred* under his jurisdiction, and a white red-eared bull for every hundred cows among them. . . . If it happens that a man from another *gwlad* commits *sarhaed* against him, his *sarhaed* is three score and three pounds (and that is his own *mechdeyrn ddylyed* ["sovereign tribute"] to the king of London when he takes land from him, and apart from that, he [the king of London] is not entitled to anything else from him [the king of Aberffraw] except dogs and hawks and horses).

This lengthy paragraph on the king is nearly as long as the entire status list given in Ior E, and yet it still constitutes only a portion of the whole. As in Ior E, the discussion in Ior B continues down the list through the queen and royal children to the *caeth*, or slave, and although the compensation for homicide (the word used here is *guerth*) is usually given, the focus is clearly on *sarhaed*. The passage is more narrative than list-like in tone, and the piece in general reads much like a subtractate on *sarhaed*—one that includes, among other things, a paragraph-long digression on the role of the kindred in denying *sarhaed*. As Charles-Edwards has shown, this latter exists largely to counter problems created by its own shift in focus away from *galanas* in favor of *sarhaed*.[88]

At first glance, the decision to highlight *sarhaed* rather than *galanas* in a subtractate originally devoted to the abetments of *galanas* seems a most curious one. But we have seen this sort of harkening back to earlier sections of the lawbook before. In its wording, imagery, and content, the Ior B *sarhaed* list draws heavily on the discussion of the king's *sarhaed* in the Laws of Court—though not, curiously, on Ior B's own version of that passage. Rather, the author uses an expanded version of the text, one that includes not only the golden plate (dropped out of Ior B's Laws of Court), but the *mechdeyrn ddylyed*, "sovereign tribute," found in some lawbook versions.[89] The redactor's disregarding of his own text seems rather odd on the face of it; possibly a fuller version of this passage had come into his hands by the time he was constructing his subtractate, and he decided to use it. Regardless of how he came by his sources, however, the effect of his reiterating the earlier discussion of *sarhaed* is the same: to return the reader to the timeless royal court with which the lawbook began. Here again, we meet the golden treasures paid to Hywel and his successors, the red-eared bull and attendant bovines, the long-serving tillers of the land. Even the striking of the queen, with its reflexes in contemporary tales such as *Peredur*,[90] is not only repeated here, but is also expanded on in ways that encompass the king's daughter as well as his wife.

It is hard to imagine a reiteration of this kind being inadvertent or accidental. And while one cannot be certain about the redactor's intent in repeating this material, it may be possible to infer from the impact of his actions what his motives may have been. Charles-Edwards speaks of the Ior B redactor wishing to expand his account of the king's status and turning naturally to *sarhaed* instead of *galanas* because the amount of the latter was defined with reference to the former.[91] This is quite plausible, although it does not explain why the redactor might have decided to expand his discussion in the first place. Another possibility, one that accords with what we have seen previously in Ior, is deliberate intertextual referencing. Reiterating the section on the royal *sarhaed* inevitably underscores the connection between the Laws of Court (known already as the first part of the lawbook) and the Test Book (created to serve as its final part by a compiler identified in some manuscripts as Iorwerth ap Madog himself[92]). Exactly this sort of deliberate tying together of lawbook sections also occurs in the land measurements attributed in the Laws of Country to Dyfnwal Moelmud and later repeated in the Test Book. In those passages, thematic as well as textual coherence was clearly a priority. Dyfnwal's measurements in the Laws of Country constitute the historical foundation for Welsh claims to jurisdiction over the island of Britain; his measurements in the Test Book are the basis on which the land itself is to be exploited for agriculture. This double invocation of Dyfnwal functions both to unite the individual sections of the lawbook, and to emphasize the antiquity and independence of the political system underlying its production.[93]

A similar thematic coherence may well be at work in Ior B's shift in focus from *galanas* to *sarhaed*.[94] The Laws of Court (along with the preface) open the lawbook as a whole; the Three Columns (along with the preface) open the Test Book that is Ior's principal structural innovation to the lawbook tradition. Implicit in the *sarhaed* passages incorporated into both of these are the lawbook's most prominent themes and images: the wealth, order, and prerogatives of the prince's court; the long historical tradition claimed for Welsh sovereignty and independence; and the vesting of royal authority in the bodies of the ruled. In both, the jurisdictional supremacy of the prince of Aberffraw is asserted in numerous ways. As in the Laws of Court version of the *sarhaed* passage, the prince alone is said in Ior B to receive the golden regalia allotted to kings in cases of *sarhaed*. Additionally, he is portrayed as occupying the same position relative to men from other regions in Wales that he himself occupies with respect to the "king of London." The orderly nature of his court is underscored by the careful way in which its hierarchy is described; the clear presumption of the Ior B *sarhaed* list is that the ruler's authority is sufficiently widely accepted as to ensure that payments due to those who have been injured will ultimately be made and that peace will be restored. Political unity is implied here as well. Indeed, unity is a significant theme of the subtractate as a whole: the passage immediately preceding the paragraph on *sarhaed* in Ior B (and only in B) makes clear that practices regarding the payment of compensation paid for homicide, like those governing inheritance, extended across all regions of Wales.[95]

Ior B's account thus differs from that found in Ior E in several ways. Perhaps its most significant departure, however, is one we have not yet mentioned: Ior B's dramatically increased emphasis on the powers of the lord at the expense of the wider kindred.[96] Charles-Edwards has already outlined the major changes the Ior B redactor makes in this direction. Whereas the Ior E redactor acknowledges (before examining at length and ultimately rejecting) the fact that some believe that the fines due for abetments should go to the kindred of the victim, the Ior B redactor focuses all his attention on the monies due to the lord and simply passes over the idea that such fines might be paid to the kindred.[97] Ior B explicitly permits the lord to plunder the killer on the day of the killing (or on the day it first comes to the lord's attention); Ior E says nothing about such a lordly prerogative.[98] Like all principal redactions, Ior B and Ior E examine the corporate liability of the kindred in great detail. However, Ior B provides a considerably more expanded role than does Ior E for the lord in compelling distant kinsmen to make the payments for which they are liable.[99] In short, while Ior E already puts the lord in charge of the peace-making process, Ior B significantly expands that role.[100]

Charles-Edwards suggests that Ior B's increased emphasis on lordly authority may reflect the ambitions of a young lawyer seeking to enhance his status in the profession by revising *Llyfr Iorwerth*, the premier redaction of Gwynedd; alternatively, he proposes, these provisions may reflect local practice in the region of Gwynedd Is Conwy.[101] Both of these explanations are plausible. It only stands to reason that practices might vary from region to region in Wales, and it is certainly true that personal motives can reshape a text in significant ways. Indeed, if we are dealing here with an enterprising young jurist looking to leave his personal mark, this might also account for his apparent downplaying of the authority of Iorwerth ap Madog.[102] However, it is also possible that what we are seeing here is a deliberate attempt by the redactor to accommodate an expanded vision of lordly authority. This may constitute an acknowledgment of changes in lordship that were already under way; alternatively, it may reflect the redactor's own hopes for the internal stability of Welsh society. Either stance would be entirely in keeping with the emphasis on (judiciously exercised) lordly power that we have seen elsewhere as a theme in Ior B. We already know that interfamilial violence was a major problem in Wales at the time Ior B was redacted and that families of *uchelwyr* status were among the most seriously affected. Perhaps in Ior B's shift in emphasis from kin to lord we are seeing not only the redactor's desire to downplay the fractiousness of internal Welsh politics, but also his personal conviction that the best hope for healing these rifts lay in strong and effective lordship.

This is not to say that the Ior B redactor regards the kin as unimportant. Indeed, quite the contrary: Ior B is one of the Ior manuscripts that includes an entirely new section on family law at the end of the Laws of Country (*Ior* §§97–103). However, lordship is also a principal theme of this text, which focuses otherwise on the constitution and proper workings of the kin.[103] And with respect to *galanas*, Ior B's portrayal of the relationship between them leaves no doubt as to where its redactor perceives the ultimate responsibility to lie. Everything is to proceed under the authority of the lord, who forestalls further violence by ensuring that kindreds receive the compensation due to them. As we saw earlier with kingship, the point is underscored by the structure of the lawbook itself. Ior's Laws of Court establish the image of a peaceful *gwlad* in which violence takes place only outside court and kingdom. The tractate on family law immediately precedes the Test Book and hence the Three Columns with their treatment of *galanas*; this has the effect of embedding such violence as the Ior B redactor is willing to acknowledge firmly within the structures of lord and kin. Even occasions of disunity and division such as homicide become instead celebrations of the fundamental stability of Welsh society.

Depicting Violence

Some redactors clearly went further down the road of refocusing their discussions on homicide than others did. Even with respect to these texts, however, the relative paucity of material on homicide and violence is striking: the failure of the dog to bark in circumstances where one might have expected it. At a time when jurists in England and other regions of Europe were devoting considerable attention to such subjects, Welsh redactors remained seemingly hesitant either to add new materials on violence to their existing lawbooks, or to compile entirely new texts out of traditional materials. They did do this with some subjects, as Ior's section on family law clearly illustrates. But they did not do it with violence, and what makes their silence especially significant is the fact that we know for certain that, by the thirteenth century, there were in circulation a number of passages on homicide, wounding, violent trespass, and assault from which they could have chosen. Contemporary legal texts outside the lawbooks such as the *Llyfr y Damweiniau*, "Book of Eventualities," and *Llyfr Cynghawsedd*, "Book of Pleadings,"[104] contain many provisions on these subjects—indeed, so many that one could easily piece together a detailed discussion of homicide from this material alone. Extant *damweiniau* cover several of the distinctions made in other contemporary laws, such as the role of insanity in prosecutions of homicide;[105] killings by animals, women, foreigners, or persons who die prior to compensation being paid;[106] the difference between homicide and deaths caused by negligence or accident;[107] and the killing of an innocent man as retribution for a crime he did not commit.[108] The *cynghawsedd* similarly detail several kinds of violent assault (*sarhaed*, *trais*) and give detailed pleadings for cases of this sort.[109]

To be sure, these texts are not always easy to date. Many of them occur in manuscripts contemporaneous with the principal redactions, but the fact that they existed does not guarantee that every lawbook redactor would have had access to them. Still, it does seem very curious that in a culture concerned with (and often accused of) excessive violence, one does not really get from the lawbooks the sort of focused discussion one might have expected even on topics that should have resonated very strongly, such as kin-slaying. After all, even apart from the provisions just mentioned, redactors would likely also have had access to oral or written accounts of actual court proceedings.[110] The *cwynion*, "plaints," made by prosecuting parties are extant today only in much later (fifteenth-century) manuscripts; it seems hard to imagine, however, that counts or judicial decisions would not have been available to the lawbook redactors, if only in oral form. Indeed, as we have seen, such a source may well lie behind the provision on going armed into an assembly, which includes what purports to be direct speech. Supplementary matter of this sort, perhaps rewritten as traditional genres such as triads and *damweiniau*,[111] would have been easy to integrate into existing lawbook discussions, not least because there was already a place—the Three Columns tractate itself—into which additional materials relating to homicide could easily have been introduced.[112] In other words, had the lawbook redactors wished to treat homicide and violent assault more thoroughly, they would almost certainly have had materials available to them to use. We are dealing with a deliberate silence here rather than an absence of evidence.

Of course, there are many possible reasons for which redactors might choose to present—or not present—subjects in the way that they did. Perhaps customs surrounding *galanas* were sufficiently well known as not to require further explication; perhaps the existing lawbook provisions, especially when joined to the *damweiniau* and *cynghawsedd* collections also in circulation, were regarded as sufficient for educating those new to the legal field (believed to have been the main purpose of the lawbook redactions). However, our examination to this point raises further possibilities, particularly with respect to certain manuscripts of Ior.[113] It has been argued that Ior's depiction of landscapes interior and exterior to the *gwlad* intentionally underscores the importance of Welsh unity and the stability and centrality of the prince's court. Might not Ior's (and especially Ior B's) portrayal of homicide and violent assault have been governed by exactly those same priorities? No one suffered more from anarchy and disorder than did the Welsh themselves; no one was more affected by the stereotypes of barbarousness and incivility foisted upon them by outsiders than those who had to defend themselves against them. What the lawbooks, and particularly Ior and Ior B, provide for the Welsh is a very different vision of their own culture, one in which a strong and united people live peacefully under the rule of a just and law-abiding prince.

For although Ior undoubtedly constitutes, as Charles-Edwards has remarked, "the richest collection of texts on *galanas*"[114] in terms of its length and complexity, what is missing is as important as what it covers. With the exception of Col,[115] Ior manuscripts omit all mention of *cynllwyn*, "secret killing, ambush," and there are indications that this might have been deliberately done.[116] Similarly, Ior says nothing about *cyrch cyhoeddog*, "public attack" (Cyfn, Lat B, Lat D, and the *Llyfr y Damweiniau*),[117] and does not include the triad *tri argae gwaet*, "three stays of blood," which has strong connections to the pleading literature of the day and is cited (in most cases outside the Three Columns tractate) in Cyfn, Lat A, Lat B, Lat D, and Lat E.[118] Ior E (but not Ior B) makes reference to a "killing by 'ferocity'" (*llad o fyrnygruyd*); however, it nowhere defines this term,[119] and in general, the point still holds that the primary focus of the Ior accounts of *galanas* is not homicide itself but, rather, the abetments, the status lists, and the manner in which payments made with respect to incidents of *galanas* and *sarhaed* are to be divided, paid, and received. Indeed, Ior's accounts are so singular in comparison to the southern texts that it is hard to resist the conclusion that the decision not to enlarge upon issues pertaining to homicide was deliberate.

Also important is the question of imagery—the language and tropes used to talk about *galanas* and similar acts of violence. Here again, we see differences not only between Ior and the other lawbook versions, but within the Ior tradition itself. The picture of Welsh society communicated in Ior B, undoubtedly the most pointed in this respect, is one in which the problem of personal violence is minimal and actual killing rare. Ior B rarely even refers to blood, and when it does, the referent is not usually the violent spilling of it.[120] The contrast with Cyfn and Bleg, and most especially with nonlawbook Welsh legal texts of the period, is striking. The latter display little reticence in their discussions of violent crime; indeed, their language is often brutally reminiscent of the language used in the poetry of the time. The detailed *cynghawsedd*, "pleadings," pertaining to *sarhaed* and *galanas*, for example, are linguistically as graphic as anything found elsewhere in contemporary Welsh literature: *g6eli egoret*, "open vein"; *ath6nn ar groen ac ar gic*, "cutting on skin and on flesh"; *a g6aet gellyngedic llithredic colledic, o benn hyt rann, or rann hyt lenn, o lenn hyt lin, o lin hyt troet, o droet hyt la6r*, "and blood flowing and pouring and spilling from head to brow, from brow to vest, from vest to knee, from knee to foot, from foot to ground."[121]

The desire to minimize the emotional impact of potentially disturbing passages may also help explain one of the other major structural differences between Ior and the other lawbook traditions. Across all redactions, by far the most implicitly graphic passages on personal violence occur not in the subtractate on *galanas*, but in the short text we have already referred to on the worth of body parts that have been injured, destroyed, or severed from the person to whom they belong: *Gwerth Aelodau*, the "Value of Limbs."[122] In the Model Lawbook, the Value of Limbs was linked to a paragraph on status contained somewhere (we do not know exactly where) in the Laws of Country (the connection being that whereas *sarhaed* payments varied according to rank, payments made to compensate a person for the loss of a limb did not).[123] Some redactions (Cyfn Mk and V, Latin D) subsequently appear to have moved the Value of Limbs to a position following closely after *galanas* and the Three Columns of Law.[124] This move was likely deliberate—prompted presumably by the thematic proximity between homicide and assault and the desire to underscore the relationship between compensation for wounding and compensation for *sarhaed*. In Ior, by contrast, whereas the paragraph on status was joined to the *galanas* subtractate, the Value of Limbs is now to be found in a totally different part of the lawbook, at the end of the tractate on the replacement value of animals and items of household equipment. It thus follows directly not after homicide, but after a consideration of what one should pay to replace the sticks one uses to clean a plow.[125]

There is a logic to this, of course: body parts, like plow paraphernalia, can be compensated for with material goods. On the other hand, the same can be said of homicide generally. Because we do not know where precisely the Value of Limbs was situated in the Model Lawbook, we cannot be absolutely certain whether the Ior redactor deliberately moved it to the position it currently occupies or not. However, an intentional resituating of that sort remains a distinct possibility; moreover, the fact that the Ior redactor *did* move the status list into the *galanas* subtractate, but did *not* move the Value of Limbs tractate to which it was traditionally linked, must surely raise the question of why.[126] If it is right to suspect that the redactors of Ior and especially Ior B are deliberately downplaying violence as a theme, then this may help us approach the problem. For the rhetorical impact of situating the Value of Limbs in the position it currently occupies, whether or not it was deliberately moved there by the Ior redactor, is considerable. Contextualizing grievous bodily wounds alongside broken tools and damaged dishes blunts the horror of what is actually being described. The bloody reality of the types of wounds under discussion is almost completely obscured by the lengthy lists of domestic items and animals to which the passage has been appended. Scars and woundings and lopped-off ears cannot be replaced in the same way a blanket might be mended, and yet this almost seems to be the implication of the text. Only in the triads of *Ior* §147—*try guaet ny dywygyr*, *try arperygyl den*, *teyr kreyth gogyuarch*; "three [types of] blood that are not compensated," "three dangerous woundings," and the "three visible scars"—does the language give us any sense of the nature of the violence lurking behind the otherwise matter-of-fact prose.[127] And yet, even these are exceptions which seemingly prove the rule, in that their impact is muted by being followed almost immediately by the regulations governing joint-plowing.

Another aspect of the depiction of violence is the manner in which weapons are discussed in Ior. Weapons are conceptualized consistently in this text as items of equipment to be bestowed, possessed, paid for, or repaired rather than as tools with which violent deeds might be committed.[128] Apart from the provision on the *rhingyll*, for example, the only passages in Ior B relating to spears, swords, and shields are as follows:

> *Ior* 39/2: Ef a dele guneythur reydyeu e llys oll en rat, eythyr try peth: sef yv e rey henne, kant kvllter a pen guaeu a thedyf bvyall kennut.
>
> He (the court smith) ought to make all the necessities of the court free, except for three things: these are those, the rim of a coulter, and the head of a spear and the socket of the fuel-axe.
>
> *Ior* 93/6: Herwyd rey, er alltudyon henne kemeynt ac a dangossont o da pan delhoent y ty e mab eyllt a deleant e gaffael pan elhoent ohanau; ac o chyll dym, e talu udunt, eythyr try peth a deleant y gadu ganthunt ehun dyd a nos: sef eu henne, eu llodreu ac eu kledyueu ac eu menyc.
>
> According to some, those *alltud*s are entitled to have whatever they display by way of goods when they come to the house of an *aillt* ["unfree person"] when they depart from it, and if [they[129]] lose something, to be compensated for them (the lost goods), except for the three things that they ought to keep with them day and night, in other words, their trousers and their swords and their gloves.
>
> *Ior* 141/18–22 (very similar in Cyfn is *WML* 105.6–12): *Gvayu, iiii.* Bua a deudec saeth, iiii.k'. Buyall aryf, ii.k'. Kledyf, o byd breulyf, xii.k'; o byd gurymseyt, xvi.k'; o byd guynseyt, xxiiii.k'. Taryan, viii.k'; o byd kalch llassar neu eurgalch, pedeyr ar ugeynt.
>
> A spear [is valued at] four pence; a bow and twelve arrows, four pence; a battle-axe, two pence. A sword, if it is quern-ground, twelve pence; if it be dark-handled, sixteen pence; if it be white-handled, twenty-four pence. A shield, eight pence; if it be painted in blue or in gold, twenty-four.

Axes, which could serve as weapons as well as domestic tools, are treated similarly. Of the five passages in which axes (*bwyall,* pl. *bwyeill*) appear in Ior B (in addition to those just cited), one pertains to the fuel axe used by the court fueler (*Ior* 37/5); two to the axe due to the king as dues from each villain settlement (*Ior* 43/5, 93/8), and two to the domestic axes used in husbandry (*Ior* 44/10–11, 140/39–41).

The contrast with the manner in which weapons are featured in English lawbooks of the period is striking:

> *Leges Edwardi Confessoris*: Emendationem faciat parentibus uel guerram patiatur, unde Angli prouerbium habebant: "Búge spere of síde ođer bere," quod est dicere: "Lanceam eme de latere aut fer eam."
>
> He shall pay compensation to the relatives or endure a feud, for which the English had the proverb, "*Buge spere of side ođer bere*," that is to say, "Buy the lance from the side or bear it."[130]
>
> Bracton, *De legibus*, II, 383: Videtur ergo quod ordinarius loci sicut archidiaconus vel officialis suus, decanus vel persona, hoc facere possent et deberent, scilicet compellere eum exire, quia gladius debet iuvare gladium et iuris executio non habet iniuriam.
>
> It would seem then that the ordinary of the place, the archdeacon or his official, dean or person, may and ought to do so, that is compel [the wrongdoer] to come out [of sanctuary after forty days], for sword ought to aid sword, nor does the execution of the law constitute a wrong.
>
> Bracton, *De legibus*, II, 32: GLADIUS autem significant defensionem regni et patriæ. Sunt et alii potentes sub rege, qui barones dicuntur, hoc est robur belli.
>
> What the sword signifies. For the sword signifies the defence of the realm and the country. There are other powerful persons called barons, that is *belli robur*, 'the strength of war.'
>
> Bracton, *De legibus*, IV, 327: De capiendo excommunicatum ut sic gladius iuvet gladium.
>
> Of arresting an excommunicate: thus sword aids sword.[131]

Weapons occupy a very different role in English legal texts of the period than they do in the Welsh. In Ior, weapons are passive rather than active, things to be valued rather than used. In the *Leges Edwardi* and Bracton, by contrast, they spark feuds, take offenders out of sanctuary by force, and wage war.

Equally telling is the comparison between the role weapons play in the lawbooks and the manner in which they figure in contemporary Welsh poetry and prose. Weapons are anything but passive in the work of the "Poets of the Princes," for example. The late twelfth-century poet Cynddelw Brydydd Mawr's "Arwyrain Owain Gwynedd," cited here in Joseph Clancy's stirring translation, is fairly typical of the verse of the period:

Oedd cleudaer, oedd claer cleddyf uch gwain
A llinon yng ngnif a llif rhag llain,
Llafn yn llaw a llaw yn lladd pennain,
Llaw ar llafn a'r llafn ar llu Norddmain.

Ardent, shining, was sword above sheath,
And spear in strife, and bloodflow from blade,
Sword held in hand and hand hewing heads,
Hand on sword and the sword on Norman hosts.[132]

Similarly, in Bleddyn Fardd's lament for Llywelyn ap Gruffudd (d. 1282), the slain prince is praised for having been a *gŵr gwaywrudd*, "red-speared man," and a *gẃreiddlafn esgud*, "quick, valiant (literally: manly) sword."[133] And Gwalchmai ap Meilyr (d. 1180), court poet to Owain Gwynedd, speaks of his sword flashing in battle like lightning and of the gleam of gold on his shield (*Llachar fy nghleddyf, lluch ei annwyd—yng nghad / Llewychedig aur ar fy ysgwyd*).[134]

Poetry of this sort was largely authored in praise of prominent Welsh princes for whom success in battle was critical to establishing one's reputation, so it might be argued that the contrast between poetic imagery and that of the laws is only to be expected. However, the phenomenon of depicting weapons and armor in thematically deliberate ways is found elsewhere in the period. A nearly exact parallel to what I am suggesting for Ior can be seen in the Latin life of Gruffudd ap Cynan, which Russell has dated to the mid-twelfth century.[135] Given the up-and-down nature of Gruffudd's political career, and the frequency with which he found himself engaged in armed conflict, one might expect the imagery of this work to be similar to that of the poetry of the period, and indeed, many of the passages are quite gruesome, as we have already seen.[136] However, the manner in which the text depicts Gruffudd's own comportment in war (as opposed to that of his enemies) is considerably more complex than one might have anticipated from a life of a warrior prince. Gruffudd is certainly presented as a heroic leader in battle, a king who rules his people with a "rod of iron" (*populum suum virga ferrea gubernabat*).[137] As a warrior, he is fearless, rushing into battle *non secus ac gigas vel leo cuncto gladio inimicos prosternens,* "just like a giant or a lion laying low enemies with every blow of his sword,"[138] wielding his "death-dealing sword" among the "tightly packed enemy . . . as if he was harvesting traitors and enemies" (*inter confertissimos hostes gladio mortifero quasi metere proditores ac inimicos videtur*).[139]

However—and this is where the deliberate manipulation of images of violence becomes visible—Gruffudd is also depicted as cultivated and gently reared,[140] a ruler who acts humbly with respect to others, a man of peace and builder of churches.[141] In war, he fights singly, a rightful lord betrayed by his enemies and a fighter against incredible odds. He is Agamemnon rather than Achilles,[142] and David hunted by Saul fighting against the overwhelming forces of the Philistines.[143] A notable conceit running throughout the work is that it is Gruffudd's enemies (or occasionally his foreign allies) rather than he himself who go into battle heavily armed. Thus, Robert, warden of the castle of Rhuddlan, is defeated by Gruffudd's forces despite the former's "armoured and helmeted cavalry" (*equites illi loricati galeatique*).[144] Hugh, earl of Chester, garrisons castles in Wales with cavalry, infantry, and archers;[145] Gruffudd rushes alone into the crush of battle so that he might "lay low the French in their armour, their helmets and armed with two-headed axes" (*ut Francos loricatos, galeatos bipennibusque armatos prosterneret*).[146] The king of England, "William of the long sword" (*Willelmus ensis longi rex Angliae*) has companies of cavalry and infantry,[147] while Gruffudd's French enemies are imagined as "more fearful than little women" (*quamvis timidiores mulierculis, loricati, et pro more suo in equis sedentes*) even though they are explicitly said to be mounted and in full armor.[148] Similarly, a single arrow was enough to kill Hugh, earl of Shrewsbury, "though he was in full armour."[149]

Gruffudd's vita thus does not portray him as eschewing violence altogether or conceptualize this much-set-upon prince as never wielding a weapon in pursuit of his rights. However, its author deliberately uses weapons and, even more significantly, a lack of weapons, as a rhetorical device intended to portray Gruffudd as an underdog and would-be man of peace fighting against tremendous odds an enemy more numerous and better armed than he is. When he does wield a weapon—and frequently no weapon at all is specified for him—it is alone against the multitudes; when hostile forces gather against him, they are inevitably holding spears and swords, garbed in helmets and mail, and often mounted to boot. The parallels with the manner in which the Ior redactor manipulates the imagery of warfare are evident, despite the differing goals of these two texts. In Ior, the absence or passivity of the few weapons that are mentioned highlights the peaceful and unified nature of the redactor's idealized vision of Wales. In Gruffudd's biography, they underscore not only the hero's would-be adherence to peace, but his stature as underdog and the magnitude of the challenges facing him.

There are other similarities between these two works. In Ior, the relative absence of conflict and the inactivity of the weapons described in the text parallel the manner in which the redactor depicts the animals of the *gwlad*. As we saw earlier, only a very few wild animals are mentioned; when they do appear, it is made clear that they have already been domesticated or made ready for human use and no longer exist as threatening forces in the *gwlad*. The animal imagery of Gruffudd's vita may seem at first to depart substantially from what we see in the legal texts. In fact, however, the symbolic import of the images employed is almost exactly the same, not least because Gruffudd is so often pictured as asserting his rights from outside a settled position as king. When Gruffudd is hard-pressed from within Gwynedd by attacking forces, for example, he is a stag fleeing hunting dogs or a shepherd whose sheep have been scattered into the wilds: in other words, an animal (or caretaker of animals) of the *gwlad* wrongfully threatened within his own realm.[150] When he attacks from a position of exile, by contrast, he is imagined as a giant or a lion: a ferocious aggressor whose strength will inevitably triumph over those who have presumed to lay claim to his kingdom. At Mynydd Carn, it is Trahaearn, his enemy, who ends up sliced, preserved, and domesticated "like pork turned into bacon," and Gruffudd who pursues the remnant of his enemies through "forests, valleys, marshes and mountains" across the borders of his kingdom.[151] As in the laws, while in possession of his kingdom, Gruffudd is the consummate man of the *gwlad*, defending what is his but otherwise living in peace within its borders. Once ousted from his rightful territory, however, he himself becomes the threat, attacking as a wild creature from outside.

Changing Times

Another way to contextualize the treatment of violence in Ior is to step back from the specifics of homicide and weapons and return to the questions raised earlier about kingship and rule. As we have seen, Gruffudd's vita was not the only prose work of the period concerned with the nature of power in a rapidly changing political world. The goddess of sovereignty remained a familiar conceit in the era of the lawbooks, one to which appeal could be made without fear of incomprehension. However, she was no longer the principal vehicle through which Welshmen of the twelfth and thirteenth centuries imagined what it meant to govern. Nor for that matter was the feasting hall peopled with carousing warriors champing at the bit for war. Gruffudd the historical king may have spent much of his career on the battlefield asserting his power, but his vita is far more concerned to present him as a wise and discerning caretaker of his people than as a rampaging hero. It is surely not accidental that the Ior redactor—who is usually reluctant to expand the traditional framework of the lawbooks with new materials—ends his version of the Laws of Court with a special section laying claim on behalf of the king to financial and jurisdictional prerogatives of a very contemporary nature—albeit often couched in traditional garb.[152]

The shift away from an archaic view of kingship grounded in heroic endeavor or the fertility of the land toward a more recognizably administrative type of rule is a major theme in other literary works of the period. Andrew Welsh speaks of the "new civilization" taking shape after the "terrible destruction" of the Second Branch, for example: "It will not be like the old one, with giant warriors such as Bendigeidfran or violently unpredictable ones such as Efnisien. It is not the warrior Pryderi who frees the land from its spell, but Manawydan, who does it in the process of establishing a new way of life with new values. . . . Manawydan is no warrior-hero but a man of crafts and a man of agriculture. He is also a man of law, as we see in the careful details of his charging the mouse with theft and settling its ransom."[153] Manawydan is not "a mythic hero restoring fertility to nature, and certainly not an epic hero recklessly risking death for the sake of honor"; he uses his wits rather than his sword to ensure the future prosperity of his people.[154] By contrast, Math is a "failed king" by contemporary standards precisely because he "rules by aura rather than by action." He is a virtual "parody of the ancient myth of Celtic kingship," whose reign "exemplifies the inadequacy" of earlier models of kingship.[155] Bendigeidfran, too, provides a negative example of what kings ought to be in the Welsh here and now. His inability to maintain order and keep his own relatives in line leads to a cataclysmic war from which only he and a few followers will return—in McKenna's words, "disturbingly fragmented."[156]

Similar ideas are also visible in another text of the era, the tale of *Peredur vab Efrawc*.[157] As Susan Aronstein has noted, this tale exists both in shorter and longer versions, each of which demonstrates a markedly different stance on the touchy subject of how best to adapt to the newly Anglo-Norman reality of Wales without losing touch with the legacy of the native past. The short version, she argues, embraces the idea of a return to the epic heroism of bygone days—not to prolong or instigate war, but rather for defensive purposes, the policing "of territorial and cultural borders."[158] The longer version, by contrast, rejects "a return to the old ways—symbolized by the feminine otherworld" in favor of "an assertion of a centralized male order—symbolized by Arthur's court, an order that actually represents the true past of Wales." This latter stance is consonant both with the "hybrid cultural and political agenda first advanced by Llewelyn ap Iorwerth, who adopted English political and economic narratives to consolidate power and resources, and the aspirations the native aristocracy of *uchelwyr* who commissioned the Red and White Books as part of their self-appointed task as guardians of Welsh literary culture, a task that did not prevent them from embracing the Anglo-Norman ideal of the good life—a settled and prosperous manor home—made possible by assimilation."[159] If Aronstein is right, one would not be hard-pressed to see a reflection of Ior's footholder in this highly gendered vision of the changing nature of rule in postcolonial Wales: a figure who, like Wales itself, has made the transition from female fertility symbol to male bodyguard of the king.

Helen Fulton suggests that the Four Branches as a whole were intended to function as a type of Prince's Mirror aimed at rulers and *uchelwyr*, modeling both what it meant to be an effective ruler in a newly cosmopolitan world, and the advantages that would accrue to princely followers who consented to serve faithfully under the new dispensation. Her observations on the Four Branches encapsulate almost without need for alteration what also emerges from Ior as the paradigmatic relationship between a ruler and his people: "strong leadership, wise judgment, the importance of good counsel, and a consultative relationship between an overlord and his vassals, between a regional prince and his men."[160] One cannot help but see the similarities here. As in the tales, so also in the lawbooks we are offered a type of rule vested not in archaic notions of sovereignty, nor in the outmoded swagger and vainglory of epic heroism. Rather, we are presented with an aristocracy that defends its borders but does not foment civil war within them, and a court that is united around the body of the ruler. Like Manawydan's realm, the society pictured in Ior is ruled by law and grounded in agriculture rather than violence and war. This is why the booty taken by the *teulu* in its predatory raids is imagined in Ior as always having been taken from the *gorwlad*, an external realm. It is also why the king's body is depicted as essentially immune to injury or violent assault, and why the *penteulu*, though a relative of the king and historically frequently a rival for his power, is imagined as perennially loyal and integrated into the rituals of the court rather than as a potential contender for the crown.[161] In Ior's idealized Wales, lords only plunder realms other than their own.

CONCLUSION

Law and the Imagination

York claims to be the most haunted city in Europe, so when I found myself there one summer with a chance to visit a haunted house on one of its oldest streets, I did not hesitate. I had expected to tour the house in a group with a guide scaring us silly with tales of ghostly apparitions; instead, my companion and I were left entirely on our own to progress through a series of pitch-black rooms guided only by a prerecorded voice. This was not at all what we had bargained for. We did not actually want to see a ghost. And yet there we were, alone in the dark in a house that had reputedly caused experienced ghost-hunters to run screaming into the streets. As the tension mounted, I began taking photos, suspecting—correctly, as it turned out—that the flash on my camera would illuminate our surroundings sufficiently to allow us to see what was actually in there with us. We were in a late medieval house that had clearly been lovingly occupied well into the twentieth century. Blackened oak beams ran the length of the rooms; creaking steps led to once-elegant parlors adorned with faded Victorian murals and colorful tiled fireplaces. In many rooms, faces loomed out of the darkness. African masks, mounted stag-heads, an old baby carriage, even a suit of armor—all had been carefully positioned to suggest to impressionable visitors that they were not alone. I took photo after photo, increasingly aware that what we were experiencing was a performance of a very particular kind. The house as a physical structure might or might not be the site of paranormal activity; the haunted house we were touring, however, owed its existence largely to staging and props designed to reinforce the expectations brought into it by visitors. It took only a simple change in perspective—in this case, the odd flash of light—to reveal the two different realities cohabiting the space: one, an interesting historic house I would have paid money to tour on its own, and the other, its dramatically constructed counterpart, created in large part by the anxieties of those who had come to see it.

I was already thinking about this book at the time I took the tour, and I had been struggling with how to put into words the new ideas I was having about the sources I was working with. Monographs often develop in directions impossible to foresee at the outset. However, this book, more than most, had evolved piecemeal rather than as a focused piece of research. For quite a few years, every subject I tackled seemed always to lead back in the same direction regardless of where it had begun; eventually I could no longer help noticing that what I was producing was more a thematic whole than a series of unrelated projects. Moreover, as I worked, my perspective on the sources was shifting dramatically. Texts I had once thought I knew reasonably well seemed suddenly susceptible to a variety of interpretations, while possibilities that I had never before imagined began to emerge into my line of vision. Even more distressing, many of the anomalies I believed myself to be uncovering seemed distinctly at odds with my earlier preconceptions as to the nature of written Welsh law as a genre. I had always presumed law to be intrinsically more "real" than other contemporary forms of narrative. Medieval redactors themselves kept the laws separate from other forms of *cyfarwyddyd* in the manuscripts, and this seemed to underscore the extent to which they were taken seriously, in their day, as sources of judicial authority.[1] Indeed, many early manuscripts display evidence of being portable and well-thumbed in precisely the manner one would expect had they been frequently carried about by practitioners.[2] Even the fact that one often finds the pleading texts—of all extant legal sources, those most closely associated with thirteenth-century court procedure—appended to the lawbook versions in the manuscripts seemed to emphasize the link between Hywel's book and the world of actual legal practice.[3]

And yet I also did not think that I was imagining what I was finding in my research. It had become clear to me that whatever the Welsh lawbooks may have looked like when they were first written down, whoever had compiled them, and whatever purposes they might have served at that time and in subsequent years, many had become by at least the thirteenth century, and quite possibly earlier, additionally a venue for political writing of a very particular kind. As my research had shown, lawbooks of this period could communicate ideas and opinions as well as information; they could convey outrage and resentment as well as the stability of long usage. Their authors and redactors could and did indulge themselves in humorous asides and scathing parody, playing with themes and tropes and images in a manner that would have seemed very familiar to the storytellers and poets of their day. Ideas about violence, about bodies—male, female, and animal—and about movement across landscapes, both internal and external, informed the lawbooks in much the same way that they did the poetry or the tales of the Mabinogion. For all intents and purposes, law had come, by the time of the Edwardian Conquest, to constitute a form of literature that had far more in common with other types of contemporary narrative than I, at least, had hitherto suspected. And yet, these were also unquestionably legal sources, with all that implies about the attributes traditionally accorded to the body of custom by which societies are governed. How best to reconcile such a paradox?

My experiences in York gave me a language with which to characterize what I was finding in my work. The importance of expectations in shaping what one perceives, the coexistence of disparate and often competing realities in a single locale, the manner in which a simple change in perspective can illuminate otherwise unseen aspects of a familiar venue—all seemed as pertinent to the lawbooks as to the darkened corridors I had toured that day. For what I believe we have in these sources—or in many of them, at least, since it is clear that redactions and manuscripts can differ significantly from one another—is a manner of presentation that resists easy classification into categories like literal or fictional, objective or subjective, true or false. This is political writing of the broadest possible sort—and in this respect fully comparable to other forms of Welsh narrative in this period, which recent scholarship has shown to be anything but hard and fast in terms of boundaries between genres. It is well known that verse frequently acted as a vehicle through which political views could be articulated,[4] and the same is also true of prose. Patricia Malone has pointed recently to the important role played by politically loaded rhetorical conventions even in putatively disinterested genres like biography and historical narrative.[5] K. L. Maund has identified similar concerns with respect to politically oriented charter collections such as the *Liber Landauensis*.[6] Prophecy—secular or ecclesiastical, Galfridian or native in origin—had such a marked political component in the Middle Ages that it has been explicitly characterized as "a type of political literature."[7] Both *Peredur* and *Branwen* actively comment on colonialism and the Anglo-Norman settlement of Wales,[8] and the Four Branches likely functioned as a type of Prince's Mirror designed to educate kings and members of the *uchelwyr* class on the characteristics of good rule. Indeed, the vision of kingship they promoted was, much like that in the Aristotelian-inspired works mentioned in an earlier chapter, a feudal model instructing rulers to rely on the counsel provided by their subjects rather than the theocratic model embraced by, among others, John of Salisbury in the *Policraticus*.[9]

But if we are to include the lawbooks in this broader category of political writing, as I have been arguing throughout this book that we should, if we are to have a hope of accessing the multiple realities inhabiting these texts, then we will need to broaden our thinking in some rather fundamental ways. Significant methodological questions will inevitably arise when we attempt to put these legal sources side by side with other types of narrative sources. Law has a practical aspect to it and claims a type of authority that these other types of texts do not. If it is true that the lawbook authors drew on many of the same ideas and images as we find in the poetry and prose literature, if it is true that some of what we are reading here is as much purposeful fiction as fact, then in what sense ought these sources to be considered law? How ought we to imagine redactors creating and using them, and how ought we as historians to make use of them if—to put it bluntly—we cannot always trust what they say? These are not easy questions, and their potential implications are disturbing. After all, much of what we know about the workings of medieval Welsh society comes from these sources, just as much of our ability to understand allusions in the literature of the period rests on knowledge gleaned largely from their pages. How then to proceed?

These are questions that can be tackled on a variety of levels. From the strictly methodological point of view, it seems important to note that even if one accepts that the lawbooks constituted real law in their day, and that judges were encouraged to defend controversial verdicts by referring to them, one still does not have to acknowledge as a necessary conclusion that judges were bound to enforce everything in a lawbook or decide all cases in exactly the same way in accordance with it. If nothing else, medieval ideas about the manner in which matters like social status, gender, or states of anger or enmity ought—quite properly, and not as a matter of corruption or injustice—to influence the progression and outcome of disputes would suggest that cases were likely to be decided very differently regardless of what the written law said.[10] A written text can be regarded as generally authoritative even if some sections of it must be read differently (and as differently authoritative) from others; similarly, the fact that a written text is regarded as authoritative need not mean that it will inevitably be regarded as the only, or the best, or even a relevant, source of authority in a given dispute. Presumptions to the contrary reflect a modern rather than medieval view of written law; they are ideas that derive more from our world than from theirs.

Another helpful way to think about such matters is to think further about the processes that lay behind the composition of our extant texts and about what fact and fiction might mean in the medieval Welsh context. Even apart from the many issues on which historians continue to disagree—the likely date(s) of origin of the lawbooks, when they first took on the form they have today, how they usually circulated and became known as texts, who revised and redacted them and at what stages and how often, and so on—there are inconsistencies among the various versions that must complicate any notion of legal fact considerably. Even the briefest of glances at the materials discussed in this book reveals a multitude of contradictions. The award given in Cyfn to the eloping woman (the steer with the greased tail) is instead assigned in Ior and the Latin and Bleg texts to the false virgin.[11] In Cyfn (and certain of the Latin texts), by contrast, the false virgin gets nothing at all.[12] Similarly, Latin A, B, and E stipulate three beasts with horns and ears equal in length for a woman who is slept with openly for three days and three nights and subsequently abandoned; Latin A awards the same to a woman who elopes, or who acts on her own without the involvement of her kindred.[13] Ior agrees with this with respect to the woman who elopes, but has a slightly different tradition regarding the woman slept with openly for three nights, demanding three steers in ascending order of value as payment for each night.[14] Cyfn, many of the Latin texts, and Bleg differentiate the payment to be made to an eloping woman according to status, with a *breyr*'s daughter receiving six steers, and a *taeog*'s three.[15]

Of course, some of these differences may reflect regional variations in custom. Latin D and Bleg acknowledge, for example, that Venedotian practices regarding the eloping woman differ from those of the men of the south.[16] Similarly, some discrepancies among redaction traditions may be attributable to differences in textual preservation or patterns of transmission: the passages on the Seven Bishops' Houses and the provisions from the early Irish canons are clear cases in point.[17] It was also apparently quite common for clauses to be added to or omitted from one redaction but not another, or phrased in different terms, or moved from one place to another.[18] And of course, there is no reason why the explanation behind one contradiction or inconsistency must be the same as for the next. However, rationales like these do not seem to adequately explain a lot of the differences we have been discussing in this work. In the Laws of Court, for example, some of the most symbolically evocative figures or gifts appear either in one lawbook version only (e.g., the eyes given to the watchman and the necks to the fueler in Ior,[19] the spleens and rectums assigned to the porter in Cyfn[20]), or in certain manuscripts only of a given version (e.g., the tongues given to the judge in Cyfn V and W[21]). In at least two instances, a payment appears in two redactions but not in the rest, and these pairings of redactions are not always the same. Thus, the heads and feet of the cattle slaughtered in the kitchen go to the smith in Cyfn, the Latin texts, and Bleg, but not in Ior;[22] the hearts of animals killed in the kitchen go to the falconer in Ior and Cyfn, but not in the Latin texts or Bleg.[23] Moreover, it is not uncommon for the political ideas implicit in a particular narrative structure to be hinted at in one redaction, but only fully developed in another. While the queen is associated with the private sphere in Cyfn, she is not entirely relegated to it as she is in Ior, and while Cyfn's division of goods by divorcing spouses is not entirely pragmatic, the passage is not yet clearly a full-blown condemnation of divorce.[24]

Discrepancies like these seem less like regional variations in custom or individual floating passages than a different order of textual fluidity altogether. What they most closely resemble are the tropes one finds in more forthrightly literary compositions—recognized narrative structures that authors might choose to adapt or ignore depending on their larger purposes for their works. To return briefly to the haunted-house metaphor: images can function interchangeably within a narrative if approached within a particular and known frame of reference. An empty cradle in a darkened corner or an eerie mask above a squeaking staircase can evoke similar feelings of terror in a person assessing them within a given context, such as a ghost story or a haunted house. In most circumstances, it will not really matter which item is chosen—if the appeal is broad enough, and the referent sufficiently well known, either one will do the job. Moreover, when the context in which these items are being interpreted changes, the range of responses changes as well. The same empty cradle that can trigger fears of demon babies or homicidal dolls in one setting can evoke profound feelings of grief and loss in another. Similarly, an animal mask that in a horror movie would conjure up fears of a devouring demonic spirit can be deployed in an English cozy as a symbol of armchair colonialism and white game hunters in Africa. The meaning of the object in a given context is dependent not only on the nature of the object itself, but on the manner in which it is presented, the associations it is designed to evoke, and the resonance it has for onlookers—which resonance itself might be shaped by factors external to the immediate situation.

It may seem as though, with such musings, we have strayed some distance from our appointed topic. However, I would suggest that these insights may provide us with additional ways to read our sources and gain access to the legal truths expressed in them. Perhaps for the lawbook redactors we are discussing, the point was often less to record who actually would get what in compensation or payment for services than it was to evoke a particular frame of reference. The frame within which items were to be interpreted mattered more than the individual objects themselves because it was within the frame that the deeper meaning of the text was carried forward. Possible examples of such interpretative frames abound in the materials we have surveyed to this point: the idea of the court as a fragmented body, the notion of internal and external landscapes as metaphors for safety and peril, the equation of maleness with the judicious exercise of authority and of femaleness and childishness with weakness or injustice. There were literal frames as well: recognized cultural traditions of sexualized social ridicule as a behavioral corrective, for example, that could be evoked or enlarged upon as circumstances dictated. Most importantly for our purposes, as in the haunted house with which we began, the individual components of these frames would have been to a large degree—albeit also presumably within limits—interchangeable. Innovation would thus have been possible at any stage of the redaction process, from the itemizing of individual details to the internal structuring of tractates and the organizing of the lawbook itself. The ideas implicit in the organic analogy, for example, could be evoked in a variety of ways, from the introduction by Ior of eyes as a gift for a watchman,[25] to the association of skins with the steward and the doorkeeper[26] or the giving of stomachs to the *maer*.[27] Similarly, the ideological landscapes around which the lawbooks are structured could be evoked by having characters move (or not move) within certain spaces, or restricting violence to particular venues only, or reading wild animals out of a realm altogether.

Such a process would explain much about what our extant texts look like; it would also broaden our understanding as to what concepts like "truth" might mean in the lawbook context. Was it literally true that the watchman received eyes as his reward from the court or the porter the rectums of cattle slaughtered in the kitchen? On one level, this is not inconceivable as a historical practice. Any inclination to reject such an idea out of hand because of its grotesque nature must be resisted as being rooted more in modern squeamishness than in medieval attitudes toward animal body parts. Performative gift-giving and humorous exchange were obviously very real parts of courtly and judicial life in this period, and it is all but impossible from this distance to distinguish the performative from the strictly textual. Those eyes and rectums might well have been real, at least once upon a time. On another level, however, there may be different notions of truth operating here. The idea of a porter piling up rectums or a watchman wrangling hundreds of cattle eyeballs into submission could be totally fictional as an actual practice even while the political ideal this conceit was intended to express—the notion of the court as a unified body working together in the interests of a righteous prince—was anything but. We are dealing here with smaller and larger truths.

Moreover, when one adds into the mix the use of the laws as a venue for political protest, questions of fact and fiction get even more complicated. It was evidently a cultural trope to equate femininity in an aristocratic male with injustice and the reversal of hierarchy, just as it was to equate femininity in a queen sitting quietly in her chamber with politics properly conducted. Embedded in such associations are a whole host of beliefs not merely about maleness and authority, but about court and kingdom as a form of household, about fertility as an indication of rightful rule, and about the feminine as a source of disorder. So when we read that sergeants were to carry their spears high on the shaft up near the spearpoint, or receive a single quernstone after the death of a tenant, or dress nonsensically in winter, how then are we to understand this? When we hear about porters pulling short sticks out of carts of wood as they pass through the gate and being rewarded with tailless steers, do we believe that this actually happened? Are these provisions reflecting truth in any meaningful sense? Again, from a strictly literal perspective, who knows? It is slightly easier to imagine a porter profiting from kindling than it is a sergeant prancing about in his underwear during the winter as he goes to collect his dues. But from a perspective that prioritizes the larger political truth being expressed over the question of whether these particular details are historically accurate, then yes, absolutely. There are different types of reality residing in these texts. To see one instead of the other, or to assume that truths and falsehoods of this sort cannot logically coexist, does a disservice to what these texts and their authors were all about.

So what, then, are the implications for us as historians, as persons who have no choice but to rely on legal sources for information about the past? First, from a strictly pragmatic point of view, it would be wise to stop using the laws as a way to test the historical accuracy of the medieval Welsh tales. The law is not an immutable standard against which to measure literary texts; in fact, in most cases of similarity or overlapping content, we may never know which came first or who borrowed what from whom. The question is unlikely to be that simple anyway. As Paul Russell's study of the regalia shows, one might be able to distinguish simpler from more complex articulations of a given concept (or object, in this case) and thus track the evolution of an idea over time and across different genres. One might even be able to suggest a line of development that would make sense of the intentions of the authors in question.[28] However, in the absence of some sort of textual smoking gun, direct borrowing and a strictly linear line of development would be almost impossible to prove. Even the closest of parallels might reflect nothing more than authors working in different narrative genres drawing on similar cultural traditions. This might strike some as frustrating, but I would argue that in fact it enriches rather than diminishes our sense of the relationship between the legal and the literary in medieval Wales. For we are dealing here not only with familial connections, but with actual similarities in narrative intent and technique: the willingness to speak in symbols, to make use of shared tropes, and to imagine the intersection between the natural and political worlds in particular ways. The question going forward ought to be less that of who took what from whom, than of how authors in all these narrative traditions made use of the symbolic vocabularies available to them.

Such a perspective leaves open the question of why the lawbooks were such a popular venue for the type of political commentary we have been describing and whether legal sources conveyed meaning in ways that were different from other prose genres. In part, the use of the lawbooks as a venue for the expression of these ideas likely reflects the concerns of those for and by whom they were authored. Basic concepts like inheritance, divorce and legitimacy, the nature of kingship, relations with the outside world, and Welsh identity itself—all were changing rapidly and all were issues in which the lawyers themselves had clearly vested interests. There were also perceived and long-standing connections between law and identity and between the right to adjudicate and the right to rule.[29] In an era in which sovereignty of all kinds, national and regional, appeared to be under threat, and in which the idea of the nation was itself in flux, a genre that was so intimately connected to these issues would surely have seemed an especially powerful forum for political expression. But in the end, it may have been the lawbooks' claims to an association with Hywel that made them particularly appealing as a vehicle for *uchelwyr* concerns about threats to traditional patterns of rule. For regardless of the role these texts might have played in court, regardless—or perhaps even because—of their importance to the education of future jurists, it is impossible for them not to have constituted political documents in the context in which they were produced. In this they differed sharply not only from the tales, but from other contemporary legal texts not associated with Hywel, like the *Llyfr Cynghawsedd.* Within the covers of Hywel's book, complaints against the oppressive extension of princely power could be—quite literally in the case of the sergeant—cloaked in the exemplary garb of the past.

Second, it would be useful when confronted with a disagreement among legal traditions not simply to assume that we are dealing with floating passages, regional variations, or issues of age or textual preservation. Obviously such things do matter. There are chronological layers within the lawbooks, and there are obvious indications that redactors often differed in the extent of their access to particular bodies of materials. There were clearly also differences in custom and judicial practice in the various parts of Wales—indeed, as we have seen, the texts themselves often alert us to these.[30] We hear about divergences in views among judges as to what the law ought actually to be,[31] and occasionally we even hear about rulers changing the law, although this is relatively rare.[32] However, despite all these very real factors to take into account, we should never close our eyes to other possibilities. Even a tractate composed largely of old law can be edited to make it relevant to modern-day controversies. Moreover, lawbooks can reflect reality without necessarily reproducing it. We know, for example, that the porter is said to get the rectums in Cyfn, but the money for removing cattle skins in Ior.[33] Rather than trying to figure out which is right, or concluding that traditions must have varied on this between north and south, we ought to at least consider the idea that these passages might be addressing something altogether different from what purports to be their main subject. For it may be that implicit in both provisions is the organic analogy as a political ideal: the notion of the court as an animal entity, a unified system into which access from outside is restricted by command of the prince. One version communicates this by evoking the image of the skin holding everything together, while the other focuses instead on entrances and exits. Both may even be attempting to also convey the idea that princely rule is not all it could be. Given the cultural potency of excrement as a symbol, this is more certain in Cyfn than it is in Ior. But the possibility is there in them both: in one case, the lord's representative expels excrement from the system; in another he literally fleeces those who would enter it. Neither agrees with the other from a literal point of view, and yet both could be saying the same thing.

In fact, it may even be useful as a practical rule of thumb for scholars tackling the Welsh lawbooks to pay particular attention to passages that appear on the surface to be bizarre or out of keeping with the rest. Why is the sergeant dressed like he is? Why do so many of the prince's officers act in ridiculous ways, and why is his court imagined as full of protruding tongues and oddly detached body parts? Why does the judge sleep on the king's seat cushion? Why are so many of the objects mentioned in the divorce process shaped like phalluses? Why is the lawbook as a whole so relatively bloodless? Why do violent events seem to take place only in the *gorwlad* in some redactions and why is there no mention of the March? And why, of course, might a baker or a laundress throw her tools into the air? Usually, scholars have either ignored such peculiarities altogether or interpreted them as leftovers from a different and more primitive time. Such a tendency is, of course, quite understandable. It is difficult to know what to do with such oddities anyway, and the sorts of interpretations that might be put forward to explain them can easily end up sounding as outlandish as the passages themselves. There is simply no way to attempt to discuss a grouping of bovine rectums without risking something of one's scholarly dignity. Scholarship, like law, is a serious business, and it takes a foolhardy person indeed to venture voluntarily into such perilous realms. But it is a primary argument of this book that there is no necessary conflict between imaginative writing and a seriousness of purpose. In a culture like that of medieval Wales, in which ridicule was a recognized form of social sanction, and in which there already existed a rich tradition of texts communicating simultaneously on a variety of levels, we will miss a great deal if we insist on texts "meaning" in only one way. The language of symbols was already a powerful language of political critique, and humor and whimsy were already being used to call out the trespasses of the great in ways that more straightforward forms of attack could not. Our challenge as scholars is to read in ways that allow us to fully get whatever jokes these authors might be telling.

Such reflections return us to the question of imagination with which we began. Some of what has been proposed here may strike readers as completely preposterous, or as a manner of treating the law that is inherently disrespectful and wrong. Law and literature may seem too different as genres to be amalgamated in this way; interpretative approaches adopted by literary scholars may seem ill-adapted to historical sources and problems. This is certainly a defensible point of view: a manner of reading that has its grounding in tradition and long usage. However, that it is the only or inevitably most fruitful manner of accessing sources from the past is an idea with which I must respectfully disagree. Like the other forms of contemporary narrative we have considered—tales, chronicles, hagiographical accounts, poetry—the lawbooks had their origins in particular places and times. All were authored and redacted by stakeholders in a rapidly changing political world who were themselves united to one another by the closest of personal and cultural ties. It would be surprising indeed had these authors not shared similar symbolic lexicons or evinced a similar regard for the use of humor and sexuality in pursuit of their goals. For us as scholars to show similar breadth in approaching these texts seems to me to be only common sense. Does this mean that every section of every lawbook version will have a meaning larger than it purports on the surface to have? Certainly not. But does it mean that we as readers must always be attuned to the possibility that the text before us is more complex than it appears to be, and that we must be prepared to use all the tools in our interpretative arsenal to try to approach it? I believe so. What we have in the Welsh lawbooks is an invitation to use our own imaginations as creatively as the redactors used theirs.

ABBREVIATIONS

ALW	*Ancient Laws and Institutes of Wales.* Ed. Aneurin Owen. London: Record Commission, 1841. This was published in both single- and double-volume forms, so references are to book.chapter.paragraph as delineated by Owen.
AWR	*The Acts of Welsh Rulers, 1120–1283*. Ed. Huw Pryce. Cardiff: University of Wales Press, 2005.
BBCS	*Bulletin of the Board of Celtic Studies*
Bleg	Blegywryd Redaction of the Welsh laws. See *Bleg* for one version.
Bleg	*Cyfreithiau Hywel Dda yn ôl Llyfr Blegywryd*. Ed. Stephen J. Williams and J. Enoch Powell. 2nd ed. Cardiff: University of Wales Press, 1961. References are to page.line.
ByT (*RBH*)	*Brut y Tywysogyon or The Chronicle of the Princes: Red Book of Hergest Version*. Ed. Thomas Jones. Cardiff: University of Wales Press, 1955.
CBT	*Cyfres Beirdd y Tywysogion*. Gen. ed. R. Geraint Gruffydd. For volumes referred to, see individual titles. Poems referred to frequently are also cited separately in the bibliography.
CCC	R.R. Davies. *Conquest, Coexistence, and Change: Wales 1063–1415*. Oxford: Clarendon Press, 1987.
CLP	*Celtic Law Papers Introductory to Welsh Medieval Law and Government. Studies Presented to the International Commission for the History of Representative and Parliamentary Institutions*, 42. Ed. Dafydd Jenkins. Brussels: Les Éditions de la Librairie Encyclopédique, 1973.
CMCS	*Cambridge/Cambrian Medieval Celtic Studies*
Col	*Llyfr Colan*. Ed. Dafydd Jenkins. Cardiff: University of Wales Press, 1963. References are to numbered provisions as delineated by Jenkins.

Cyfn Cyfnerth Redaction of the Welsh laws. See *WML* for one version.

DwCol *Damweiniau Colan: Llyfr y Damweiniau yn ôl Llawysgrif Peniarth 30*. Ed. Dafydd Jenkins. Aberystwyth: Cymdeithas Lyfrau Ceredigion, 1973. References are to numbered provisions as delineated by Jenkins.

EIWK *Early Irish and Welsh Kinship*. By T. M. Charles-Edwards. Oxford: Oxford University Press, 1993.

GPC *Geiriadur Prifysgol Cymru*. Ed. R. J. Thomas et al. 1st ed. Cardiff: University of Wales Press, 1952–2002. 2nd ed. Ed. G. A. Bevan et al. Cardiff: University of Wales Press, 2003.

Ior *Llyfr Iorwerth*. Ed. Aled Rhys Wiliam. Cardiff: University of Wales Press, 1960. References are to section/sentence.

Ior Iorwerth Redaction of the Welsh laws. For one version, see *Ior*.

LAL *Lawyers and Laymen: Studies in the History of Law Presented to Professor Dafydd Jenkins on His Seventy-Fifth Birthday Gŵyl Ddewi 1986*. Ed. T. M. Charles-Edwards, Morfydd E. Owen, and D. B. Walters. Cardiff: University of Wales Press, 1986. References are either to article and page number or, with respect to primary texts, to version, section/numbered provision, page number.

Lat Latin tradition of the Welsh Laws, comprising Lat A, Lat B, Lat C, Lat D, and Lat E. Lat A has been translated in *Latin Redaction A of the Law of Hywel*. Trans. Ian Fletcher. Pamffledi Cyfraith Hywel. Aberystwyth: Canolfan Uwchefrydiau Cymreig a Cheltaidd Prifysgol Cymru, 1986.

LlPom *Llawysgrif Pomffred: An Edition and Study of Peniarth MS 259B*. Ed. Sara Elin Roberts. Leiden: Brill, 2011.

LT *The Legal Triads of Medieval Wales*. Ed. Sara Elin Roberts. Cardiff: University of Wales Press, 2007. References are to page and numbered provision as delineated by the editor.

LTMW *The Law of Hywel Dda: Law Texts from Medieval Wales Translated and Edited*. Ed. Dafydd Jenkins. Welsh Classics, vol. 2. Llandysul: Gomer Press, 1986.

LTWL *The Latin Texts of the Welsh Laws*. Ed. Hywel Emanuel. Cardiff: University of Wales Press, 1967. References are to version, page.line.

Mabinogi *The Mabinogi: A Book of Essays*. Ed. C. W. Sullivan III. New York: Garland, 1996.

MPW	*Medieval Prince of Wales: The Life of Gruffudd ap Cynan*. Ed. D. Simon Evans. Lampeter: Llanerch Enterprises, 1990.
MWM	*Medieval Welsh Manuscripts*. Ed. Daniel Huws. 2000. Reprint, Cardiff: University of Wales Press and the National Library of Wales, 2002.
PKM	*Pedeir Keinc y Mabinogi*. Ed. Ifor Williams. 1930. Reprint, Cardiff: University of Wales Press, 1975. References are to page.line.
TCC	*Tair Colofn Cyfraith. The Three Columns of Law in Medieval Wales: Homicide, Theft and Fire.* Ed. T. M. Charles-Edwards and Paul Russell. Bangor: Cymdeithas Hanes Cyfraith Cymru, 2005. References are either to article and page number or, with respect to primary texts, to version, section/numbered provision, page number.
Tome	*Tome: Studies in Medieval Celtic History and Law in Honour of Thomas Charles-Edwards.* Ed. Fiona Edmonds and Paul Russell. Woodbridge: Boydell Press, 2011.
WKC	*The Welsh King and His Court.* Ed. T. M. Charles-Edwards, Morfydd E. Owen, and Paul Russell. Cardiff: University of Wales Press, 2000. References are either to article and page number or, with respect to primary texts, to version, section/numbered provision, page number.
WLMA	*Welsh Law in Medieval Anglesey: British Library Harleian MS 1796 (Latin C).* Ed. Paul Russell. Cambridge: Seminar Cyfraith Hywel, 2011. References are either to article and page number or, with respect to primary texts, to section/numbered provision, page number.
WLW	*The Welsh Law of Women: Studies Presented to Professor Daniel A. Binchy on His Eightieth Birthday.* Ed. Dafydd Jenkins and Morfydd E. Owen. Cardiff: University of Wales Press, 1980. References are either to article and page number or, with respect to primary texts, to version, section/numbered provision, page number.
WML	*Welsh Medieval Law.* Ed. A. W. Wade-Evans. Oxford: Clarendon Press, 1909. Reprint, Aalen: Scientia, 1979. References are to page.line.
ZCP	*Zeitschrift für celtisiche Philologie*

NOTES

INTRODUCTION

1. *Ior* 38/3, and see Pryce, *Native Law*, 163–203, on secular and ecclesiastical sanctuary.

2. *Ior* 41/2.

3. Porsdam, "Doing What Comes Naturally, 496; Brooks, "Law, Literature," 61.

4. Weisberg, "Law-Literature Enterprise"; Porsdam, "Doing What Comes Naturally," 503.

5. J. S. Peters, "Law, Literature, and the Vanishing Real," 83.

6. Dolin, *Critical Introduction*, 10–11.

7. Binder, "Law-as-Literature Trope," 64–67.

8. Following Robert Weisberg, "Law-Literature Enterprise"; Page, "Place of Law and Literature." Works that have helped me in my thinking about these issues include Alford and Seniff, *Literature and Law*; Cormack, "Practicing Law and Literature"; Davenport, *Medieval Narrative*; Dworkin, "Law as Interpretation"; Firth Green, *Crisis of Truth*; Firth Green, "Literature and Law"; Firth Green, "Nede ne hath"; Fish, "Don't Know Much"; Kahn and Hutson, *Rhetoric and Law*; and J. White, *Heracles' Bow*.

9. Steiner and Barrington, *Letter of the Law*, 2.

10. Bloch, *Medieval French Literature*.

11. W. I. Miller, *Bloodtaking and Peacemaking*, 45–47 and 231.

12. S. D. White, "Ambiguity of Treason"; S. D. White, "Prosecuting and Proving"; and S. D. White, "Protection, Warranty, and Vengeance."

13. Menuge, *Medieval English Wardship*; Marvin, *Hunting Law*. For additional topics, see Dunn, "Language of Ravishment"; Pencak, *Conflict of Law*; E. Peters, *Shadow King*; and Burgwinkle, *Sodomy, Masculinity*.

14. J. B. White, "Judicial Opinion and the Poem."

15. Gewirtz, "Narrative and Rhetoric," 4; see also Weisberg and Barricelli, "Literature and the Law," 150.

16. Goodrich, *Law in the Courts of Love*, 112.

17. Sheen and Hutson, *Literature, Politics and Law*, 2.

18. Porsdam, "Doing What Comes Naturally," 497.

19. The father of the law and literature movement is generally held to be James Boyd White, *Legal Imagination*. An excellent bibliography and general introduction is Dolin, *Critical Introduction*; a fair sampling of the debate to date can be found in Ledwon, ed., *Law and Literature*. See particularly on the contrary side the reservations expressed by Posner (Ledwon, *Law and Literature*, 61–89), and Posner, *Law and Literature*. Very similar is Thomas, "Reflections," 533.

20. For example, Hibbitts, "'Coming to Our Senses'"; Stacey, *Dark Speech.*

21. Firth Green, "Medieval Literature and Law," 407; and see also R. West, "Economic Man and Literary Woman," 134.

22. Brooks, "Law as Narrative and Rhetoric," 14–17. Farber and Sherry also use "movement": "Legal Storytelling," 38.

23. Gewirtz, "Narrative and Rhetoric," 3.

24. Dolin, *Critical Introduction*, 10–11.

25. Despite complaints about Bacon similarly "bracketing off the medieval centuries as unworthy of notice": Dolin, *Critical Introduction*, 75.

26. Firth Green, "Medieval Literature and Law," 408–10.

27. Menuge, *Medieval English Wardship*, 21. Especially valuable is the explanation on p. 22 of his use of the word "fiction."

28. Menuge, *Medieval English Wardship*, 17.

29. Gravdal, *Ravishing Maidens*, 18–19. See also Sheen and Hutson, *Literature, Politics and Law.*

30. Alford, "Literature and Law in Medieval England"; Firth Green, "Medieval Law and Literature"; Steiner and Barrington, *Letter of the Law*, 1; Visconsi, *Lines of Equity.*

31. Firth Green, "Medieval Literature and Law," 407.

32. Steiner and Barrington, *Letter of the Law*, 1–2; Steiner, *Documentary Culture.*

33. Marvin, *Hunting Law*, 15.

34. Gravdal, *Ravishing Maidens*, 131–40; see also Hanawalt, "Whose Story Was This?"

35. Gravdal, *Ravishing Maidens*, 135, 140.

36. Alford, "Literature and Law in Medieval England," 941–42.

37. Habermann, "'She Has That in Her Belly,'" 101.

38. Menuge, *Medieval English Wardship*, 21.

39. Wormald, *Making of English Law.*

40. O'Brien, *God's Peace*, 4. Other parts of the lawbook speak to twelfth-century debates about custom versus the will of the king: O'Brien, *God's Peace*, 33–35. Rosemarie McGerr's recent study of a fifteenth-century manuscript of the "Statutes of England" shows the "work" a legal manuscript might do and the rhetorical strategies it might share with medieval manuscripts in other genres: *Lancastrian Mirror*, 1–2.

41. Wormald, *Making of English Law*, 480. Wormald's essay on early medieval law remains one of his most influential pieces: "*Lex Scripta*," 1–43.

42. Pollard, *Imagining Robin Hood*, 57–81.

43. Tardif, "'Mistery' of Robin Hood." See also Keen, *Outlaws*; Holt, *Robin Hood*; Knight, *Complete Study*; Knight, *Mythic Biography*; and H. Phillips, *Robin Hood.*

44. Pollard, *Imagining Robin Hood*, 80–81.

45. *Giraldi Cambrensis Opera, Itinerarium Cambriae.*

46. Douglas, *Leviticus as Literature*; see also Bartor, *Reading Law.*

47. See Goodrich above, *Law in the Courts of Love*, 112; and Gravdal, *Ravishing Maidens*, 140.

48. S. E. Roberts, *LT*, 1; S. E. Roberts, "Iorwerth Triads," 155–64.

49. Owen, '*Meddygon Myddfai*," 232–33. See also her distinction between "technical" and "literary" with respect to the early legal text *Excerpta de Libris Romanorum et Francorum* in Owen, "*Excerpta*," *TCC*, 174.

50. Owen, "Y Cyfreithiau—(1) and (2)," 220. See also, on Irish law, L. Breatnach, "Law," 116; Kelly, *Early Irish Farming*, 8–9; and Kelly, *Guide to Early Irish Law*, 237–38.

51. There are exceptions: J. B. White, *Legal Imagination*; Sheen and Hutson, *Literature, Politics and Law*, 2.

52. Firth Green, "Medieval Literature and Law," 407.

53. Marvin, *Hunting Law*, 4–5.

54. Even while speaking in terms of "law-codes as 'literature'" (Wormald, *Making of English Law*, 431).

55. Steiner and Barrington, *Letter of the Law*, 10–11.

56. Goodrich, *Law in the Courts of Love*, 97.

57. R. R. Davies, *First English Empire*, 113–41. I owe the image of the "traveler" to this work.

58. Fulton, "Class and Nation," 191–212.

59. *Registrum Epistolarum Fratris Johannis Peckham*, letter 66 (1:77–78, October 20, 1279).

60. Barrell and Davies, "Land, Lineage, and Revolt," 39–45; Jacobs, "Animadversions," 54–57; and, for post-Conquest relationships, Barrell and Brown, "Settler Community." Dower traditions were also in flux: Richards, *Welsh Noblewomen*, 59–94, 152–80.

61. Many of the manuscript complexities are outlined by Russell in "Scribal (In)competence," and Russell, "Scribal (In)consistency."

62. See, for example, R. R. Davies, "Status of Women"; and Stephenson, "Laws of Court." Earlier studies were more confident about the laws as a source for institutional history: T. P. Ellis, *Welsh Tribal Law*.

63. R. R. Davies, "Status of Women," *WLW*, 93–94.

64. See, for example, Benveniste, *Vocabulaire*; Puhvel, *Comparative Mythology*; Mallory, *In Search of the Indo-Europeans*; Watkins, *How to Kill a Dragon*; Mallory and Adams, *Oxford Introduction to Proto-Indo-European*; M. E. West, *Indo-European Poetry*; Fortson, *Indo-European Language*.

65. With the exception of Rawlinson B 502 (early twelfth century), medieval Irish law manuscripts date from the fourteenth through the sixteenth century and medieval Welsh from the thirteenth through the sixteenth century: Kelly, *Guide to Early Irish Law*, 225–31; Charles-Edwards, *Welsh Laws*, 100–102.

66. See particularly Thurnseysen, "Celtic Law," and Binchy, "Linguistic and Historical Value"; Binchy, "Linguistic and Legal Archaisms"; Binchy, "Celtic Suretyship"; and Binchy, "Celtic Legal Terms." Similar questions have been raised about the tales, although there is much disagreement on this issue. Hamp, "Mabinogi and Archaism"; Koch, "Some Suggestions"; Hemming, "Ancient Tradition"; and Hutton, "Medieval Welsh Literature."

67. Most notably, *EIWK*; Charles-Edwards, "Nau Kynywedi Teithiauc"; Charles-Edwards, "Some Celtic Kinship Terms"; Charles-Edwards, "Heir-Apparent"; Stacey, *Road to Judgment*; and McAll, "Normal Paradigms."

68. Sims-Williams, "Celtomania and Celtoscepticism"; Sims-Williams, "Celtic Civilization"; and Sims-Williams, "Post-Celtoscepticism."

69. Sims-Williams, "Celtomania and Celtoscepticism," 34; see also Sims-Williams, *Irish Influence*.

70. Pryce, "Prologues," 167. Excellent introductions to the lawbooks include D. Jenkins, *Cyfraith Hywel*, and D. Jenkins, "Medieval Welsh Idea of Law."

71. Charles-Edwards, *Welsh Laws*, 26–37, 68–86; Charles-Edwards, *Wales and the Britons*, 268–72.

72. Pryce, "Lawbooks and Literacy"; Pryce, "Context and Purpose"; Harding, "Legislators, Lawyers," 249; R. R. Davies, "Peoples," 8.

73. Charles-Edwards, *Wales and the Britons*, 270–71.

74. Scholars have not yet settled on a single term to use in describing these groups and their relationship both to their constituent manuscripts and to the legal tradition as a whole. This is due in part to the fact that the nature of the groups themselves varies considerably, Cyfn manuscripts being a much looser textual family than Ior, for example. Sometimes Ior, Cyfn, and Bleg are referred to as "versions" or "Versions" (e.g., Charles-Edwards, *Welsh Laws*, 26); sometimes as "redactions" or "Redactions" (e.g., Paul Russell, "Arrangement and Development," *TCC*, 60; Pryce, *Native Law*, 5); sometimes as "groups" (e.g., Jenkins, "Excursus," *WKC*, 11); and sometimes as "traditions" (e.g., Charles-Edwards, *Wales and the Britons*, 269). Often one will see these terms being used interchangeably, or at least side by side (e.g., S. E. Roberts, *LT*, 2–3; Jenkins, "Excursus," *WKC*, 12; Stacey, "Archaic Core," *LAL*, 17, etc.). I will draw on all of these, but will make most frequent use of "redaction" and "redactor" because these terms seem best to capture what I believe to be the activist role taken by jurists and scribes in revising and reshaping their materials. At some points, I will speak of the "Ior (or Bleg or Cyfn) redactor" as though only a single person was involved along the way. This is a shorthand term of convenience, however—it seems almost certain that while the original Ior redaction may well have been the work of Iorwerth ap Madog, the various lawbook versions extant today were reworked to some degree by a variety of redactors or scribes.

75. Exceptions include Charles-Edwards, "*Cynghawsedd*"; S. E. Roberts, "Law Texts"; Stacey, "Learning to Plead"; and Stacey, "Legal Writing."

76. Charles-Edwards, *Wales and the Britons*, 269 (*llyfr* means "book," so that *Llyfr Iorwerth* means the "Book of Iorwerth," *Llyfr Cyfnerth*, the "Book of Cyfnerth," and so on); see also Pryce, *Native Law*, 17–36; and S. E. Roberts, *LT*, 1–38.

77. I have chosen additionally in this work to use the italicized versions of these abbreviations—*Ior*, *Bleg*—as shorthand for the currently standard editions of these works; for details, see the List of Abbreviations.

78. Sigla provided by Charles-Edwards in *Welsh Laws*, 100–102, and see fuller description of the Ior texts in Charles-Edwards, "'Iorwerth' Text," *LAL*, 137, and of the Cyfn texts in Owen, "'Cyfnerth' Text," *LAL*, 179–82.

79. A full listing of these sigla and the manuscripts they represent (up to c. 1500) can be found in Charles-Edwards, *Welsh Laws*, 99–102.

80. Huws, "Descriptions," *WKC*, 418; Charles-Edwards, *Welsh Laws*, 43.

81. Charles-Edwards, *Welsh Laws*, 43.

82. Jenkins, "Excursus," *WKC*, 13; and see S. E. Roberts, *LlPom*, 10–20.

83. Huws, "Descriptions," *WKC*, 420.

84. Emanuel, "Book of Blegywryd"; Russell, "Arrangement and Development," *TCC*, 76–84, 91.

85. Charles-Edwards, *Welsh Laws*, 91–93.

86. S. E. Roberts, *LlPom*.

87. Pryce, "Lawbooks and Literacy," 38–39; Charles-Edwards, *Welsh Laws*, 91–93, 102; Charles-Edwards, *Wales and the Britons*, 269.

88. Jenkins, "Significance," 74–75; Stacey, *Road to Judgment*, 179–98; Charles-Edwards, *Wales and the Britons*, 269.

89. Huws, "Earliest Version," 177–92.

90. *WLMA*, xv, xli–xliii.

91. R. R. Davies, "Administration," *LAL*, 262–66; Stacey, *Road to Judgment*, 191–95.

92. Charles-Edwards, *Welsh Laws*, 92, and see more generally 90–93, 100–102.

93. Pryce, "Context and Purpose," 43–46; Charles-Edwards, *Welsh Laws*, 26–37, 68–86; Charles-Edwards, *Wales and the Britons*, 268–72; Owen, "Y Cyfreithiau—(1) and (2)," 210.

94. Charles-Edwards, "Seven Bishop-Houses"; Pryce, "Early Irish Canons"; Owen, "*Excerpta*."

95. Charles-Edwards, "Nau Kynywedi Teithiauc."

96. Note also the archaic terms *gwrthrych* and *gwrthrychiad*, which Jenkins argues were finally replaced by *edling* in the context of Llywelyn the Great's designation of his younger son Dafydd as heir: *LTMW*, 222; Dumville, "*Ætheling*"; T. M. Charles-Edwards, "Heir-Apparent."

97. *LTMW*, 337.

98. *EIWK*, 211–15, 274–303, 520–27; Charles-Edwards, *Wales and the Britons*, 271; Pryce, "Duw yn Lle Mach"; Stacey, *Road to Judgment*, 199–221.

99. Pryce, "Context and Purpose," 43, and see more generally 43–45.

100. Charles-Edwards, *Wales and the Britons*, 269, and see Owen, "*Excerpta*," *TCC*, 178–79. The *nau kynywedi teithiauc* occur only in Lat B and E: Charles-Edwards, "Nau Kynywedi Teithiauc," *WLW*, 23–26.

101. Charles-Edwards, *Wales and the Britons*, 270; see also Charles-Edwards, *Welsh Laws*, 68–86.

102. Charles-Edwards, *Welsh Laws*, 79–83.

103. Charles-Edwards, *Wales and the Britons*, 269.

104. Charles-Edwards, *Welsh Laws*, 26–37, 76–86; Charles-Edwards, *Wales and the Britons*, 269–71. Russell makes suggestions about how the Model Lawbook version of this tractate might have been ordered: Russell, "Arrangement and Development," *TCC*, 84–85.

105. Pryce, "Context and Purpose," 46, 52; Pryce, "Prologues," 158–60.

106. Stacey, "Hywel in the World," 200–201.

107. Charles-Edwards: *Wales and the Britons*, 270; see also Stacey, "Hywel in the World," 202; and Kirby, "Hywel Dda: Anglophil?"

108. H. D. Emanuel supports the idea that Hywel might have brought together a written compilation of Welsh custom; however, he also makes the point that the nature of Hywel's book and the extent of his own contribution remain uncertain: *LTWL*, 84–85.

109. Stacey, "Archaic Core," *LAL*, 34–37.

110. Owen, "'Cyfnerth' Text," *LAL*, 179–82.

111. Pryce, "Context and Purpose," 46–49. For other examples of the creative redeployment of earlier texts, see Stacey, *Road to Judgment*, 141–221; and *WKC*, 29–62, 167–90, 224–54, 400–414.

112. Pryce, "Context and Purpose," 46.

113. Pryce, "Context and Purpose," 54–63; Stephenson, "Laws of Court"; Owen, "Royal Propaganda," *WKC*, 230–32, 238–46; Pierce, "Social and Historical Aspects," 37–38. See also on the *uchelwyr* and literary production: Johnston, *Llên yr Uchelwyr*; and Fulton, "Poetic Construction."

114. Pryce, "Context and Purpose," 56–61; Stephenson, "Laws of Court," *WKC*, 400–409.

115. I am grateful to Paul Russell for this point.

116. Helpful treatments on the subject of foreign elements in Welsh law are *LTWL*, 2–92; Pryce, *Native Law*; and Walters, "Roman and Romano-Canonical Law."

117. See, for example, Pennington, *Prince and the Law*; and Sturges, *Law and Sovereignty*.

118. O'Brien, "Becket Conflict," 12, 16; see also O'Brien, *God's Peace*, 35.

119. R. R. Davies, "Law and National Identity"; R. R. Davies, "Law of the March"; Pryce, "Context and Purpose," 50–52; and Pryce, "British or Welsh." Andrews and Stephenson give a good sense of how complex the issue of identity could become in "Draig Argoed," and see also Suppe, "Interpreter Families."

120. Pryce, "Context and Purpose," 48–52; Pryce, "Origins," 7–9, following D. Simon Evans, "Iaith y Gododdin," 85; Owen, "Gwŷr Dysg."

121. Pryce, "Context and Purpose," 48.

122. Brundage, *Medieval Origins of the Legal Profession*; Brand, *Origins of the English Legal Profession*; Brand, "Judges and Judging"; Schäfer and Wulf, "Jurists, Clerics."

123. On "professional" in this context, see Stacey, *Dark Speech*, 54.

124. Jenkins, "Family of Welsh Lawyers"; Stephenson, *Welsh Law Courts*; R. R. Davies, "Administration of Law"; J. Beverley Smith, "*Ynad Llys*"; J. Beverley Smith, "Judgement"; Ll. Beverley Smith, "Cannwyll Disbwyll"; Ll. Beverley Smith, "Disputes and Settlements"; S. E. Roberts, "Addysg Broffesiynol"; S. E. Roberts, "Legal Practice."

125. Stacey, "Hywel in the World."

126. Stacey, *Road to Judgment*, 141–78.

127. Unlike the "Anomalous Laws," which cover only certain subjects and are organized as books defined primarily according to genre (*damweiniau*, *cynghawsedd*), the lawbooks attributed to Hywel all follow a single, comprehensive pattern and self-consciously present themselves as purveyors of the historical legal tradition as a whole. The "Anomalous Laws" also had a didactic purpose and content; however, they complemented the lawbooks ascribed to Hywel by making room for materials additional to the Hywelian tradition and allowing the latter to maintain its traditional nature and shape: Stacey, "Legal Writing," 85, and further 60–62, 65–74, 81–85; Charles-Edwards, *Welsh Laws*, 49–56.

128. Charles-Edwards, "*Cynghawsedd*"; Stacey, "Learning to Plead."

129. Stacey, "Legal Writing."

130. Stacey, "Instructional Riddles"; Brynmor-Jones, "Foreign Elements"; and see also Wahlgren, "Swedish-Latin Parallel."

131. *Ior* §58–67 and 72–81 respectively.

132. Charles-Edwards, *EIWK*, 274–303.

133. *Ior* 73/7–8. The court depicted in *Ior* 73/10–11 is reminiscent of the eighth-century Irish *airecht* discussed by Kelly in "Old-Irish Text."

134. Jenkins, "Family of Welsh Lawyers."

135. Charles-Edwards, *Wales and the Britons*, 270.

136. See discussion at http://bracton.law.harvard.edu/ (home page), accessed February 26, 2016.

137. *Saxon Mirror*, bk. 3, 45, 53a, for examples of history, and 202n11, for literature.

138. *LTWL*, 260, notes to p. 193, lines 14, 17–18.

139. Pryce, "Prologues," 173–76; *LTWL*, 29.

140. Jenkins, "Family of Welsh Lawyers"; S. E. Roberts, "Addysg Broffesiynol"; Lynch, "Court Poetry."

141. Jenkins, "Family of Welsh Lawyers"; Charles-Edwards, *Wales and the Britons*, 269.

142. Stephenson, *Governance of Gwynedd*, 14; see also the National Library of Wales introduction to *Llyfr Gwyn Rhydderch*.

143. B. F. Roberts, "Oral Tradition and Welsh Literature"; Owen, "Y Cyfreithiau"; Owen, "Gwŷr Dysg"; Pryce, "Lawbooks and Literacy," 45.

144. *Liber Landavensis*, *Text of the Book of Llan Dâv*, xlv. Wendy Davies translates this term as "historians": "Latin Charter-Tradition," 263.

145. Jenkins and Owen, "Welsh Marginalia," pt. 1, 5:54n75.

146. Jenkins and Owen, "Welsh Marginalia," pt. 1, 5:53–54, and pt. 2, 7:109–11; Stacey, "Hywel in the World," 200–201. On early Irish ideas about legal origins, see McCone, "Pseudo-Historical Prologue"; McCone, "Dubthach maccu Lugair"; and Stacey, *Dark Speech*, 55, 84–85, 90–91, 141–42, 163–65.

147. *PKM*, 1–3, and see Jenkins, "Hawk and Hound"; Fife, "Legal Aspects."

148. *PKM*, 33; and see *Math uab Mathonwy*, 21n5; McKenna, "Revising Math," 107–8; and Russell, "From Plates and Rods."

149. *PKM*, 67, 74; McKenna, "Revising Math." Other intriguing topics include virginity and chastity tests and the punishment of Rhiannon: Cartwright, "Virginity and Chastity Tests"; Hemming, "*Sellam Gestare*"; Lloyd-Morgan, "Gender and Violence," 68–70; B. Roberts, "Penyd Rhiannon"; and Wood, "Calumniated Wife."

150. *PKM*, 60–65; Charles-Edwards, "Welsh Law of Theft," *TCC*, 120, 122.

151. Several of these are discussed in *WKC*: the *teulu* and *penteulu*, for example (63–81), the *bardd* (142–66), the *meddyg* (116–41), etc., and see also Jenkins, "Distain," 127–28; Jenkins, "*Cynghellor* and Chancellor," 115–18; Jenkins, "Pencerdd a Bardd Teulu"; Owen, "Bwrlwm Llys Dinefwr." See also Larson, *King's Household*.

152. Charles-Edwards, "Honour and Status"; and M. Phillips, "Defod a Moes y Llys," *WKC*, 347–61.

153. Walters, "Société et Droit."

154. For example, homage, foresters, *gweission cyhain* or *macwyaid* ("young male servants, esquires"), and fosterage: T. P. Ellis, "Legal References," 92–95, 97, 104–6, 138–40. I am grateful to Paul Russell for calling my attention to one particularly important example not treated by Ellis: *trwydded*, "permission [to stay freely in a locale with the support of a lord]," which appears only once in Latin C, but occurs in *Peredur*, *Etmic Dinbych*, the *Historia Gruffud vab Kenan*; the triads; and the poetry of Llywarch Hen and of Prydydd y Moch.

155. Ellis, "Legal References, Terms." The word "Mabinogion" comprises the Mabinogi itself together with a number of narratives from the White Book of Rhydderch and the Red Book of Hergest: Bollard, "What Is the Mabinogi?"

156. Examples here are too numerous to cite, but include, on the legal side, *WLW*; *LAL*; *WKC*; *TCC*; *WLMA*; Pryce, and *Native Law and the Church*; and on the literary side, Charles-Edwards, "Date of the Four Branches"; McKenna, "Learning Lordship"; McKenna, "Revising Math"; McKenna, "Colonization of Myth"; and Goetinck,"Pedair Cainc y Mabinogi," 258.

157. Ellis, "Legal References," 143.

158. Goetinck, "Pedair Cainc y Mabinogi."

159. Cichon, *Violence and Vengeance*, 215–17. See also Cichon, "Mishandled Vessels"; and Cichon, "Insult and Redress."

160. Humphries, "Limits of the Law."

161. Harris, "Dychwelyd," 33.

162. Harris, "Dychwelyd," 35.

163. Harris, "Dychwelyd," 34. For *cwynion*, see S. E. Roberts, "Plaints"; and S. E. Roberts, "More Plaints."

164. Harris, "Dychwelyd," 30.

165. Humphries, "Limits of the Law," 1.

166. Humphries, "Limits of the Law," 13 and 7–9 respectively.

167. Cichon, *Violence and Vengeance*, 78–79.

168. Cichon, "Mishandled Vessels," 231.

169. Harris, "Dychwelyd," 24–25.

170. Welsh, "Traditional Narrative Motifs"; Welsh, "Traditional Tales"; Russell, "Texts in Contexts, 60–61"; and Sims-Williams, "Clas Beuno."

171. Russell, "From Plates and Rods."

172. Owen, "Royal Propaganda."

173. Owen, "Royal Propaganda," in *WKC*, 229–32. A different type of fictionalizing is visible in the charters: Insley, "Fact and Fiction."

174. Cichon, *Violence and Vengeance*, 97; M. Phillips, "Defod a Moes y Llys," 361.

175. Russell, "Canu i Swyddogion Llys y Brenin," *WKC*, 552–60.

176. Although the term *cyfraith Hywel* ("law of Hywel") is also known from nonlawbook sources (albeit late thirteenth century and legal in context): Goronwy Edwards, "Hywel Dda," 139–41; and see *The Welsh Assize Roll*, 173, 226, 286; and Pryce, "Prologues," 151–52, 176–79, 181–82.

177. Pryce, "Context and Purpose," 50–51.

178. Stephenson, "Laws of Court," *WKC*, 400–409.

179. Owen, "Royal Propaganda," *WKC*, 225; see also Stacey, "Law and Literature."

180. Stacey, "Divorce"; Stacey, "King, Queen, and *Edling*."

181. In the White Book of Rhydderch and the Red Book of Hergest, which date to the mid-fourteenth to early fifteenth century respectively. Their political content is outlined in McKenna, "Learning Lordship"; McKenna, "Revising Math"; McKenna, "Colonization of Myth"; McKenna, "Theme of Sovereignty"; and Fulton, "Education of Princes."

182. W. I. Miller, *Bloodtaking and Peacemaking*, 45.

CHAPTER 1

1. R. A. Breatnach, "Lady and the King"; Mac Cana, "Aspects of the Theme of King and Goddess"; Bhreathnach, "Sovereignty Goddess"; Ford, "Celtic Women"; Herbert, "Goddess and King."

2. H. A. Roberts, "Court and *Cyuoeth*," 59–60, 66–72; Lloyd-Morgan, "Medieval Welsh Tales," 54.

3. Classic studies include W. J. Gruffydd's *Rhiannon*; Mac Cana, *Branwen*; Jackson, "Some Popular Motifs"; and Andrews, "Rhai Agweddau." See also Koch, "Some Suggestions"; and Koch, "Welsh Window." Outside the Four Branches per se, probably the best-known examples of this approach are Goetinck, *Peredur*, 129–55; Goetinck, "Sofraniaeth"; and Goetinck, "*Peredur* and the Three Functions." Lovecy takes issue with Goetinck's approach in "Celtic Sovereignty." An excellent recent discussion is Charles-Edwards, *Wales and the Britons*, 324–30.

4. McKenna, "Learning Lordship," 112–16, is a valuable survey, and see also Bollard, "Structure," 175; and Fulton, "Trading Places," 228.

5. Place names and descriptions abound in many Welsh tales, including *Breuddwyd Rhonabwy*, *Breuddwyd Maxen*, and *Ystoria Gereint uab Erbin*: B. F. Roberts, "Where Were the Four Branches," 62. Precise attention to geographical locale appears to be one of the differences between the Welsh and French Arthurian tales: H. A. Roberts, "Court and *Cyuoeth*," 59–60, 66–72; Lloyd-Morgan, "Medieval Welsh Tales," 54. The Mabinogi has proven especially difficult to localize, not least because the question is inevitably bound up with the issue of when and by whom the Four Branches were written. On locale, see B. F. Roberts "Where Were the Four Branches"; and Sims-Williams, "Clas Beuno," 112–16 and 122–25. On dating, see Charles-Edwards, "Date of the Four

Branches"; Sims-Williams, "Submission of Irish Kings"; and Sims-Williams, *Irish Influence*, which brings together a number of relevant earlier studies. On authorship, see Bollard, "Pedeir Keinc"; B. F. Roberts, "Where Were the Four Branches"; and the very different tack taken by S. Davies in her "Pedeir Keinc." Breeze's suggestion that the Four Branches were authored by Gwenllian, daughter of Gruffydd ap Cynan, has been met with considerable skepticism: Breeze, "Did a Woman Write the Four Branches"; and Breeze, *Medieval Welsh Literature*. A tale by tale *status quaestionis* of the Mabinogion and related prose texts to 2007 is provided by Rodway in "Where, Who, When"; the best recent survey with full references is Charles-Edwards, *Wales and the Britons*, 653–55. Other thought-provoking studies include S. Davies, *Crefft y Cyfarwydd*; S. Davies, "Storytelling"; R. M. Jones, "Narrative Structure"; Sturzer, "Inconsistencies"; Russell, "Texts in Contexts"; and R. M. Davies, *Moral Structure*.

6. See, for example, several important essays now reprinted in Sullivan's *Mabinogi*, including Ford, "Prolegomena"; Welsh, "*Manawydan fab Llŷr*"; McKenna, "Theme of Sovereignty"; Valente, "Gwydion and Aranrhod"; and Sullivan, "Inheritance and Lordship." Fulton points out that there is no evidence that historical Welsh rulers were looked upon as sacral kings: "Education of Princes," 230–31, 245–46. She and McKenna both stress the manner in which traditional motifs were used to make contemporary points about kingship and rule: McKenna, "Learning Lordship"; McKenna, "Revising Math"; McKenna, "Colonization of Myth"; Fulton, "Education of Princes."

7. For example, Siewers, "Icon of the Land," 194–95, and Siewers, *Strange Beauty*. Nor are the Four Branches alone in this respect; see Aronstein, "Becoming Welsh," 152–54. Similar attention is accorded to the symbolic significance of landscape in Welsh poetic tradition: Fulton, "Trading Places"; Fulton, "Poetic Construction," 20–27; and see also Fulton, "Class and Nation." Very similar also are cross-cultural or mixed-genre works such as *De laude Cestrie*, the *Chronicle of Lanercost*, and the writings of Gerald of Wales: McAvoy, *Medieval Anchoritisms*, ix, 201.

8. Ellis, "Legal References," 95, 145–48; Pryce, "Context and Purpose," 48–50; Harris, "Dychwelyd," 33–35; Cichon, *Violence and Vengeance*, 41–42, 97, 215–16; McKenna, "Revising Math," 116–17. For more on the background and training of the lawbook authors, see Jenkins, "Family of Welsh Lawyers"; Owen, "Gwŷr Dysg," 60–61; and S. E. Roberts, "Addysg Broffesiynol."

9. Pryce, "Prologues," 152–58; and see also Owen, "Laws of Court from Cyfnerth," *WKC*, 428–30.

10. Stacey, "King, Queen, and *Edling*," *WKC*, 34–46.

11. *LTWL*, 2–12, 40–41, 48–53, 68–70, 81; Pryce, "Prologues," 158–65; Stacey, "King, Queen, and *Edling*," *WKC*, 40–44; *WLMA*, xxxvi–xliii.

12. Owen, "Royal Propaganda"; Pryce, "Prologues," 167–68.

13. What follows draws heavily on (and reproduces prose from) earlier published studies: Stacey, "King, Queen, and *Edling*"; and Stacey, "Clothes Talk," *WKC*, 29–62 and 338–46 respectively. I am grateful to the University of Wales Press for permission to reprint passages from these articles. On the space of the court, see also Charles-Edwards, "Food, Drink and Clothing," *WKC*, 324–25.

14. *TCC*, xi and 84.

15. In the Ior prologue and in (certain manuscripts of) the preface to the Test Book in Ior: *Ior* 1/6; and *TCC* Ior §§104/7 and 105/7–9, pp. 260–63.

16. A closely contemporary poem by Prydydd y Moch characterizes Marcolf, Cato, and Solomon as the *tair colofyn y celfyddodion*, "three columns of the arts": "Mawl Rhodri ab Owain o Wynedd," 39–49, p. 44, lines 11–14; and *Welsh Court Poems*, poem 4, lines 12–14, p. 6.

17. Russell raises the possibility that the referent here might be columns in a manuscript rather than a building. However, as he notes, there are problems with this interpretation—not least that in no Welsh law manuscript do the columns appear three across in this way: Russell, "*Y Naw Affaith*," 147–49. See further, on the issue of dating and development, Russell, "Arrangement and Development."

18. M. T. Davies, "Metaphorics of Carpentry"; M. T. Davies, "Death of Dafydd ap Gwilym," 67–69; and see the following discussion. On the metaphor of the hall in early Welsh poetry, see also Sweetser, "Figurative Harmony," 351–52.

19. *WML* 4.6–11, 19–21 (=*WKC* Cyfn §4/5–8, 15, pp. 440–41); *LTWL* Lat A 110.34–38, 111.7–13; Lat B 194.24–28, 194.35–195.2 (=*WKC* Lat B §1.5/4–7, §1.5/14–18, pp. 486–87); Lat C 277.31–278.3, 278.11–16 (=*WLMA* §§1.8–1.9, pp. 10–11); Lat D 318.9–13, 29–34; Lat E 437.12–15, 438.5–11; *Bleg* 4.20–25 and 5.20–28; and *Ior* 5/1–8, and see 4/3. I am following here Dafydd Jenkins's reconstruction of the hall, which can be found in *LTMW*, 223–24, and see also introduction, *WKC*, 1–9, p. 3, and diagrams on 570–71.

20. Russell, "*Y Naw Affaith*," *TCC*, 148–49.

21. *Dialogus de Scaccario*, 1.5 (pp. 40–41) and, on the question of authorship and date, pp. xiv, xviii–xx.

22. *Dialogus de Scaccario*, 41n56; J. Hudson, "Administration, Family," 77–79.

23. *WML* 1.24–2.3 (=*WKC* Cyfn §1/6, pp. 436–37); 36.21–24; and cf. Ior B: *Lleuer Llys*, the "Book of the Court" (*Ior* 43/13); *keureythueu e wlat*, "the laws of country" (*Ior* 56/1). Lat C, the earliest of the Latin versions, reads: *De quibus legibus . . . principales sunt curiales*, "of these laws the most important are those pertaining to the court" (*LTWL* Lat C 276.12=*WLMA* §1.2, pp. 4–5). For discussion, see Charles-Edwards, *Welsh Laws*, 26–33; and Pryce, "Context and Purpose," 59–60.

24. The attribution of the Test Book to Iorwerth ap Madog comes from the lengthy prologue to that text found in Ior manuscript C, fol. 180r.

25. *Leges Henrici Primi*, 5–10, 34–37.

26. *Leges Henrici Primi*, c. 6, 1 and 6, 2 (pp. 96–97).

27. O'Brien, *God's Peace*, 36–44.

28. Glanvill, *Treatise on the Laws and Customs*. A new edition is currently being prepared by Paul Brand and John Hudson under the auspices of the Early English Laws Project: http://www.earlyenglishlaws.ac.uk/laws/texts/synopsis/Glanvill/.

29. *Bracton*, 2:26–29.

30. Goronwy Edwards, "Royal Household." For other comparisons, see Jenkins, "Prolegomena," *WKC*, 17–18. Hincmar's work is available in *De ordine palatii*, and has been translated into English by Herlihy, *History of Feudalism*, 208–36. For the *Constitutio*, see *Dialogus de Scaccario, and Constitutio Domus Regis*, ed. Amt and Church.

31. *Dialogus de Scaccario*, bk. 1, chaps. 1–8.

32. Walters, "Comparative Aspects," *WKC*, 389; introduction, *WKC*, 3.

33. *Dialogus de Scaccario*, bk. 1, chap. 1.

34. Walters, "Comparative Aspects," *WKC*, 385.

35. Walters, "Comparative Aspects," *WKC*, 390–96, 398–99.

36. His main priority being to remind kings that it was to God and the church rather than to their armies that Carolingian rulers owed their thrones: Nelson, "Kingship, Law," 138–39.

37. Walters, "Comparative Aspects," *WKC*, 389–90.

38. For example, regarding Wales, see *Ior* 1/1; cf. Cyfn's *brenhin Kymry* in *WML* 1.1–2 (=*WKC*, Cyfn §1/1, pp. 436–37). Regarding provinces, see *WML* 1.1–6 and 3.7–8 (=*WKC*, Cyfn

§1/1, pp. 436–37 and §3/3, pp. 438–39); *Ior* 3/4; *Bleg* 2.1–5 (which mentions Powys as well); *LTWL* Lat A 109.3–4 and 110.20–21 (which also mentions Powys); Lat B 194.11–12 (= *WKC* Lat B §1.2/7, pp. 484–85); Lat C 276.1–3 (= *WLMA* §1.1/1, pp. 2–3) and 277.7, 23 (= *WLMA* §§1.4/3 and 1.7/1, pp. 6–9); Lat D 316.18–21 and 317.30–37; Lat E 435.15–20. The best recent discussion is Charles-Edwards, *Wales and the Britons*, 1–4, 14–21, 31–36, 75–76, 89–95, 238–41.

39. Owen, "Royal Propaganda."

40. *WML* 22.15–19 (= *WKC*, Cyfn §18/1–2, pp. 458–59); *Ior* 13/7; *Bleg* 22.24–25; *LTWL* Lat A 118.18–21; Lat B 206.13–16 (= *WKC* Lat B §1.31/1, pp. 514–15); Lat D 328.34–39; Lat E 445.29–32.

41. *GPC*, 3704, s.v. "unben."

42. For discussion and references, see McKenna, "Colonization of Myth," 113–14; and Lynch, "Court Poetry," *WKC*, 181–86.

43. *Ior* 1/1; cf. Cyfn's *brenhin Kymry* in *WML* 1.1–2 (= *WKC*, Cyfn §1/1, pp. 436–37); and see Pryce, "Prologues," 156; and Charles-Edwards, *Wales and the Britons*, 268–72.

44. R. R. Davies, "Law and National Identity," 56; Pryce, "Prologues"; Charles-Edwards, *Welsh Laws*, 40–45; Goronwy Edwards, "Hywel Dda and the Welsh Lawbooks"; Over, *Kingship, Conquest*, 83–88.

45. E.g., the complex notions of identity in the poetry of the *Gogynfeirdd*: Lynch, "Court Poetry," *WKC*, 181–86.

46. Charles-Edwards, *Welsh Laws*, 25–48.

47. See discussion below and Siewers, "Icon of the Land"; Fulton, "Trading Places"; McKenna, "Colonization of Myth," and Owen, "Literary Convention."

48. Ior manuscripts C, G, and Col are defective, and do not contain the prologue.

49. Pryce, "Prologues," 167.

50. Pryce, "Prologues," 156, 167–68.

51. *Ior* §1/1–6; *WML* 1.1–24 (= *WKC* Cyfn §1, pp. 436–37); *Bleg* 1.1–2.13; *LTWL* Lat A 109.1–18; Lat B 193.1–18; Lat C 276.1–11 (= *WLMA* §§1.1, pp. 2–3); Lat D 316.1–29; Lat E 434.1–435.37. See discussion in Pryce, "Prologues," 152–65.

52. Carey, "Edition of the Pseudo-Historical Prologue"; *Pactus Legis Salicae*; and see also *Lex Salica* for the later Carolingian version; III Aethelred and I Canute can be found in *Laws of the Kings of England*, 64–65, 154–55; *Leges Henrici Primi*, 80–81; and O'Brien, *God's Peace*, 158–61.

53. Thomas Charles-Edwards suggests to me that there is also a progression of status here: from those whose status pertains to the king, to the country ruled by him, to those whose status does not derive from him (pers. comm., July 2016).

54. The "Laws of Court" are absent from Ior manuscripts F, G, K, Col, and Peniarth 163.

55. *WKC*, 3–6; and see discussion by Charles-Edwards, "*Gorsedd*, *Dadl*, and *Llys*."

56. For seating arrangements, see *WML* 4.6–11, 19–21 (= *WKC* Cyfn §4/5–9, 15–16, pp. 440–41); *LTWL* Lat A 110.34–38 and 111.7–13; Lat B 194.24–28, 194.35–195.2 (= *WKC* Lat B §1.5/4–7, §1.5/14–18, pp. 486–87); Lat C 277.31–278.3, 278.11–16 (= *WLMA* §§1.8/3–1.9/5, pp. 10–11); Lat D 318.9–13, 29–34; Lat E 437.12–15, 438.5–11; *Bleg* 4.20–25 and 5.20–28; and *Ior* 5/1–8, and see 4/3.

57. *WML* 6.11–13 (= *WKC* Cyfn §5/22, pp. 442–43), and the bakeress in *Ior* 38/3.

58. Sigston, "'*As Far as His Horn May Be Heard*,'" 32. I am very grateful to the author for making this work available to me in advance of publication.

59. Taken largely from Charles-Edwards, *Welsh Laws*, 27–28, and based on Cyfn manuscript Mk and Ior manuscripts other than Ior B. Helpful conspectuses showing some of these differences at a glance are available in *Ior*, xlii–xliv; *LlPom*, 49–65; *Col*, xlii–xliii; and Jenkins, *Conspectus*; and see more generally Charles-Edwards, *Welsh Laws*, 26–31.

60. Ior manuscript C, fol. 180r, and similarly attributed to Iorwerth in manuscripts D, K, and Ll: see *ALW* V.C. bk. 3, "Rhaglith," with translation in *LTMW*, 141, and see also *Col* §§237–41. For the idea that the preface was once contained in all Ior manuscripts apart from A and E, see *TCC*, 102–4.

61. Charles-Edwards, *Welsh Laws*, 29–31; Jenkins, "Family of Welsh Lawyers," 130–31.

62. Charles-Edwards, *Welsh Laws*, 26–28, 49–50, 53–67; and see Pryce, "Lawbooks and Literacy," 40; Stacey, *Road to Judgment*, 182–85; Stacey, "Legal Writing," 59, 74–83. Other types of texts include the triads and the plaints: S. E. Roberts, *LT*; S. E. Roberts, *Welsh Legal Triads*; S. E. Roberts, "Iorwerth Triads"; S. E. Roberts, "Plaints"; and S. E. Roberts, "More Plaints."

63. Title taken from Ior Ms. C: *ALW* III.iv. See below for discussion on the Wild and Tame tractate.

64. *Ior* 73/3.

65. *Ior* §§33–35 (the discussion of court officers ends with §41; the Laws of Women begin with §44); *Ior* §§91–96; *WML* 27.22–31.5, 32.1–18, 33.4–13 (the discussion of court officers ends with 34.5 and the Laws of Country begin with 36.21); *WML* 43.8–17, 56.10–11, 57.9–13; *LTWL* Lat A 119.11–29, 120.13–41 (the Laws of Country begin on 121.7); Lat B 203.36–204.2; 209.3–11 (the Laws of Country begin on 209.12, but see also 227.14–15; 253.1–30; 254.12–15); Lat D 332.3–12 (the Laws of Country begin on 332.13, but see also 346.22–347.39; 349.19–25); Lat E 447.17–448.9 (the Laws of Country begin on 448.10, but see also 467.26–27; 502.18–24; 504.25–26); *Bleg* 24.21–23, 27.17–29.12 (the Laws of Country begin on 29.26).

66. *LTWL* Lat D 346.21.

67. Pryce, "Prologues," 152–69.

68. *Llyfr Gwyn Rhydderch*, 229, col. 458.

69. *Llyfr Gwyn Rhydderch*, 112, col. 223; *Ystoria Gereint uab Erbin*, 1, line 19.

70. For Ior B, see discussion below.

71. Stephenson, "Laws of Court," *WKC*, 400–404.

72. T. M. Charles-Edwards, "Seven Bishop-Houses"; Charles-Edwards, "Nau Kynywedi Teithiauc"; Pryce, "Duw yn Lle Mach"; Stacey, *Road to Judgment*, 141–221. See the useful discussion by Charles-Edwards (who argues for the historical veracity of the ascription to Hywel) in his *Wales and the Britons*, 268–72.

73. Owen, "*Excerpta*"; Dumville, "Dating of the Early Breton Lawcodes"; Pryce, "Early Irish Canons."

74. Charles-Edwards suggests that the Laws of Court constitutes one of the sections of the laws "most likely to have been written or rewritten in the tenth century" on the basis of the strikingly early concepts and terms preserved in it: *Wales and the Britons*, 271.

75. *WML* 2.23–3.11 (=*WKC* Cyfn §3/2–3, pp. 438–39); *Ior* 3/4–5; *LTWL* Lat A 110.9–21; Lat B 194.1–12 and 207.18–29 (=*WKC* Lat B §1.2/4–7, pp. 484–85; §2.3, pp. 518–19); Lat C 277.5–12 and 277.19–26 (=*WLMA* §§1.4/3–4 and 1.7/1–3, pp. 6–9); Lat D 317.19–37; Lat E 436.17–31; *Bleg* 3.17–4.6. Paul Russell has traced the development from its simplest incarnation in *Branwen* and Ior to its most elaborate form in the Latin texts and Bleg: *WLMA*, xxxix–xli; Russell, "From Plates and Rods." Ior B omits the golden plate or cover (*klaur eur*) mentioned elsewhere (Aled Rhys Wiliam has supplied it from manuscript E); however, since it is mentioned later in the Test-Book list of *sarhaed* payments to the king of Aberffraw, this was probably not a deliberate omission: *Ior* 110/1–3. The following discussion reiterates points made earlier in Stacey, "King, Queen, and *Edling*," *WKC*, 34–40; and Stacey, "Law and Literature," 75–81. See references there, and Loth, "Un genre particulier."

76. *PKM*, 33, and see *PKM*, 29, for the setting of the tale; *Branwen uerch Lyr*, 111–14. The

best discussions of this passage are *WLMA*, xxxix–xli; and Russell, "From Plates and Rods." In the Llandaff charters, the price of the golden plate is adjudged to a bishop's *familia* in a narrative that projects the bishop into the position of secular ruler in order to underscore the freedom of the church in judicial matters: *Liber Landavensis*, 233. For discussion of the Llandaff charters, see Charles-Edwards, *Wales and the Britons*, 245–67; on the golden plate, see Pryce, *Native Law*, 158–62; and Stacey, "King, Queen, and *Edling*," *WKC*, 38.

77. See esp. Ford, "Prolegomena," 197–200; Welsh, "*Manawydan fab Llŷr*," 121–27; McKenna, "Theme of Sovereignty," 35–39; McKenna, "Learning Lordship," 101–3; McKenna, "Colonization of Myth," 105–19; and Fulton, "Education of Princes," 242–43.

78. Fulton, "Education of Princes"; McKenna, "Theme of Sovereignty"; McKenna, "Revising Math"; and see also on the *Branwen* passage specifically, *WLMA*, xxxix–xli, and Russell, "From Plates and Rods."

79. See further Stacey, "King, Queen, and *Edling*," *WKC* 34–46.

80. Stacey, "King, Queen, and *Edling*," *WKC*, 45; *WLMA*, xxxix–xli; Russell, "From Plates and Rods," 17–18.

81. Aronstein, "Becoming Welsh," 149–50, drawing upon Bhabha, *Location of Culture*. See also McKenna, "Colonization of Myth," 117.

82. *LTMW*, 221–22, note 6.6.

83. *PKM* 29.1–3 (*Branwen uerch Lyr*); see further Fulton, *Welsh Prophecy*; and Fulton, "Education of Princes," 242–44.

84. *Ior* 13/7.

85. *Ior* 110/1–5.

86. *Ior* 90/1–9; and see discussion, text, and translation in Owen, "Royal Propaganda," *WKC*, 229–32, 250–51. The genealogies place him in Northern Britain around 500 CE: Owen, "Royal Propaganda," *WKC*, 230–31, and references there. Dyfnwal also appears in the early Welsh genealogies, in *Culhwch ac Olwen*, and in Geoffrey of Monmouth's *Historia Regum Britanniae*: see discussion and references in Stacey, "Law and Literature," 77–78.

87. *Ior* 90/1.

88. The redactor attributes contemporary Welsh law to Hywel rather than to Dyfnwal in order to establish the native legal tradition as separate and independent from that of England. Geoffrey's point is the opposite, and forms part of his general appropriation of native tradition in the interests of Anglo-Norman rulers: *Historia Regum Britanniae*, ii, 17. See also Fulton, *Welsh Prophecy*, 5–14; B. F. Roberts, "Geoffrey of Monmouth"; and Curley, *Geoffrey of Monmouth*, 7–47.

89. *Ior* 90/3–4, and cf. text of manuscript D in Owen, "Royal Propaganda," *WKC*, 250. The notion that Hywel changed all the old laws he found in place contradicts what is said in the Ior prologue, where he is said to have kept or emended some: *Ior* 1/4.

90. Unless otherwise noted, all translations are my own.

91. *Ior* 90/5; edition and translation from D by Owen, "Royal Propaganda," *WKC*, 250–51.

92. *Ior* 90/7.

93. R. R. Davies, *First English Empire*, 34. R. R. Davies has several excellent treatments of this period: *Conquest, Coexistence, and Change*; *Age of Conquest*; and *Domination and Conquest*. Also helpful are Stephenson, *Governance of Gwynedd*; and T. Jones Pierce, "Age of the Princes."

94. Stacey, "Law and Literature," 77–78.

95. *Alltudyon*, defined by implication in *Ior* 86/11 as persons from outside Wales: see *LTMW*, 264, note 108.18. Dylan Foster Evans cites this clause as evidence for the ethnically mixed nature of Welsh life in this period: Evans, "On the Lips of Strangers," 26.

96. *Ior* §§89–90, and see Jenkins, "Conspectus," xliv.

97. *Ior* 89/1–5.

98. Literally "the fourth man."

99. *Ior* 86/11.

100. *Ior* 89/5; *GPC*, 384–86, s.vv. "caeth," "caethiwed."

101. Cf. also the interpretations offered in Owen, "Royal Propaganda," *WKC*, 230–32.

102. Pryce, *Native Law*, 96–112, 127, 202–3, 241–58; Stacey, "Divorce," 1124–25.

103. *Ior* 13/7; *WML* 22.17–19 (= *WKC* Cyfn §18/2, pp. 458–59); *LTWL* Lat A 118.19–21; Lat B 206.13–16 (= *WKC* Lat B §1.31/1, pp. 514–15); Lat D 328.6–9; Lat E 445.30–32; *Bleg* 22.21–25.

104. Charles-Edwards, *Welsh Laws*, 85: "The propaganda value of Hywel appears to be an accretion to the original tradition."

105. Cereal grains, including the barleycorn, are also found as units of measurement in early Ireland: Kelly, *Early Irish Farming*, 560–61.

106. Welsh, "*Manawydan fab Llŷr*," 135.

107. McKenna, "Colonization of Myth," 117–19. See also, for an exploration of similar themes in *Peredur*, Aronstein, "Becoming Welsh," 144–47.

108. McKenna, "Colonization of Myth," 119.

109. Charles-Edwards, *EIWK*, 292–93, and see the plea of *ymwrthryn* in *ALW* VII.i.22.

110. McKenna, "Colonization of Myth," 113.

111. *CCC*, 12–20; R. R. Davies, *First English Empire*, 31–53; R. R. Davies, "Law and National Identity"; Charles-Edwards, *Wales and the Britons*, 1–74.

112. Bhabha, *Location of Culture*, 2, 5, 113; Aronstein, "Becoming Welsh," 145–51, 164–68; McKenna, "Colonization of Myth," 117–19; Pryce, "Context and Purpose"; Fulton, "Education of Princes," 241–47.

113. For example, in addition to the prologue: references to Gwynedd, Powys, and/or Deheubarth in *Ior* 86/1, 11; *WML* 113.7–8; *LTWL* Lat A 140.18–19; Lat B 251.12; Lat D 349.31–32; and to *Cymru/Cymro/Cymraes/Wallia* in *Ior* 87/4; *WML* 121.15; *LTWL* Lat A 148.23; Lat B 207.22 (= *WKC* Lat B §2.3/4, pp. 518–19); Lat C 277.25 (= *WLMA* §1.1, pp. 2–3); Lat D 380.28; Lat E 438.1; 466.21, and so on. On inheritance practices, see *Ior* 86/11.

114. E.g., *CCC*, 18–19.

115. Ior frequently acknowledges debates within the legal community with the phrase *rey a deweyt . . . e keureyth a deweyt eyssyoes*, "Some say . . . the law says, however." See, for example, *Ior* 64/6; 65/7–9; 66/1; 80/1; 86/7–9; and so on. In some cases, variations in legal practice are characterized in regional terms—e.g., *Ior* 86/1.

116. The Cyfn redactor seems here to be using *brenin* in a manner intended to encompass local kings as well as major rulers. The term *rhi*—often used elsewhere for rulers of smaller units (*WKC*, 214–15, for example, with respect to the poetry of Cynddelw)—never occurs in Cyfn, and when the redactor does refer to a principal ruler, he uses the term *arglwydd* instead of *brenin*: *WML* 3.8 (= *WKC* Cyfn §3/3, pp. 438–39). However, it must be acknowledged that the terminology of rulership is variable across texts of the period, so the matter is far from clear. Many texts distinguish major and minor rulers in this way (*brenin* vs. *rhi*), but others do not: Charles-Edwards, "Dynastic Succession," 78–79, 83–85, and n. 66.

117. Worth noting is the likely emendation in Lat BI, where the scribe appears to have added Aberffraw into a text that originally mentioned only Dinefwr: Russell, "Laws of Court from Latin B," *WKC*, 479, referring to Lat B §1.2/7 (pp. 484–85).

118. *WML* 3.7–11 (= *WKC* Cyfn §3/3, pp. 438–39), and see a fuller discussion in Stacey, "King, Queen, and *Edling*," *WKC*, 34–46, and references there.

119. Pryce, "Prologues," 153.

120. This point is made also by Pryce, "Context and Purpose," 51.

121. R. R. Davies, "Law of the March"; R. R. Davies, "Kings, Lords, and Liberties"; R. R. Davies, *Lordship and Society*; and see most recently, Lieberman, *Medieval March of Wales.*

122. Stacey, "King, Queen, and *Edling*," *WKC*, 39–40.

123. Pryce, "Context and Purpose," 50–51.

124. Meecham-Jones, "Where Was Wales?"; Davenport, "Wales and Welshness"; and Kennedy and Meecham-Jones, *Authority and Subjugation.*

125. Stacey, "King, Queen, and *Edling*," *WKC*, 40–46, on the portrayal of kingliness in the Latin texts and Ior.

126. *Ny thelyr eur namyn y urenhyn Aberfrav*, "gold is not paid except to the king of Aberffraw": *Ior* 3/5, and see also *Ior* 110/1–5.

127. Jenkins, "Kings, Lords and Princes"; Stephenson, "Laws of Court," 400; and see also Fulton, "Education of Princes," 233–34. Ior B (the basis for Wiliam's edition) and Ior A use *tywysog* for Hywel in their version of the prologue, but Ior D uses *brenin*; in Cyfn, he appears as *brenhin Kymry*: *Ior* 1/1; *WML* 1.1 (= *WKC* Cyfn §1/1, pp. 436–37).

128. This is evident even at a glance from the index: *Ior*, pp. 144–45.

129. *LTMW* 250, note to 72.21–23; and see also Stephenson, "Laws of Court," *WKC*, 400–401.

130. *Ior* 90/1–2; 110/1–9.

131. *Ior* 4/8–9; Stacey, "King, Queen, and *Edling*," *WKC*, 50.

132. *Ior* 4/8–9.

133. *Ior* 110/5, though cf. readings in Ior E, C, D, and K, which do not mention the *mechdeyrn ddylyed*: *TCC*, Ior E and B §110, pp. 274–76.

134. *Ior* 4/5–6; 6/30.

135. J. Beverley Smith, *Llywelyn ap Gruffudd*, 17–19, 285–86.

136. Charles-Edwards, *Wales and the Britons*, 321–22. Tribute (albeit under a different name) is mentioned as being exacted from Wales at an earlier date. See, for example, the tribute noted in the D version of the Anglo-Saxon Chronicle (under 1062/1063, fol. 78r).

137. Though probably not any extant version of that book: *WLMA*, xxxvii–xxxix. For Ior, see *Ior* 110/5. For Latin C, see *LTWL* Lat C, 277.19–26 (= *WLMA*, §1.7, pp. 8–9); for Latin BII: see *LTWL* Lat B 207.19–26 (= *WKC*, Lat B §2.3/1–3, pp. 518–19) and discussion by Russell in *WKC*, 478–79. On the *mechdeyrn ddylyed*, see *WLMA*, xxxvi–xxxix, 54; *WKC*, 42–43; *CCC*, 292–307; J. Beverley Smith, *Llywelyn ap Gruffudd*, 17–18, 285–86; *WLMA*, xvi, xxiv, xxxvii–viii, xli, 54; and Andrews, "Nomenclature of Kingship," 99–101.

138. *WLMA*, xxiv, 54.

139. *GPC*, 2389, s.v. "ced"; W. Davies, "People and Places in Dispute," 72; W. Davies, "Suretyship in the *Cartulaire de Redon*"; W. Davies, "Holding Court," 147–48, 153–54.

140. Lat C's "king of London" suggests that the pseudohistoricizing of this due already existed in its sources. On London as a principal seat, see also Charles-Edwards, *Wales and the Britons*, 322–24.

141. As is the superiority of the prince of Aberffraw to other Welsh rulers, as evidenced by Lat C and Lat B's comment that the other kings of Wales must render *mechdeyrn ddylyed* to the prince of Aberffraw when they take their land, and that his authority (*verbum*) prevails over them in all matters: *LTWL* Lat B 207.22–26; Lat C 277.19–26 (= *WLMA* §1.7, pp. 8–9) and see also the text edited by Pryce in "Prologues," 186–87.

142. *LTWL* Lat C 277.27–29 (= *WLMA* §1.8, pp. 10–11, with discussion and notes at

pp. xxxvii, 54–55); Stacey, "King, Queen, and *Edling*," *WKC*, 42–44; and Charles-Edwards, "Heir-Apparent."

143. Dafydd Jenkins, introduction, *LTMW*, xxix–xxxvii; Jenkins, "Lawbooks of Medieval Wales"; Jenkins, "Medieval Welsh Idea"; Charles-Edwards, "Nau Kynywedi Teithiauc"; Charles-Edwards, "Seven Bishop-Houses"; Pryce, "Duw yn Lle Mach"; and see Stacey, *Road to Judgment*, 179–98.

144. Stephenson, "Laws of Court," *WKC*, 400–409.

CHAPTER 2

1. On the *gwlad*, see *CCC*, 12–13; *EIWK*, 566; Charles-Edwards, *Wales and the Britons*, 321; *LAL*, 348; *WKC*, 159–60; Charles-Edwards, "Date of *Culhwch ac Olwen*"; Pryce, *Native Law*, 105. On the *cymwd* and *cantref*, see Rh. Jones, "Formation." The essays in Hanawalt and Kobialka's *Medieval Practices of Space* were helpful to me in thinking about these issues.

2. See *LTMW*, 270, note to 124.5, for some of the difficulties caused by this usage.

3. *WML* 36.21–24, and cf. *LTWL* Lat B 209.12–18; Lat D 332.3–14.

4. Ior manuscripts A and D read *eythyr egulad* and *odieithyr y wlat*, "from outside the *gwlad*" here.

5. *WML* 10.17–18 (= *WKC* Cyfn §8/2, pp. 446–47).

6. *LTWL* Lat A: *Si familiares regis predam fecerint* (113.37); and cf. Lat B 197.19–22 (= *WKC* Lat B §1.9/3, pp. 492–93), Lat D 321.28–31, Lat E 441.22–23; and *Bleg* 10.18–19 (*Or keiff teulu brenhin anreith*). Lat C, likely the earliest extant northern text, has *De preda vero quam facit familia, si erit cum eis*: *LTWL* Lat C 281.15–16 (= *WLMA* §1.13/3, pp. 18–19).

7. *LTWL* Lat A 114.27–28: *terciam partem que regis est de preda*, and cf. Lat B 200.28–29 (= *WKC* Lat B §1.15/9, pp. 500–501); Lat D 322.29–31; Lat E 442.10–11; *Bleg* 12.10. Lat C 285.7–8 has this passage in Welsh (= *WLMA* §1.18/7, pp. 30–31).

8. *WML* 13.5–6 (= *WKC* Cyfn §11/10, pp. 448–49).

9. Manuscript D reads *or wlat* here.

10. *WML* 15.24–25 (= *WKC* Cyfn §12/8, pp. 450–51).

11. *LTWL* Lat A 115.27–28 (*Ipse debet habere partem viri de preda quam familia regis fecerit, licet domi sit*); cf. Lat B 198.32–34 (= *WKC* Lat B §1.11/5, pp. 496–97); Lat C 283.2–3 (= *WLMA* §1.15/5, pp. 22–23); Lat D 198.32–34; Lat E 443.12–13; and *Bleg* 15.15–16 (which grants him the shares of two men: *rann deuwr*).

12. Compare *Ior* 13/7 (on the poet of the warband) with *WML* 22.15–16 (*WKC* Cyfn §18/1, pp. 458–59); *LTWL* Lat A 118.18–19; Lat B 206.13–14 (= *WKC* Lat B §1.31/1, pp. 514–15); Lat D 328.36–37; Lat E 445.29–30; *Bleg* 22.21–23; and *Ior* 34/9 (on the *rhingyll*) with *WML* 30.22–23 (= *WKC* Cyfn §38/19, pp. 472–73); *LTWL* Lat A 119.23–25; Lat B 207.2 (= *WKC* Lat B §1.33/5, pp. 516–17); *Bleg* 28.30.

13. With reference to the porter and chief grooms: *Ior* 35/7, 11/7, and 24/6 respectively. Outside the Laws of Court, *anrhaith* is used in the laws on homicide and theft to designate judicial spoils taken by law from offenders: *Ior* 105/2; 111/14; 112/4 (Ior E).

14. Ior manuscript B: *Ior* 6/21; 8/22; 10/11; 13/7; 34/9; and 24/6 on the chief groom of the queen.

15. *Ior* §§42 and 43; it is explicitly marked as an addition in *Ior* 42/1.

16. *Ior* 43/4; and cf. *LTWL* Lat B 204.20–22 (= *WKC* Lat B §1.25/2, pp. 510–11).

17. *LTWL* Lat A 119.35–38; very similar is Lat D 328.25–27=*Bleg* 22.14–17, which also speaks

of taking *anreith ygwlat y brenhin*. Cf. also Lat B's version, which is not explicit about the *opus* a king might need help with in his own *patria*: *LTWL* Lat B 204.20–22 (= *WKC* Lat B §1.25/2, pp. 510–11); and Lat D 377.22–24; *Bleg* 47.12–14.

18. This seems to me the most likely explanation, given Ior's consistency and the departure it represents from the other lawbook traditions. However, one other possibility is that *gorwlad* is being using predicatively, as a way of distinguishing booty (*anrhaith*) from judicial fines (also *anrhaith*). The effect of associating the *gorwlad* with predation would nonetheless be the same in any case.

19. The only exceptions are *WML* 57.10–15, which envisages hosting both within and without the *gwlad*, and *WML* 138.18–21, omitted from manuscripts U and X (see pp. 322–24), which speaks of the horns of the host raised against the army of a *gorwlad* as being an excuse not to respond to a legal summons.

20. *LTWL* Lat D 328.24–25; *Bleg* 22.13–14; 47.12–14. *Bleg* 58.15–16 mentions a man killed in a *gorwlat*, but murder rather than war is implied. *Anrhaith* occurs elsewhere in the Latin texts, once in the meaning of "booty" but without any specified connection to the *gorwlad* (*LTWL* Lat C 285.7–8 = *WLMA* §1.18/7, pp. 30–31) and twice in the meaning of "judicial spoil" (*LTWL* Lat B 259.21; Lat E 505.17–18).

21. For example: *WML* 33.21–23; 99.9–10; 119.13; *LTWL* Lat B 209.1–2 (= *WKC* Lat B §2.13/4, pp. 520–21); Lat C 288.4–6 (= *WLMA* §2.1/3, pp. 38–39); Lat D 331.4–6; and Lat E 446.2–3; *Bleg* 26.6–8; 39.16–17.

22. *CCC*, 239–51.

23. As implied by *Ior* §86/11's denial of "mother-right" to a person from Powys who happens to be in Gwynedd, or a person from Gwynedd who happens to be in Powys (and similarly with respect to Deheubarth). See *LTMW* 264, note to 108.18.

24. McKenna, "Colonization of Myth"; Aronstein, "Becoming Welsh," 144–47; Bhabha, "World and the Home."

25. McKenna, "Colonization of Myth," 117.

26. Patricia Malone argues convincingly that the text constitutes deliberate fictionalizing rather than objective history: "Treachery from the Beginning"; and Malone, "'Entirely Outside the World.'" Paul Russell suggests a date of 1137 x 1148 for the composition of the Latin *Vita Griffini filii Conani*, on which he argues the early thirteenth-century Welsh translation was based: *Vita Griffini*, 46–47; and see D. Simon Evans, *Historia Gruffud vab Kenan*. For further discussion, see Maund, *Collaborative Biography*.

27. Malone, "Entirely Outside the World."

28. *Medieval Prince of Wales*, 32, with translation on 62; and cf. *Vita Griffini* §14, pp. 64–65.

29. *Vita Griffini* §18, pp. 68–71, and note the reference to *regni sui* of §19, pp. 70–71; *Medieval Prince of Wales*, 36.5–9, 37.13–16, and see 38.5–6, with translation of all cited passages on pp. 67–69.

30. *WML* 4.6–11 (= *WKC* Cyfn §4/5–9, pp. 440–41), but see further *WML* 4.19–21 (= *WKC* Cyfn §4/15–16, pp. 440–41); 19.17–19 (= *WKC* Cyfn §15/12, pp. 456–57); 21.20–21 (= *WKC* Cyfn §13/12, pp. 452–53, and see also §13/13); 22.24–25 (= *WKC* Cyfn §18/9, pp. 458–59); 24.25–25.1 (= *WKC* Cyfn §22/1, pp. 462–63); 26.19–20 (= *WKC* Cyfn §28/1, 464–65). See also discussion in *WKC* 570–71. For seating arrangements in the Bleg and Latin texts, see *LTWL* Lat A 110.34–38 and 111.7–13; Lat B 194.24–28 and 194.35–195.3 (= *WKC* Lat B §1.5/4–7, §1.5/14–18, pp. 486–87); Lat C 277.31–278.3 and 278.11–16 (= *WLMA* §1.8/3–6, pp. 10–11, and §1.9/1–5, pp. 10–11); Lat D 318.9–13 and 318.29–34; Lat E 437.12–15 and 438.5–11; *Bleg* 4.21–25 and 5.20–28. In Latin A and

Latin D, the second of these discussions is given a separate title: *De dignitate regis* (Latin A) and *De rege* (Latin D).

31. *Ior* 12/3–8.

32. Charles-Edwards, "Food, Drink and Clothing," *WKC*, 320–27, and see also *WKC*, 570–71.

33. Charles-Edwards, "Food, Drink and Clothing," *WKC*, 320.

34. L. A. Butler, "Domestic Building in Wales"; G. R. Smith, "Manor of Aberffraw"; Johnstone, *Llys and Maerdref: An Investigation*; Johnstone, "Investigation into the Location"; Johnstone, "*Cae Llys Rhosyr*"; Johnstone, "*Llys* and *Maerdref*: Royal Courts"; and Charles-Edwards, "*Gorsedd, Dadl.*" Another important source of information is Welsh poetry of the period, on which see Owen, "Literary Convention," 72–73.

35. Hauck, "Rituelle Speisegemeinschaft"; Woolgar, *Great Household*, 111–65; Effros, *Creating Community*.

36. Charles-Edwards suggests in a private note that *celfi*, "screen," is singular in meaning before the seventeenth century. I am grateful to him for his insights and have translated it accordingly here.

37. Roughly, "chancellor," but see *LTMW*, 331–32.

38. *Ior* 5/1–8, and see diagram and discussion in *WKC*, 570–71.

39. Charles-Edwards, "Food, Drink and Clothing," *WKC*, 323–28.

40. E.g., the killing of a notable bird: *Ior* 9/12. See Charles-Edwards, "Food, Drink and Clothing," *WKC*, 327–36.

41. *WML* 12.15–18 (= *WKC* Cyfn §11/12, pp. 448–49). Note that Cyfn U and V speak only of the *penteulu*'s gift to the steward. *Ior* 6/14, 8/4, 13/3, 19/5, and see also *LTWL* Lat A 114.22–23, Lat D 322.21, and Lat E 442.2–3.

42. Charles-Edwards, "Food, Drink and Clothing," *WKC*, 335–36.

43. This point and others that follow draw heavily from Stacey, "Clothes Talk," *WKC*, 338–46.

44. Labarge, *Baronial Household*, 131; Mertes, *English Noble Household*, 45, 103, and 132; Dyer, *Standards of Living*, 78–79, 88–89, 175–77, and 205–7; Coss, *Lordship, Knighthood*, 173.

45. Stacey, "Clothes Talk," *WKC*, 338–46.

46. E.g., *Ior* 7/1, 8/1, 9/1, etc.

47. Sweetser, "Figurative Harmony," 351–52.

48. Owen, "Literary Convention," 71, and see Sweetser, "Figurative Harmony," 351–52; B. F. Roberts, "*Breuddwyd Maxen Wledig*," 310–11; and G. Gruffudd, "'Praise of Tenby,'" 97–99.

49. Williams, "Two Poems from the Book of Taliesin," 155–72.

50. "*Canu Owain Cyfeiliog*," in *Gwaith Llywelyn Fardd I ac Eraill*, no. 14.

51. M. T. Davies, "Metaphorics of Carpentry," 75–77; M. T. Davies, "Death of Dafydd ap Gwilym," 67–69.

52. Hunter, "Feast of Words," 43.

53. Hunter, "Feast of Words," 43–46. Cichon simply presumes that redactors of the tales were drawing from and citing to the lawbooks directly: Cichon, *Violence and Vengeance*, 97–99.

54. Pryce, "Duw yn Lle Mach"; Pryce, *Native Law*; Stacey, *Road to Judgment*, 141–221; Stacey, "King, Queen, and *Edling*"; Lynch, "Court Poetry"; Owen, "Royal Propaganda"; and Stephenson, "Laws of Court."

55. A point made also by Pryce in "Context and Purpose," 59–60.

56. The following discussion on the queen and *edling* both reproduces and builds upon

Stacey, "King, Queen, and *Edling*." I am grateful to the University of Wales Press for permission to reprint this material.

57. For example, Stephenson, "Laws of Court," *WKC*, 401–2.

58. *WML* 4.23–25 (=*WKC* Cyfn §5/2, pp. 442–43); 5.11–17 (=*WKC* Cyfn §5/10–11, 13, pp. 442–43); 6.17–20 (=*WKC* Cyfn §5/25–26, pp. 442–43); 8.6–8 (=*WKC* Cyfn §5/25–26, pp. 442–43); 9.20–21 (=*WKC* Cyfn §7/4, pp. 444–45); 12.7–14 (=*WKC* Cyfn §10, pp. 446–47); *LTWL* Lat A 112.3–6, 34–35; 113.30–31; 117.14–21; Lat B 195.20–24 (=*WKC* Lat B §1.6/10–12, pp. 488–89); Lat B 196.7 (=*WKC* Lat B §1.6/25, pp. 490–91); Lat B 205.38–40 (=*WKC* Lat B §1.29/4–5, pp. 512–13); Lat C 277.13–15 (=*WLMA* §1.5/1, pp. 8–9); Lat C 278.17–19 (=*WLMA* §1.10/1, pp. 12–13); Lat C 279.2–7, 280.2 (=*WLMA* §1.10/10–11, 25, pp. 12–15), Lat D 319.11–13, 29–32; 320.2, 16–17, 33; 323.17; 328.13–32 (where the king's and queen's officers are intermixed); Lat E 439.13–16, 24–25; 440.11; 445.27–28; *Bleg* 7.6–10, 24–25; 9.3; 22.8–12.

59. Some Cyfn manuscripts also treat the queen's officers separately; it is unclear whether this represents a borrowing from Ior or an independent innovation: see Stacey, "King, Queen, and *Edling*," *WKC*, 54n99.

60. Russell translates *camerarie* in *WKC*, Lat B §1.6/12 (pp. 488–89) and 1.29/5 (pp. 512–13) as "chamberlain" instead of "chambermaid," thus suggesting that the queen was imagined in this text as having a *gwas ystafell* (Latin *camerarius*) as well as a chambermaid (*morwyn ystafell/ cameraria*). However, the association of the queen with the *morwyn ystafell* and the king with the *gwas ystafell* seems consistent across the Latin texts and Bleg: *LTWL* Lat A 117.14–21; Lat B 193.19–27 (=*WKC* Lat B §1.1/1–3, pp. 484–85); Lat D 320.33 (*morwyn ystauell brenhines*); 328.13–32 (where the king's and queen's officers have become confused); Lat E 439.23–25; 445.20–28; *Bleg* 7.24–25; 22.6–12. Lat B's *dapifer regine* in *LTWL* 193.27 (=*WKC* Lat B §1.1/3, pp. 484–85) clearly did not form part of the original Latin list.

61. *Ior* §§22–29.

62. *WLMA*, xxxvi–xliii.

63. *WML* 27.8 (=*WKC* Cyfn §30/2, pp. 466–67); and *LTWL* Lat C 279.2–5 (=*WLMA* §1.10/10, pp. 12–13), for example. Similar provisions are found elsewhere in the Latin tradition, e.g., *LTWL* Lat A 112.3–5; Lat B 195.20–22 (=*WKC* Lat B §1.6/10, pp. 488–89); 252.1–6 (=*WKC* Lat B §3.4, pp. 522–23), etc.

64. Compare *WML* 5.15–17 (=*WKC* Cyfn §5/11, pp. 442–43) and 27.8–10 (=*WKC* Cyfn §30/3–4, pp. 466–67) with *WML* 5.3–5 (=*WKC* Cyfn §5/5, pp. 442–43) and 12.20–13.2, 7–9, 17–18, 13.20–14.1 (=*WKC* Cyfn §11/4, 5, 12, 16, 17, 20, pp. 448–49). In the Latin texts and Bleg, compare *LTWL* Lat A 112.3–5 with 111.28–31; Lat B 195.20–22 (=*WKC* Lat B §1.6/10, pp. 488–89) with Lat B 195.9–11 (=*WKC* Lat B §1.6/5, pp. 448–49); Lat C 279.2–5 (*pincerne regine*) with 278.23–24 (=*WLMA* §1.10/10, pp. 12–13 with §1.10/4, pp. 12–13); Lat D 319.29–31 with 319.15–18; Lat E 439.14–16 with 439.1–2; *Bleg* 7.6–8 with 6.20–22.

65. *WML* 12.7 (=*WKC* Cyfn §10/1, pp. 446–47); *WML* 11.14–15 (=*WKC* Cyfn §9/1, pp. 446–47). The *efeirat teulu regine* mentioned in *LTWL* Lat C 279.6–7 (=*WLMA* §1.10/11, pp. 12–13) is unique and most likely an error: see *WLMA*, 58, and compare *LTWL* Lat A 112.5–6; Lat B 195.22–23 (=*WKC* Lat B §1.6/11, pp. 488–89); Lat D 319.29–32; Lat E 439.13–14; and *Bleg* 7.9–10.

66. The discussion of most officers in Ior opens with a variant of *ef a dele e tyr en ryd a'e uarch bressvyl a'e urethynwysc y gan e brenhyn a'e lyeynwysc e gan e urenhynes*, "he is entitled to his land free and to his horse in attendance, and his woolen clothing from the king and his linen clothing from the queen" (e.g., *Ior* 9/1, 10/1, 11/1, and so on). For Cyfn, see *WML* 2.12–15 (=*WKC* Cyfn §2/1, pp. 438–39), and cf. *WML* 11.12–13; 12.4–5; 13.3–4; 26.9–10, 15–16, 24–25;

27.1–3, and so on. On the gendered associations of these two types of cloth, see Herlihy, *Opera Muliebria*, 92.

67. The *morwyn ystafell*, one of the queen's officers, is said to have her lodging in the chamber of the king: *WML* 10.10–12 (=*WKC* Cyfn §7/10, pp. 444–45); *LTWL* Lat A 113.30–31; and compare Lat B 197.14–15 (=*WKC* Lat B §1.8/9, pp. 492–93); Lat C 281.10–11 (=*WLMA* §1.12/9, pp. 18–19); Lat D 321.21–22; Lat E 441.17–18); and *Bleg* 10.11–12.

68. *Ior* 22/2, 7; 23/2, 7, and contrast 25/3 with 19/4.

69. *Ior* 2/3; in 30/1 the queen's officers become part of the officers of the court in order to distinguish them from those who, like the footholder, groom of the rein, and dung *maer*, are "in the court" (*emevn llys*).

70. *Ior* 19/4 and 27/3.

71. *Ior* 25/6: *estauell e urenhynes.*

72. *Ior* 12/2; 26/4.

73. *Unbeiniaeth Prydain* is mentioned by name: *Ior* 13/6–7. Guests are implied by *Ior* 22/8 and 23/7.

74. Compare *Ior* 13/6 with *WML* 34.3–5 (=*WKC* Cyfn §34/3, pp. 466–67).

75. *Ior* 22/3–4; 23/7.

76. *Ior* 6/23.

77. *WML* 12.13–14 (in manuscripts W and X); cf. *ALW* Gwentian Code I.xi.5.

78. For the female nature of the chamber versus the generally male nature of the rest of the household, see Mertes, *English Noble Household*, 57–59, and see 42–46.

79. R. A. Brown, Colvin, and Taylor, *History of the King's Works*, i.121 and plan of the medieval palace of Westminster; Robert Stacey, *Politics, Policy*, 241–42; Labarge, *Baronial Household*, 57–58; Stacey, "King, Queen, and *Edling*," *WKC*, 60–61.

80. *WML* 4.23–25 (=*WKC* Cyfn §5/2, pp. 442–43); *LTWL* Lat A 111.25–26; Lat B 195.3–4 (=*WKC* Lat B §1.6/1, pp. 488–89); Lat C 278.17–18 (=*WLMA* §1.10/1, pp. 12–13); Lat D 319.11–13; Lat E 438.30–31; *Bleg* 6.13–15; *Ior* 3/6 and 110/6.

81. *WML* 5.3–5, 15–17 (=*WKC* Cyfn §5/5, 11, pp. 442–43); *LTWL* Lat C 278.23–24 and 279.2–5 (=*WLMA* §1.10/10, pp. 12–13).

82. Compare *Ior* 8/14–16 with 22/8 and note that traditions regarding the king's steward appear to have varied—perhaps because of the steward's increasing importance as a military leader.

83. This officer does not exist in Cyfn or the Latin tradition texts. Ior reports differing views on this issue: *Ior* 24/4–5. Compare the king and queen's groom of the rein in Cyfn and Latin C: *WML* 6.17–20 (=*WKC* Cyfn §5/25–26, pp. 442–43); *LTWL* Lat C 279.30–280.2 (=*WLMA* §1.10/24–25, pp. 14–15).

84. *Ior* 23/3; 24/3; 27/5; 28/5; 29/7; and cf. Cyfn traditions in *WML* 9.20–21 (=*WKC* Cyfn §7/4, 11, pp. 444–45).

85. Many versions that mention this practice record doubt or dissension about it: *WML* 10.1–4 (=*WKC* Cyfn §7/6, pp. 444–45); *LTWL* Lat C 281.8–9 (=*WLMA* §1.12/8, pp. 18–19) vs. Lat D 321.19–21; Lat E 441.15–17; *Ior* 10/3–4.

86. *Ior* 12/8.

87. Charles-Edwards, *Welsh Laws*, 64, and see also pp. 100–102. Huws argues that Ior C, written around the middle of the thirteenth century, is the earliest extant version of *Llyfr Iorwerth*. Since it contains a version of the Test Book, the latter had clearly come into existence by the time Ior C was written: Huws, "The Texts. ii. The Manuscripts," *LAL*, 123–25; and Huws, "Earliest Version." Jenkins dates the compilation of *Llyfr Iorwerth* to sometime after 1240: Jenkins, "Family of Welsh Lawyers," 123–33.

88. *AWR*, §252, pp. 412–14 (1222); *ByT* (*RBH*), 191–93.

89. Sources show her accompanying Einion Fychan and Ednyfed Fychan to negotiate with the government of Henry III in 1232 and writing to Henry III defending the cleric Instructus from rumors that he was disloyal to the king: Stephenson, *Governance of Gwynedd*, 208, 210, 225. See also Walker, *Medieval Wales*, 93, 96, 107; and *AWR*, 28–29 and references there. Llywelyn was clearly concerned about the potential impact of the execution of de Braose on his relations with the English Crown and certain noble families; shortly after the execution, he wrote to William's widow saying that he wished the betrothal agreement between them to continue and explaining that he could not have prevented the *magnates terre nostre* from issuing the verdict they had on her husband: *AWR* §261, pp. 428–29, and see also Crump, "Repercussions."

90. *AWR*, 28–29 and references there.

91. Stephenson, "Laws of Court," *WKC*, 402; and see also the many legal and political activities undertaken by women in Richards, *Welsh Noblewomen*; Johns, *Gender*.

92. Stacey, "King, Queen, and *Edling*"; and Stephenson, "Laws of Court."

93. *Brut y Tywysogyon* for the year 1230, *ByT* (*RBH*), 228–29.

94. Marie de France, "Lay of Guigemar."

95. Jennifer Smith, "Women, Land and Law," 26–27, with fuller discussion on 23–27; see also Cholakian, *Troubadour Lyric*, 101–6; and Gaunt, *Gender and Genre*.

96. *Ior* 86/1; *Col* 600; and see discussions in Jenkins, "Property Interests," *WLW*, 75; and Jenkins, "Lawyer Looks at Welsh Land Law," 236–40.

97. *Bleg* 75.24–25, but cf. *LTWL* Lat D 387.27–29.

98. R. R. Davies, "Status of Women," *WLW*, 100–101; Richards, *Welsh Noblewomen*, 59–94, 152–80; Cavell, "Aristocratic Widows"; Cavell, "Intelligence"; Cavell, "Welsh Princes." Under Welsh law, widows had only nine days in the marital home before departing with their belongings to whatever home would take them: Jenkins, "Property Interests," *WLW*, 85–86.

99. R. R. Davies, "Status of Women"; *WLW*, 100–111.

100. Barrell and Davies, "Land, Lineage," 41–45.

101. R. R. Davies, "Law and National Identity"; Pryce, "Prologues," 176–79; Pryce, "Context and Purpose," 55–63; Charles-Edwards, *Welsh Laws*, 9–13; Stacey, *Road to Judgment*, 179–82.

102. R. R. Davies, "Status of Women," *WLW*, 101.

103. C. W. Sullivan III, "Inheritance and Lordship," 361–63.

104. Valente, "Gwydion and Aranrhod," 342.

105. Part of what follows replicates Stacey, "King, Queen, and *Edling*," *WKC*, 47–53. I am grateful to the University of Wales Press for permission to reprint this material.

106. A point made explicitly with respect to both men in Ior, Cyfn, and Latin D. The Latin texts generally characterize the *edling*, but not the *penteulu*, in this way: *Ior* 4/2; 6/1; *WML* 3.25–4.1 and 11.3–5 (= *WKC* Cyfn §4/2 and §8/5, pp. 440–41 and 446–47 respectively); *LTWL* Lat A 110.33–34; Lat B 194.23–24 (= *WKC* Lat B §1.5/3, pp. 486–87); Lat B 207.30–35 (= *WKC* Lat B §2.4, pp. 518–19); 238.25–38; Lat C 277.30 (= *WLMA* §1.18/2, pp. 10–11); Lat D 318.9 and 321.38–39; Lat E 437.12; *Bleg* 4.20–21 and 11.1–2.

107. *WML* 9.14–18; 10.13–11.13 (= *WKC* Cyfn §7/1 and §8, pp. 444–47); and cf. *LTWL* Lat A 113.17–19, 113.33–41; Lat B 197.1–3, 17–22 (= *WKC* Lat B §1.8/1; §1.9/1–3, pp. 492–93); Lat C 278.2–3 (= *WLMA* §1.8/6, pp. 10–11), 280.30–33 (= *WLMA* §1.12/2, pp. 18–19), 281.13–18 (= *WLMA* §1.13/1–3, pp. 18–19); Lat D 321.7–10, 321.25–33; Lat E 441.6–8, 20–25; *Bleg* 9.17–21, 10.15–11.9.

108. *WML* 10.20–11.3 (= *WKC* Cyfn §8/3, pp. 446–47); *LTWL* Lat A 114.1–7; Lat B 200.16–20 (= *WKC* Lat B §1.15/2–5, pp. 500–501); 255.8–10; Lat C 284.26–29 (= *WLMA* §1.18/2–3,

pp. 30–31); Lat D 321.34–322.5; 329.4; 331.10–11; Lat E 441.25–28, 442.2–3; 444.15–16; *Bleg* 10.24–29, 19.28–31. The upper precinct also, according to Ior, if the *teulu* had been the ones to apprehend the offender: *Ior* 6/12–13, and cf. *WML* 11.1–3 (=*WKC* Cyfn §8/3–4, pp. 446–47).

109. For the *edling*, see *WML* 4.1–2 (=*WKC* Cyfn §4/3, pp. 440–41); and *LTWL* Lat E 438.31–32. For the *penteulu*, see *WML* 4.25–5.1 (=*WKC* Cyfn §5/3, pp. 442–43); *LTWL* Lat A 111.26–27; Lat B 195.4–5 (=*WKC* Lat B §1.6/2, pp. 488–89); Lat C 278.18–19 (=*WLMA* §1.10/2, pp. 12–13); Lat D 319.13–14; Lat E 438.32–33; and *Bleg* 6.16–17.

110. Cf. *Ior* 4/13 with 6/6—both *hyt yn dyogel*, "to a place of safety."

111. *Ior* 6/14.

112. *Ior* 6/30.

113. Thus, it is said that the ruler of Aberffraw owed *mechdeyrn ddylyed* to the English king, did not owe *ebediw*, and gave only dogs, hawks, and horses to the English ruler thereafter: *LTWL* Lat B 207.19–26 (=*WKC* Lat B §2.3/2–3, pp. 518–19); Lat C 277.19–26 (=*WLMA* §1.7/1–3, pp. 8–9); Lat E 437.30–438.4; and cf. *Ior* 110/1–5.

114. *Ior* 6/18.

115. *Ior* 6/18; 6/26–29.

116. *WML* 4.6–11 (=*WKC* Cyfn §4/5–9, pp. 440–41); *LTWL* Lat A 110.34–38; Lat B 194.24–28 (=*WKC* Lat B §1.5/4–7, pp. 486–87); Lat C 277.31–278.3 (=*WLMA* §1.8/3–6, pp. 10–11); Lat D 318.9–13; Lat E 437.12–15; *Bleg* 4.21–25; Charles-Edwards, "Heir-Apparent," 186–90; and, most recently, Charles-Edwards, *Wales and the Britons*, 329–33.

117. *WML* 4.11–13, 15–18 (=*WKC* Cyfn §§4/10, 4/12–13, pp. 440–41); *LTWL* Lat A 111.3–5; Lat B 194.31–33 (=*WKC* Lat B §1.5/11, pp. 486–87); Lat C 278.6–9 (=*WLMA* §1.8/9–10, pp. 10–11); Lat D 318.18–20; Lat E 437.18–19; *Bleg* 5.7–10; *Ior* 4/4.

118. Stacey, "King, Queen, and *Edling*," *WKC*, 48.

119. *Ior* 6/14, 8/4, 13/3, 19/5; *WML* 12.15–18 (=*WKC* Cyfn §11/12, pp. 448–49). Cyfn U and V speak only of the *penteulu*'s gift to the steward. See also *LTWL* Lat A 114.22–23, Lat D 322.21, Lat E 442.2–3.

120. *Ior* 4/18.

121. *Ior* 4/17 (from MSS B and D) and 4/18.

122. *Ior* 6/8, 10–12, 14–15, 21, 23–25.

123. *WML* 4.13–15 (=*WKC* Cyfn §4/11, pp. 440–41).

124. *LTWL* Lat C 278.6–7, 9–10 (=*WLMA* §1.8/8, 11, pp. 10–11); and cf. *LTWL* Lat A 111.2–3, 5–6 (*omnem sumptum et omnia necessaria*); Lat B 194.30–31, 33–34 (=*WKC* Lat B §1.4/11, 14, pp. 440–41); Lat D 318.17–18, 20–21; Lat E 437.17–18 and cf. 19–20; *Bleg* 5.6–7, 10–11.

125. The passage on the *edling*'s dinner, where he is said to eat without measure but "to a sufficiency," may speak also to the issue of dependency, in that it seems like a deliberate attempt to put boundaries around the *penteulu*'s consumption, which may be why Latin E omits it.

126. *LTWL* Lat C 277.28–29 (=*WLMA* §1.8/1, pp. 10–11).

127. *Ior* 4/4; the other Ior redactions have *ffrwyn*, "bridle," in place of *offrwm*: *LTMW*, 223, note to 6.30.

128. *Ior* 4/5.

129. *Ior* 4/4, and see further Stacey, "King, Queen, and *Edling*," *WKC*, 47–53, which the following discussion largely summarizes. On the *edling*, see Stephenson, *Governance of Gwynedd*, 152–53; and J. Beverley Smith, "Dynastic Succession," 218–24.

130. *WML* 4.6–11, 19–21 (=*WKC* Cyfn §4/5–9, 15–16, pp. 440–41); *LTWL* Lat A 110.34–38 and 111.7–13; Lat B 194.24–28, 194.35–195.2 (=*WKC* Lat B §1.5/4–7, 14–18, pp. 486–87); Lat C

277.31–278.3, 278.11–16; Lat D 318.9–13, 29–34; Lat E 437.12–15, 438.5–11; *Bleg* 4.21–25 and 5.20–28; and *Ior* 4/3 and 5/1–8.

131. *Ior* 4/3; 4/10.

132. See, for example, Warren, *Henry II*, 580–84; and Abulafia, *Frederick II*, 229–42.

133. *Ior* 6/1–3, the clear implication of which is that he remains on the list in other regions. See further Russell, "*Swydd, Swyddog, Swyddwr.*"

134. *Ior* 4/7–9. The failure to mention the king's brothers is likely not significant: *EIWK*, 217–18.

135. Stephenson, *Governance of Gwynedd*, 138–39; Charles-Edwards, "Heir-Apparent," 185–86; Charles-Edwards, *Wales and the Britons*, 329–34; *LTMW* 222; *WLMA*, 54–55.

136. J. Beverley Smith, "Dynastic Succession," 218–21; *CCC*, 192–93, 245–50; and Stephenson, *Governance of Gwynedd*, 138–39.

137. Stacey, "King, Queen, and *Edling*," *WKC*, 50–51, and references there.

138. See, for example, the opinions expressed in *Ior* 61/6–7; 64/5–8; 66/1, and so on. On succession patterns, see Charles-Edwards, *Wales and the Britons*, 329–37.

139. J. Beverley Smith, "Dynastic Succession," 199–232, 210–30.

140. Pryce, "Context and Purpose," 57–63.

141. J. Beverley Smith, "Dynastic Succession," 205–10; Stephenson, *Governance of Gwynedd*, chap. 8.

142. *Ior* 4/16. This occurs outside the tractate in *LTWL* Lat B 238.25–38, and in the *edling* section in Lat D 318.23–27; Lat E 437.27–29; and *Bleg* 5.12–19.

143. *CCC*, 300–301.

144. Carr, "*Teulu* and *Penteulu*," *WKC*, 78–79.

145. *Cronica de Wallia*, 15.

146. Charles-Edwards, "Food, Drink and Clothing," *WKC*, 324–25.

147. Assuming that *Ior* 87/6–7 can be interpreted as also extending to the question of kingship. This is not to say that Gruffudd would claim thereby to be the *only* heir, merely that he might insist on his own rights as outlined in 87/7.

148. Fulton, "Education of Princes," 234–35, 243–44.

149. Pryce, "Household Priest," *WKC*, 83–85; Pryce, *Native Law*, 147–62, 192–233.

150. Pryce, "Household Priest," *WKC*, 85.

151. Pryce, *Native Law and the Church*, 163–233, 241–51.

152. Pryce, "Household Priest," *WKC*, 84, and references there. The queen's priest is allotted a *nawdd*, one that aligns him with the church (*Ior* 23/8). The tractate on ecclesiastical sanctuary in *Ior* §71 follows immediately after the discussion of the *gorfodog* surety; for discussion, see Pryce, *Native Law and the Church*, 192–251.

153. *Ior* 7/12–13, with which compare *WML* 12.6–7 (= *WKC* Cyfn §9/6, pp. 446–47). Why this might be is suggested by *Ior* 7/9 and *Bleg* 13.15–20.

154. The extent of princely claims in Gwynedd may be reflected in the fact that the only definitive boundaries imagined for the *gwlad* in Ior (but not Cyfn, Bleg, or the Latin texts) are those where two kings meet to parley: J. Beverley Smith, *Llywelyn ap Gruffudd*, 1–2, 139–86.

155. *Ior* xxxv; Huws, "Earliest Version," 185–86.

156. Ior §104, *TCC*, 260–61, and cf. *Ior* 1/6 and 104/2.

157. *Ny dyly neb varnu ar ny 6yppo teir colofyn kyfreith a g6erth pop aneueil kyfreitha6l*, "no one should act as judge who does not know the three columns of law and the value of every legal animal": *WML* 16.13–15 (= *WKC* Cyfn §12/16, pp. 450–51), but cf. Cyfn manuscript U. In Lat A,

this sentence introduces the *nau affeyth galanas* and thus the Laws of Country; elsewhere in the Latin tradition, it occurs in the subtractate on the *iudex curie*.

158. The sole exception here is the sheep, which seems to be valued at a surprisingly low rate, on which see Charles-Edwards, "Three Columns of Law: Comparative Perspective," *TCC*, 44–45.

159. *WLMA* §§5.1 and 5.3, pp. 44–45, with notes on pp. 74–75; see also C. Eska, "Problematic Pigs."

160. Huws, "Earliest Version," 185.

161. *WLMA*, xlii–xliii, 74.

162. E.g., the value of animals used in the hunt, the laws on which are situated in the Laws of Court in Cyfn manuscripts W, X, and Y, but grouped together with the other animal regulations in Cyfn V and Mk: Jenkins, *Conspectus*, 23–28, 35.

163. In Cyfn V and Mk, for example, the tractate follows (roughly) after the provisions on land, which in turn follow the tractate on the Three Columns of Law: *WML*, lxxix–lxxxiii; Charles-Edwards, *Welsh Laws*, 27–30; Jenkins, *Conspectus*, 23–28; and see further on the ordering of tractates Charles-Edwards, "Relationship of the Tractates," *WLW*, 182–85; Russell, "Laws of Court from Latin B"; Owen, "Laws of Court from Cyfnerth"; Russell, "Arrangement and Development"; Charles-Edwards, "*Galanas* Tractate." In Lat A, most fall near the end of the lawbook, but hunting animals are treated separately from the others, as they are in certain Cyfn texts (*LTWL*, 107–8). In Lat B, material on animals is scattered throughout the redaction in a way that makes placement difficult to characterize (*LTWL*, 176–92, and see also 231–36). In Lat C, the laws on hunting appear to have been part of the Laws of Court, but the fragmentary nature of the manuscript makes it difficult to say much about the placement of the rest (*WLMA* §1.21 [pp. 34–37], and see §1.19–1.20 [pp. 30–33]; §§4.4, 5.1, and 5.3 [pp. 42–45]; *LTWL*, 273–75). Lat D's Wild and Tame tractate follows a collection of triads on judgment (*LTWL*, 300–315; and see also 358–62). Bleg's tractate follows texts on women, land, and status, while Lat E's follows after the provisions on land (*Bleg* 87–98; *LTWL*, 419–33, and see also 483–89).

164. Entitled in Ior C: *Gwerth Gwyllt a Dof*, "The Worth of Wild and Tame." Whether Wild and Tame was originally the final tractate of the Test Book is difficult to say; tractates on Joint-Ploughing and Corn-Damage follow Wild and Tame as the text is extant today. Ior manuscript B implies that the tractates that follow after Wild and Tame formed part of an appendix to the Test Book proper (*Ior* 138/13, 139/1; appendix is Wiliam's term in *Ior* xxxv–xxxvi, and see *Ior* 1/6 and 104/2). Huws suggests on the basis of Ior C, the earliest of the Ior manuscripts, that the Test Book might originally have ended with the tractates on Joint-Ploughing and Corn-Damage rather than with Wild and Tame (Huws, "Earliest Version," 185–86).

165. Powell, "Floating Sections"; Jenkins, "'Cyfnerth' Text," *WLW*, 134–35; S. E. Roberts, *LlPom*, 52–53.

166. Bracton, *De legibus*, 2:42–43.

167. See, for example, Hywel ab Owain Gwynedd's "Boast," in *Gwaith Llywelyn Fardd*, p. 121, lines 3–18.

168. *Ior* §§121–35; *WML* 67.3–85.3; *LTWL* Lat A 147.11–150.5, 152.24–158.2; Lat B 232.7–236.23; Lat D 358.1–362.30; Lat E 483.6–489.38; *Bleg* 87.23–94.27.

169. *WML* 80.2–10, 16–19 and 113.11–18, and cf. *LTWL* Lat A 127.17–30; Lat B 203.14–20 (= *WKC* Lat B §1.20/19, pp. 506–7); 244.1–3; Lat D 376.15–16; 390.12–13; Lat E 467.20–25; 495.1–2. On the issue of utility, see *LTWL* Lat A 121.7–10; Lat B 199.4–6 (= *WKC* Lat B §1.11/11, pp. 496–97, *precium omnium animalium que necesse sunt ad opus hominum*); Lat C 283.12–14 (= *WLMA* §1.15/10, pp. 24–25); Lat D 325.21–23 (*precia omnium animalium domesticorum et quorundam sil-*

vestrium quibus homo utitur); Lat E 444.1–3 (*et precium omnium animalium ad homines pertinencium*); and *Bleg* 16.22–24 (a *gwerth holl anyueileit dof, ac ereill gwyllt a aruerho dynyon ohonnunt*).

170. *Ior* §137.

171. Jenkins, "Hawk and Hound," *WKC*, 265, and 258–59 and 280 on possible changes in princely hunting practices contemporary with the lawbooks.

172. *Art of Falconry*.

173. Oggins, *Kings and Their Hawks*, 139–44; and Cummins, *Hound and the Hawk*.

174. Jenkins, "Hawk and Hound," *WKC*, 262–64, and references there.

175. Jenkins, "Hawk and Hound," *WKC*, 274–80, and references there. For medieval hunting generally as a courtly diversion, see Cummins, *Hound and Hawk*; and cf. Marvin, *Hunting Law*.

176. *WML* 34.6–36.20 (=*WKC* Cyfn §35, pp. 468–69); and see also *LTWL* Lat A 147.11–149.35; Lat C 285.9–287.29 (=*WLMA* §§1.19–1.21, pp. 30–37); Lat E 465.25–467.25.

177. *Ior* 90/10–11; 148/3. Translation closely based on *LTMW*, 120–21 and 198–99.

178. Compare *Ior* 3/1–7, 4/12, and 6/4–5 with *Ior* 110/1–10.

179. *Ior* 158/1.

180. The chief falconer was honored publicly in the hall for special kills made by his birds: *Ior* 9/6, 9/12; *WML* 17.14–23, 18.15–19 (=*WKC* Cyfn §14/1–3, 16–18, pp. 454–55); *LTWL* Lat A 114.39–115.5; Lat B 199.21–26 (=*WKC* Lat B §1.13/1–3, pp. 498–99); Lat C 283.29–34 (=*WLMA* §1.16/1–2, pp. 26–27); Lat D 323.27–32, 323.35–324.1; Lat E 442.20–25; *Bleg* 13.24–14.2; 14.6–10.

181. *Ryd yw y'r brenhin hela ym pob lle yn y wlat*, "the king is free to hunt anywhere in his *gwlad*": *Bleg* 51.1, and see discussion in Jenkins, "Hawk and Hound," *WKC*, 274–78. His animals likewise: *Ior* 136/5–9; *WML* 36.14–17 (=*WKC* Cyfn §35/31 pp. 468–69), for example, and see further Jenkins, "Hawk and Hound," *WKC*, 274–78.

182. This point is made most clearly in Ior, but occurs (sometimes to a lesser extent) in the southern redaction texts as well, suggesting that this placement was not entirely an innovation on the part of the Ior redactor: see discussion above.

183. *WML* 27.22–29.4; very similar is *Ior* §33 (the quote is from *Ior* 33/13) and §§91–96.

184. *WML* 29.5–16; *Ior* §§91–96.

185. *WML* 29.17–31.5; *Ior* §34.

186. *LTWL* Lat A 121.7–10; Lat B 199.4–6 (=*WKC* Lat B §1.11/11, pp. 496–97); Lat C 283.12–14 (=*WLMA* §1.15/10, pp. 24–25); Lat D 325.21–23; Lat E 444.1–3; and *Bleg* 16.23–24. Wild animals are not entirely excluded from the Latin texts, though the focus is on domesticated beasts: *LTWL* Lat A 127.17–30; Lat B 203.14–20 (=*WKC* Lat B §1.20/19–23, pp. 506–7); 244.1–3; Lat D 376.15–16; 390.12–13; Lat E 467.20–25; 495.1–2. Something similar is also implied in Cyfn, although it is nowhere stated as directly as it is in the Latin texts: *WML* 80.16–19.

187. *Glân*: defined in *Ior* 57/1; and see *LTMW*, 247, note to 63.5.

188. Goodrich, *Law in the Courts of Love*, 98.

189. Bracton, *De legibus*, 2:42–43.

190. Pryce, "Context and Purpose," 50–51.

191. Stephenson, "Laws of Court," *WKC*, 404–9.

CHAPTER 3

1. Bynum, *Holy Feast and Holy Fast*; Bynum, *Fragmentation and Redemption*; Bynum, "Why All the Fuss About the Body?" Not all critics found themselves in agreement with Bynum's approach: Biddick, "Genders, Bodies, Borders"; Aers, "Figuring Forth the Body of Christ"; Biddick, "Response to David Aers."

2. For example, Bynum, "Mysticism and Asceticism"; Elliott, *Spiritual Marriage*; Wogan-Browne, "Chaste Bodies"; Karras, *Sexuality in Medieval Europe*; Rousseau, *Cultural Turn*; Kroll and Bachrach, *Mystic Mind*; Newman, "Considerations on Life and Death."

3. P. Brown, *Cult of the Saints*; P. Brown, "Relics and Social Status"; P. Brown, "Society and the Supernatural"; Van Dam, *Leadership and Community*; Bynum and Gerson, "Body-Part Reliquaries"; Freeman, *Holy Bones*; Rollo-Koster, "Politics of Body Parts."

4. For example, Borsje, *Chaos to Enemy*; Borsje, "Meaning of *Túathcháech*"; Bynum, "Gerald and the Werewolf"; Bynum, *Metamorphosis and Identity*; Cohen, *Of Giants*; Cohen, "Hybrids, Monsters, Borderlands"; Cohen, *Hybridity, Identity*; Lowe, "Kicking over the Traces"; Lowe, "Contagious Violence"; Huot, *Madness*; Harper, *Insanity, Individuals and Society*; S. A. Miller, *Medieval Monstrosity*; Crawford and Lee, *Bodies of Knowledge*; Eichhorn-Mulligan, "*Togail Bruidne Da Derga*"; Eichhorn-Mulligan, "Anatomy of Power"; Ó Cathasaigh, "Body in *Táin Bó Cúailnge*."

5. For example, Bynum, *Fragmentation and Redemption*; Cadden, *Meanings of Sex Difference*; Coakley, *Religion and the Body*, 111–54; Lochrie, McCracken, and Schultz, *Constructing Medieval Sexuality*; Cohen and Wheeler, *Becoming Male*; Karras, *From Boys to Men*; Farmer and Pasternack, *Gender and Difference*.

6. For example, Elliott, *Fallen Bodies*; Thibodeaux, *Negotiating Clerical Identities*; Coon, *Dark-Age Bodies*.

7. Oliver, *Body Legal*.

8. Scott, "Gender: A Useful Category of Historical Analysis"; and subsequent reassessments in Feree, Lorber, and Hess, *Revisioning Gender*; Scott, "Gender: Still a Useful Category of Analysis?"; J. Butler and Weed, *Question of Gender*.

9. P. Brown, *Body and Society*, 28–29.

10. Kantorowicz, *King's Two Bodies*; Post, *Studies in Medieval Legal Thought*.

11. John of Salisbury, *Policraticus*, bk. 5, chaps. 1–2. For discussion, see Hale, "Analogy of the Body Politic," 1:68–70; Le Goff, "Head or Heart?," 13–27; and Stevens, "Secular Heart," 262–82.

12. Nederman and Forhan, *Medieval Political Theory*, 24–25.

13. Harvey, *Body Politic*, 15–16.

14. For biblical references, see Douglas, *Leviticus as Literature*, 14–18, 67–86, 176–94; O'Connor, "Body in the Bible," 29–33; and Douglas, "Body of the World," 395–99. The metaphorical equation of the body of Christian believers with the *corpus Christi* would have been familiar to any literate Christian of the period: 1 Cor. 12:12–28; Eph. 4:23 and 4:30. For medieval examples, see LeGoff, "Head or Heart?," 16–17, and references there.

15. As also the later struggles between Philip the Fair and Boniface VIII: see Le Goff, "Head or Heart?," 16–17.

16. Brunetto Latini, *Li Livre dou Tresor*, bk. 3, chaps. 75, 87.

17. Thomas Aquinas, *De Regimine Principum*, bk. 1, chaps. 1, 2, 3, 12, 13, 15; 4.23.

18. John of Paris, "On Royal and Papal Power," chap. 1.

19. William of Pagula, *Mirror of King Edward III*, 11.

20. Marsiglio of Padua, *Defensor Pacis*, chap. 17, no. 8.

21. Wyclif, *On the Duty of the King*, chap. 5.

22. Oresme cites Aristotle as his precedent in his *De moneta*, written around 1356. The illustration can be found in Pierpont Morgan manuscript 456 (fol. 99v), and is reproduced and discussed in Sherman, *Imagining Aristotle*, 216–17, and see also pt. 3, "Paradigms of the Body Politic," 175–302.

23. Christine de Pisan, *Book of the Body Politic*, 3.1–2, 9–10.

24. Le Goff, "Head or Heart?," 18, and see further M. D. Johnston, *Medieval Conduct Literature*, no. 111; Born, "Perfect Prince"; Krynen, *L'Idéal du prince*; Ferster, *Fictions of Advice*; Meens, "Politics, Mirrors of Princes and the Bible"; Anton, *Fürstenspiegel und Herrscherethos*; Anton, *Fürstenspiegel (Königsppiegel) des frühen und hohen Mittelalters*.

25. For both sides the decapitated head served as an important symbol for the removal of the ruler: Yeager, "Body Politic."

26. Yeager, "Body Politic," 151.

27. *Ior* 4/6; 6/30; *LTWL* Lat A 138.35–38; Lat B 207.31–34 (=*WKC* Lat B §2.4, pp. 518–19); 238.25–30; Lat D 318.23–26; Lat E 437.7–10; *Bleg* 5.12–15; 32.7–17; 58.7–8.

28. *LTWL* Lat B 207.31–32 (=*WKC* Lat B §2.4/2, pp. 518–19); Lat D 318.23–26; Lat E 437.7–10; *Bleg* 5.13–15.

29. *GPC*, 2726–29, s.v. "pen"; *Pwyll Pendeuic Dyuet*, ed. Thomson, 7, lines 190–91; cf. its use in *Y Gododdin*, ed. Koch, A44, line 537, pp. 96–97, and see note on p. 213. For Old Irish *cenn*, see *Dictionary of the Irish Language*, s.v. "cenn," 107–8, cols. 120–27.

30. *Branwen Uerch Lyr*, ed. Thomson, 1, lines 1–2, and 11, lines 289–95.

31. McKenna, "Colonization of Myth," 117, and see broader discussion on 112–19.

32. Russell, " 'Go and Look in the Latin Books,' " 222–24 (Peniarth 20, pp. 204–5, line 32). See also the eulogy on the prince's sepulcher on p. 223: *Cesaries quasi congeries solis radiorum / Principis et facies vertitur in cineres*. I am grateful to the author for pointing me to these texts and making the text of his article and edition available to me in advance of publication.

33. Cited from the Peniarth 20 Welsh text (138a4–139b24), to which compare the *brachium fortitudinis, largitatis manus, rationis occulus* of the Exeter fragment (also known as the *Cronica de Wallia*): Exeter, Cathedral Library MS 3514, pp. 507–23. Texts, translations, and commentary by Russell, " 'Go and Look in the Latin Books,' " 233–34.

34. *Ploratu plene vite laxantur habene* (from Peniarth 20, pp. 204–5, line 21); text and translation by Russell, " 'Go and Look in the Latin Books.' "

35. Peniarth 20, pp. 204–5, lines 13–14, cited and translation adapted from Russell, " 'Go and Look in the Latin Books,' " 222–23.

36. *Lugent corda tacent corpora resus obit / Resus obit vexilla cadunt regalia signa / Hic iam nulla leuat dextera resus obit*: from Peniarth 20, pp. 204–5, lines 8–10, all cited from Russell, " 'Go and Look in the Latin Books,' " 222–23.

37. "*Marwnad Llywelyn ap Gruffudd*," 414–33, poem no. 36, with historical introduction on 409–10.

38. J. Beverley Smith, *Llywelyn ap Gruffudd*, 568–69, 578–79.

39. "*Marwnad Llywelyn ap Gruffudd*," 424–25, lines 89–90, 93–94. For commentary, see Matonis, "Rhetorical Patterns," 192, and J. Beverley Smith, *Llywelyn ap Gruffudd*, 569–70.

40. Higley, "Forcing a Gap," 254, and 249–51, 263 on the mimetic aspects of the work generally.

41. "*Marwnad Llywelyn ap Gruffudd*," 424–25, lines 97–99; the translation is Higley's, "Forcing a Gap," 269.

42. Higley, "Forcing a Gap," 254.

43. Fulton, "Education of Princes," 232–39.

44. Fulton, "Education of Princes," 239.

45. Fulton, "Education of Princes," 239, citing James, "*Secretum Secretorum*," 158. The Latin text is available in *Secretum secretorum: Nine English Versions*.

46. Douglas, *Leviticus as Literature*, 14–18, 67–86, 176–94.

47. John of Salisbury, *Policraticus*, bk. 4, chap. 4.

48. John of Salisbury, *Policraticus*, bk. 6, chap. 24.

49. "*Castigos del Rey Don Sancho*," 214–16, §§43–46. Cf. Christine's use of the biblical metaphor of the prince as shepherd protecting his people with servants conceptualized as guard dogs: Christine de Pisan, *Book of the Body Politic*, chap. 9.

50. John of Salisbury, *Policraticus*, bk. 6, chaps. 20, 24, and see also chap. 26.

51. Aristotle's *De Motu Animalium*, 19–56.

52. *Ior* 110/10 (translation closely follows that of *LTMW*, 155). In Latin A, it is included in a part of a group of triads following the suretyship tractate in the Laws of Country (*LTWL* Lat A 126.1–5). In Latin B, it occurs in a section following on the main body of the Laws of Court entitled "Here are added things which pertain to the court and to the officials": *LTWL* Lat B 207.13–17 (=*WKC* Lat B §2.2/1–2, pp. 516–17). By contrast, Latin D, E, and Bleg have integrated it into their main discussion of the king's *sarhaed*: *LTWL* Lat D 317.15–18; Lat E 436.9–10; *Bleg* 3.13–16. In Ior, this triad occurs in the Test Book tractate on *sarhaed*, but not in the earlier version in the Laws of Court. Cf. also S. E. Roberts, *LT*, Q2, pp. 92–93.

53. *TCC*, 315–16.

54. *Ior* 3/3, and cf. *Ior* 110/2; translation closely follows that of *LTMW*, 5. Other redactions define *sarhaed* to the king in similar ways, but with different wording. Latin D and E expand the breaking of protection clause to include the king's peace (*pacem illius violare*) as well as his *nawdd*: *WML* 2.19–3.11 (=*WKC* Cyfn §3/1–4, pp. 438–39); *LTWL* Lat A 110.1–21; Lat B 193.32–194.12 (=*WKC* Lat B §1.2, pp. 484–85; and see also §2.3, pp. 518–19); Lat C 276.27–277.12 (=*WLMA* §1.4, pp. 6–7); Lat D 317.10–37; Lat E 436.11–31; *Bleg* 3.16–4.6.

55. *Sarhaed* to the queen is defined in all redactions as breaking her protection, striking her, or snatching something violently from her hand: *Ior* 3/6–7; *WML* 3.13–18 (=*WKC* Cyfn §3/5, pp. 438–39); *LTWL* Lat A 110.22–26; Lat B 194.13–17 (=*WKC* Lat B §1.3, pp. 486–87); Lat C 277.13–15 (=*WLMA* §1.5, pp. 8–9); Lat D 317.38–318.2; Lat E 436.32–34; *Bleg* 4.7–11.

56. The status of the heir in this respect is unclear. *Sarhaed* to the *edling* is nowhere expressly defined, which may suggest that, like the king, his body is also being depicted as personally inviolable. The most notable aspect of his *sarhaed* is the disagreement among the various versions regarding its nature and manner of calculation—the same as the king's (minus the gold and silver ornaments and, in Cyfn, the herd of cattle: Cyfn, Lat A, Lat B, Lat C, Lat E) or a third of the king's (also without the gold and silver: Ior, Lat D, Bleg). All set the amount due to the *penteulu* as a third of the king's: *Ior* 4/12; 6/5; *WML* 4.3–6; 8.9–11(=*WKC* Cyfn §4/4, pp. 440–41; §6/1, pp. 444–45); *LTWL* Lat A 111.1–2; Lat B 194.29–30 (=*WKC* Lat B §1.5/8–9, pp. 486–87); 196.16–17 (=*WKC* Lat B §1.7/5, 490–91); Lat C 278.4–5; 280.7–8 (=*WLMA* §1.8/7, pp. 10–11, and §1.11/2, pp. 16–17); Lat D 318.14–17; 320.29–31); Lat E 437.15–16; *Bleg* 5.2–5; 8.27–29.

57. *Vita Griffini*, §§18–20 (pp. 68–73), and see the laudatory description of his wife and remarks on the large number of children he fathered in §24 (pp. 76–79); *Medieval Prince of Wales*, 36–39, 42–43 (trans. pp. 67–69, 70, 74). Very similar is the account of the battle of Gwaederw: *Vita Griffini*, §12 (pp. 60–63). The best study of the rhetoric of this vita is Malone, "Entirely Outside the World."

58. "*Arwyrain Owain Gwynedd*," p. 8, lines 2, 5, and 36.

59. "*Arwyrain Owain Gwynedd*," p. 8, lines 21–24, 41–45, and p. 9, lines 45–46. I owe this evocative translation to Clancy, *Medieval Welsh Poems*, 148.

60. "*Arwyrain Owain Gwynedd*," p. 9, line 59.

61. *Ior* 42/2–4; *LTWL* Lat A 126.15–17; Lat D 370.28–31; Lat E 503.18–19; *Bleg* 108.31–109.2.

62. *Ior* 6/29; 7/12; 10/15; 42/2; *WML* 12.6–7; 16.7–8 (=*WKC* Cyfn §9/6, pp. 446–47; §12/12, pp. 450–51); 124.2–3; *LTWL* Lat A 126.10–14; Lat B 199.11–15 (=*WKC* Lat B §1.12/1, pp. 496–97); Lat C 283.20–23 (=*WLMA* §1.15/14, pp. 24–25; Lat D 370.24–27); Lat E 464.34–465.4; *Bleg* 108.27–30.

63. *Ior* 3/4; 110/1–3; *WML* 3.7–11 (=*WKC* Cyfn §3/3, pp. 438–39); *LTWL* Lat A 110.9–16; Lat B 194.1–7 (=*WKC* Lat B §1.2/4, pp. 484–85); Lat C 277.5–12 (=*WLMA* §1.4/3, pp. 6–7); Lat D 317.19–29; Lat E 436.17–27; *Bleg* 3.17–18, 3.26–4.4. For the distance involved, see *LTMW*, 221–22.

64. Some Ior versions have nine years: *Ior* 3/4 and note 3 on p. 2.

65. After seven years a marriage is deemed to be sufficiently well established that the two parties divide their property equally should they divorce, for example: *Ior* 44/1–2 (=*WLW* Ior §44/1–2, pp. 162–63); *WML* 90.7–9 (=*WLW* Cyfn §73/8, pp. 136–37); *LTWL* Lat A 141.31–34 (=*WLW* Lat A §51/1–2, pp. 148–49); Lat B 221.6–10; Lat D 344.15–18; Lat E 470.7–11; *Bleg* 60.23–61.4.

66. *Ior* 146/1–2; cf. *WML* 41.24–42.2.

67. *Ior* §4.

68. *Ior* 6/2–3, and Jenkins, "Prolegomena," *WKC*, 24–28.

69. *Ior* §6; *GPC*, 1556–57, s.vv. "gwahan, gwahanu."

70. *Ior* 6/26–28.

71. *Ior* 6/29.

72. Because they return to him when they die: see discussion below.

73. *Ior* 4/4; 6/14, 30.

74. *Ior* 4/4–7; 6/30.

75. Payment in currency rather than in kind has become the norm by the thirteenth century: see the note to 11.23 in *LTMW*, 225. However, it is the relationship with the king that matters most: *Ior* 6/30.

76. *Ior* 3/4–5; *WML* 2.25–3.7 (=*WKC* Cyfn §3/2, pp. 438–39); *LTWL* Lat A 110.9–21; Lat B 194.1–12 (=*WKC* Lat B §1.2/4–7, pp. 484–85); Lat C 277.5–12 (=*WLMA* §1.4/3, pp. 6–7); Lat D 317.19–29; Lat E 436.17–28; *Bleg* 3.17–25.

77. *Ior* 3/7; 4/12; 6/4–5; 110/7–8 (and see also 110/9 on the king's daughter). Compare this with *WML* 3.16–18; 4.3–6; 8.9–12 (=*WKC* Cyfn §§3/5; 4/4; 6/1–2, pp. 438–45); *LTWL* Lat A 110.25–26; 111.1–2; 113.3–5; Lat B 194.15–17; 194.29–30; 196.16–18 (=*WKC* Lat B §§1.3/3; 1.5/9; 1.7/5, pp. 486–91); Lat C 277.14–15; 278.4–5; 280.7–8 (=*WLMA* §1.5/2, pp. 8–9; §1.8/7, pp. 10–11; §1.11/2, pp. 16–17). Lat D and Bleg assign the *edling* a compensation equivalent to two-thirds that of the king, distinguishing him from "others who belong to the kingdom" who are entitled to only a third: *LTWL* Lat D 318.14–17; 320.29–31; *Bleg* 4.9–11; 5.1–5; 8.27–29. In Latin E, the *edling*'s price is the same as the king's (but without gold or silver), while the other royal relatives are level with the queen and *penteulu*: *LTWL* Lat E 436.33–34; 437.15–16; 437.27–28; 440.19–20.

78. *Ior* 110/11–14 (=Ior manuscript B only; all other Ior manuscripts read as Ior E 110/4–9a in *TCC*, pp. 274–75); and cf. the slightly different rates cited in *WML* 8.12–9.7 (=*WKC* Cyfn §6/3–11, pp. 444–45); *LTWL* Lat A 113.5–10; Lat B 196.18–34 (=*WKC* Lat B §1.7/6–13,

pp. 490–91); Lat C 280.8–25 (=*WLMA* §1.11/2–9, pp. 16–17); Lat D 320.21–39; Lat E 440.21–34; *Bleg* 9.1–10. The translation here closely follows that of *LTMW*, 155.

79. *Ior* 110/16 (=Ior B; for other Ior manuscripts see Ior E 110/11, *TCC*, pp. 274–75). The translation here closely follows that of *LTMW*, 155.

80. *WML* 45.18–24.

81. *WML* 45.24–46.2.

82. *Ystoria Gereint uab Erbin*, 17–18; *Pwyll Penduic Dyuet*, 390–31.

83. *Ior* 2/4; 4/4, 17; 6/14 (note that the clothing referred to here is the special clothing given at the three principal feasts rather than livery); 8/4; *WML* 2.12–15; 4.13–15; 12.15–16 (=*WKC* Cyfn §2/1, §4/11, and §11/1 , pp. 438–39, 440–41, and 448–49 respectively); *LTWL*, Lat A 109.33–35; 111.2–3; 114.22–23; Lat B 193.28–30; 194.30–31 (=*WKC* Lat B §1.1/4; §1.5/10, pp. 483–87); Lat C 276.23–25; 278.6 (=*WLMA* §1.3/1, pp. 6–7, and §1.8/8, pp. 10–11); Lat D 317.3–5; 318.17–18; 322.21; Lat E 436.6–8; 437.17–18; 442.2–3; *Bleg* 2.25–28; 5.6–7; 11.29–12.1.

84. *Ior* 4/4.

85. In *Ior* 6/1, the *penteulu* is identified as the son or nephew of the king *neu y kywuvch gvr ac y galler penteylu ohanav*, "or a man sufficiently noble that he can be made *penteulu*."

86. *Ior* 6/14.

87. Stacey, "King, Queen, and *Edling*," *WKC*, 57–58.

88. See also Charles–Edwards, "Food, Drink and Clothing," *WKC*, 335–36; Stacey, "Clothes Talk," *WKC*.

89. Two parts of them according to Ior and Cyfn, and the share of two men according to the Latin traditions and Bleg: *Ior* 8/8; *WML* 13.18–20 (=*WKC* Cyfn §11/19, pp. 448–49); *LTWL* Lat B 197.28–30 (=*WKC* Lat B §1.10/5, pp. 494–95); Lat C 281.22–24 (=*WLMA* §1.14/3, pp. 20–21); Lat D 322.32–34; Lat E 441.30–31; *Bleg* 12.13–14.

90. *Ior* 9/7; *WML* 18.19–20 (=*WKC* Cyfn §14/19, pp. 454–55). Cyfn has "hearts" only; Ior specifies that the animals in question are wild.

91. On the nature of the *anrheg*, see Charles–Edwards, "Food, Drink and Clothing," *WKC*, 330–34. See *WML* 161, note 1, on the corrupt reading of the text.

92. *WML* 17.5–10=Cyfn V, but the sentence is better preserved (as an addition in the margin) in Cyfn W. The sentence does not occur in the other Cyfn manuscripts and is not therefore in the *WKC* version; however, a similar tradition is found in Cyfn X: *WKC* Cyfn X §39/1–2, pp. 474–75. I am grateful to Thomas Charles-Edwards for this information and for sharing with me his proposed reconstruction of the passage in question. Manon Phillips explains the *anrec y pen* in "Defod a Moes y Llys," *WKC*, 349–50.

93. *Ior* 11/10; *WML* 21.1–2 (=*WKC* Cyfn §13/2, pp. 452–53); *LTWL* Lat A 116.7–8; Lat B 198.10 (=*WKC* Lat B §1.10/18, pp. 494–95); Lat C 282.11–12 (=*WLMA* §1.14/13, pp. 20–23); Lat D 326.24–25; Lat E 444.10–11; *Bleg* 18.25–27.

94. *Ior* 36/3 (*Rey a dyweyt*, "some say").

95. *WML* 32.24–25 (=*WKC* Cyfn §41/5, pp. 474–75).

96. *Ior* 37/5.

97. *WML* 31.6–8 (=*WKC* Cyfn §39/1–2, pp. 474–75) in the kitchen; *LTWL* Lat A 119.1–3; Lat B 206.20–21 (=*WKC* Lat B §1.32/1, pp 514–15); Lat D 331.20–21; Lat E 447.4–5; *Bleg* 26.25–26 in the court.

98. He gets one third of the skins: *Ior* 8/9, 20/4.

99. *WML* 26.3–6.

100. *LTWL* Lat A 118.13–15 (two men's part of sheep and goat skins killed in kitchen); Lat B 203.34 (=*WKC* Lat B §1.23/1, pp. 508–9); Lat D 330.24–25; *Bleg* 25.8–9; Lat E 446.25–28.

101. *Ior* 20/6.

102. *WML* 26.3–6.

103. *LTWL* Lat D 330.8–9, 24–25; Lat E 446.25–28; *Bleg* 25.3–5, 8–9.

104. *WML* 33.4–6 (= *WKC* Cyfn §42/1–2, pp. 476–77).

105. Or, conceivably, a reference to stomach fat, and thus essentially parallel with the reading in Cyfn?

106. *LTWL* Lat B 203.36–204.2 (= *WKC* Lat B §1.23/3, pp. 508–9).

107. *Ior* 33/11–12.

108. *LTWL* Lat A 120.37–38 (slaughtered in kitchen); Lat D 349.19–20 (slaughtered in court); Lat E 447.33–448.1 (slaughtered in court); *Bleg* 27.17–18 (slaughtered in court).

109. *WML* 32.15–17 (= *WKC* Cyfn §40/7, pp. 474–75), and see also *WML* 26.3–6 (= *WKC* §26/1, pp. 464–65).

110. *Ior* 35/6.

111. *Ior* 35/4, 7, 8; *WML* 32.3–17 (= *WKC* Cyfn §40/3–7, pp. 474–75); and cf. *LTWL* Lat A 118.4; Lat B 206.26–28 (= *WKC* Lat B §1.32/6, pp. 514–15); Lat D 330.2–6; *Bleg* 24.21–22.

112. *WML* 24.8–11 (= *WKC* Cyfn §19/6–7, pp. 460–61).

113. *LTWL* Lat A 117.32–35; Lat B 206.9–12 (= *WKC* Lat B §1.30/5, pp. 514–15); Lat D 329.15–17; Lat E 446.14–16; *Bleg* 23.17–19 (*dryswr neuadd*, "doorkeeper of the hall").

114. *Ior* 19/13.

115. Patterson, "Honour and Shame," 83; Charles–Edwards, "Food, Drink and Clothing," *WKC*, 321, 334; Cichon, *Violence and Vengeance*, 100–101n332.

116. *WML* 17.5–8.

117. *Ior* 8/8–9; 20/2–3; 33/2; and contrast also 8/11–12 with 33/5. See Jenkins's comments on the *maer* and dung *maer* in *LTMW*, 363–64. Stephenson argues that the *stiwart* in 33/2 refers to the usher rather than to the *distain*: Stephenson, *Governance of Gwynedd*, 46n26. Patterson suggests that the skins and entrails given to the cook reflect his work in butchering the animals brought in to him: Patterson, "Honour and Shame," 83.

118. Charles-Edwards seems inclined to see the falconer's payment in symbolic terms: Charles–Edwards, *WKC*, "Food, Drink and Clothing," *WKC*, 334 and 334n71.

119. Jenkins, "Prolegomena," *WKC*, 17–18; Charles–Edwards, "Food, Drink and Clothing," *WKC*, 334; Stacey, "King, Queen, and *Edling*," *WKC*, 29–31; and see also Stephenson, "Laws of Court," who argues that the Laws of Court emphasize the festive, "good works" element of the king's rule in preference to the more "onerous developments" in government, which were regarded by those who suffered through them as abuses. Patterson's views admit for interpretations that are both literal and symbolic in nature, though even she seems to take these payments more or less at face value: "Honour and Shame," 83, 89–91.

120. Jenkins, "Prolegomena," *WKC*, 18. These payments are, however, conceptualized as entitlements due from the king to his officers rather than as hospitality renders due from subordinates to their lord. An interesting parallel is the Dinnshenchas poem "Temair III," on which see Charles–Edwards, "Another Reading."

121. Jenkins, "Hawk and Hound," *WKC*, 274–78.

122. *Ior* 9/7; Charles–Edwards, "Food, Drink and Clothing," *WKC*, 334n71.

123. *Ior* 37/5.

124. As implied by the provisions on handling a kill on land that belongs to another: *Ior* §§136–37.

125. As suggested by Patterson, "Honour and Shame," 83; and see also Cichon, *Violence and Vengeance*, 100–101n332.

126. For example, the *penteulu* (*Ior* 4/21); chief groom (11/7); *bard teulu* (13/7), and so on. The judge gets a share (Cyfn says two shares) even though he did not go on the raid himself: *WML* 15.23–25 (= *WKC* Cyfn §12/8, pp. 450–51), and cf. *Ior* 10/11.

127. *LTWL* Lat D 330.8–9, 24–25; Lat E 446.25–28; *Bleg* 25.3–5, 8–9.

128. Le Goff, "Head or Heart?," 20–23.

129. John of Salisbury, *Policraticus*, bk. 5, chap. 2; Harvey, *Body Politic*, 15.

130. *Ior* 6/7.

131. It is unclear when knowledge of Aesop's fable on the body and its members would have reached Britain, but since it was used by both John of Salisbury and Marie de France, it seems likely that it could have been known in Wales by the time the lawbooks were composed. Harvey observes that, by the fifteenth century, "the fable of the Belly and its Members must have been one of the most familiar of political analogies": Harvey, *Body Politic*, 17.

132. The text was widely known and read in the medieval period: Harvey, *Body Politic*, 16–17.

133. Pryce, "Context and Purpose," 59; Stephenson, "Laws of Court," *WKC*, 406.

134. Pryce, "Context and Purpose," 52–63; Stephenson, "Laws of Court," *WKC*, 404–9.

135. Fulton, "Individual and Society," 25.

136. Fulton, "Individual and Society," 23–24.

137. Fulton, "Individual and Society," 27, 49.

138. *WML* 17.5–10 (Cyfn V and W, but not in X, U, Y); 31.6–8. The same tradition (though worded differently) appears in manuscript Cyfn X in the passage on the smith: *WKC* Cyfn X §39/1–2, pp. 474–75.

139. Stacey, "Clothes Talk," *WKC*, 343–46; Charles-Edwards, "Food, Drink and Clothing," *WKC*, 335–36.

140. Patterson, "Honour and Shame," 94–103. Thus, a bard who wasted his talent on a low-status audience would receive only derisory compensation if he was insulted: "Honour and Shame," 93–94.

141. *WML* 16.1–3.

142. *WML* 33.4–5.

143. John of Salisbury, *Policraticus*, bk. 5, chap. 2.

144. *Bleg* 115.9–10.

145. Patterson, "Honour and Shame," 90.

146. *Ior* 34/1, 4. Cf. *WML* 30.1–8 (= *WKC* Cyfn §38/6–10, pp. 472–73), in which the ankle is a marker of the amount of hide he receives rather than the height of the boots he can make with that hide; and *LTWL* Lat A 119.23; Lat B 207.1 (= *WKC* Lat B §1.33/4, pp. 516–17); Lat D 348.6–14; Lat E 447.22–23; *Bleg* 28.7–15.

147. A *kyuelin* is defined in Cyfn and elsewhere as measuring approximately the length of a man's (presumably) forearm, from elbow joint to the tip of the middle finger: *WML* 30.3–5 (= *WKC* Cyfn §38/8, pp. 472–73), and see the parallel passage in *LTWL* Lat D 348.8–11; *Bleg* 28.9–14.

148. *WML* 30.6–7 (= *WKC* Cyfn §38/9, pp. 472–73).

149. *LTMW*, 233, 237.

150. *Ior* 34/6, 8, closely following Jenkins's translation in *LTMW*, 34. Cf. *WML* 30.9–22 (= *WKC* Cyfn §38/12–18, pp. 472–73); *LTWL* Lat A 119.14–23; 120.1–5; Lat B 206.33–207.1 (= *WKC* Lat B §1.33/1–4, pp. 516–17); Lat D 348.17–25; Lat E 447.17–23; *Bleg* 28.17–29.

151. Latin E does not offer this explanation, saying only *lancea eius non erit longior quam tres ulne*: *LTWL* Lat E 447.22.

152. *LTMW*, 233, notes 34.30 and 34.34; Patterson, "Honour and Shame," 89–91, 94–103.

153. All references are to the manuscript illustrations on the National Library of Wales Digital Gallery site, accessed July 13, 2011, http://www.llgc.org.uk/index.php?id=570, with discussion and commentary; Huws, "Peniarth 28."

154. These are the two times during the year he is said to receive clothing from the court: *WML* 30.2–8 (=*WKC* Cyfn §38/8–10, pp. 472–73); *Ior* 34/4; Lat B 207.1 (=*WKC* Lat B §1.33/4, pp. 516–17); Lat D 348.8–13, 24–25; Lat E 447.22–23; *Bleg* 28.9–15, 28–29.

155. *WML* 30.3–6 (=*WKC* Cyfn §38/8, 18, pp. 472–73); and compare *Ior* 34/4; *LTWL* Lat A 119.23; Lat B 207.1 (=*WKC* Lat B §1.33/4, pp. 516–17); Lat D 348.25; Lat E 447.22–23; *Bleg* 28.28–29.

156. *LTMW*, 233, note to 34.22.

157. See discussion above. *Lliein* can mean simply "cloth," but given the prohibition against *tenllif* and the consistent link between *lliein* and underclothing elsewhere in the tractate, the reference is almost certainly to linen.

158. *Ior* 44/11.

159. *Ior* 34/11; *WML* 30.24–31.1; 110.19–21; *LTWL* Lat A 119.26–29; Lat D 348.31–33; Lat E 447.27–28; *Bleg* 29.3–6; and cf. Latin B, where the provision has been placed outside the Laws of Court: 257.29–31.

160. Patterson, "Honour and Shame," 90, with full discussion on 89–91.

161. Stacey, "Divorce," 1114–15.

162. *Ior* 35/4, 7, 8; *WML* 32.3–8, 12–17; and cf. *LTWL* Lat A 118.2–3; Lat B 206.26–30; Lat D 330.2–6.

163. *Canu Maswedd*, poems 7, 20, 22, 27, 28, 29 (tail). See *WML* 96.10–97.4; *Ior* 47/5 (for woman of bush and brake).

164. National Library of Wales Peniarth 28, accessed July 13, 2011, http://www.llgc.org.uk /index.php?id=570.

165. Aigremont argues that fingers were so commonly used in the period as symbols for the penis that the latter was actually referred to as the *digitus virilis* in the eleventh and twelfth centuries: Aigremont, "Beiträge sur Hand– und Finger–Symbolik," 328.

166. Ziolkowski, *Obscenity*, 13.

167. "Illustrations of Welsh Soldiers from the *Littere Wallie*." Peniarth 28 was almost certainly the manuscript that inspired Pecham's denunciation of Welsh law: Huws, "Peniarth 28: Illustrations," 1–2. The *nota delens* placed beside the passage on the bedclothes suggests that Pecham "got" this joke; might he have "gotten" (and intensely disapproved of) this joke as well?

168. Ll. Beverley Smith, "*Gravamina*," 11 (§63), 12 (§64), 14–15 (§§66–67), 29–30 (§§81–82), and 34 (§86). See also Charles-Edwards and Jones, "*Breintiau Gwŷr Powys*," 210.

169. "*Breintiau Gwŷr Powys*," §14 (pp. 217 and 220).

170. *Llyfr Du Caerfyrddin*, p. 32, line 124, and p. 30, line 47, respectively.

171. All three alternatives are mentioned in *Ior* 34/9; *LTWL* Lat D 348.25–28; Lat E 447.23–24; *Bleg* 28.30–32. Latin A mentions a bull or an animal *sine cauda*: *LTWL* Lat A 119.23–25, while Cyfn and Latin B mention only the bull: *WML* 30.22–23 (=*WKC* Cyfn §38/19, pp. 472–73); *LTWL* Lat B 207.2 (=*WKC* Lat B §1.33/5, pp. 516–17).

172. In this brief fable, the other members of the body decide that the belly is taking in too much food and refuse to feed it, whereupon (in Marie's version), the entire body sickens and dies.

173. Marie de France, "*De ventre et membris*," xxvii, pp. 92–93.

174. O'Brien, *God's Peace*, 5–7.

175. Yeager, "Body Politic," 146.

176. Walters, "Comparative Aspects," *WKC*, 386. The lawbook redactors do not place the same emphasis on the peasantry as John of Salisbury does, for example: John of Salisbury, *Policraticus*, bk. 5, chap. 2, and bk. 6, chap. 20; Harvey, *Body Politic*, 16.

177. Radner, "Interpreting Irony"; McKenna, "What Dreams May Come"; McKenna, "Learning Lordship"; Fulton, "Education of Princes"; Sturzer, "Purpose of *Culhwch and Olwen*"; Sweetser, "Figurative Harmony."

CHAPTER 4

1. Goodrich, *Law in the Courts of Love*, 112.

2. Ziolkowski, *Obscenity*, 13.

3. Here following D. Johnston, "Erotica and Satire," 60–61.

4. McKenna, "Revising Math"; McKenna, "Colonization of Myth"; McKenna, "Theme of Sovereignty"; McKenna, "Learning Lordship"; Fulton, "Education of Princes"; Aronstein, "Becoming Welsh"; Siewers, "Icon of the Land"; but see also Hutton, "Medieval Welsh Literature."

5. Hywel ab Owain Gwynedd, "Gorhoffedd Hywel ab Owain," in *Gwaith Llywelyn Fardd*, 114–30.

6. Gwalchmai ap Meilyr, "Gorhoffedd Gwalchmai," in *Gwaith Meilyr Brydydd*, 203, lines 40–42.

7. Gwalchmai ap Meilyr, "Gorhoffedd Gwalchmai," in *Gwaith Meilyr Brydydd*, 192–224, lines 19, 31–33, 43, 75, 96 (*arfau*, "arms").

8. Prydydd y Moch, "Mawl Llywelyn ab Iorwerth o Wynedd," in *Gwaith Llywarch ap Llywelyn*, 201–9; contrast lines 15–28 with 29–32, for example.

9. Prydydd y Moch, "Mawl Gwenllïan ferch Hywel o Wynllŵg," in *Gwaith Llywarch ap Llywelyn*, 137–45, line 29.

10. There is such a high degree of variation in the Laws of Women tractate, both within the tractate itself and within the lawbook as a whole, that Dafydd Jenkins has recently wondered whether the tractate as a whole ought to be considered "floating": Jenkins, "'Cyfnerth' Text," *WLW*, 132–35. See also S. E. Roberts, *LlPom*, 52–53; and Powell, "Floating Sections."

11. Charles-Edwards, *Welsh Laws*, 27–29.

12. Russell, "Arrangement and Development," *TCC*, 61–64, 83–85; and see Wiliam's schema (which needs now to be revised to take Russell's work into account) in *Ior*, xxix.

13. Charles-Edwards, *Welsh Laws*, 27–28; Russell, "Arrangement and Development," *TCC*, 61–62; and compare *Ior* §§44–55 with *ALW* V.C. bk. II, and see Owen's note 9 on p. 80. See also "Appendix IV" on the ordering of Ior A in *Ior* 139–40; and *Col* xxvi–xxxiii. The Laws of Women are missing altogether from Ior C, F, K, and Peniarth 163 (*Ior*, xxx).

14. Ior B also marks other major transitions in the lawbook: e.g., *Ior* 104/1, where Test Book begins, and *Ior* 138/14, where it ends; *Ior* 139/1 where the appendix on Joint-Ploughing and Corn-Damage begins, and *Ior* 160/9, where the Corn-Damage tractate ends (and with it the lawbook as a whole.)

15. Drawing on schemas provided by Charles-Edwards, *Welsh Laws*, 27–28 (and see more generally 26–31); Russell, "Arrangement and Development," *TCC*, 84; and Wiliam, *Ior* xxii. Cf. also the conspectuses available in *Ior*, xlii–xliv; *LlPom*, 49–65; *Col*, xlii–xliii; and Jenkins, *Conspectus*.

16. See, for example, Charles-Edwards, *Welsh Laws*, 27–28, on Cyfn manuscript Mk; and *WML*, lxxiii–lxxxvi on manuscripts V and W.

17. The exception here is manuscript G (Peniarth 35), which is a complex manuscript made up of two different and unrelated sections; it is independent of all other Ior manuscripts, and thus cannot be viewed as typical: *Ior* xxix; Charles-Edwards, "'Iorwerth' Text," *WLW*, 161; Charles-Edwards, "NLW Peniarth MS 35 (G) and the Textual Tradition of Llyfr Iorwerth," unpublished article made available by the kind offices of the author, *Llyfr Cynog*, ii–xx. Manuscript A (The Black Book of Chirk, NLW Peniarth 29) has a complicated collation history, on which see Wiliam, "Appendix IV," *Ior*, 139–40.

18. Russell, "Arrangement and Development," *TCC*, 62–64.

19. *Ior* xxviii–xxix (Wiliam thought that Ior B's order was likely the original, which Russell has shown not to be correct: *Ior* xxii; Russell, "Arrangement and Development," *TCC*, 62–65).

20. At least to judge from those Ior manuscripts that are complete. Col is missing folios at the beginning and end and starts in the middle of the Laws of Women. Since the divorce passage is not contained in what it has of the tractate, however, it seems probable that in Col also, the divorce passage would have come at the beginning: xxvi–xxxiii; and see *Col* §§1–68.

21. *Ior* 44/8, 15, and cf. also 43/1 (= *WLW* Ior 44/8, 15, pp. 162–63). For the sergeant's confiscation of goods from a *marwdy*, "dead-house," see *LTMW*, 233, note 34.30, and 237, note 40.35–39.

22. *LTMW*, 233, note 34.30.

23. Lat A and Lat B appear to derive from a text drawing on early versions of Cyfn and Ior and may have gotten the cut meat and butter from it: Charles-Edwards, "Relationship of the Tractates ," *WLW*, 180–82.

24. *WML* 95.6–12 (= *WLW* Cyfn §73a/8–9, pp. 140–41).

25. It would be easier to make this case for the Latin and Bleg texts than for Cyfn, although Lat A's dependence on a text drawing on Ior muddies the waters somewhat.

26. Scott, "Gender: A Useful Category of Historical Analysis."

27. The household as a microcosm for the state occurs in a variety of historical works and contexts: Ozment, *When Fathers Ruled*; Roper, *Holy Household*; Mertes, *English Noble Household*; Gobetti, *Private and Public*; Hardwick, *Practice of Patriarchy*; Nagle, *Household as the Foundation*; Cooper, *Fall of the Roman Household*; Kendall, *Lordship and Literature*.

28. P. Brown, *Body and Society*, 5–32; Pomeroy, *Goddesses, Whores*, 206–26.

29. Roper, *Holy Household*.

30. McSheffrey, *Marriage, Sex, and Civic Culture*, 137–63, esp. 138.

31. Fulton, "Individual and Society," 23–24, 27–30.

32. Although, as we have seen, there is some disagreement as to what these traditional practices might be: *Ior* 4/7–9, 16.

33. See, for example, Andrews, "Rhai Agweddau"; Charles-Edwards, *Wales and the Britons*, 323–26; Goetinck, "*Peredur*"; Goetinck, "Sofraniaeth" (but see also Lovecy, "Celtic Sovereignty Theme"); Hughes, "King's Nephew"; Valente, "Gwydion and Aranrhod"; Winward, "Some Aspects"; McKenna, "Theme of Sovereignty"; McKenna, "Revising Math"; Siewers, "Icon of the Land"; Bollard, "Role of Myth"; Cichon, "Violence and Vengeance"; Stacey, "King, Queen, and *Edling*," *WKC*, 35–37; and Fulton, "Education of Princes." Also very helpful is Ní Chonaill's *Place of the Child*, 138–39. For an alternative (though ultimately unpersuasive, in my opinion) view, see Hutton, "Medieval Welsh Literature."

34. "Marwnad Llywelyn ap Gruffudd," in *Gwaith Bleddyn Fardd*, pp. 414–33, lines 49–100.

35. Charles-Edwards, *Wales and the Britons*, 325; Andrews, "Rhai Agweddau."

36. *WML* 2.23–3.7 (= *WKC* Cyfn §3/2–3, pp. 438–39); *Ior* 3/4–5; *LTWL* Lat A 110.9–21;

Lat B 194.1–12, and 207.18–29 (=*WKC* Lat B §1.2/4–7, pp. 484–85; §2.3, pp. 518–19); Lat C 277.5–12 and 277.19–26 (=*WLMA* §1.4/3, pp. 6–7, and §1.7/1–3, pp. 8–9); Lat D 317.19–37; Lat E 436.17–31; *Bleg* 3.17–4.6.

37. Stacey, "Ancient Irish Law Revisited."

38. *Pwyll Pendeuic Dyuet*, 16–18, lines 449–60 and 491–99.

39. *DwCol* 314–16, and see discussions in Jenkins, "Property Interests," *WLW*, 73–75; and Patterson, "Wife as Vassal," 37–40.

40. Patterson, "Wife as Vassal," 39–40.

41. *Ior* 54/4–6 (=*WLW* §54/4–6, pp. 176–77); *LTWL* Lat E 437.21–26; *Col* 47.

42. Stacey, "King, Queen, and *Edling*," *WKC*, 38n35.

43. *WML* 2.23–3.7 (=*WKC* Cyfn §3/2–3, pp. 438–39); *Ior* 3/4–5; *LTWL* Lat A 110.9–21; Lat B 194.1–12 and 207.18–29 (=*WKC* Lat B §1.2/4–7, pp. 484–85; §2.3, pp. 518–19); Lat C 277.5–12 and 277.19–26 (=*WLMA* §§1.4/3, pp. 6–7, and 1.7/1–3, pp. 8–9); Lat D 317.19–37; Lat E 436.17–31; *Bleg* 3.17–4.6.

44. Cyfn U and W: *WML* 97.12–21 (=*WLW* Cyfn U §73/19–22, pp. 142–43). Only Lat B and E of the Latin texts mention the taking of the testicles: *LTWL* Lat A 144.29–37 (=*WLW* Lat A §52/37–39, pp. 154–55); Lat B 224.17–26 and 243.21–22; Lat D 338.10–14; Lat E 473.8–15 and 470.33–35; *Bleg* 43.31–44.1.

45. *Bleg* 63.31–32: *Nyt oes yg kyfreith Hywel Da yspadu gwr yr treissaw gwreic*, "There is no castrating of a man for the rape of a woman in the law of Hywel Dda"; *LlPom*, 21–22.

46. McKenna, "Revising Math," 112. See *PKM*, 57, for Manawydan's promise to Cigfa.

47. Fulton, "Education of Princes," 230–32.

48. McKenna, "Theme of Sovereignty," 46–47, and see discussion below.

49. Welsh, "Manawydan," 129.

50. Welsh, "Manawydan," 129, 135–36, here following Koch, "Welsh Window."

51. Fulton, "Education of Princes," 245–47, here following McKenna, "Revising Math," 95–103.

52. *Críth Gablach*, 542–47; and see further Stacey, "Ancient Irish Law Revisited."

53. "Mawl Llywelyn ab Iorwerth," in *Gwaith Llywarch ap Llywelyn*, 208, line 29; and see also the "Mawl Hywel ap Goronwy," where the comparison to Garwy seems intended to speak mostly to the latter's military prowess: *Gwaith Meilyr Brydydd a'i Ddisgynyddion*, 8, line 3, and 12n3.

54. Patterson, "Honour and Shame"; and see also Cichon, *Violence and Vengeance*, 100–101n332.

55. *WML* 22.19–22 (not in *Ior*); Patterson, "Honour and Shame," 93–94.

56. *Kroessan*: *Ior* 11/6; *WML* 21.13–15. Patterson concludes that the testicles in question belong to the horse: "Honour and Shame," 91n1.

57. Patterson, "Honour and Shame," 90–91.

58. Cichon (rightly) includes the smith and the porter in his list of burlesques, although he does not explain why they might have been treated in this way: Cichon, *Violence and Vengeance*, 100–101n332.

59. *Ior* §34, and see arguments in Chapter 3.

60. *Ior* §33; *WML* 33.4–13.

61. *Ior* 12/6, 8; and cf. *LTWL* Lat A 111.38–112.2; 113.30–31; 117.14–19; Lat B 195.16–19 (=*WKC* Lat B §1.6/9, pp. 488–89); 197.14–15 (=*WKC* Lat B §1.8/9, pp. 492–93); Lat C 278.32–279.2; 281.10–11 (=*WLMA* §§1.10/9, pp. 12–13, and 1.12/9, pp. 18–19); Lat D 319.25–28; 321.21–22; 328.14–27; Lat E 439.10–12; 441.17–18; 445.22–26; *Bleg* 7.3–5; 10.11–12; 21.27–22.17.

62. *WML* 22.13–15 (=*WKC* Cyfn §16/6, pp. 458–59).

63. Patterson, "Honour and Shame," 80–84. Sheringham offers an age-related explanation in "Bullocks with Horns."

64. *WML* 96.10–97.4 (=*WLW* Cyfn §73a/14–15, pp. 140–41); *Ior* 47/2–5 (=*WLW* Ior §47/2–5, pp. 166–67); D. Johnston, *Canu Maswedd*: poems 1, 24 (horn), and 7, 20, 22, 27, 28, 29 (tail).

65. Patterson, "Honour and Shame, 84.

66. National Library of Wales Peniarth 28, fol. 5r, accessed July 13, 2011, http://www.llgc.org.uk/index.php?id=570. The main discussions of these figures are also contiguous in Lat A, Lat D, and Lat E, but not in Lat B, where the chamberlain is preceded in the *nawdd* and lodging lists by the judge, nor in Cyfn (chief groom) or Ior (also chief groom).

67. Fulton, "Education of Princes," 239.

68. *LTWL* Lat D 328.24–27; *Bleg* 22.13–17; and cf. Lat E, which grants him the *minuta animalia, id est, man yscrybyl*, taken from the *gorwlat*: Lat E 445.23–24. Lat D and Bleg say nothing about cattle with horns as long as their ears and are thus not as forthrightly sexual in their symbolism as is Cyfn.

69. *Porthavr*: *Ior* 35/4, where it is described as a stick that he can draw easily out of the bundle without holding up the horse, which implies that it is small in size (cf. *WML* 32.3–8); *Ior* 35/8–9 (cf. *WML* 32.12–15=a tailless steer; *Bleg* 24.21–22 has "the last beast"). Sticks are metaphors for the penis in the poetry of the period—indeed, the linking of the rod paid to the king to the taking of testicles suggests that the idea is present also in the laws themselves: *WML* 97.12–21 (=*WLW* Cyfn U §73/19–22, pp. 142–43); Lat B 224.17–26; Lat E 473.8–15; Johnston, *Canu Maswedd*, poems 7, 20, 22, 27, 28, 29.

70. National Library of Wales Peniarth 28, fol. 5v, accessed July 13, 2011, http://www.llgc.org.uk/index.php?id=570.

71. *WML* 10.1–4 (=*WKC* Cyfn §7/6, pp. 444–45); *Ior* 10/3–4; *LTWL* Lat A 113.29–30; Lat B 197.12–14 (=*WKC* Lat B §1.8/7–8, pp. 492–93); Lat C 281.8–9 (=*WLMA* §1.12/8, pp. 18–19); Lat D 321.19–21; Lat E 441.15–17; *Bleg* 10.6–10.

72. *WML* 17.5–10 (also in Cyfn V and W, but not in X or U). The same tradition appears in manuscript Y, but in the passage on the smith: *WKC* §39/1–2, pp. 474–75.

73. Johnston, *Canu Maswedd*, poem 1, line 21 (pp. 28–31); poem 27, line 8 (pp. 120–23).

74. *Ior* 9/6. Elsewhere, the falconer is said to handle his birds rather than urinate: *WML* 17.14–19 (=*WKC* Cyfn §14/1, pp. 454–55); *LTML* Lat A 114.39–115.5; Lat B 199.21–26 (=*WKC* Lat B §1.13/1–2, pp. 498–99); Lat C 283.29–33 (=*WLMA* §1.16/1, pp. 26–27); Lat D 323.25–31; Lat E 442.19–25; *Bleg* 13.24–14.2. For discussion, see Jenkins, "Hawk and Hound," *WKC*, 252–68. *Guassanaeth* is the word used in the Ior text. Cyfn and the Latin texts minimize the reversal of hierarchy by not mentioning urination and instead tying the king's action to special achievements on that day.

75. Pacaut, *Frederick Barbarossa*, 68. This story became famous in the late medieval and early modern period, existing in different versions and used for different political purposes. One seventeenth-century English example is Bridgeman Images, Image STC469126.

76. Sturzer, "Purpose of *Culhwch and Olwen*," 145.

77. Recent studies of humor in the Middle Ages include Classen, *Laughter in the Middle Ages*; and Allen, *On Farting*.

78. McKenna, "Colonization of Myth," 108–10; Fulton, "Trading Places"; R. R. Davies, *First English Empire*, 141–71.

79. R. R. Davies, *First English Empire*, 113–41; Meecham-Jones, "Where Was Wales?." Fulton points out the role played by social class in complicating Welsh reactions to their conquerors post 1282: Fulton, "Class and Nation."

80. Surridge, "Words of Romance Origin," 249.

81. Stacey, "King, Queen, and *Edling*," *WKC*, 55–61; and see R. R. Davies on the process of Anglicization in the British Isles in general, *First English Empire*, 141–71.

82. Aronstein, "Becoming Welsh," 149–50; McKenna, "Colonization of Myth"; Fulton, "Education of Princes"; Owen, "Literary Convention"; Owen, "Archaism."

83. M. Phillips, "Defod a Moes y Llys"; Lloyd-Morgan, "Medieval Welsh Tales"; Fulton, "Individual and Society"; Lloyd-Morgan, "Crossing the Borders."

84. Fulton, "Education of Princes"; Stephenson, "Laws of Court," *WKC*, 406–8; Stacey, "Clothes Talk," *WKC*, 342–43.

85. The term employed by Fulton (following Bhabha) to describe postconquest aristocratic attitudes toward English culture: Fulton, "Class and Nation," 195, 199–201. See also McKenna, "Colonization of Myth," and Aronstein, "Becoming Welsh," both of whom also draw on Bhabha's insights.

86. Aronstein, "Becoming Welsh," 146, and see also 163–64. Wales was consistently depicted in English literature of the period as backward and servile, in every way a "barbarous land": R. R. Davies, *First English Empire*, 115–34; Meecham-Jones, "Erasure of Wales," 27–55.

87. Stephenson, "Laws of Court," *WKC*, 407–8.

88. *Ior* 35/4 (and see also 35/7).

89. *Ior* 21/3–4, 6.

90. Reported of the bakeress and laundress in Ior (*Ior* 38/3; 41/2); of the bondman (*caeth*) and dung *maer* in Cyfn (*WML* 46.2 [MS. V]; 94.5–7 [MS. W]), and of the slave (*refugium captivi*) in Lat B (*LTWL* Lat B 196.7–8=*WKC* Lat B §1.6/26, pp. 488–91).

91. *Ior* 9/6; Jenkins, "Hawk and Hound," *WKC*, 252–68.

92. Fulton, "*Breuddwyd Rhonabwy*," 48, and see also Chandler, "Humour in *Breuddwyd Rhonabwy*."

93. Pryce, "Context and Purpose," 52–63; Stephenson, "Laws of Court," *WKC*, 404–9.

94. Fulton, "Education of Princes," 230–32, 245. McKenna, "Revising Math," 95–103, provides an excellent survey with bibliography of earlier approaches.

95. Radner, "Interpreting Irony."

96. Sturzer, "Purpose of *Culhwch and Olwen*."

97. B. F. Roberts, "Where Were the Four Branches," 71. A particularly elegant statement of this point is Welsh's "Manawydan fab Llŷr."

98. McKenna, "Revising Math."

99. But see McKenna, "Revising Math," 102.

100. The fullest descriptions of his office are in *Ior* §32 and *WML* 26.19–25 (=*WKC* Cyfn §28/1–5, pp. 464–65). See also *WML* 2.10–11 (=*WKC* Cyfn §1/6, pp. 436–37); *WML* 5.23–24 and 7.4–6 (=*WKC* Cyfn §5/16, pp. 442–43); 20.24–21.1 (=*WKC* Cyfn §13/13, pp. 452–53); 23.6 (=*WKC* Cyfn §17/1, pp. 458–59); *LTWL* Lat A 111.12–13; 112.27–29; Lat B 195.1–2, 28–30 (=*WKC* Lat B §1.5/17; §1.6/15, pp. 486–89); Lat C 276.22 (=*WLMA* §1.2/4, pp. 4–5); 278.14–15 (=*WLMA* §1.9/4, pp. 10–11); 279.11–13 (=*WLMA* §1.10/15, pp. 12–15); Lat D 317.2, 318.33–34; 320.13–14; 326.37–39; Lat E 436.1; 438.8–9; 439.35–37; 441.36–442.1.

101. Discussion and references in McKenna, "Revising Math," 102–8, and see also Carey, "Myth of Origins."

102. Hughes, *Math uab Mathonwy*, 21n5; McKenna, "Revising Math," 107–8; and see Harris, "Dychwelyd," 30. See also Patrick Ford's comments on the changing genders of the Celtic war deity: Ford, "Branwen," 37.

103. McKenna, "Revising Math," 104–17; Fulton, "Education of Princes," 245–46; Hughes, "King's Nephew."

104. *Ior* 32/2; and see Russell's note to *truidedaut* in *WLMA*, 50.

105. Stacey, "King, Queen, and *Edling*," *WKC*, 44–46.

106. McKenna, "Revising Math," 107.

107. Fulton, "Education of Princes," 245–47.

108. Sullivan, "Inheritance and Lordship," 363.

109. McKenna, "Revising Math," 116–17.

110. Fulton, "Individual and Society"; Fulton, "Education of Princes"; McKenna, "Theme of Sovereignty"; McKenna, "Revising Math"; McKenna, "Learning Lordship"; McKenna, "Colonization of Myth"; Aronstein, "Becoming Welsh"; Hughes, "King's Nephew"; and cf. Sullivan, "Inheritance and Lordship."

111. Fulton, "Education of Princes," 245.

CHAPTER 5

1. For a discussion of ecclesiastical criticism of native Welsh law, see Pryce, *Native Law*, 71–81.

2. Cheney, "Council of Westminster 1175."

3. *uxores legitimae Howelisda patrocinio contra Evangelium dato repudio, fama teste vel potius infamia, repelluntur*: *Registrum Epistolarum Fratris Johannis Peckham*, 2:473–77, letter 360, November 14, 1282; Cheney, "Council of Westminster 1175."

4. Huws, "Leges Howelda," 341; Pryce, *Native Law*, 82n2. Pecham cited this manuscript in a letter to Llywelyn ap Gruffudd in 1282; by the early fourteenth century at least, it was one of the holdings of the library of St. Augustine's Canterbury: Huws, "Peniarth 28."

5. Pryce, "Welsh Custom and Canon Law"; Pryce, "Yr eglwys a'r gyfraith"; Pryce, "Ecclesiastical Sanctuary." On women and marriage specifically, see Pryce, *Native Law*, 82–112; Charles-Edwards, "Nau Kynywedi Teithiauc"; R. R. Davies, "Status of Women"; and Ll. Beverley Smith, "View."

6. See further Cheney, "Council of Westminster 1175"; and Gerald of Wales, *Descriptio Kambriae* 2.6 in *Giraldi Cambrensis Opera*, 6:213–14. It was to be many centuries before church regulations on marriage were uniformly enforced elsewhere in Europe: Helmholz, *Marriage Litigation*; and see comments by R. R. Davies, "Status of Women," *WLW*, 97–98; Pryce, *Native Law*, 70–92; and, with respect to the late Middle Ages, Ll. Beverley Smith, "View."

7. Even post-Conquest attempts by Welsh landowners to pass on their lands by English rather than native custom resulted in dispossessed Welsh heirs siding with English lords in their efforts to fight back: Barrell and Davies, "Land, Lineage," 43–45.

8. Patterson, "Honour and Shame," 74–86 ("dishonourable women" is Patterson's phrase).

9. What follows in these next two sections ("Divorce, Medieval Welsh Style" and "Law or Literature?") is slightly revised from my earlier article, "Divorce." I thank the Medieval Academy of America for permission to reprint this piece.

10. A wife was entitled in the case of a (justified) separation to take her *agweddi*, a sum determined by her natal status, from the property owned by the couple: *WLW*, 187–88, and see R. R. Davies, "Status of Women," *WLW*, 99–100, 112–14, and Pryce, *Native Law*, 82–95.

11. B.M. Harleian MS 1796 is a defective text, and both of the other two manuscripts of Latin C descend directly or indirectly from it: *LTWL*, 269–75; *WLMA*, xix–xxii.

12. On the character of these different redactions, see Charles-Edwards, *Welsh Laws*, 17–48; and Stacey, *Road to Judgment*, 179–98.

13. Charles-Edwards, "Relationship of the Tractates," *WLW*, 180–85, also outlines the relationship of the tractates in Lat D and Lat E to the (no longer extant) archetype from which both Lat A and Lat B drew their material. Lat B, D, and E also had access to a text or texts of the Ior tradition, since *LTWL* Lat B 225.38–39 (cf. Lat E 474.25–26) draws on Ior §45/1; Lat D 344.19 (cf. Lat E 474.4; *Bleg* 65.4) on Ior §44/3; Lat E 474.12–13 on Ior §44/12; and Lat E 474.24–25 on Ior §44/19.

14. As they are arguably also in Peniarth 35 (G), the least elaborate of the Ior versions of this passage. The passage is missing altogether from Cyfnerth U, the most "senior" of the Cyfn manuscripts, and "floats" in various places in the others: Jenkins, *WLW*, "'Cyfnerth' Text," 132–35.

15. He appears to have done exactly the same thing in his treatment of the royal family: Stacey, "King, Queen, and *Edling*."

16. Jenkins, *WLW*, "'Cyfnerth' Text," 134; *Ior* introduction, xliii.

17. The amount the wife would take from the property owned by a married couple upon a justified separation, which sum varied according to her birth status.

18. Text and translation of Ior §44 from manuscript G (Peniarth MS 35, of the first half of the fourteenth century), with italicized sentences §44/7–8, 10–19 supplied from D (Peniarth MS 32, c. 1400) by Charles-Edwards, "'Iorwerth' Text," *WLW*, 162–63.

19. Jenkins, "Property Interests," *WLW*, 84; and see also comments on divorce by R. R. Davies and by Walters on pp. 112–13 and 121 of *WLW*.

20. *Ior* 44/11 (= *WLW* Ior §44/11, pp. 162–63); *LTWL* Lat A 143.11–15 (= *WLW* Lat A §52/14–15, pp. 150–51); Lat B 225.21–24; Lat D 344.30–33; Lat E 474.11–13; *Bleg* 65.17–22.

21. *Ior* 45/1 (= *WLW* Ior §45/1, pp. 164–65); *LTWL* Lat B 225.38–39; Lat E 474.25–26.

22. *Ior* 44/18 (= *WLW* Ior §44/18, pp. 162–63); *LTWL* Lat A 143.26–27 (= *WLW* Lat A §52/20, pp. 152–53); Lat B 225.33–34; Lat D 345.1–2; Lat E 474.20–21; *Bleg* 65.31–32.

23. *Cáin Lánamna*, §§10–19, pp. 138–91, with discussion on pp. 20–24, 31–32. See also McAll, "Normal Paradigms," and, most recently, Breatnach, "Collective and Abstract Nouns."

24. This was kept separate from the joint possessions of the couple until the seven-year period had elapsed. For more on the *priodas* form of marriage, see Charles-Edwards, "Nau Kynywedi Teithiauc," *WLW*, 28–29.

25. *WLW*, 187–88.

26. Charles-Edwards, "Nau Kynywedi Teithiauc," *WLW*, 27–30. *Ior* 44/2 (= *WLW* Ior §44/2–3, pp. 162–63) makes clear the nature of the relationship in question in the passage; for contrast, see *LTWL* Lat A 142.24–30 (= *WLW* Lat A §51/14–16, pp. 148–51).

27. *Ior* 48/2–8 (= *WLW* Ior §48/2–8, pp. 166–69).

28. *Ior* 44/11 (= *WLW* Ior §44/11, pp. 162–63); *LTWL* Lat A 143.11–13 (= *WLW* Lat A §52/14, pp. 150–51); Lat B 225.21–23; Lat D 344.30–34; Lat E 474.11–13; *Bleg* 65/17–22. The making of linen—and hence the connection with flax—was associated primarily with women in the medieval period: Herlihy, *Opera Muliebria*, 92–97, 147–48, 161–62, 189.

29. *Ior* 44/5 (= *WLW* Ior §44/5, and §44/5/4, pp. 162–63); *WML* 95.3–6 (= *WLW* Cyfn §73a/7, pp. 140–41); *LTWL* Lat A 143.2–4 (= *WLW* Lat A §52/8, pp. 150–51); Lat B 225.15–16; Lat D 344.20–22; Lat E 474.7–8; *Bleg* 65.5–8. For the gendering of work in the rural economy, see Bennett, *Women in the Medieval English Countryside*, 115–29; Bennett, "Village Ale-Wife"; and Bennett, *Ale, Beer, and Brewsters*.

30. *WML* 95.6–8 (= *WLW* §73a/8, pp. 140–41).

31. *Ior* 44/5, 10 (= *WLW* Ior §44/10 and §44/5/4, pp. 162–63); *WML* 94.17–21 (= *WLW* Cyfn §73a/5, pp. 138–39); *LTWL* Lat A 143.5, 9–11 (= *WLW* Lat A §52/13 and §52/10, pp. 150–51);

Lat B 225.19–21 and 225.17–18; Lat D 344.27–30 and 344.22–23; Lat E 474.8–11; *Bleg* 65.13–17 and 65.8–9.

32. *Ior* 44/3 (=*WLW* Ior §44/3, pp. 162–63); *LTWL* Lat A 142.40–143.1 (=*WLW* Lat A §52/5–6, pp. 150–51); Lat B 225.11–12, 35–38; Lat D 344.18–19; Lat E 474.3–4, 22–26; *Bleg* 65.3–4. On the relative value of pigs and sheep, see *Ior* §§129–30; *WML* 75.1–11 and 76.2–77.3; *LTWL* Lat A 155.30–156.36; Lat B 235.10–236.8; Lat D 361.16–362.5; Lat E 486.32–488.12; *Bleg* 93.1–94.5. On goats, *Ior* §130; *WML* 75.12–76.1; *LTWL* Lat A 156.37–40; Lat B 235.14–16; Lat D 361.21–23; Lat E 486.36–487.1; *Bleg* 93.6–10. On medieval Welsh farming and land law, see Jenkins, "Lawyer Looks at Welsh Land Law."

33. Ó Flaithearta, "An Chulaith Nua," 100.

34. *Ior* 44/3 (=*WLW* Ior §44/3, pp. 162–63), §130; *LTWL* Lat A 142.40–143.1 (=*WLW* Lat A §52/5–6, pp. 150–51), 156.37–40; Lat B 225.11–12, 35–38, 235.14–16; Lat E 474.3–4, 22–26 (in a passage likely borrowed from Ior), 486.36–487.1; and *Bleg* 93.1–10.

35. *Ior* 44/3 (=*WLW* Ior §44/3, pp. 162–63); *LTWL* Lat B 225.11–12; Lat D 344.19; Lat E 474.4. On oldest and youngest sons, see *Ior* 82/6–7; *WML* 50.11–15; *LTWL* Lat A 133.4–6; Lat B 227.26–29; Lat D 387.7–9; Lat E 478.25–29; *Bleg* 74.26–28.

36. *Ior* 44/10–11 (=*WLW* Ior §44/10–11, pp. 162–63); *WML* 94.17–95.3 (=*WLW* Cyfn §73a/5–6, pp. 138–41, which assigns the small hand axe to the husband as well); *LTWL* Lat A 143.9–13 (=*WLW* Lat A §52/13–14, pp. 150–51); Lat B 225.19–23; Lat D 344.27–32; Lat E 474.8–13; *Bleg* 65.13–20. On women's role in the fields, see Bennett, *Women in the Medieval English Countryside*, 116–18; and M. Roberts, "Sickles and Scythes."

37. *Ior* 44/11 (=*WLW* Ior §44/11, pp. 162–63).

38. Found only in Ior: *Ior* 44/12 (=*WLW* Ior §44/12, pp. 162–63: *Y pelleneu y'r meibyon or bydant*). Lat B and Lat E read *globos filorum* (Lat E: *glomeres filorum*), "balls of yarns": *LTWL* Lat B 225.23; Lat E 474.12–13.

39. *Ior* 44/10–11 (=*WLW* Ior §44/10–11, pp. 162–63); *WML* 94.17–95.3 (=*WLW* Cyfn §73a/5–6, pp. 138–41); *LTWL* Lat A 143.9–13 (=*WLW* Lat A §52/13–14, pp. 150–51); Lat B 225.19–23; Lat D 344.27–32; Lat E 474.8–13; *Bleg* 65.13–20.

40. *Ior* 44/7 (=*WLW* Ior §44/7, pp. 162–63).

41. *Ior* 44/13 (=*WLW* Ior §44/13, pp. 162–63); *LTWL* Lat A 143.17–20 (=*WLW* Lat A §52/17, pp. 150–51); *WML* 94.16–17 (=*WLW* Cyfn §73a/4, pp. 138–39, where the wife is said to own the prepared flour and the husband the corn); *LTWL* Lat B 225.25–27; Lat D 344.35–37; Lat E 474.14–15; *Bleg* 65.22–24.

42. *Ior* 44/14 (=*WLW* Ior §44/14, pp. 162–63); *LTWL* Lat A 143.17–20 (=*WLW* Lat A §52/17, pp. 150–51, where he also gets the geese); *LTWL* Lat B 225.25–27; Lat D 344.35–37; Lat E 474.14–17; *Bleg* 65.22–25.

43. *Ior* 44/3, 11–12 (=*WLW* Ior §44/3, 11–12, pp. 162–63); *LTWL* Lat A 142.40–143.2, 11–13, 15–16 (=*WLW* Lat A §52/5, 14, 16, pp. 150–51); Lat B 225.11, 21–23; Lat D 344.18–20, 30–34; Lat E 474.1–2, 11–13; *Bleg* 65.2–4, 17–22.

44. *Ior* 44/3–11 (=*WLW* Ior §44/3–11, 15, pp. 162–63); *WML* 95.3–12 (=*WLW* Cyfn §73a7–9, pp. 140–41); *LTWL* Lat A 142.40, 143.2–5, 11–13, 20–26 (=*WLW* Lat A §52/5, 8, 10, 13–14, 18–19, pp. 150–53); Lat B 225.11, 15–33; Lat D 344.18–19, 21–23 (which parallels *Bleg* and thus differs from the rest of the Latin tradition), 27–30; Lat E 474.1–12; *Bleg* 65.3–9 (where the man gets only one dish), 13–18, 25–29.

45. In Cyfn, the contrast is between seed vs. prepared flour, and processed vs. unprocessed cheese: *WML* 94.16–17, 95.6–12 (=*WLW* Cyfn §73a/4, §73a/9, and see §73a/8 on the butter, pp. 138–41).

46. *Ior* 44/9 (=*WLW* Ior §44/9, pp. 162–63); *WML* 94.14–16 (=*WLW* Cyfn §73a/3, pp. 138–39); *LTWL* Lat A 143.5–8 (=*WLW* Lat A §52/11–12, pp. 150–51); Lat B 225.12–15; Lat D 344.23–26; Lat E 474.5–7; *Bleg* 65.8–13.

47. Note the contrast with early Irish law: McAll, "Normal Paradigms," *WLW*, 9–10. On false virgins, see discussion below and Patterson, "Honour and Shame."

48. *Ior* 46/4 (=*WLW* Ior §46/4, pp. 164–65); *LTWL* Lat A 142.35–39 (=*WLW* Lat A §52/22, 152–53); Lat B 224.38–41; Lat D 345.10–13; Lat E 473.31–33; *Bleg* 66.9–13.

49. *Ior* 44/8 (=*WLW* Ior §44/8, pp. 162–63).

50. I am grateful to Eve Sweetser for this point.

51. *Ior* 44/15–16 (=*WLW* Ior §44/15–16, pp. 162–63); *WML* 95.8–12 (=*WLW* Cyfn §73a/9, pp. 140–41). The Latin and Bleg redactions vary, with Lat A, B, D, and E following Ior in giving it to the woman, and Bleg assigning it to the man (despite Bleg's customary reliance on Latin D): compare *Bleg* 65.25–29 with *LTWL* Lat A 143.22–26 (=*WLW* Lat A §52/18–19, pp. 150–53); *LTWL* Lat B 225.27–31; Lat D 344.37–40; Lat E 474.15–18.

52. *Ior*, note to *pergyg* on 108.

53. *Ior* 44/11 (=*WLW* Ior §44/11, pp. 162–63); D. Johnston, *Canu Maswedd*, poem 4, lines 51–52 (pp. 38–39).

54. D. Johnston, *Canu Maswedd*, 23–24. It may have originated as a strategy associated with satire: *Gramadegau'r Penceirddiaid*, 6.36, 38=25.38, 30=46.15, 17.

55. Prydydd y Moch, "Mawl Gwenllïan," in *Gwaith Llywarch ap Llywelyn*, poem 14, lines 9–12 (p. 142).

56. *WML* 94.16–17 (=*WLW* Cyfn §73a/4, pp. 138–39).

57. Cyfn attaches the provision on the departure of the wife with her goods to the passage on divorce: *WML* 95.12–14 (=*WLW* Cyfn §73a/10, pp. 140–41). Ior and the Latin/Bleg texts have differing traditions here: *Ior* 45/9 (=*WLW* Ior §45/9, pp. 164–65); *Ior* 51/9 (=*WLW* Ior §51/9, pp. 172–73); *LTWL* Lat A 142.35–39 (=*WLW* Lat A §52/3–4, pp. 150–51); *LTWL* Lat B 224.32–35; Lat D 345.3–7; Lat E 473.26–29; *Bleg* 66.1–6.

58. She notes that the burlesques cluster in the Laws of Court and the Laws of Women: Patterson, "Honour and Shame," 73.

59. Patterson, "Honour and Shame."

60. Owen, "Shame and Reparation," *WLW*, 40–46, 52; *CCC*, 128; *LTWL* Lat A 144.42–145.4 (=*WLW*, "Latin Redaction A," §52/42–43, pp. 154–55: *quia dominus eius est*). See also Patterson, "Wife as Vassal."

61. *Ior* 46/4 (=*WLW* Ior §46/4, pp. 164–65); and see Pryce, *Native Law*, 89–95.

62. Although the passage in question may refer to marriages lasting less than seven years. See also *WML* 92.20–93.2 (=*WLW* Cyfn §73/15b, pp. 138–39).

63. *Col* §§1–2; and compare *WML* 93.7–10 (=*WLW* Cyfn §73/23a, pp. 138–39). See discussion in Owen, "Shame and Reparation," 50–54.

64. Patterson, "Honour and Shame," 74–86.

65. McAll, "Normal Paradigms," 9, 15.

66. Patterson, "Honour and Shame," 89–94.

67. Ultimately, she concludes that the burlesques were "archaic survivals" preserved either because "they were memorable, or because their meaning still was not lost upon an early medieval audience": Patterson, "Honour and Shame," 74.

68. Pryce, *Native Law*, 91.

69. *PKM*, 19–21. Discussions of the dating of the Four Branches include Charles-Edwards, *Wales and the Britons*, 653–55; Charles-Edwards, "Date of the Four Branches"; B. F. Roberts,

"Where Were the Four Branches," 71–72; Sims-Williams, "Submission of Irish Kings" (revised in his *Irish Influence*, 209–29); S. Davies, *Crefft y Cyfarwydd*, 7–9, 28–29; S. Davies, "Pedeir Keinc"; Rodway, "Where, Who, When," 58–59, esp. n. 52; Fulton, "Education of Princes," 230–32.

70. Gerald of Wales, *Descriptio Kambriae*, 2.6, in *Giraldi Cambrensis Opera*, 6:213–14. Ecclesiastical regulations regarding marriage were not yet uniformly enforced even elsewhere in Europe: Helmholz, *Marriage Litigation*. For the later period, see Ll. Beverley Smith, "View."

71. Pryce, *Native Law*, 84–86.

72. R. R. Davies, "Status of Women," 94; and see also *CCC*, 127–28, and Jack, *Medieval Wales*, 127–60.

73. Pryce, *Native Law*, 82–95.

74. Pryce, *Native Law*, 90–91.

75. Pryce, *Native Law*, 163–233, 241–51.

76. *Ior* 87/5–6, and see Pryce, *Native Law*, 96–100.

77. Pryce, *Native Law*, 96–112, 127, 202–3, and 241–58.

78. Joan was declared legitimate by the pope as part of Llywelyn's campaign to ensure that his son Dafydd was recognized as Llywelyn's lawful heir in preference to his older son Gruffudd, born of an earlier union: see discussion in *CCC*, 192–93 and 249–50.

79. *ByT* (*RBH*), 228–29.

80. Walker, *Medieval Wales*, 96, outlines the dangers in Llywelyn's decision.

81. John had imprisoned many prominent members of the de Braose family in 1210, putting William the Younger and his mother to death: *ByT* (*RBH*), 188.

82. *CCC*, 248–51.

83. Huws, "Earliest Version," 182–86; Huws, "Manuscripts," *LAL*, 123–25; Charles-Edwards, *Welsh Laws*, 64, and 100–102. The section on the *edling* makes reference to events taking place in the 1220s (and possibly to Gruffudd ap Llywelyn's taking of lands in Powys Wenwynwyn in 1234). Jenkins dates the compilation of *Llyfr Iorwerth* to sometime after 1240: Jenkins, "Family of Welsh Lawyers," 123–33.

84. *ByT* (*RBH*), 190–93; Stephenson, *Governance of Gwynedd*, document summaries on 208 and 210.

85. Aronstein, "When Arthur Held Court."

86. Doan, "Sovereignty Aspects"; Ford, "Celtic Women"; Ford, *Mabinogi*, 4–26; Ford, "Prolegomena"; Hanson-Smith, "*Pwyll Prince of Dyfed*"; Goetinck, *Peredur*, 129–85; McKenna, "Theme of Sovereignty"; and Stacey, "King, Queen, and *Edling*," *WKC*, 35–36.

87. *ALW* II.i.5, note 29. The exception is manuscript B, on which Wiliam's edition is based, which reads *a guedy e dyrchauer e gur byeu*, "and after it is hung up, it belongs to the man."

88. *ByT* (*RBH*), 228–29.

89. Presumably the "raised" meat and cheese are freshly slaughtered meat hung for draining, and cheese in the beginning stages of preparation hung to drain off the whey, rather than foods that have been fully preserved.

90. Pryce, "Ecclesiastical Sanctuary," 1–3; Pryce, *Native Law*, 163–203.

91. Pryce, "Ecclesiastical Sanctuary," 7–9.

92. Outlined and discussed in Charles-Edwards, "Nau Kynywedi Teithiauc."

93. Charles-Edwards, "Nau Kynywedi Teithiauc," *WLW*, 35–37.

94. *Priodas* relationships, on which see note on *WLW*, 214. As this note points out, *gwraig briod* is actually used in *Ior* 87/5 to designate the woman recognized by the church as a wife.

95. *Ior* 45/9 (=*WLW* Ior §45/9, pp. 164–65); *Ior* 51/9 (=*WLW* Ior §51/9, pp. 172–73); *WML* 95.12–14 (=*WLW* Cyfn §73a/10, pp. 140–41); *LTWL* Lat A 142.35–39 (=*WLW* Lat A §52/3–4,

pp. 150–51); Lat B 224.32–35; Lat D 345.3–7; Lat E 473.26–29; *Bleg* 66.1–6. Note that in Ior the parting is lawful (*kyureythyaul*), while in the Latin tradition and *Bleg*, it is unlawful (*sine lege/agkyfreithawl*). Cyfn does not stipulate one way or the other, but the fact that the sentence is placed in the middle of its divorce passage suggests that the parting is a lawful one.

96. *Ior* 46/3–4 (=*WLW* Ior §46/3–4, pp. 164–65); *LTWL* Lat A 143.31–35 (=*WLW* Lat A §52/22, 152–53); Lat B 224.35–41; Lat D 345.7–13; Lat E 473.29–33; *Bleg* 66.6–13.

97. She is entitled to compensation for insult on the first two occasions: *Ior* 51/4–5 (=*WLW* Ior §51/4–5, pp. 170–73); *WML* 93.7–10 (=*WLW* Cyfn §73/23a, pp. 138–39); *LTWL* Lat A 146.1–4 (=*WLW* Lat A §52/60, pp. 158–59); Lat B 222.21–25; Lat D 343.31–37; Lat E 471.13–14; *Bleg* 64.3–7.

98. Wives could also lawfully separate from their husbands on the grounds of leprosy, bad breath, and impotence—all concerns relevant to the issue of ongoing sexual relations between spouses: *Ior* 45/4 (=*WLW* Ior §45/4, pp. 164–65); *WML* 92.20–93.2 (=*WLW* Cyfn §73/15b, pp. 138–39); *LTWL* Lat A 145.23–25 (=*WLW* Lat A §52/54, pp. 156–57); Lat B 222.3–5; Lat D 343.28–30; Lat E 471.4–6; *Bleg* 64.1–3; and see *Ior* 54/1–3 (=*WLW* Ior §54/1–3, pp. 176–77); and discussion by Pryce, *Native Law*, 82–95. Recent studies of sexuality and marriage elsewhere in Europe include Karras, *Sexuality in Medieval Europe*, 59–86; McSheffrey, *Marriage, Sex, and Civic Culture*.

99. *Ior* 48/3–7 (=*WLW* Ior §48/3–7, pp. 168–69). Cyfn and the Latin versions differentiate the daughter of the freeman (*breyr/optimatus*), who gets six cows in such circumstances, from the daughter of the *taeog* (Latin *villanus*) who gets only three: *WML* 89.21–25 (and cf. *WML* 43.14–22); *LTWL* Lat B 221.19–23; Lat D 342.19–22; Lat E 470.18–22; *Bleg* 62.4–8; and compare also *LTWL* Lat A 142.24–29 (=*WLW* Lat A §51/14–16, pp. 148–51); Lat B 223.17–20; Lat D 343.10–13; Lat E 472.7–9; *Bleg* 63.10–14.

100. By contrast, the chamberlain in Cyfn receives *gwartheg*, "cattle," not *eydyon*—perhaps because his relationship with the king is ongoing: *WML* 22.13–14 (=*WKC* Cyfn §16/6, pp. 458–59), but cf. Lat D and Bleg discussion above.

101. *WML* 97.5–11 (=*WLW* Cyfn §73a/16–17, pp. 140–41).

102. Patterson, "Honour and Shame," 79–80.

103. D. Johnston, *Canu Maswedd*, poem 1, line 34 (pp. 28–31); poem 6, line 6 (pp. 44–45).

104. Some judges allowed the man to attempt a denial in such circumstances, while others did not: *Ior* 50/1–3 (=*WLW* Ior §50/1–3, pp. 170–71); *WML* 97.12–21 (=*WLW* Cyfn U §73/19–22, pp. 142–43); *LTWL* Lat A 144.23–30 (=*WLW* Lat A §52/35–37, pp. 154–55); Lat B 221.39–222.2; Lat D 343.19–27; Lat E 470.36–471.3; *Bleg* 63.23–32. See also Johns, *Gender*, 32–34.

105. Cyfn W, Mk, X, Z. Text and translation are from Dafydd Jenkins, "'Cyfnerth' Text": *WLW* Cyfn §73a/15, pp. 140–41.

106. Patterson, "Honour and Shame," 79–80.

107. D. Johnston, *Canu Maswedd*, poem 7, lines 30 and 36 (pp. 46–48); poem 20, line 31 (pp. 94–97); poem 22, line 71 (pp. 102–5); poem 27, line 28 (pp. 120–23); poem 28, line 10 (pp. 124–29); poem 29, line 64 (pp. 130–33). The word used in all these poems for "tail" is *llost* rather than *loscwrn*, but the image is unmistakable.

108. I would like to thank Amy Mulligan for helpful suggestions about this passage.

109. Argued also regarding rape by Johns, *Gender*, 32–34. By contrast, Patterson characterizes this as focusing entirely on the woman: "Honour and Shame," 79–82.

110. Lloyd-Morgan argues that violence against women in the Four Branches serves to reinforce traditional social values and hierarchy: "Gender and Violence," 72.

111. He was speaking specifically of the wife with one foot out of bed provision: R. R. Davies, "Status of Women," *WLW*, 94.

112. An expression coined by Jenkins: "Legal and Comparative Aspects," 56; and see also Stacey, *Road to Judgment*, 19–20.

113. *Ior* 47/2–5 (= *WLW* Ior §47/2–5, pp. 166–67) and discussion below.

114. *Self and Society*, 10–30.

115. Stacey, "King, Queen, and *Edling*," *WKC*, 34–46.

116. Ior follows the paragraphs on divorce and separation (§§44–45) with a section focused on offenses within marriage (§46) and a lengthy discussion of the consequences of clandestine unions (§§47–49) and of rape (*Ior* §50). Together with the passage on divorce, these sections constitute half the tractate as a whole.

117. *Ior* 47/1–4 (= *WLW* Ior §47/1–4, pp. 166–67) is perhaps the most striking in this regard. See also *Ior* 50/1–3 (= *WLW* Ior 50/1–3, pp. 170–71); *Ior* 54/4–7 (= *WLW* Ior 54/4–7, pp. 176–77); *WML* 92.10–20 (= *WLW* Cyfn §73/14–15a, pp. 138–39, and see also Cyfn U §73/16–24, pp. 142–43); *LTWL* Lat A 143.36–40 (= *WLW* Lat A §52/23–24, pp. 152–53); Lat A 144.4–8 (= *WLW* Lat A §52/27–28, pp. 152–53); Lat A 144.24–37 (= *WLW* Lat A §52/35–39, pp. 154–55); Lat A 145.13–17 (= *WLW* Lat A §52/49–51, pp. 156–57); Lat A 146.5–8 (= *WLW* Lat A §52/62, pp. 158–59); Lat B 221.39–222.2; 222.17–25, 28–30; 223.17–20; 223.41–224.10 (which distinguishes between customs in northern and southern Wales); 224.17–31; Lat D 341.36–40; 343.4–27; 345.14–15; Lat E 470.36–471.3, 15–18; 472.29–32, 472.35–473.1, 8–25; *Bleg* 63.15–32; 64.11–17; 66.14–17.

118. *Ior* 51/1–5 (= *WLW* Ior §51/1–5, pp. 170–73, and cf. *WLW* Lat A §52/65, pp. 158–59).

119. Defined as giving away an item she is not permitted to alienate, being found with a man (presumably in circumstances that might suggest infidelity), and *una6 meuel ar y uaraf*, "wishing shame upon his beard": *Ior* 51/3–4 (= *WLW* Ior §51/3–4, pp. 170–73).

120. *Ior* 46/5–11 (= *WLW* Ior §46/5–11, pp. 164–67).

121. *Ior* 47/1 (= *WLW* Ior §47/1, pp. 166–67, and cf. *WLW* Lat A §52/23–24, pp. 152–53).

122. *Ior* 48/8 (= *WLW* Ior §48/8, pp. 168–69, and cf. *WLW* Lat A §51/14, pp. 148–51).

123. *Ior* 49/1–4 (= *WLW* Ior §49/1–4, pp. 168–71).

124. See, in addition to the passages on eloping and on false virgins cited above and below: *Ior* 46.5–8 (= *WLW* Ior §46/5–8, pp. 164–67); *WML* 93.7–10 (= *WLW* Cyfn §73/24a, pp. 138–39); *WLW* Cyfn §73a/38/10c, pp. 140–41 (manuscript Mk); *LTWL* Lat A 145.8–20 (= *WLW* Lat A 52/46–52, pp. 156–57); Lat B 222.21–25; Lat D 344.11–14; Lat E 471.19–21; *Bleg* 66.14–21.

125. Barrell and Davies, "Land, Lineage," 34, 44–51; and see also R. R. Davies, "Status of Women," 100–103; Richards, *Welsh Noblewomen*, 59–94, 152–80.

126. Paraphrasing *WLW* Ior §49/1, pp. 168–69.

127. *WLW*, notes to *gwraig llwyn a pherth*, 36, 206.

128. *Ior* 49/1–5 (= *WLW* Ior §49/1–5, pp. 168–71); and see also *DwCol* §153; *WLW* Cyfn §44/5, pp. 142–43; *LTWL* Lat A 142.4–15 (= *WLW* Lat A §51/7–10, pp. 148–49); and Jenkins, "Property Interests, Excursus II," in *WLW*, pp. 90–92.

129. *Ior* §§97–103. Some of this is new, and some represents passages found elsewhere in other versions that have been brought together by the Ior redactor.

130. Ní Chonaill, *Place of the Child*, 239, and chap. 5 generally; *Ior* §§90–96.

131. *Ior* 47/2–5 (= *WLW* Ior §47/2–5, pp. 166–67); *WML* 132.10–19; *LTWL* Lat A 143.41–144.10 (= *WLW* Lat A §52/25–30, pp. 152–53); Lat B 224.3–13; Lat D 342.13–16; Lat E 472.33–473.4; *Bleg* 61.27–31 (and cf. *LTWL* Lat D 374.23–32; *Bleg* 116.24–117.6). These latter are located in the triads rather than in the tractate on women. See S. E. Roberts, "Emerging from the Bushes."

132. McAll, "Normal Paradigms," 9–10. See also the discussion of these issues in Owen, "Shame and Reparation," 44–54.

133. Bracton, *De legibus*, 2:403, 415–16. The explanation given there for the king's interest in the crime is the preservation of the king's peace.

134. Glanvill, *Treatise on the Laws and Customs*, 14.6, p. 175.

135. K. M. Phillips, "Written on the Body," 130–35.

136. Oliver, *Body Legal*, 183–88, 200–201.

137. McAll, "Normal Paradigms," 9–10.

138. On such issues even Welsh bishops tended to appeal more to native rules and precedents rather than to "foreign"—e.g., English or ecclesiastical—systems of law lest they be seen as abandoning native tradition: Pryce, *Native Law*, 127, and see also 82–112.

139. Or lady (*argl6ydes*), likely a reflection of another way that lordship was changing with the pressure of English settlement: *Ior* 55/9–10 (=*WLW* Ior §55/9–10, pp. 178–79).

140. *WLW*, 190, 203.

141. *Ior* 48/1–2 (=*WLW* Ior §48/1–2, pp. 166–69); 51/11 (=*WLW* Ior §51/11, pp. 172–73); 52/5 (=*WLW* Ior §52/5, pp. 174–75); *WML* 89.18–90.7 (=*WLW* Cyfn §73/1–7a, pp. 136–37); 92.4–11 (=*WLW* Cyfn §73/13a–14, pp. 136–39); 93.21–94.5 (=*WLW* Cyfn U §73/26–27, 33/2, pp. 142–43); *LTWL* Lat A 146.9–13 (=*WLW* Lat A §52/63–64, pp. 158–59); Lat A 146.19–28 (=*WLW* Lat A §53/1–10, pp. 158–59); Lat B 222.28–223.2; Lat C 287.25–27, 30; 288.1–3 (=*WLMA*, Fragment 2, §2.1, pp. 38–39); Lat D 345.41–346.11; Lat E 471.24–31; *Bleg* 67.6–19.

142. *DwCol* §124; *WLW* Cyfn §73/16, 17, pp. 142–43.

143. Jenkins, "Property Interests," *WLW*, 73–75. Other interpretations associate it with the *ius primae noctis/droit de seigneur*.

144. *Ior* 52/5 (=*WLW* Ior §52/5, pp. 174–75); and compare with Ior 51/11 (=*WLW* Ior §51/11, pp. 172–73); *WML* 23.13–15; 43.11–13; *Col* 19.

145. *Ior* 52/2 (=*WLW* Ior §52/2, pp. 172–73), here following Jenkins on the meaning of this phrase: *LTMW*, 244, note 57.6.

146. Strasser, *State of Virginity*, 120, 178.

147. P. Brown, *Body and Society*, 8–9; Pomeroy, *Goddesses, Whores*, 206–26.

148. Pomeroy, *Goddesses, Whores*, 206–9, and see 209–14 on cults pertaining to virginity.

149. The two classic treatments are Roper, *Holy Household*; and Ozment, *When Fathers Ruled*.

CHAPTER 6

1. Doyle, "Silver Blaze."

2. Glanvill, *Treatise on the Laws and Customs*, bk. 14, pp. 171–77.

3. Bracton, *De legibus*, 2:340–48.

4. Violent crimes in general are treated under *De Placitis Coronae*: Bracton, *De legibus*, 2:327–449.

5. All available in translation: *Saxon Mirror*; *Établissements*; *Laws of Early Iceland*. Excellent secondary studies include W. I. Miller, *Bloodtaking and Peacemaking*; Grant, "Murder Will Out"; Hyams, *Rancor and Reconciliation*; W. Brown, *Violence in Medieval Europe*.

6. *Laws of Early Iceland: Grágás I*, 139–85, and see also the "Additions" on homicide, 208–38.

7. *Établissements*, "The Customs of Touraine and Anjou," §27, p. 22; §§30–31, pp. 24–25; §§35–37, pp. 26–27; §§40–41, p. 28; §53, p. 36; §62, p. 40; §108, p. 70; §§ 156–57, p. 99; §171, p. 105; "The Customs of the Orléans District," §38, p. 161.

8. Caviness, "Bad Name."

9. R. R. Davies, "Survival of the Bloodfeud," 342; T. Jones Pierce, "Laws of Wales"; and Ll. Beverley Smith, "A Contribution." See also Cichon, *Violence and Vengeance*; L. Johnson, *Kinship and Violence*; S. E. Roberts, "*Tri Dygyngoll Cenedl*"; Lloyd-Morgan, "Gender and Violence"; and, more generally, W. Brown, *Violence.*

10. *Ior* 50/1–5; 53/5; 55/6, 11 (= *WLW* Ior §50/1–5; §53/5; §55/6, 11, pp. 170–71, 174–79); *WML* 92.10–20; 95.20–96.5 (= *WLW* Cyfn §73/14–15a; §73a/12–13, pp. 138–41; and cf. manuscript U §73/16–23, pp. 142–43); *LTWL* Lat A 144.23–41 (= *WLW* §52/35–41, pp. 154–55); Lat B 221.39–222.2; 224.17–31; Lat D 343.19–27; Lat E 470.36–471.3, 472.29–32, 473.8–20; *Bleg* 63.23–32.

11. R. R. Davies, "Survival of the Bloodfeud," 342.

12. Cichon, *Violence and Vengeance*, 78–79. Ellis and Thomson thought similarly: Ellis, "Legal References," 92; and Thomson, *Owein*, 33–34n22.

13. R. R. Davies, *First English Empire*, 134.

14. *Giraldi Cambrensis Opera, Descriptio Kambriae*, 2.4. See also R. R. Davies, *First English Empire*, chap. 5, esp. 131–34.

15. R. R. Davies, *First English Empire*, 123–24.

16. Suppe, "Cultural Significance"; Johnson, "Mutilation"; Eska, "'Imbroued.'"

17. Johnson, "Mutilation"; Eska, "'Imbroued.'"

18. E.g., the killing of Hywel ap Goronwy in 1106 by Gwgan ap Meurig, fosterer of Hywel's son (*ByT* [*RBH*], 48–49); the betrayal and burning of Iorwerth ap Bleddyn by his nephew Madog ap Rhiddid (*ByT* [*RBH*], 72–77); and the blinding of Llywelyn ap Cadwallon by his brothers in 1187 (*ByT* [*RBH*], 170–71). For other examples, see Charles-Edwards, *Wales and the Britons*, 552–69.

19. Idwal Foel dies in 942; Gruffudd ap Cynan in 1137, Rhys ap Gruffudd in 1197, and Llywelyn ap Gruffudd in 1282. Summary taken from Johnson, *Kinship and Violence.*

20. Johnson, "Mutilation"; and see also Eska, "'Imbroued.'"

21. McKenna, "Colonization of Myth," 115.

22. *PKM*, 74–77; Valente, "Gwydion and Aranrhod," in Sullivan, *Mabinogi*, 337–38.

23. The translation is Russell's: *Vita Griffini*, §18, pp. 70–71; and cf. the Welsh version of this passage in D. Simon Evans, *Medieval Prince of Wales*, 37 (translation on 68).

24. "Arwyrain Owain Gwynedd," p. 8, lines 12, 28–29; p. 9, line 46. Translations by J. Clancy, *Medieval Welsh Poems*, 147–49.

25. "Marwnad Llywelyn ap Gruffudd," Poem 36, lines 87–100, pp. 424–25.

26. Five sentences in Cyfn (twelve in Cyfn U); ten in Ior; and seven in Lat A, for example: Cyfn §73/14–15a and cf. §73a/12–13 (*WLW*, pp. 138–41), and from U only: §73/16–22 (*WLW*, pp. 142–43); Ior §50/1–4 (*WLW*, pp. 170–71), §53/5 (rape by a foreigner, *WLW*, pp. 174–75), §54/4–6 (virginity test by the *edling*, *WLW*, pp. 176–77), §55/6, 11 (rape of a prostitute, which entails no compensation, *WLW*, 178–79); Lat A §52/35–41 (*WLW*, pp. 154–55).

27. Twelve sentences in Cyfn (thirteen in Cyfn U); twenty-five in Ior; and twenty-one in Lat A, for example: Cyfn §73/3–4, 13a, 13b, 13c (*WLW*, pp. 136–39); §73a/12, 14–18, 38/10c (*WLW*, pp. 138–41), and from U only: §73/26 (*WLW*, pp. 142–43); Ior §46/5–11, §47/1 (*WLW*, pp. 164–67); §48/2–8, §49/1–5 (*WLW*, pp. 166–69); §50/5, §51/3 (*WLW*, pp. 170–71); §51/10, §52/1 (*WLW*, pp. 172–73), §52/7 (*WLW*, pp. 174–75); Lat A §51/14–16 (*WLW*, pp. 148–51); §52/23–24, 33–34, 40, 46–53, 55, 57–58, 63–64 (*WLW*, pp. 152–59). For a comparative perspective, see K. M. Phillips, "Written on the Body." Also helpful is Saunders, "Matter of Consent."

28. *TCC*, xii–xiii.

29. I use the term "subtractate" here not in order to suggest that the account of *galanas* is

lacking in length or significance, but in recognition of the fact that it forms part of the Three Columns of Law tractate. See Stacey, "Further Musings."

30. Russell, "Etymology." The redactions vary in their particulars: *Ior* 106 (= *TCC* Ior §106, pp. 264–65); *WML* 37.4–17 (= *TCC* Cyfn X §4/1–14, pp. 244–45); *LTWL* Lat A 121.12–28; Lat B 209.19–32; Lat D 332.25–333.3 (= *TCC* Lat D §2, pp. 214–15); Lat E 448.13–29; *Bleg* 30.11–28. For a quick comparison, see *TCC*, 163.

31. Owen suggested that Lat B, here, was preserving an older sense of the term *affaith* (Owen, "Shame and Reparation," *WLW*, 61–65), but Russell, "*Y Naw Affaith*," *TCC*, 151–59, dates the use of *affaith* to mean "cause" rather than "abetment" to the second half of the thirteenth century and later.

32. Bracton, *De legibus*, 2:389–92.

33. Bracton, *De legibus*, 2:389.

34. Discussion and references in Russell, "*Y Naw Affaith*," *TCC*, 159–62.

35. Discussion and references in Kelly, *Guide to Early Irish Law*, 125–29.

36. Russell, "*Y Naw Affaith*," *TCC*, 147.

37. *TCC*, x–xii, Jenkins, "Crime and Tort," *TCC*, 1–3.

38. *TCC*, xi.

39. *TCC*, x–xi; Russell, "Arrangement and Development," and Charles-Edwards, "*Galanas* Tractate," *TCC*, 60–91 and 92–107 respectively; Charles-Edwards, *Welsh Laws*, 26–31.

40. As observed also by the *TCC* editors: x–xii.

41. Jenkins's suggestion: "Crime and Tort," *TCC*, 2–3.

42. Stacey, *Road to Judgment*, 179–98.

43. Charles-Edwards, *Welsh Laws*, 49–53; Pryce, "Lawbooks and Literacy," 40; Stacey, *Road to Judgment*, 182–84; Stacey, "Legal Writing," 59–66, 84–85. Early medieval passages in the lawbooks include the Seven Bishop Houses, the *Nau Kynywedi Teithiauc*, and the Irish canons, on which see, respectively, Charles-Edwards, "Seven Bishop-Houses of Dyfed"; Charles-Edwards, "Nau Kynywedi Teithiauc"; Pryce, "Early Irish Canons"; and Owen, "*Excerpta*."

44. Russell, "Arrangement and Development," *TCC*, 67.

45. Russell, "Arrangement and Development," *TCC*, 76–84.

46. Russell, "Arrangement and Development," *TCC*, 86–87, provides a useful conspectus of the Three Columns. On Cyfn, see Charles-Edwards, *Welsh Laws*, 17–24, 35–38; Jenkins, "'Cyfnerth' Text," *WLW*, 132–35; Owen, "'Cyfnerth' Text," *LAL*, 179–82; Owen, "Laws of Court from Cyfnerth," *WKC*, 425–28; Owen, "Three Columns," *TCC*, 240; Charles-Edwards, "Textual Tradition," 9–30.

47. See conspectus in Russell, "Arrangement and Development," *TCC*, 86–87.

48. In all Cyfn manuscripts: *TCC* Cyfn X §11, pp. 250–51; and Russell, "Arrangement and Development," *TCC*, 86–87.

49. Compare Cyfn X (*TCC* §4/16, pp. 244–45) with the more expanded reflection in Cyfn V (*WML* 37.20–39.21; not in Cyfn W or U).

50. See conspectus in Russell, "Arrangement and Development," *TCC*, 86–87, and note the placement of this in MSS. X and U.

51. *Gweli a chraith*: Russell, "Arrangement and Development, *TCC*, 86–87.

52. Russell, "Arrangement and Development," *TCC*, 84.

53. In Cyfn W, a short section on *galanas* follows on from the tractate on Joint-Ploughing. Both this and the sentence on *oergwymp galanas* are also found in Cyfn U, W, Mk, and Z, but outside the tractate itself: *WML* 109.6–110.3 (= *TCC* Cyfn X §3, pp. 242–43); *Ior* 109 (= *TCC* Ior B §109, p. 273, and cf. Ior E §109, pp. 272–73). This provision represents an addition in Ior B; it

appears in the *damweiniau* attached to Ior E, but not in the lawbook itself: *ALW* IV.iii.1–12; *TCC*, note to Ior B §109, pp. 304–5.

54. *WML* 110.4–11 (=*TCC*, Cyfn X §2, pp. 242–43); *LTWL* Lat A 122.22–25; Lat B 210.26–30; Lat D 335.27–29 (=*TCC* Lat D §8/6, pp. 222–23); Lat E 450.15–19; *Bleg*, 33.18–23. This provision is also found in Cyfn U, V, W, and Mk, but outside the tractate itself: Russell, "Arrangement and Development," *TCC*, 86–87.

55. *TCC* Cyfn X §§12/1–12/5, 12/8–12/10, pp. 250–55.

56. Russell argues that the better-organized Lat A and Lat E derive from a Latin version that is no longer extant, while Lat B reflects material from a variety of sources, including an early medieval text known as the *Excerpta de Libris Romanorum et Francorum*. Lat D stands apart in many ways: Russell, "Arrangement and Development," *TCC*, 66–74, 88–90.

57. Russell, "Arrangement and Development," *TCC*, 88–91 (on Latin D and *Bleg*).

58. On *cynllwyn*, see Owen, "Cynllwyn a Dynyorn"; *TCC*, 314; *WML* 46.16–21, 120.21–121.13 (cf. *TCC* Cyfn X §11, pp. 250–51); *LTWL* Lat A 122.39–123.2; Lat B 214.32–37; Lat D 335.32–34 (=*TCC* Lat D §9/2, pp. 222–23); Lat E 456.14–15; *Bleg* 33.27–29; and cf. *TCC* Lat D §19/8–9, pp. 236–37; *ALW* IV.iii.12–13.

59. *WML* 110.4–11 (=*TCC* Cyfn X §2, pp. 242–43); *LTWL* Lat A 122.22–25; Lat B 210.26–30; Lat D 335.27–29 (=*TCC* Lat D §8/6, pp. 222–23); Lat E 450.15–19; *Bleg* 33.18–23.

60. *WML* 46.19–22 (=*TCC* Cyfn X §11/3–4, pp. 250–52); Lat A 122.39–123.2; Lat B 214.32–37; Lat D 337.18–20 (=*TCC* Lat D §12/14–15, pp. 228–29); Lat E 455.28–30; *Bleg* 36.6–8; and cf. *DwCol* 243 (=*ALW* V.ii.19).

61. *WML* 122.1–13 (=*TCC* Cyfn X §12/1/1–4, pp. 250–53), in the triads, not the tractate; *LTWL* Lat B 210.19–30, in the tractate; Lat D 335.15–26 (=*TCC* Lat D §8/1–5, pp. 222–23), in the tractate; Lat E 450.8–19, in the tractate; *Bleg* 33.4–17, in the tractate; and cf. *Col* 280–82, 291; and *LT* X14 and Q19 (S227), pp. 46–47 and 102–3 respectively.

62. *WML* 122.14–123.1 (=*TCC* Cyfn X §12/2, pp. 252–53), couched in triadic form, and not in the tractate; *LTWL* Lat B 211.7–17, not couched in triad form, and is in the tractate; Lat D 335.38–336.6 (=*TCC* Lat D §10/2–5, pp. 224–25), phrased as triad and is in the tractate; Lat E 450.34–451.3, phrased like Lat B, but is in the tractate; *Bleg* 109.30–110.9; and cf. *LT* X15 and Q20, pp. 46–47 and 102–3 respectively.

63. *WML* 125.16–24 (=*TCC* Cyfn X §12/4, pp. 252–53), in the triads rather than the tractate; *LTWL* Lat B 257.32–38 (not in the main tractate, though is together with other provisions pertaining to the Three Columns); Lat D 336.7– 11 (=*TCC* Lat D §10/6–7, pp. 224–25); Lat E 449.30–38 (in tractate); *Bleg* 110.15–22; and cf. *LT* Q22, pp. 104–5. Some texts (e.g., Cyfn V, but not Cyfn X) have *yn dadleu*, "in [court] sessions" (Lat: *in consistorio*). Cf. also *LTWL* Lat A 140.40–141.14 (not in the tractate); Lat B 210.12–18; Lat E 449.21–29 (in the tractate); *Col* 292–93; and discussion below.

64. *Teir gwarthrud kelein*, "three shames of dead body": *WML* 137.13–15 (=*TCC* Cyfn X §12/10, pp. 254–55; and *LT* X71, pp. 78–79); *LTWL* Lat A 128.7–8; Lat B 243.8–9; Lat D 373.36–37; Lat E 494.17–18; *Bleg* 116.3–5. This provision is always found in the triads rather than the Three Columns tractate. Cf. also *LT* Q100, pp. 140–41; and Q246, p. 232. *Teir sarhaed kelein*, "three insults of a dead body": *WML* 137.11–13 (=*TCC* Cyfn X §12/9, pp. 254–55; and *LT* X70, pp 78–79); *LTWL* Lat A 128.18–19; Lat B 243.7; Lat D 373.34–35; Lat E 494.15–16; *Bleg* 116.1–2. Cf. also *Ior* 112/7; and *LT* Q99, pp. 140–41.

65. Russell, "Arrangement and Development," *TCC*, 81.

66. *LTWL* Lat B 245.17–246.16; and Lat E 451.4–16, 496.3–14, 498.29–30; with which compare *Irish Penitentials*, 136–140, 150–53, and see also Owen, "*Excerpta*."

67. I am grateful to Thomas Charles-Edwards for pointing out an interesting parallel in the *Vita Tripartita* of Patrick, in which a great slaughter and "trembling of arms" (*armchrith*) arises suddenly in an assembly in response to Patrick's curse: Stokes, *Tripartite Life*, 46–47, lines 487–502.

68. Lat E's version has been enlarged and joined to an expanded version of a triad on carrying arms *in consistorio* (the latter in Lat B is located outside of the tractate): *LTWL* Lat A 140.40–141.5; Lat B 210.12–18; Lat E 449.21–29, and cf. Lat E 449.30–450.7.

69. *LTWL* Lat A 122.34–36; Lat B 209.36–37; Lat D 335.30–31 (=*TCC* Lat D §9/1, pp. 222–23); Lat E 448.31–32; *Bleg* 33.24–26 (*y mywn llu*). I am grateful to Paul Russell for this suggestion.

70. *Llyfr Colan* is the exception here: see discussion below.

71. *LTWL* Lat B 209.13–19. Even simpler is Lat E: *LTWL* Lat E 448.10–12, and cf. Lat A 121.7–11.

72. Text and translation by Russell: *TCC* Lat D §1, pp. 214–15 (=*LTWL* 332.15–24).

73. *LTWL* Lat B 210.31–40.

74. Charles-Edwards, "*Galanas* Tractate," *TCC*, 104.

75. Charles-Edwards, "*Galanas* Tractate," *TCC*, 92–93.

76. *TCC* Ior E, §109, pp. 272–73; and cf. Ior E, §107/10–11, pp. 274–75; *Ior* 106–7 (=*TCC* Ior §§106–107, pp. 265–69); and *Col* 270–71 and 299–303.

77. *Ior* 109 (=*TCC* Ior B §109, pp. 272–73), and see note on *TCC*, 304–5; and *ALW* IV.iii.

78. *Col* 292–93; *LTWL* Lat B 210.12–18; Lat E 449.21–29.

79. *Col* 282; and cf. *WML* 110.4–11 (=*TCC* Cyfn X §2/1–2, pp. 242–43); *LTWL* Lat A 122.22–25; Lat B 210.26–30; Lat D 335.27–29 (=*TCC* Lat D §8/6, pp. 222–23); Lat E 450.15–19; *Bleg* 33.18–23.

80. *Col* 283–88; *LTWL* Lat B 231.16–28; Lat D 335.35–37; Lat E 482.23–33; *LT* X23, pp. 52–53; Q63, pp. 124–25; Q168, pp. 174–77; Z89, pp. 364–65.

81. *Col* 277, 290, and cf. *WML* 46.20–22; *LTWL* Lat B 214.32–35; Lat D 337.18–20 (=*TCC* Lat D 12/14, pp. 228–29); Lat E 28–30; *Bleg* 36.6–8, 131.4–7; *DwCol* 243 (=*ALW* V.ii.19); and cf. *TCC* Ior E §108/10, pp. 270–71. See also *TCC* 314–15.

82. *Col* 285, 290.

83. He acknowledges that the evidence for this clause having been part of the Model Lawbook is less than for the other passages he is proposing: Russell, "Arrangement and Development," 84.

84. See discussion *TCC*, 314.

85. Text and translation by Charles-Edwards, "Iorwerth E and B," *TCC* Ior §110/1–3, 274–75.

86. *Col* 304–28.

87. *Ior* 110/1–3, 5 (=*TCC* Ior B §110/1–3, 5, p. 276).

88. Charles-Edwards, "Iorwerth E and B," *TCC*, 305–6.

89. Charles-Edwards, "Iorwerth E and B," *TCC*, 305.

90. *Historia Peredur*, 11.21–12.11.

91. Charles-Edwards, "Iorwerth E and B," *TCC*, 305.

92. Though not in Ior B: contrast *Ior* 105 with *TCC* Ior B §105/7, pp. 262–63.

93. See discussion in Chapter 1.

94. That Ior B does not actually delimit the complete measure of *sarhaed* is evident from Ior B §108/1–2: *TCC* p. 272.

95. *Ior* 109/1–3 (=*TCC* Ior B §109/1–3, p. 273) and *TCC* Ior E §109/1–3, pp. 272–73, with notes on pp. 304–5; and cf. *Ior* 86/11.

96. *TCC*, note to Ior B §110 on pp. 305–6.

97. *Ior* 104/14–18 (=*TCC* Ior B §104, pp. 265–67) and *TCC* Ior E §106, pp. 264–65, with notes on pp. 297–98.

98. *Ior* §105 (=*TCC* Ior B §105, p. 267) and *TCC* Ior E §106, pp. 264–65, with notes on pp. 298–99.

99. Compare *TCC* Ior E §§106–7, pp. 264–69) with *TCC* Ior B §§106–7, pp. 268–69; notes on pp. 299–301.

100. Charles-Edwards, "Iorwerth E and B," *TCC*, 306, note to §110: "The broad tendency of *B*'s version was to lessen the claims of the wider kindred and to enhance the powers of the Lord. The Lord's officers already supervised the process of making peace in E's account (108/2), but his position is even more central in B's version."

101. Charles-Edwards, "Iorwerth E and B," *TCC*, 306.

102. Charles-Edwards, "Iorwerth E and B," *TCC*, 306.

103. *Ior* §§97–103; Ní Chonaill, *Place of the Child*, makes the argument on lordship in detail.

104. See discussion and references in Stacey, "Legal Writing," 57–61.

105. *DwCol* 2, 3.

106. *DwCol* 20, 240, 309, 313.

107. *DwCol* 6, 130, 169–72, 246.

108. *DwCol* 300–302.

109. *ALW* VIII.vii.2, VIII.xi.31; IX.iv–v.

110. Charles-Edwards, *Welsh Laws*, 49–60; Stacey, "Legal Writing," 57–61. On triads and triad collections, see *LT*, 11–38. Later texts make reference to the increasing use of written records in court: Stacey, *Road to Judgment*, 156–62; S. E. Roberts, "Legal Practice," 307–23, and see also S. E. Roberts, "Plaints" and "More Plaints."

111. Presumably with respect to *ALW* XII.xi, the pleading developed from the triad rather than the other way around: *LTWL* Lat A 122.13–18 (in tractate); Lat B 241.3–5, 257.22–28 (not in the main tractate, though in the second section addressing homicide); Lat D 373.13–14 (in triads) and cf. also Lat D 396.25–27; Lat E 492.26–31(in triads) and cf. Lat 463.7–10; *Bleg* 118.26–119.5 (in triads). This provision also occurs in many Cyfn triad collections in what may be its earliest form: *WML* 135.10–12 (not in tractate); *LT* Mk71, pp. 84–85); and cf. *LT* Q116, pp. 150–51. For more on triad development, see S. E. Roberts, *LT*, 7–15; S. E. Roberts, *Welsh Legal Triads*, 19–22; and S. E. Roberts, "Iorwerth Triads."

112. Russell, "Arrangement and Development," and Charles-Edwards, "*Galanas* Tractate."

113. Col's treatment of *galanas* (*Col* 242–333) differs substantially from that of Ior E and B and does not follow what I am suggesting here for Ior B. Indeed, Col is probably as close as one gets to a detailed treatment of the primary offense. Col's redactor seems to draw on material from outside the Ior tradition here, including in his *galanas* subtractate provisions not only on secret killings and ambushes (*Col* 285, 290), but also on killing in war (*Col* 279); killing with borrowed weapons (*Col* 292–93, with which compare *LTWL* Lat B 210.12–18; Lat E 449.21–29); and the financial consequences of killing a lord or kindred head (*Col* 283–90). For differences between Ior and Col, see "Rhagymadrodd," *Col*, xxvi–xxxiii.

114. Charles-Edwards, "*Galanas* Tractate," *TCC*, 92.

115. *Col* 277, 285, 290; and see also *DwCol* 243 and 394.

116. Russell, "Arrangement and Development," *TCC*, 84.

117. *WML* 46.20–22; *LTWL* Lat B 214.32–35; Lat D 337.18–20 (=*TCC* Lat D 12/14, pp. 228–29); Lat E 28–30; *Bleg* 36.6–8, 131.4–7; *Col* 277, 290; *DwCol* 243 (=*ALW* V.ii.19). See also the discussion in *TCC*, 314–15. The possible exception here is Ior E, which speaks of an as yet ill-understood *llad o fyrnygruyd*, "killing by ferocity": *TCC* Ior E §108/10, pp. 270–71, with note on p. 316.

118. *WML* 135.10–12; *LTWL* Lat A 122.13–18 (in the tractate); Lat B 241.3–4, 257.22–28 (not in the main part of the tractate, but in a second section on homicide); Lat D 373.13–14 (in the triads), and cf. also Lat D 396.25–27; Lat E 492.26–31, and cf. Lat E 463.7–10; *Bleg* 118.26–119.5 (in triads). For the use of this triad in pleas, see *ALW* VIII.vii.2; XII.xi; and discussion and references below.

119. *TCC* Ior E §108/10, pp. 270–71), with additional commentary on p. 316.

120. *Ior* 17/5–6 (the context here is physicians' fees); 100/6 (membership in a given family); 104/15 (fighting); 147/1–2 (released blood, as from a nosebleed or a scab); 147/5, 15–17 (payment for injuries caused by another).

121. *ALW* XII.xi, with translation there, and cf. also the *sarhaed* plea in *ALW* VIII.vii.2, which uses a truncated version of this latter; and triad Q116 (=*LT*, pp. 150–51). The shortest version of this provision appears in *DwCol* 138 and Mk71 (=*LT*, pp. 84–85, with notes on 280). Other examples include *ALW* VII.i.44, 46 on surreption (*agkyuarch*), and VII.i.43 on rape (*treis*).

122. Russell, "Arrangement and Development," *TCC*, 82–85; and see on such matters Harris, "Compensation for Injury."

123. Russell, "Arrangement and Development," *TCC*, 82–85.

124. Russell, "Arrangement and Development," *TCC*, 82–85; *WML*, lxxiii.

125. *Ior* §146 following on §145.

126. Russell, "Arrangement and Development," *TCC*, 84.

127. It may be significant that the most graphic passages in Ior and Cyfn relating to violence are all triads—for example, in Cyfn W the *tri argae guaet*, *teir sarhaed kelein*, and *teir guarthrut kelein*, "three stays of blood," "three [types of] of *sarhaed* done to a corpse," and the "three reproaches of a corpse" (*WML* 135.10–12; 137.11–15). Triads are floating almost by definition, and thus are less likely to have formed a part of the original lawbook core.

128. For weapons in medieval poetry, see Day, *Arfau yn yr Hengerdd*.

129. Literally "he."

130. Text and translation from O'Brien, *God's Peace*, 170–71, 12.6.

131. Text and translation of all Bracton passages from Bracton online, http://bracton.law.harvard.edu/Common/index.htm.

132. Andrews, *Welsh Court Poems*, text 2, p. 3, lines 17–20; Cynddelw Brydydd Mawr, "Arwyrain Owain Gwynedd," 8. The translation here is by Clancy, *Medieval Welsh Poems*, 148. An excellent study is Day, *Arfau yn yr Hengerdd*.

133. Andrews, *Welsh Court Poems*, Text 12, p. 16, lines 25 and 14.

134. Gwalchmai ap Meilyr, "Gorhoffedd Gwalchmai," Poem 9, p. 203, lines 33–34.

135. Russell, *Vita Griffini*, 46–47.

136. Particularly relating to the battle of Mynydd Carn: Russell, *Vita Griffini*, 68–71, §18; and cf. parallel passages in the Welsh life of Gruffudd, *MPW*, 36.5–38.4. Two excellent studies of the narrative themes of Gruffudd's biography are Malone, *Entirely Outside the World*, and Malone, "There Has Been Treachery."

137. Russell, *Vita Griffini*, 62–63, §12/9; 86–87, §33/5; and cf. *MPW*, 31.8–9; 50.12.

138. Russell, *Vita Griffini*, 68–71, §18/8; and cf. *MPW*, 36.26–31. As Russell remarks, the intent here is to portray him as a biblical hero in the vein of Iudas Maccabaeus: *Vita Griffini*, 147, note to §18/8.

139. Russell, *Vita Griffini*, 64–65, §14/10; and cf. *MPW*, 32.25–29.

140. Russell, *Vita Griffini*, 58–59, §9/1–2; and cf. *MPW*, 28.2–8.

141. Russell, *Vita Griffini*, 86–89, §33; and cf. *MPW*, 50.1–11.

142. Russell, *Vita Griffini*, 64–65, §14/10; and cf. *MPW*, 32.25–29.

143. Russell, *Vita Griffini*, 60–63, §12/4; 74–75, §22/8; 74–75, §23/7; 78–79, §25/9; and cf. *MPW*, 41.6–10, 44.1–2.

144. Russell, *Vita Griffini*, 62–63, §13/3; and cf. *MPW* 31.10–21.

145. Russell, *Vita Griffini*, 72–73, §21/2; and cf. *MPW*, 34.15–19.

146. Russell, *Vita Griffini*, 74–75, §23/7; and cf. *MPW*, 41.6–10.

147. Russell, *Vita Griffini*, 78–79, §25/1; and cf. *MPW*, 43.6–13.

148. Russell, *Vita Griffini*, 82–83, §28/4; and cf. *MPW*, 46.13–17.

149. Russell, *Vita Griffini*, 82–83, §28/7; and cf. *MPW*, 46.22–26.

150. Because the rightful realm is always where Gruffudd himself is: see Chapter 2; Russell, *Vita Griffini*, 72–73, §19/7; 74–75, §22/9; and cf. *MPW* 38.24–27, 40.17–20.

151. Russell, *Vita Griffini*, 68–71, §18/8, 13–14 (and see also the characterization of Gruffudd's brother at 56–59, §6/6, and of his enemies as wandering intruders at 68–69, §17/6–9), and cf. *MPW* 36.26–28, 37.3–16.

152. *Ior* §§42–43.

153. Welsh, "*Manawydan*," in Sullivan, *Mabinogi*, 136.

154. Welsh, "*Manawydan*," in Sullivan, *Mabinogi*, 135.

155. Fulton, "Education of Princes," 242.

156. McKenna, "Colonization of Myth," 117; Fulton, "Education of Princes," 244.

157. Most would put the dating of this tale c. 1200: S. Davies, *Crefft*, 12; B. F. Roberts, *Studies*, 60; Lloyd-Morgan, "Narrative Structure"; and Breeze, "Windmills," 61–62.

158. Aronstein, "Becoming Welsh," 164.

159. Aronstein, "Becoming Welsh," 167–68.

160. Fulton, "Education of Princes," 245–47.

161. This depiction forms a striking contrast with the tales, in which male relatives of the king—including the *penteulu*—appear frequently as they were in real life, potentially a dangerous source of rebellion: see McKenna, "Revising Math," 109–11.

CONCLUSION

1. As does the statement in some manuscripts of the Test Book enjoining judges to learn its contents: *ALW* III, *Llyvyr Pra6v*.

2. Including Latin C (British Library Harleian MS 1796): *WLMA*, xliii. Peniarth 28 itself may have been a presentation copy, perhaps intended for an ecclesiastic: Huws, "Peniarth 28: Illustrations"; Huws, "Leges Howelda"; Pryce, *Native Law*, 28n47. For individual manuscripts, see the Cyfraith Hywel website.

3. For example, the pleadings in manuscripts B, G, and Lew, which are attached to versions of Ior.

4. See, for example, Lynch, "Court Poetry," *WKC*, 167–90; Owen, "Archaism"; Caerwyn Williams, *Court Poet*; Caerwyn Williams, *Poets of the Welsh Princes*; E. I. Rowlands, "Bardic

Lore"; Carr, "Patrons"; Caerwyn Williams, "Meilyr Brydydd"; and Br. Roberts and Owen, *Beirdd a Thywysogion.*

5. Malone, "Treachery from the Beginning," 61; Morse, "Medieval Biography." See also Bowen, *Y Traddiodiad Rhyddiaith*; Br. Roberts, "Historical Writing"; Owain Wyn Jones, *Historical Writing*; Mac Cana, "On the Early Development"; and T. Jones, "Historical Writing."

6. Maund, "Fact and Narrative Fiction."

7. Fulton, *Welsh Prophecy*, 4; and see also her "Owain Glyn Dŵr."

8. McKenna, "Colonization of Myth"; Aronstein, "Becoming Welsh."

9. Fulton, "Education of Princes," 238–40. See also McKenna, "Theme of Sovereignty"; McKenna, "Learning Lordship"; McKenna, "Revising Math"; Ford, "Prolegomena"; and on the sovereignty aspects of the Welsh tale *Peredur*: Goetinck, *Peredur*; and Goetinck, "Peredur and the Three Functions."

10. For example, see Dean, *Crime in Medieval Europe*; Smail, *Consumption of Justice*. The argument is laid out for the early Middle Ages in Stacey, "Law and Order."

11. *Ior* 47/2–5 (= *WLW* Ior §47/2–5, pp. 166–67); *LTWL* Lat A 143.41–144.10 (= *WLW* Lat A §52/25–30, pp. 152–53); Lat B 224.3–13; Lat D 342.13–16; Lat E 472.33–473.4; *Bleg* 61.27–31.

12. *WML* 132.10–19; *LTWL* Lat D 374.26–32; *Bleg* 116.29–117.6.

13. *LTWL* Lat A 142.24–30 (= *WLW* Lat A §51/14–16, pp. 148–51); Lat B 223.17–20; Lat E 472.8–10.

14. *Ior* 48/3, 8 (= *WLW* Ior §48/3, 8, pp. 168–69).

15. *WML* 89.21–25 (= *WLW* Cyfn §73/3–4, pp. 136–37); *LTWL* Lat B 221.19–23; Lat D 342.19–22; Lat E 470.18–22; *Bleg* 62.4–8.

16. In that while the former award such a woman her steers, the latter give her the *agweddi* to which she would have been entitled had she been given in marriage by her kin: *LTWL* Lat D 343.10–13; *Bleg* 63.10–14.

17. Charles-Edwards, "Seven Bishop-Houses of Dyfed"; Charles-Edwards, "Nau Kynywedi Teithiauc"; Pryce, "Early Irish Canons"; and Owen, "*Excerpta.*"

18. Powell, "Floating Sections."

19. *Ior* 36/3 (*Rey a dyweyt*, "some say") and 37/5, respectively; Cyfn awards him the aitchbone: *WML* 32.24–25 (= *WKC* Cyfn §41/5, pp. 474–75).

20. *WML* 32.15–17 (= *WKC* Cyfn §40/7, pp. 474–75), and see also *WML* 26.3–6 (= *WKC* Cyfn §26/1, pp. 464–65).

21. *WML* 17.5–10, and cf. *WKC* Cyfn Y §39/2, pp. 474–75.

22. *WML* 31.6–8 (= *WKC* Cyfn §39/1, pp. 474–75) in the kitchen; *LTWL* Lat A 119.1–3; Lat B 206.20–21 (= *WKC* Lat B §1.32/1, pp 514–15); Lat D 331.20–21; Lat E 447.4–5; *Bleg* 26.25–26 in the court.

23. *Ior* 9/7; *WML* 18.19–20 (= *WKC* Cyfn §14/19, pp. 454–55). Cyfn has "hearts" only; Ior specifies that the animals in question are wild.

24. Stacey, "King, Queen, and *Edling*"; Stacey, "Divorce."

25. *Ior* 36/3, vs. the aitchbone in Cyfn: *WML* 32.24–25 (= *WKC* Cyfn §41/5, pp. 474–75).

26. Albeit in different ways across the various lawbook versions: *WML* 24.8–11 (= *WKC* Cyfn §19/6–7, pp. 460–61); *LTWL* Lat A 117.32–35; Lat B 206.9–12 (= *WKC* Lat B §1.30/5, pp. 514–15); Lat D 329.15–17; Lat E 446.14–16; *Bleg* 23.17–19 (*dryswr neuadd*, "doorkeeper of the hall"); *Ior* 19/13.

27. In Cyfn and Lat B: *WML* 33.4–6 (= *WKC* Cyfn §42/1–2, pp. 476–77); *LTWL* Lat B 203.36–204.2 (= *WKC* Lat B §1.23/3, pp. 508–9). Ior and other Latin texts and Bleg associate him also or instead with the skins: *Ior* 33/11–12; *LTWL* Lat A 120.36–39 (of cattle slaughtered in

kitchen that are in his care for three nights); Lat D 349.19–20 (slaughtered in court), 349.22; Lat E 447.33–448.1 (slaughtered in court); *Bleg* 27.17–21 (slaughtered in court).

28. Russell, "From Plates and Rods."

29. R. R. Davies, "Law and National Identity."

30. E.g., *Ior* 86/1: *herwyd guyr Guyned*, "according to the men of Gwynedd."

31. E.g., *Ior* 64/6; 65/7–9; 66/1; 80/1; 86/7–9; and so on.

32. E.g., *Ior* 82/1–3, 115/6.

33. *WML* 32.15–17 (=*WKC* Cyfn §40/7, pp. 474–75), and see also *WML* 26.3–6 (=*WKC* §26/1, pp. 464–65); *Ior* 35/6.

BIBLIOGRAPHY

PRIMARY SOURCES AND BIBLIOGRAPHICAL AIDS

The Acts of Welsh Rulers, 1120–1283. Ed. Huw Pryce. Cardiff: University of Wales Press, 2005.

Ancient Laws and Institutes of Wales. Ed. Aneurin Owen. London: Record Commission, 1841.

Anglo-Saxon Chronicle, Version D: British Museum, Cotton MS. Tiberius B iv. Accessed October 8, 2016. http://www.bl.uk/manuscripts/Viewer.aspx?ref=cotton_ms_tiberius_b_iv_f003r.

Annales Cambriae, A Version. "The *Annales Cambriae* and the Old Welsh Genealogies from Harleian MS 2859." Ed. E. Phillimore. *Y Cymmrodor* 9 (1888): 141–83. *Annales Cambriae*, A, B, and C Versions. Ed. J. Williams ab Ithel. London: Rolls Series, 1860.

Aquinas, Thomas. *De Regimine Principum*. In *Medieval Political Theory—A Reader: The Quest for the Body Politic, 1100–1400*, ed. Cary Nederman and Kate Forhan, 100–116. London: Routledge, 1993.

Aristotle. *De Motu Animalium*. Ed. and trans. Martha Nussbaum. Princeton, NJ: Princeton University Press, 1978. Another version consulted is *De Motu Animalium, On the Motion of Animals*. Trans. A. S. L. Farquharson. eBooks@Adelaide. Adelaide, South Australia: University of Adelaide Library, 2007, last updated August 25, 2010. Accessed June 28, 2011. http://ebooks.adelaide.edu.au/a/aristotle/motion/.

———. *Politics, Books V and VI*. Trans. David Keyt. Oxford: Oxford University Press, 1999.

The Art of Falconry by Frederick II of Hohenstaufen. Trans. Casey Wood and F. Marjorie Fyfe. Stanford, CA: Stanford University Press, 1943.

"*Arwyrain Owain Gwynedd*." Ed. Nerys Ann Jones and Ann Parry Owen. In *CBT*, vol. 4, *Gwaith Cynddelw Brydydd Mawr II*, 1–16. Cardiff: Univ. of Wales Press, 1995.

Bethu Phátraic: The Tripartite Life of Patrick. Ed. K. Mulchrone. Dublin: Hodges, Figgis, 1939. Earlier print edition: *The Tripartite Life of Patrick with Other Documents Pertaining to That Saint*. Ed. Whitley Stokes. London: H.M. Stationery Office, 1887. Electronic version prepared by Henar Velasco. Madrid: 1997–2000. TITUS version prepared by Jost Gippert. Frankfurt: 2000–2002. Available at: http://titus.uni-frankfurt.de/texte/etcs/celt/mir/vitatrip/vitat.htm.

Bracton. De legibus et consuetudinibus Angliae. 4 vols. Ed. G. E. Woodbine. Trans. Samuel E. Thorne. London: Publications of the Selden Society, 1968–77. Accessed September 30, 2011. http://bracton.law.harvard.edu/.

Branwen uerch Lyr: The Second of the Four Branches of the Mabinogi edited from the White Book of Rhydderch with Variants from the Red Book of Hergest and from Peniarth 6. Ed. Derick S. Thomson. Dublin: Dublin Institute for Advanced Studies, 1976.

Brenhinedd y Saeson or The Kings of the Saxons. Ed. and trans. T. Jones. Cardiff: University of Wales Press, 1971.

Bridgeman Images, Image STC469126. Accessed January 3, 2014. http://www.bridgemanart.com/en-GB/asset/469126/English-School-17th-century/Frederick-I-Emperor-holding-ye-Popes-stirrup-on.

Brunetto Latini. *Li Livre dou Tresor*. In *Medieval Political Theory—A Reader: The Quest for the Body Politic, 1100–1400*, ed. Cary Nederman and Kate Forhan. London: Routledge, 1993.

Brut y Tywysogyon or The Chronicle of the Princes: Red Book of Hergest Version. Ed. Thomas Jones. Cardiff: University of Wales Press, 1955.

Cáin Lánamna: An Old Irish Tract on Marriage and Divorce Law. Ed. Charlene M. Eska. Leiden: Brill, 2010.

Calendar of Various Chancery Rolls: Supplementary Close Rolls, Welsh Rolls, Scutage Rolls, 1277–1326. Ed. H. C. Maxwell Lyte. London: HMSO, 1912.

Canu Maswedd yr Oesoedd Canol/Medieval Welsh Erotic Poetry. Ed. Dafydd Johnston. Cardiff: Tafol, 1991.

"*Canu Owain Cyfeiliog*." In *Gwaith Llywelyn Fardd I ac Eraill*, ed. Gruffydd Aled Williams, 14. Cardiff: University of Wales Press, 1994.

"*Castigos del Rey Don Sancho* and *Castigos y Dotrinas que un sabio dava a sus hijas*." Ed. and trans. Emily C. Francomano. In *Medieval Conduct Literature: An Anthology of Vernacular Guides to Behaviour forYouths, with English Translations*, ed. Mark D. Johnston, 185–284. Medieval Academy of America Books, no. 111. Toronto: University of Toronto Press, 2009.

Christine de Pisan. *The Book of the Body Politic*. Ed. Kate Langdon Forhan. Cambridge: Cambridge University Press, 1994.

Constitutio Domus Regis. In *Dialogus de Scaccario, and Constitutio Domus Regis*.

Críth Gablach. Ed. D. A. Binchy. Dublin: Dublin Institute for Advanced Studies, 1979.

Cronica de Wallia. "Cronica de Wallia and Other Documents from Exeter Cathedral Library MS 3514." Ed. T. Jones. *BBCS* 12 (1948): 27–44. Reprinted separately by University of Wales Press, 1948, 1–24.

"Culhwch ac Olwen." *Culhwch ac Olwen: An Edition and Study of the Oldest Arthurian Tale*. Ed. R. Bromwich and D. Simon Evans. Cardiff: University of Wales Press, 1997.

Cyfraith Hywel website. Accessed October 6, 2016. http://www.cyfraith-hywel.org.uk/.

Cyfranc Lludd a Llefelys. Ed. Brynley Roberts. Dublin: Dublin Institute for Advanced Studies, 1975.

Cyfreithiau Hywel Dda yn ôl Llawysgrif Coleg yr Iesu LVII. Ed. Melville Richards. 2nd ed. Cardiff: University of Wales Press, 1990.

Cyfreithiau Hywel Dda yn ôl Llyfr Blegywryd. Ed. Stephen J. Williams and J. Enoch Powell. 2nd ed. Cardiff: University of Wales Press, 1961.

Cyfres Beirdd y Tywysogion. Gen. ed. R. Geraint Gruffydd. For volumes referred to, see individual titles. Poems referred to frequently are also cited separately in the bibliography.

Cynddelw Brydydd Mawr. "Arwyrain Owain Gwynedd." In *CBT*, vol. 4, *Gwaith Cynddelw Brydydd Mawr II*, ed. Nerys Ann Jones and Ann Parry Owen, 1–16. Cardiff: University of Wales Press, 1995.

Damweiniau. See *ALW* and *Damweiniau Colan*.

Damweiniau Colan: Llyfr y Damweiniau yn ôl Llawysgrif Peniarth 30. Ed. Dafydd Jenkins. Aberystwyth: Cymdeithas Lyfrau Ceredigion, 1973.

Dialogus de Scaccario, and Constitutio Domus Regis/The Dialogue of the Exchequer and The Establishment of the Royal Household. Ed. Emilie Amt and Stephen Church. Oxford: Oxford

University Press, 2007. The text can also be accessed online in English translation via the Yale Law School's Avalon Project. Accessed May 20, 2014. http://avalon.law.yale.edu/medieval/excheq.asp#b1p5.

Dictionary of the Irish Language Based Mainly on Old and Middle Irish Materials. Compact ed. Dublin: Royal Irish Academy, 1998. Accessed July 6, 2016. Now most easily accessible online through eDIL: http://www.dil.ie/.

Early English Law Project. Accessed March 28, 2011. http://www.earlyenglishlaws.ac.uk/laws/texts/synopsis/Glanvill/.

Edmyg Dinbych. "Edmyg Dinbych:" Cerdd Lys Gynar o Ddyfed. Ed. R. Geraint Gruffydd. Aberystwyth: Canolfan Uwchefrydiau Cymreig a Cheltaidd Prifysgol Cymru, 2002. For translation into English, see Gruffydd, " 'The Praise of Tenby.' "

The Établissements of Saint Louis: Thirteenth-Century Law Texts from Tours, Orléans, and Paris. Trans. F. R. P. Akehurst. Philadelphia: University of Pennsylvania Press, 1996.

Facsimile of the Chirk Codex of the Welsh Laws. Ed. J. Gwenogvryn Evans. Llanbedrog, North Wales: National Library of Wales, 1909.

Geiriadur Prifysgol Cymru. Ed. R. J. Thomas et al. Cardiff: University of Wales Press, 1952–2002. 2nd ed. Ed. G. A. Bevan et al. Cardiff: University of Wales Press, 2003.

Gesetze der Angelsachsen. Ed. F. Liebermann. 3 vols. Halle: Max Niemeyer, 1903–16. Reprint, Aalen: Scientia, 1960.

Giraldi Cambrensis Opera. Ed. J. S. Brewer, J. F. Dimock, and G. F. Warner. Rolls Series. 8 vols. London: HMSO, 1861–91. *The Journey Through Wales* and *The Description of Wales* have been translated by Lewis Thorpe. London: Penguin Books, 1978. Reissued 2004.

[Attributed to] Glanvill. *The Treatise on the Laws and Customs of the Realm of England Commonly Called Glanvill.* Ed. G. D. G. Hall. 1965. Reprint, Oxford: Clarendon Press, 2002.

Y Gododdin. Y Gododdin: Llyfr Aneirin: A Facsimile/Llyfr Aneirin: Facsimile. Ed. Daniel Huws. Cardiff: University of Wales Press, 1989. Editions and translations: *Canu Aneirin: Gyda rhagymadrodd a nodiadau.* Ed. Ifor Williams. Cardiff: University of Wales Press, 1961; *The Gododdin.* Trans. Kenneth Jackson. Edinburgh: Edinburgh University Press, 1969; *The Gododdin of Aneirin: Text and Context from Dark-Age North Britain.* Ed. John T. Koch. Cardiff: University of Wales Press, 1997.

Gramadegau'r Penceirddiaid. Ed. G. J. Williams and E. J. Jones. Cardiff: University of Wales Press, 1934.

Gruffudd ab yr Ynad Coch. "Marwnad Llywelyn ap Gruffudd." In *CBT*, vol. 7, *Gwaith Bleddyn Fardd a Beirdd Eraill Ail Hanner y Drydedd Ganrif ar Ddeg*, ed. Rhian Andrews, 414–33. Cardiff: University of Wales Press, 1996.

Gwaith Bleddyn Fardd a Beirdd Eraill Ail Hanner y Drydedd Ganrif ar Ddeg. Ed. Rhian Andrews. Vol. 7 of *CBT*. Cardiff: University of Wales Press, 1996.

Gwaith Cynddelw Brydydd Mawr I. Ed. Nerys Ann Jones and Ann Parry Owen. Vol. 3 of *CBT*. Cardiff: University of Wales Press, 1991.

Gwaith Cynddelw Brydydd Mawr II. Ed. Nerys Ann Jones and Ann Parry Owen. Vol. 4 of *CBT*. Cardiff: University of Wales Press, 1995.

Gwaith Llywarch ap Llywelyn 'Prydydd y Moch.' Ed. Elin M. Jones. With the assistance of Nerys Ann Jones. Vol. 5 of *CBT*. Cardiff: University of Wales Press, 1991.

Gwaith Llywelyn Fardd I ac Eraill o Feirdd y Ddeuddegfed Ganrif. Ed. Kathleen Anne Bramley, Nerys Ann Jones, Morfydd E. Owen, Catherine McKenna, Gruffydd Aled Williams, and J. E. Caerwyn Williams. Vol 2 of *CBT*. Cardiff: University of Wales Press, 1994.

Gwaith Meilyr Brydydd a'i Ddisgynyddion. Ed. J. E. Caerwyn Williams. With the assistance of Peredur I. Lynch. Vol. 1 of *CBT*. Cardiff: University of Wales Press, 1994.

Gwalchmai ap Meilyr. "Gorhoffedd Gwalchmai." In *CBT*, vol 1, *Gwaith Meilyr Brydydd a'i Ddisgynyddion*, ed. J. E. Caerwyn Williams, with the assistance of Peredur I. Lynch, 192–224, poem 9. Cardiff: University of Wales Press, 1994.

Hincmar. *De Ordine Palatii*. Ed. and trans. (into German) T. Gross and R. Schieffer. Monumenta Germania Historia, Fontes iuris 3. Hanover: Hahnsche Buchhandlung, 1980.

Historia Gruffud vab Kenan. Ed. D. Simon Evans. Cardiff: University of Wales Press, 1977. See also *Vita Griffini Filii Conani*.

Historia Peredur vab Efrawc. Ed. Glenys Goetinck. Cardiff: University of Wales Press. 1976.

The Historia Regum Britanniae of Geoffrey of Monmouth. Ed. Neil Wright. 5 vols. Cambridge: D. S. Brewer, 1985.

Hywel ab Owain Gwynedd. "Gorhoffedd Hywel ab Owain." In "Gwaith Hywel ab Owain Gwynedd," in *CBT*, vol. 2, *Gwaith Llywelyn Fardd I ac Eraill o Feirdd y Ddeuddegfed Ganrif*, ed. Kathleen Anne Bramley, Nerys Ann Jones, Morfydd E. Owen, Catherine McKenna, Gruffydd Aled Williams, and J. E. Caerwyn Williams, 114–30. Cardiff: University of Wales Press, 1994.

Icelandic Sagas. *Law and Literature in Medieval Iceland: Ljósvetninga saga and Valla-Ljóts saga*. Ed. and trans. Theodore M. Andersson and William Ian Miller. Stanford, CA: Stanford University Press, 1989.

"Illustrations of Welsh Soldiers from the *Littere Wallie*, preserved in Liber A of the Public Record Office (1280s)." Accessed July 12, 2016. http://www.warfare.altervista.org/13/Chapter_House-Liber_A.htm.

The Irish Penitentials. Ed. L. Bieler. Scriptores Latini Hiberniae, vol 5. Dublin: Dublin Institute for Advanced Studies, 1963.

Itinerarium Cambriae. See *Giraldi Cambrensis Opera*.

John of Paris. "On Royal and Papal Power." In *Medieval Political Theory—A Reader: The Quest for the Body Politic, 1100–1400*, ed. Cary Nederman and Kate Forhan, 221–29. London: Routledge, 1993.

Latin A: *Latin Redaction A of the Law of Hywel*. Trans. Ian Fletcher. Pamffledi Cyfraith Hywel. Aberystwyth: Canolfan Uwchefrydiau Cymreig a Cheltaidd Prifysgol Cymru, 1986.

Latin C: Edition by Paul Russell in *WLMA*. References are to numbered provision (and to page number when appropriate).

The Latin Texts of the Welsh Laws. Ed. Hywel Emanuel. Cardiff: University of Wales Press, 1967.

The Law of Hywel Dda: Law Texts from Medieval Wales Translated and Edited. Ed. Dafydd Jenkins. Welsh Classics, vol. 2. Llandysul: Gomer Press, 1986.

The Laws of Early Iceland: Grágás I and II. Trans. Andrew Dennis, Peter Foote, and Richard Perkins. 2000. Reprint, Winnipeg: University of Manitoba Press, 2007.

The Laws of the Earliest English Kings. Ed. F. I. Attenborough. Cambridge: Cambridge University Press, 1922.

The Laws of Edward the Confessor. *God's Peace and King's Peace: The Laws of Edward the Confessor*. Ed. Bruce R. O'Brien. Philadelphia: University of Pennsylvania Press, 1999.

The Laws of Howel Dda: A Facsimile Reprint of Llanstephan MS 116 in the National Library of Wales, Aberystwyth. Ed. Timothy Lewis. London: Sotheran, 1912.

The Laws of Hywel Dda (The Book of Blegywryd). Trans. Melville Richards. Liverpool: Liverpool University Press, 1954.

The Laws of the Kings of England from Edmund to Henry I. Ed. A. J. Robertson. Cambridge: Cambridge University Press, 1925.

The Legal Triads of Medieval Wales. Ed. Sara Elin Roberts. Cardiff: University of Wales Press, 2007.

Leges Henrici Primi. Ed. L. J. Downer. Oxford: Clarendon Press, 1972.

Liber Landavensis: The Text of the Book of Llan Dâv. Ed. J. Gwenogvryn Evans and John Rhys. Oxford: Clarendon Press, 1893. Reprint, Aberystwyth: National Library of Wales, 1979.

Life of Gruffudd ap Cynan. See *Medieval Prince of Wales: The Life of Gruffudd ap Cynan* and *Vita Griffini Filii Conani.*

Llawysgrif Pomffred: An Edition and Study of Peniarth MS 259B. Ed. Sara Elin Roberts. Leiden: Brill, 2011.

Llyfr Blegywryd. See *Cyfreithiau Hywel Dda yn ôl Llyfr Blegywryd.*

Llyfr Colan. Ed. Dafydd Jenkins. Cardiff: University of Wales Press, 1963.

Llyfr Cyfnerth. See *Welsh Medieval Law.*

Llyfr Cynghawsedd. Ed. Aled Rhys Wiliam. *BBCS* 35 (1988): 73–85.

Llyfr Cynog. Ed. A. R. Wiliam. Pamffledi Cyfraith Hywel. Aberystwyth: Canolfan Uwchefrydiau Cymreig a Cheltaidd Prifysgol Cymru, 1990.

Llyfr Du Caerfyrddin: The Black Book of Carmarthen. Ed. A. O. H. Jarman. Cardiff: University of Wales Press, 1982.

Llyfr Gwyn Rhydderch: Y Chwedlau a'r Rhamantau. Ed. J. Gwenogvryn Evans. With an introduction by R. M. Jones. Cardiff: University of Wales Press, 1973

Llyfr Iorwerth. Ed. Aled Rhys Wiliam. Cardiff: University of Wales Press, 1960.

The Mabinogion

Manuscript texts and commentary:

Llyfr Gwyn Rhydderch: Y Chwedlau a'r Rhamantau/The White Book Mabinogion. Ed. J. Gwenogvryn Evans. With an introduction by R. M. Jones. Cardiff: University of Wales Press, 1973.

National Library of Wales introduction to the *Llyfr Gwyn*, accessed October 11, 2016. https://www.llgc.org.uk/discover/digital-gallery/manuscripts/the-middle-ages/white-book-of-rhydderch/.

The Text of the Mabinogion from the Red Book of Hergest. Ed. John Rhŷs and J. Gwenogvryn Evans. Oxford: Clarendon Press, 1887.

Translations into English:

Davies, Sioned. *The Mabinogion*. Oxford: Oxford University Press, 2007.

Ford, Patrick K. *The Mabinogi and Other Medieval Welsh Tales*. Berkeley: University of California Press, 1977.

Individual tales and romances:

Branwen verch Lyr: The Second of the Four Branches of the Mabinogi edited from the White Book of Rhydderch with Variants from the Red Book of Hergest and from Peniarth 6. Ed. Derick S. Thomson. Dublin: Institute for Advanced Studies, 1976.

Breudwyt Maxen Wledic. Ed. B. F. Roberts. Dublin: Dublin Institute for Advanced Studies, 2005.

Breudwyt Ronabwy. Ed. Melville Richards. Cardiff: University of Wales Press, 2001.

Culhwch and Olwen: An Edition and Study of the Oldest Arthurian Tale. Ed. Rachel Bromwich and D. S. Evans. Cardiff: University of Wales Press, 1992.

Cyfranc Lludd a Llefelys. Ed. B. F. Roberts. Dublin: Dublin Institute for Advanced Studies, 1975.

Manawydan uab Llyr: Trydedd Gainc y Mabinogi. Ed. Ian Hughes. Cardiff: University of Wales Press, 2007.

Math uab Mathonwy: Pedwaredd Gainc y Mabinogi. Ed. Ian Hughes. Aberystwyth: Department of Welsh, University of Wales, 2000.

Owein or Chwedyl Iarlles y Ffynnawn. Ed. R. L. Thomson. Dublin: Dublin Institute for Advanced Studies, 1975.

Pedeir Keinc y Mabinogi. Ed. Ifor Williams. 1930. Reprint, Cardiff: University of Wales Press, 1975.

Pwyll Pendeuic Dyuet. Ed. R. L. Thomson. Dublin: Dublin Institute for Advanced Studies, 1957.

Ystorya Taliesin. Ed. P. K. Ford. Cardiff: University of Wales Press, 1992.

Marie de France. "The Lay of Guigemar." In *The Lais of Marie de France*, ed. and trans. Glyn S. Burgess and Keith Busby, 43–55. 2nd ed. Harmondsworth, Middlesex, England: Penguin, 1999.

———. "*De ventre et membris*." "*Of the Belly and the Members*." In *The Fables of Marie de France: An English Translation*, ed. and trans. Mary Lou Martin, xxvii, 92–93. Birmingham, AL: Summit, 1984.

Marsiglio of Padua. *Defensor Pacis*. In *Medieval Political Theory—A Reader: The Quest for the Body Politic, 1100–1400*, ed. Cary Nederman and Kate Forhan, 205–6. London: Routledge, 1993.

"*Marwnad Llywelyn ap Gruffudd*." In *CBT*, vol. 7, *Gwaith Bleddyn Fardd a Beirdd Eraill Ail Hanner y Drydedd Ganrif ar Ddeg*, ed. Rhiain Andrews, 414–33, no. 36. Cardiff: University of Wales Press, 1996.

Medieval Prince of Wales: The Life of Gruffudd ap Cynan. Ed. D. Simon Evans. Lampeter: Llanerch Enterprises, 1990.

Medieval Welsh Poems. Ed. Joseph Clancy. Dublin: Four Courts Press, 2003.

The Metrical Dinnsenchas. Ed. Edward J. Gwynn. Vol. 1. 1906. 2nd reprint, Dublin: Dublin Institute for Advanced Studies, 1991. See also CELT. Accessed September 6, 2016. http://www.ucc.ie/celt/published/G106500A/index.html.

National Library of Wales. Introduction to the Llyfr Gwyn Rhydderch. Accessed February 27, 2016. https://www.llgc.org.uk/index.php?id=whitebookofrhydderchpeniart.

Peniarth 28. Illustrations from Peniarth 28. National Library of Wales Digital Mirror. Accessed July 13, 2011. http://www.llgc.org.uk/index.php?id=570.

Plaints. "Plaints in Welsh Medieval Laws." Ed. Sara Elin Roberts. *Journal of Celtic Studies* 4 (2004): 219–61. See also "More Plaints in Welsh Medieval Law." Ed. Sara Elin Roberts. *Studia Celtica* 48 (2014): 171–99.

Pleas/pleadings. See *ALW* and *Llyfr Cynghawsedd*. Ed. Aled Rhys Wiliam. *BBCS* 35 (1988): 73–85.

Policraticus. In John of Salisbury, *Policraticus: of the Frivolities of Courtiers and the Footprints of Philosophers*, ed. and trans. C. J. Nederman. Cambridge: Cambridge University Press, 1990.

Princes' Mirrors. See Anton, Hans Hubert. *Fürstenspiegel (Königsspiegel) des frühen und hohen Mittelalters: Ein Editionsprojekt an der Universität Trier*. Accessed June 16, 2011. http://www.ahf-muenchen.de/Forschungsberichte/Jahrbuch2003/Anton.pdf.

Prydydd y Moch. "Mawl Gwenllïan ferch Hywel o Wynllŵg." In *CBT*, vol. 5, *Gwaith Llywarch ap Llywelyn 'Prydydd y Moch,'* ed. Elin M. Jones, with the assistance of Nerys Ann Jones, 137–45. Cardiff: University of Wales Press, 1991.

———. "Mawl Llywelyn ab Iorwerth o Wynedd." In *CBT*, vol. 5, *Gwaith Llywarch ap Llywelyn 'Prydydd y Moch,'* ed. Elin M. Jones, with the assistance of Nerys Ann Jones, 201–9. Cardiff: University of Wales Press, 1991.

———. "Mawl Rhodri ab Owain o Wynedd." In *CBT*, vol. 5, *Gwaith Llywarch ap Llywelyn 'Prydydd y Moch,'* ed. Elin M. Jones, with the assistance of Nerys Ann Jones, 39–49. Cardiff: University of Wales Press, 1991.

Registrum Epistolarum Fratris Johannis Peckham, Archepiscopi Cantuariensis. Ed. Charles T. Martin. 2 vols. London: Longman, 1882.

Sachsenspiegel. Digitalisierung historischen Kulturgutes—Sachsenspiegel online. http://www.sachsenspiegel-online.de/export/ssp/index.html. A translation into English of one version can be found in *The Saxon Mirror: A Sachsenspiegel of the Fourteenth Century.* Trans. Maria Dobozy. Philadelphia: University of Pennsylvania Press, 1999.

Salic law. *Pactus Legis Salicae.* Ed. K. A. Eckhardt. *Monumenta Germaniae Historica, Legum Sectio I, Leges Nationum Germanicarum*, vol. 4, pt. 1. Hanover: Hahnsche Buchhandlung, 1962. *Lex Salica. Monumenta Germaniae Historica.* Ed. K. A. Eckhardt. *Monumenta Germaniae Historica, Legum Sectio I, Leges Nationum Germanicarum*, vol. 4, pt. 2. Hanover: Hahnsche Buchhandlung, 1969. Translated by T. J. Rivers in *Laws of the Salian and Ripuarian Franks.* New York: AMS Press, 1986.

Secretum secretorum: Nine English Versions. Ed. M. A. Manzalaoui. Early English Text Society, no. 276. Oxford: Oxford University Press, 1977.

Self and Society in Medieval France: The Memoirs of Abbot Guibert of Nogent. Trans. John F. Benton. New York: Harper and Row, 1970. Revised and reprinted by University of Toronto Press, 1984.

The Statutes of Wales. Ed. Ivor Bowen. London: T. Fisher Unwin, 1908.

Tair Colofn Cyfraith. The Three Columns of Law in Medieval Wales: Homicide, Theft and Fire. Ed. T. M. Charles-Edwards and Paul Russell. Bangor: Cymdeithas Hanes Cyfraith Cymru, 2005.

"Temair III." Ed. Edward J. Gwynn. In *The Metrical Dinnsenchas*, 1:24–27. 1906. 2nd reprint, Dublin: Dublin Institute for Advanced Studies, 1991. Accessed September 6, 2016. CELT. http://www.ucc.ie/celt/published/G106500A/index.html.

The Text of the Book of Llan Dâv. Ed. J. Gwenogvryn Evans and J. Rhys. Oxford: Clarendon Press, 1893. Reprint, Aberystwyth: National Library of Wales, 1979.

Trioedd Ynys Prydein. Ed. Rachel Bromwich. 1961. 3rd ed. Cardiff: University of Wales Press, 2006.

Vita Griffini Filii Conani: The Medieval Latin Life of Gruffudd ap Cynan. Ed. and trans. Paul Russell. Cardiff: University of Wales Press, 2005. See also *Historia Gruffud vab Kenan.*

The Welsh Assize Roll, 1277–1284. Ed. J. Conway Davies. Cardiff: University of Wales Press, 1940.

Welsh Court Poems. Ed. Rhian M. Andrews. Cardiff: University of Wales Press, 2007.

Welsh Genealogies, A.D. 300–1400. Ed. Peter Bartrum. 8 vols. Cardiff: University of Wales Press, 1974.

Welsh Law in Medieval Anglesey: British Library Harleian MS 1796 (Latin C). Ed. Paul Russell. Cambridge: Seminar Cyfraith Hywel, 2011.

The White Book Mabinogion. Ed. J. Gwenogvryn Evans. Llanbedrog: National Library of Wales, 1907. Reissued 1973 as *Llyfr Gwyn Rhydderch: Y Chwedlau a'r Rhamantau.*

Welsh Medieval Law. Ed. A. W. Wade-Evans. Oxford: Clarendon Press, 1909. Reprint, Aalen: Scientia, 1979.

William of Pagula. *The Mirror of King Edward III.* In *Medieval Political Theory—A Reader: The*

Quest for the Body Politic, 1100–1400, ed. Cary Nederman and Kate Forhan, 205–6. London: Routledge, 1993.
Wyclif, John. "On the Duty of the King." In *Medieval Political Theory—A Reader: The Quest for the Body Politic, 1100–1400*, ed. Cary Nederman and Kate Forhan, 225–29. London: Routledge, 1993.
Ystoria Gereint uab Erbin. Ed. R. L. Thomson. Dublin: Dublin Institute for Advanced Studies, 1997.

SECONDARY SOURCES

Abulafia, David. *Frederick II: A Medieval Emperor*. Oxford: Oxford University Press, 1992.
Aers, David. "Figuring Forth the Body of Christ." In *Figures of Speech: The Body in Medieval Art, History, and Literature*, ed. Allen J. Frantzen and David A. Robertson, 1–14. Essays in Medieval Studies 11. Morgantown: West Virginia University Press, 1994.
Aigremont [pseud.]. "Beiträge zur Hand- und Finger-Symbolik und Erotik." *Anthropophyteia* 10 (1913): 314–29.
Alford, John A. "Literature and Law in Medieval England." *Proceedings of the Modern Language Association* 92.5 (October 1977): 941–51.
Alford, John A., and Dennis P. Seniff. *Literature and Law in the Middle Ages: A Bibliography of Scholarship*. New York: Garland, 1984.
Allen, Valerie. *On Farting: Language and Laughter in the Middle Ages*. New York: Palgrave Macmillan, 2007.
Andrews, Rhian. "The Nomenclature of Kingship in Welsh Court Poetry, 1100–1300. Part I: The Terms." *Studia Celtica* 44 (2010): 79–109.
———. "Rhai Agweddau ar Sofraniaeth yng Ngherddi'r Gogynfeirdd." *BBCS* 27 (1976–78): 23–30.
Andrews, Rhian, and David Stephenson. "*Draig Argoed*: Iorwerth Goch ap Maredudd, c. 1110–71." *CMCS* 52 (Winter 2006): 64–89.
Anton, Hans Hubert. *Fürstenspiegel und Herrscherethos in der Karolingerzeit*. Bonner Historische Forschungen 32. Bonn: Ludwig Röhrscheid Verlag, 1968.
———. *Fürstenspiegel (Königspiegel) des frühen und hohen Mittelalters: Ein Editionsprojekt an der Universität Trier*. Accessed June 16, 2011. http://www.ahf-muenchen.de/Forschungsberichte/Jahrbuch2003/Anton.pdf.
Aronstein, Susan. "Becoming Welsh: Counter-Colonialism and the Negotiation of Native Identity in *Peredur vab Efrawc*." *Exemplaria* 17.1 (2005): 135–68.
———. "When Arthur Held Court in Caer Llion: Love, Marriage, and the Politics of Centralization in *Gereint* and *Owein*." *Viator* 25 (1994): 215–28.
Barrell, A. D. M., and M. H. Brown. "A Settler Community in Post-Conquest Rural Wales: The English of Dyffryn Clwyd, 1294–1339." *Welsh History Review* 17 (1994–95): 332–55.
Barrell, A. D. M., and R. R. Davies. "Land, Lineage, and Revolt in North-East Wales, 1243–1441: A Case Study." *CMCS* 29 (Summer 1995): 27–51.
Bartor, Assnat. *Reading Law as Narrative: A Study in the Casuistic Laws of the Pentateuch*. Atlanta, GA: Society of Biblical Literature, 2010.
Bennett, Judith M. *Ale, Beer, and Brewsters in England: Women's Work in a Changing World, 1300–1600*. New York: Oxford University Press, 1996.

———. "The Village Ale-Wife: Women and Brewing in Fourteenth-Century England." In *Women and Work in Preindustrial Europe*, ed. Barbara A. Hanawalt, 20–26. Bloomington: Indiana University Press, 1986.

———. *Women in the Medieval English Countryside: Gender and Household in Brigstock before the Plague*. New York: Oxford University Press, 1987.

Benveniste, Émile. *Le vocabulaire des institutions Indo-Europèenes*. 2 vols. Paris: Les Éditions de Minuit, 1969.

Bhabha, Homi K. *The Location of Culture*. New York: Routledge Press, 1994.

———. "The World and the Home." In *Dangerous Liaisons: Gender, Nation, and Postcolonial Perspectives*, ed. Anne McClintock, Aamir Mufti, and Ella Shohat, 445–55. Minneapolis: University of Minnesota Press, 1997.

Bhreathnach, Máire. "The Sovereignty Goddess as Goddess of Death?" *ZCP* 39 (1982): 243–60.

Biddick, Kathleen. "Genders, Bodies, Borders: Technologies of the Visible." *Speculum* 68 (1993): 389–418.

———. "Response to David Aers." In *Figures of Speech: The Body in Medieval Art, History, and Literature*, ed. Allen J. Frantzen and David A. Robertson, 15–20. Essays in Medieval Studies 11. Morgantown: West Virginia University Press, 1994. Accessed June 15, 2011. http://www.illinoismedieval.org/ems/emsv11.html.

Binchy, Daniel A. "*Cáin Lánamna*." In *Studies in Early Irish Law*, ed. D. A. Binchy, 1–80. Dublin: Hodges, Figgis, 1936.

———. "Celtic Suretyship: A Fossilized Indo-European Institution?" In *Indo-European and Indo-Europeans: Papers Presented to the Third Indo-European Conference, 1966*, ed. G. Cardona et al., 355–67. Philadelphia: University of Pennsylvania Press, 1970.

———. "The Linguistic and Historical Value of the Irish Law Tracts." In *CLP*, 71–107.

———. "Linguistic and Legal Archaisms in the Celtic Law-Books." In *CLP*, 109–20.

———. "Some Celtic Legal Terms." *Celtica* 3 (1956): 221–31.

Binder, Guyora. "The Law-as-Literature Trope." In *Law and Literature*, ed. Michael Freeman and Andrew D. E. Lewis, 64–67. Oxford: Oxford University Press, 1999.

Bloch, R. Howard. *Medieval French Literature and Law*. Berkeley: University of California Press, 1977.

Bollard, J. K. "Pedeir Keinc y Mabinogi—A Case for Multiple Authorship." *Proceedings of the North American Congress of Celtic Studies*, ed. G. W. MacLennan, 185–90. Ottawa: University of Ottawa Press, 1988.

———. "The Role of Myth and Tradition in the Four Branches of the Mabinogi." *CMCS* 6 (Winter 1983): 67–86.

———. "The Structure of the Four Branches of the Mabinogi." *Transactions of the Honourable Society of Cymmrodorion* (1974–75): 250–76. Reprinted in Sullivan, *Mabinogi*, 65–196.

———. "What Is the *Mabinogi*? What Is the "Mabinogion?" Accessed March 2, 2016. https://sites.google.com/site/themabinogi/mabinogiandmabinogion.

Born, Lester Kruger. "The Perfect Prince: A Study in Thirteenth- and Fourteenth-Century Ideals." *Speculum* 3 (1928): 470–504.

Borsje, Jacqueline. *From Chaos to Enemy: Encounters with Monsters in Early Irish Texts; An Investigation Related to the Process of Christianization and the Concept of Evil*. Instrumenta Patristica 29. Turnhout: Brepols, 1996.

———. "The Meaning of *Túathcháech* in Early Irish Texts." *CMCS* 43 (2002): 1–24.

Bowen, Geraint. *Y Traddiodiad Rhyddiaith yn yr Oesau Canol*. Llandysul: Gomer Press, 1974.

Brand, Paul. "Judges and Judging, 1176–1307." In *Judges and Judging in the History of the Common Law and Civil Law: From Antiquity to Modern Times*, ed. Paul Brand and Joshua Getzler, 3–36. Cambridge: Cambridge University Press, 2012.

———. *The Origins of the English Legal Profession*. Oxford: Blackwell, 1992.

Breatnach, Liam. "Law." In *Progress in Medieval Irish Studies*, ed. Kim McCone and Katharine Simms, 107–21. Maynooth: Department of Old Irish, Saint Patrick's College, 1996.

———. "On Old Irish Collective and Abstract Nouns, the Meaning of *cétmuinter*, and Marriage in Early Mediaeval Ireland." *Ériu* 66 (2016): 1–29.

Breatnach, R. A. "The Lady and the King: A Theme of Irish Literature." *Studies* 42 (1953): 321–36.

Breeze, Andrew. "Did a Woman Write the Four Branches of the Mabinogi?" *Studi Medievali* 38 (1997): 679–705.

———. *Medieval Welsh Literature*. Dublin: Four Courts Press, 1997.

———. "*Peredur Son of Efrawg* and *Windmills*." *Celtica* 24 (2003): 58–64.

Brooks, Peter. "Law, Literature: Where Are We?" In *Teaching Law and Literature*, ed. Austin Sarat, Catherine O. Frank, and Matthew Anderson, 61–70. New York: Modern Language Association of America, 2011.

———. "The Law as Narrative and Rhetoric." In *Law's Stories: Narrative and Rhetoric in the Law*, ed. Peter Brooks and Paul Gewirtz, 14–23. New Haven, CT: Yale University Press, 1996.

Brooks, Peter, and Paul Gewirtz, eds. *Law's Stories: Narrative and Rhetoric in the Law*. New Haven, CT: Yale University Press, 1996.

Brown, Peter. *The Body and Society: Men, Women, and Sexual Renunciation in Early Christianity*. 1988. Reprinted with a new introduction. New York: Columbia University Press, 2008.

———. *The Cult of the Saints: Its Rise and Function in Latin Christianity*. Chicago: University of Chicago Press, 1981.

———. "Relics and Social Status in the Age of Gregory of Tours." The Stenton Lecture for 1976. In *Society and the Holy in Late Antiquity*, ed. Peter Brown, 222–50. Berkeley: University of California Press, 1982.

———. "Society and the Supernatural: A Medieval Change." In *Society and the Holy in Late Antiquity*, ed. Peter Brown, 302–32. Berkeley: University of California Press, 1982.

Brown, R. Allen, H. M. Colvin, and A. J. Taylor. *The History of the King's Works*. Vols. 1 and 2. London: Her Majesty's Stationery Office, 1963.

Brown, Warren. *Violence in Medieval Europe*. Harlow, England: Longman, 2011.

Brundage, James A. *The Medieval Origins of the Legal Profession: Canonists, Civilians, and Courts*. Chicago: University of Chicago Press, 2008.

Brynmor-Jones, D. "Foreign Elements in Welsh Medieval Law." *Transactions of the Honourable Society of Cymmrodorion* (1916–17): 1–51.

Burgwinkle, William E. *Sodomy, Masculinity, and Law in Medieval Literature: France and England, 1050–1230*. Cambridge: Cambridge University Press, 2004.

Butler, Judith, and Elizabeth Weed. *The Question of Gender: Joan W. Scott's Critical Feminism*. Bloomington: University of Indiana Press, 2011.

Butler, L. A. "Domestic Building in Wales and the Evidence of the Welsh Laws." *Medieval Archaeology* 31 (1987): 47–58.

Bynum, Caroline Walker, ed. *Fragmentation and Redemption: Essays on Gender and the Human Body in Medieval Religion*. New York: Zone Books, 1991.

———. *Holy Feast and Holy Fast: The Religious Significance of Food to Medieval Women*. Berkeley: University of California Press, 1987.
———. "Metamorphosis, or Gerald and the Werewolf." *Speculum* 73.4 (1998): 987–1013.
———. *Metamorphosis and Identity*. New York: Zone Books, 2001.
———. "The Mysticism and Asceticism of Medieval Women: Some Comments on the Typologies of Max Weber and Ernst Troeltsch." In *Fragmentation and Redemption: Essays on Gender and the Human Body in Medieval Religion*, ed. Caroline Walker Bynum, 53–78. New York: Zone Books, 1991.
———. "Why All the Fuss About the Body? A Medievalist's Perspective." *Critical Inquiry* 22.1 (Autumn 1995): 1–33.
Bynum, Caroline Walker, and Paula Gerson. "Body-Part Reliquaries and Body Parts in the Middle Ages." *Gesta* 3.1 (1997): 3–7.
Cadden, Joan. *The Meanings of Sex Difference in the Middle Ages: Medicine, Science, and Culture*. Cambridge: Cambridge University Press, 1993.
Caerwyn Williams, J. E. *The Court Poet in Medieval Wales: An Essay*. Lampeter: Edwin Mellen Press, 1997.
———. "Meilyr Brydydd and Gruffudd ap Cynan." In *Gruffudd ap Cynan: A Collaborative Biography*, ed. K. L. Maund, 165–86. Woodbridge: Boydell Press, 1996.
———. *The Poets of the Welsh Princes*. Rev. ed. Cardiff: University of Wales Press, 1994.
Carey, John. "A British Myth of Origins?" *Journal of the History of Religions* 31 (1991): 24–37.
———. "An Edition of the Pseudo-Historical Prologue to the *Senchas Mar*." *Ériu* 45 (1994): 1–32.
Carr, A. D. "The Patrons of the Late Medieval Poets in North Wales." *Actes du IXème Congrès international d'études celtiques*, Paris, 7–12 juillet 1991, deuxième partie: linguistique, literatures. *Études Celtiques* 29 (1992): 115–20.
———. "*Teulu* and *Penteulu*." In *WKC*, 63–81.
Cartwright, Jane. "Virginity and Chastity Tests in Medieval Welsh Prose." In *Medieval Virginities*, ed. A. Bernau, 56–79. Cardiff: University of Wales Press, 2003.
Cavell, Emma. "Aristocratic Widows and the Medieval Welsh Frontier: The Shropshire Evidence." *Transactions of the Royal Historical Society*, 6th ser. 17 (2007): 57–82.
———. "Intelligence and Intrigue in the March of Wales: Noblewomen and the Fall of Llywelyn ap Gruffudd, 1274–82." *Historical Research* 88 (February 2015): 1–9
———. "Welsh Princes, English Wives: The Politics of Powys Wenwynwyn Revisited." *Welsh History Review* 27, no. 2 (2014): 214–52.
Caviness, Madeline. "Giving 'The Middle Ages' a Bad Name: Blood Punishments in the 'Sachsenspiegel' and Town Lawbooks." *Studies in Iconography* 34 (2013): 175–235.
Chandler, Kirstie. "The Humour in *Breuddwyd Rhonabwy*." *Studia Celtica* 36 (2002): 59–71.
Charles-Edwards, T. M. "Another Reading of *Scéle Muicce Meic Dathó*." *Journal of Celtic Studies* 5 (2005): 6–7.
———. "*Cynghawsedd*: Counting and Pleading in Medieval Welsh Law." *BBCS* 33 (1986): 188–98.
———. "The Date of *Culhwch ac Olwen*." In *Bile ós Chrannaibh: A Festschrift for William Gillies*, ed. Wilson McLeod, Abigail Burnyeat, Domhnall Uilleam Stiùbhart, Thomas Owen Clancy, and Roibeard Ó Maolalaigh, 45–56. Perthshire: Clann Tuirc, 2010.
———. "The Date of the Four Branches of the Mabinogi." Reprinted in Sullivan, *Mabinogi*, 19–58.

———. "Dynastic Succession in Early Medieval Wales." In *Wales and the Welsh in the Middle Ages: Essays Presented to J. Beverley Smith*, ed. by R. A. Griffiths and P. R. Schofield, 70–88. Cardiff: University of Wales Press, 2011.

———. *Early Irish and Welsh Kinship*. Oxford: Oxford University Press, 1993.

———. "Food, Drink and Clothing in the Laws of Court." In *WKC*, 319–37.

———. "The *Galanas* Tractate in Iorwerth: Texts and Legal Development." In *TCC*, 92–107.

———. "*Gorsedd*, *Dadl*, and *Llys*: Assemblies and Courts in Medieval Wales." In *Assembly Places and Practices in Medieval Europe*, ed. Aliki Pantos and Sarah Semple, 95–108. Dublin: Four Courts Press, 2004.

———. "The Heir-Apparent in Irish and Welsh Law." *Celtica* 9 (1971): 180–90.

———. "Honour and Status in Some Irish and Welsh Prose Tales." *Ériu* 29 (1978): 123–41.

———. "III. The 'Iorwerth' Text." In *LAL*, 137–78.

———. "Nau Kynywedi Teithiauc." In *WLW*, 23–39.

———. "Relationship of the Tractates in Latin Redactions A and B to those in Llyfr Iorwerth and Llyfr Cyfnerth." In *WLW*, 180–85.

———. "The Seven Bishop-Houses of Dyfed." *BBCS* 24 (1970–72): 247–62.

———. "Some Celtic Kinship Terms." *BBCS* 24 (1970–72): 105–22.

———. "The Textual Tradition of Medieval Welsh Prose Tales and the Problem of Dating." In *150 Jahre "Mabinogion"—Deutsch-Walisische Kulturbeziehungen*, ed. Bernhard Maier and Stefan Zimmer, with Christiane Batke, 23–39. Tübingen: Max Niemeyer Verlag, 2001.

———. "The Three Columns of Law: A Comparative Perspective." In *TCC*, 26–59.

———. "The Three Columns of Law from Iorwerth Manuscripts E and B." In *TCC*, 258–307.

———. "The Welsh Law of Theft: Iorwerth versus the Rest." In *TCC*, 108–30.

———. *Wales and the Britons, 350–1064*. Oxford: Oxford University Press, 2013.

———. *The Welsh Laws*. Cardiff: University of Wales Press, 1989.

Charles-Edwards, T. M., and Nerys Ann Jones. "Breintiau Gwŷr Powys: The Liberties of the Men of Powys." In *WKC*, 191–233.

Charles-Edwards, T. M., Morfydd E. Owen, and D. B. Walters, eds. *Lawyers and Laymen: Studies in the History of Law Presented to Professor Dafydd Jenkins on His Seventy-Fifth Birthday Gŵyl Ddewi 1986*. Cardiff: University of Wales Press, 1986.

Charles-Edwards, T. M., Morfydd E. Owen, and Paul Russell, eds. *The Welsh King and His Court*. Cardiff: University of Wales Press, 2000.

Cheney, M. "The Council of Westminster 1175: New Light on an Old Source." *Studies in Church History* 2 (1975): 61–68.

Cholakian, Rouben. *The Troubadour Lyric: A Psychocritical Reading*. Manchester: Manchester University Press, 1990.

Cichon, Michael. "Insult and Redress in *Cyfraith Hywel Dda* and Welsh Arthurian Romance." *Arthuriana* 10.3 (2000): 27–43.

———. "Mishandled Vessels: Heaving Drinks and Hurling Insults in Medieval Welsh Literature and Law." *Canadian Journal of History* 43.2 (2008): 227–40. Accessed March 9, 2016. http://utpjournalsreview.com/index.php/CJOH/article/view/12270/11144.

———. *Violence and Vengeance in Middle Welsh and Middle English Narrative: Owein and Ywain and Gawain*. With a foreword by David N. Klausner. Lewiston, NY: Edwin Mellen Press, 2009.

Classen, Albrecht, ed. *Laughter in the Middle Ages and Early Modern Times: Epistemology of a Fundamental Human Behavior, Its Meaning, and Consequences*. Berlin: Walter de Gruyter, 2010.

Coakley, Sarah. *Religion and the Body*. Cambridge: Cambridge University Press, 1997.

Cohen, Jeffrey Jerome. *Hybridity, Identity and Monstrosity in Medieval Britain: On Difficult Middles*. New York: Palgrave Macmillan, 2006.

———. "Hybrids, Monsters, Borderlands: The Bodies of Gerald of Wales." In *The Postcolonial Middle Ages*, ed. Jeffrey Jerome Cohen, 85–104. New York: St. Martin's Press, 2000.

———. *Of Giants: Sex, Monsters, and the Middle Ages*. Minneapolis: University of Minnesota Press, 1999.

Cohen, Jeffrey Jerome, and Bonnie Wheeler, eds. *Becoming Male in the Middle Ages*. New York: Garland, 2000.

Coon, Lynda. *Dark-Age Bodies: Gender and Monastic Practice in the Early Medieval West*. Philadelphia: University of Pennsylvania Press, 2010.

Cooper, Kate. *The Fall of the Roman Household*. Cambridge: Cambridge University Press, 2007.

Cormack, Bradin. "Practicing Law and Literature in Early Modern Studies." Review article. *Modern Philology* 101 (2003): 79–91.

Coss, P. R. *Lordship, Knighthood and Locality: A Study in English Society, c. 1180–c. 1280*. Cambridge: Cambridge University Press, 1991. Pbk. ed., 2004.

Crawford, Sally, and Christina Lee, eds. *Bodies of Knowledge: Cultural Interpretations of Illness and Medicine in Medieval Europe*. British Archaeological Reports International Series (Book 2170). Oxford: British Archaeological Reports, 2010.

Crump, J. J. "Repercussions of the Execution of William de Braose: A Letter from Llywelyn ap Iorwerth to Stephen de Segrave." *Historical Research* 73 (2000): 197–212.

Cummins, John. *The Hound and the Hawk: The Art of Medieval Hunting*. London: Phoenix Press, 1988. Pbk. ed., 2001.

Curley, Michael. *Geoffrey of Monmouth*. New York: Twayne, 1994.

Davenport, Anthony. *Medieval Narrative: An Introduction*. Oxford: Oxford University Press, 2004.

———. "Wales and Welshness in Middle English Romances." In *Authority and Subjugation in Writing of Medieval Wales*, ed. Ruth Kennedy and Simon Meecham-Jones, 137–58. New York: Palgrave Macmillan, 2008.

Davies, Rhiannon M. (1993). *The Moral Structure of Pedeir Keinc y Mabinogi*. PhD thesis, University of Wales, 1990.

Davies, Morgan T. "Dafydd ap Gwilym and the Metaphorics of Carpentry." *CMCS* 30 (Winter 1995): 67–85.

———. "The Death of Dafydd ap Gwilym." In *Heroic Poets and Poetic Heroes in Celtic Tradition: A Festschrift for Patrick K. Ford, CSANA Yearbook* 3–4, ed. Joseph Falaky Nagy and Leslie Ellen Jones, 55–73. Dublin: Four Courts Press, 2005.

Davies, R. R. "The Administration of Law in Medieval Wales: The Role of the *Ynad Cwmwd* (*Judex Patrie*)." In *LAL*, 258–73.

———. *The Age of Conquest: Wales 1063–1415*. Reprint ed. Oxford: Oxford University Press, 1991.

———. *Conquest, Coexistence, and Change: Wales 1063–1415*. Oxford: Clarendon Press, 1987.

———. *Domination and Conquest: The Experience of Ireland, Scotland and Wales 1100–1300*. Cambridge: Cambridge University Press, 2006.

———. *The First English Empire: Power and Identities in the British Isles, 1093–1343*. Oxford: Oxford University Press, 2000.

———. "Kings, Lords, and Liberties in the March of Wales, 1066–1272." *Transactions of the Royal Historical Society*, 5th ser., 29 (1979): 41–61.

———. "The Law of the March." *Welsh History Review* 5.1 (June 1970): 1–30.

———. "Law and National Identity in Thirteenth-Century Wales." In *Welsh Society and Nationhood: Historical Essays Presented to Glanmor Williams*, ed. R. R. Davies, Ralph Griffiths, Ieuan Gwynedd Jones, and Kenneth Morgan, 51–69. Cardiff: University of Wales Press, 1984.

———. *Lordship and Society in the March of Wales, 1282–1400*. Oxford: Clarendon Press, 1978.

———. "The Peoples of Britain and Ireland, 1100–1400. III. Laws and Customs." *Transactions of the Royal Historical Society*, 6th ser., 6 (1996): 1–23.

———. "The Status of Women and the Practice of Marriage in Late-Medieval Wales." In *WLW*, 93–114.

———. "The Survival of the Bloodfeud in Medieval Wales." *History* 54 (1969): 338–57.

Davies, Sioned. "*Crefft y Cyfarwydd*. Cardiff: University of Wales Press, 1995.

———. "Pedeir Keinc y Mabinogi—A Case for Multiple Authorship." In *Proceedings of the First North American Congress of Celtic Studies*, ed. Gordon W. MacLennan, 443–59. Ottawa: Chair of Celtic Studies, University of Ottawa, 1988.

———. "Storytelling in Medieval Wales." *Oral Tradition* 7.2 (1992): 231–57.

Davies, Wendy. "Holding Court: Judicial Presidency in Brittany, Wales and Northern Iberia in the Early Middle Ages." In Edmonds and Russell, *Tome*, 145–54.

———. "The Latin Charter-Tradition in Western Britain, Brittany and Ireland in the Early Mediaeval Period." In *Ireland in Early Mediaeval Europe*, ed. Dorothy Whitelock, R. McKitterick, and D. Dumville, 258–80. Cambridge: Cambridge University Press, 1982.

———. "People and Places in Dispute in Ninth-Century Brittany." In *The Settlement of Disputes in Early Medieval Europe*, ed. Wendy Davies and Paul Fouracre, 65–84. Cambridge: Cambridge University Press, 1986.

———. "Suretyship in the *Cartulaire de Redon*." In *LAL*, 72–91.

Day, Jennifer. *Arfau yn yr Hengerdd a Cherddi Beirdd y Tywysogion*. PhD diss., Aberystwyth University, 2010. Accessed July 1, 2016. http://cadair.aber.ac.uk/dspace/handle/2160/4646.

Dean, Trevor. *Crime in Medieval Europe*. London: Routledge, 2014.

Doan, James. "Sovereignty Aspects in the Roles of Women in Medieval Irish and Welsh Society." *Proceedings of the Harvard Celtic Colloquium* 5 (1985): 87–107.

Dolin, Kieran. *A Critical Introduction to Law and Literature*. Cambridge: Cambridge University Press, 2007.

Douglas, Mary. "The Body of the World." *International Social Science Journal* 125 (1990): 395–99.

———. *Leviticus as Literature*. New York: Oxford University Press, 1999.

Doyle, Arthur Conan. "Silver Blaze." In *The Complete Sherlock Holmes*, 143–49. New York: Gramercy Books, 2002.

Dumville, David N. "The *Ætheling*: A Study in Anglo-Saxon Constitutional History." *Anglo-Saxon England* 8 (1979): 1–33.

———. "On the Dating of the Early Breton Lawcodes." *Études Celtiques* 21 (1984): 207–21.

Dunn, Caroline. "The Language of Ravishment in Medieval England." *Speculum* 86.1 (January 2011): 79–116.

Dworkin, Ronald. "Law as Interpretation." In *The Politics of Interpretation*, ed. W. J. T. Mitchell, 249–70. Chicago: University of Chicago Press, 1983.

Dyer, Christopher. *Standards of Living in the Later Middle Ages: Social Change in England, c. 1200–1520*. 1989. Reprint, Cambridge: Cambridge University Press, 1990.

Edmonds, Fiona, and Paul Russell, eds. *Tome: Studies in Medieval Celtic History and Law in Honour of Thomas Charles-Edwards*. Woodbridge: Boydell Press, 2011.

Effros, Bonnie. *Creating Community with Food and Drink in Merovingian Gaul*. New York: Palgrave, 2002.

Eichhorn-Mulligan, Amy. "The Anatomy of Power and the Miracle of Kingship: The Female Body of Sovereignty in a Medieval Irish Kingship Tale." *Speculum* 81 (2006): 1014–54.

———. "*Togail Bruidne Da Derga* and the Politics of Anatomy." *CMCS* 49 (2005): 1–19.

Elliott, Dyan. *Fallen Bodies: Pollution, Sexuality, and Demonology in the Middle Ages*. Philadelphia: University of Pennsylvania Press, 1998.

———. *Spiritual Marriage: Sexual Abstinence in Medieval Wedlock*. Princeton, NJ: Princeton University Press, 1993.

Ellis, T. P. "Legal References, Terms and Conceptions in the *Mabinogion*." *Y Cymmrodor* 39 (1928): 86–148.

———. *Welsh Tribal Law and Custom in the Middle Ages*. 2 vols. Oxford: Clarendon Press, 1926.

Emanuel, H. D. "The Book of Blegywryd and MS. Rawlinson 821." In *CLP*, 161–70.

Eska, Charlene. "'Imbroued in Their Owne Bloud': Castration in Early Irish and Welsh Sources." In *Castration and Culture in the Middle Ages*, ed. Larissa Tracy, 149–73. Cambridge: D. S. Brewer, 2013.

———. "Problematic Pigs: Swine Values in Bodleian MS Rawlinson B 506." *Celtica* 26 (2010): 23–30.

Evans, D. Simon. "Iaith y Gododdin." In *Astudiaethau ar yr Hengerdd cyflwynedig i Syr Idris Foster*, ed. Rachel Bromwich and R. Brinley Jones, 72–88. Cardiff: University of Wales Press, 1978.

Evans, Dylan Foster. "On the Lips of Strangers: The Welsh Language, the Middle Ages, and Ethnic Diversity." In *Proceedings of the Celtic Studies Association of North America Annual Meeting 2008, CSANA Yearbook* 10, ed. Morgan Thomas Davies, 16–38. Hamilton, NY: Colgate University Press, 2011.

Farber, Daniel, and Suzanna Sherry. "Legal Storytelling and Constitutional Law: The Medium and the Message." In *Law's Stories: Narrative and Rhetoric in the Law*, ed. Peter Brooks and Paul Gewirtz, 37–53. New Haven, CT: Yale University Press, 1996.

Farmer, Sharon, and Carol Braun Pasternack, eds. *Gender and Difference in the Middle Ages*. Minneapolis: University of Minnesota Press, 2003.

Feree, Myra Marx, Judith Lorber, and Beth Hess, eds. *Revisioning Gender*. Lanham, MD: Altamira Press, 2000.

Ferster, Judith. *Fictions of Advice: The Literature and Politics of Counsel in Late Medieval England*. Philadelphia: University of Pennsylvania Press, 1996.

Fife, James. "Legal Aspects of the Hunting Scene in Pwyll." *BBCS* 39 (1992): 71–79.

Firth Green, Richard. *A Crisis of Truth: Literature and Law in Ricardian England*. Philadelphia: University of Pennsylvania Press, 1998.

———. "Literature and Law." In *A Companion to Medieval English Literature and Culture, c. 1350–c. 1500*, ed. Peter Brown, 292–306. Oxford: Blackwell, 2006.

———. "Medieval Literature and Law." In *The Cambridge History of Middle English Literature*, ed. David Wallace, 407–31. Cambridge: Cambridge University Press, 1998.

———. "'Nede ne hath no lawe': The Plea of Necessity in Medieval Literature and Law." In *Living Dangerously: On the Margins in Medieval and Early Modern Europe*, ed. Barbara A. Hanawalt and Anna Grotans, 9–30. Notre Dame, IN: University of Notre Dame Press, 2007.

Fish, Stanley. "Don't Know Much About the Middle Ages: Posner on Law and Literature." *Yale Law Journal* 97.5 (1988): 777–93.

Ford, Patrick K. "Branwen: A Study of the Celtic Affinities." *Studia Celtica* 22/23 (1987–88): 29–41.

———. "Celtic Women: The Opposing Sex." *Viator* 19 (1988): 417–33.

———. "Prolegomena to a Reading of the *Mabinogi*: 'Pwyll' and 'Manawydan.'" Reprinted in *Mabinogi*, 197–216.

Fortson, Benjamin W. *Indo-European Language and Culture: An Introduction.* 2nd ed. Chichester: Wiley Blackwell, 2009.

Freeman, Charles. *Holy Bones, Holy Dust: How Relics Shaped the History of Medieval Europe*. New Haven, CT: Yale University Press, 2011.

Fulton, Helen. "Class and Nation: Defining the English in Late-Medieval Welsh Poetry." In *Authority and Subjugation in Writing of Medieval Wales*, ed. Ruth Kennedy and Simon Meecham-Jones, 191–212. New York: Palgrave Macmillan, 2008.

———. "Cyd-destun gwleidyddol *Breuddwyd Rhonabwy*." *Llên Cymru* 22 (1999): 42–56.

———. "Individual and Society in *Owein/Yvain* and *Gereint/Erec*." In *The Individual in Celtic Literatures, CSANA Yearbook* 1, ed. Joseph Falaky Nagy, 15–50. Dublin: Four Courts Press, 2001.

———. "The *Mabinogi* and the Education of Princes in Medieval Wales." In *Medieval Celtic Literature and Society*, ed. Helen Fulton, 230–47. Dublin: Four Courts Press, 2005.

———, ed. *Medieval Celtic Literature and Society*. Dublin: Four Courts Press, 2005.

———. "Owain Glyn Dŵr and the Uses of Prophecy." *Studia Celtica* 39 (2005): 105–21.

———. "The Poetic Construction of Authority: Dafydd ap Gwilym and the *Uchelwyr*." *Parergon* 10.1 (June 1992): 15–34.

———. "Trading Places: Representations of Urban Culture in Medieval Welsh Poetry." *Studia Celtica* 31 (1997): 219–30.

———. *Welsh Prophecy and English Politics in the Late Middle Ages*. Sir Thomas Parry-Williams Memorial Lecture 2008. Aberystwyth: Canolfan Uwchefrydiau Cymreig a Cheltaidd Prifysgol Cymru, 2008.

Gaunt, Simon. *Gender and Genre in Medieval French Literature*. Cambridge: Cambridge University Press, 2005.

Gewirtz, Paul. "Narrative and Rhetoric in the Law." In *Law's Stories: Narrative and Rhetoric in the Law*, ed. Peter Brooks and Paul Gewirtz, 2–13. New Haven, CT: Yale University Press, 1996.

Gobetti, Daniela, ed. *Private and Public: Individuals, Households, and Body Politic in Locke and Hutcheson*. London: Routledge, 1992.

Goetinck, Glenys. "Pedair Cainc y Mabinogi: Yr Awdur a'i Bwrpas." *Llên Cymru* 15 (1988): 249–69.

———. *Peredur: A Study of Welsh Tradition in the Grail Legends*. Cardiff: University of Wales Press, 1975.

———. "*Peredur* and the Three Functions." *Zeitschrift für celtische Philologie* 47 (1995): 201–10.

———. "Sofraniaeth yn y tair rhamant." *Llên Cymru* 8 (1964–65): 168–82.

Goodrich, Peter. *Law in the Courts of Love: Literature and Other Minor Jurisprudences*. New York: Routledge, 1996.

Goronwy Edwards, J. "Hywel Dda and the Welsh Lawbooks." Reprinted in *CLP*, 135–60.

———. "The Royal Household and the Welsh Lawbooks." *Transactions of the Royal Historical Society*, 5th ser., 13 (1963): 163–76.

Grant, Alexander. "Murder Will Out: Kingship, Kinship and Killing in Medieval Scotland." In

Kings, Lords and Men in Scotland and Britain, 1300–1625: Essays in Honour of Jenny Wormald, 193–226. Edinburgh: Edinburgh University Press, 2014.

Gravdal, Kathryn. *Ravishing Maidens: Writing Rape in Medieval French Literature and Law*. Philadelphia: University of Pennsylvania Press, 1991.

Gruffydd, Geraint. "'The Praise of Tenby': A Late-Ninth-Century Welsh Court Poem.'" In *Heroic Poets and Poetic Heroes in Celtic Tradition: A Festschrift for Patrick K. Ford, CSANA Yearbook* 3–4, ed. Joseph Falaky Nagy and Leslie Ellen Jones, 91–102. Dublin: Four Courts Press, 2005.

Gruffydd, W. J. *Rhiannon: An Inquiry into the Origins of the First and Third Branches of the Mabinogi*. Cardiff: University of Wales Press, 1953.

Habermann, Ina. "'She Has That in Her Belly will dry up your ink': Femininity as Challenge in the 'Equitable Drama' of John Webster." In *Literature, Politics and Law in Renaissance England*, ed. Erica Sheen and Lorna Hutson, 100–120. Basingstoke, Hampshire: Palgrave Macmillan, 2005.

Hale, David C. "Analogy of the Body Politic." In *Dictionary of the History of Ideas*, ed. Philip Wiener, 1:68–70. New York: Scribner, 1973.

Hamp, Eric. "Mabinogi and Archaism." *Celtica* 23 (1999): 96–110.

Hanawalt, Barbara A. "Whose Story Was This? Rape Narratives in Medieval English Courts." In *"Of Good and Ill Repute": Gender and Social Control in Medieval England*, ed. Barbara Hanawalt, 124–41. New York: Oxford University Press, 1998.

Hanawalt, Barbara A., and Michael Kobialka, eds. *Medieval Practices of Space*. Minneapolis: University of Minnesota Press, 2000.

Hanson-Smith, Elizabeth. "*Pwyll Prince of Dyfed*: The Narrative Structure." *Proceedings of the Harvard Celtic Colloquium* 5 (1985): 87–107.

Harding, Alan. "Legislators, Lawyers and Law-Books." In *LAL*, 237–57.

Hardwick, Julie. *The Practice of Patriarchy: Gender and the Politics of Household Authority in Early Modern France*. Philadelphia: University of Pennsylvania Press, 1998.

Harper, Stephen. *Insanity, Individuals and Society in Late-Medieval English Literature: The Subject of Madness*. New York: Edwin Mellen Press, 2003.

Harris, Meinir Elin. "Compensation for Injury: A Point of Contact between Early Welsh and Germanic Laws?" In *The Trial of Dic Penderyn and Other Essays*, ed. T. G. Watkin, 39–76. Cardiff: University of Wales Press, 2002.

———. "Dychwelyd at gyfeiriadau, termau a chysyniadau cyfreithiol yn y Mabinogi." *Y Traethodydd* 158 (2003): 17–39.

Harvey, A. D. *Body Politic: Political Metaphor and Political Violence*. Newcastle: Cambridge Scholars, 2007.

Hauck, Karl. "Rituelle Speisegemeinschaft im 10. und 11. Jahrhundert." *Studium Generale* 3/11 (November 1950): 611–21.

Helmholz, Richard. *Marriage Litigation in Medieval England*. Cambridge: Cambridge University Press, 1974.

Hemming, Jessica. "Ancient Tradition or Authorial Invention? The 'Mythological' Names in the Four Branches." In *Myth in Celtic Literatures, CSANA Yearbook* 6, ed. Joseph Falaky Nagy, 83–104. Dublin: Four Courts Press, 2007.

———. "*Sellam Gestare*: Saddle-Bearing Punishments and the Case of Rhiannon." *Viator* 28 (1997): 45–64.

Herbert, Máire. "Goddess and King: The Sacred Marriage in Early Ireland." In *Women and*

Sovereignty, ed. Louise Fradenburg, 264–75. Edinburgh: Edinburgh University Press, 1992.

Herlihy, David. *The History of Feudalism*. London: Macmillan, 1971.

———. *Opera Muliebria: Women and Work in Medieval Europe*. New York: McGraw-Hill, 1990.

Hibbitts, Bernard J. "'Coming to Our Senses': Communication and Legal Expression in Performance Cultures." *Emory Law Journal* 41.4 (Fall 1992): 873–960.

Higley, Sarah. "Forcing a Gap: The Stylistics of 'Amputation' in *Marwnad Llywelyn* by Gruffudd ab yr Ynad Coch." *Viator* 19 (1988): 247–72.

Holt, J. C. *Robin Hood*. London: Thames and Hudson, 1982.

Hudson, John. "Administration, Family, and Perceptions of the Past in Late Twelfth-Century England: Richard Fitz Nigel and the Dialogue of the Exchequer." In *The Perception of the Past in Twelfth-Century Europe*, ed. Paul Magdalino, 75–98. London: Bloomsbury Academic, 2003.

Hughes, Ian. "The King's Nephew." In *150 Jahre "Mabinogion"—Deutsch-Walisische Kulturbeziehungen*, ed. Bernhard Maier and Stefan Zimmer, with Christiane Batke, 55–65. Tübingen: Max Niemeyer Verlag, 2001.

Humphries, Robert. "The Limits of the Law: *Sarhaed*, Kinship and Honour in *The Four Branches of the Mabinogi*." Accessed May 9, 2014. http://www.academia.edu/4206917/The_Limits_of_the_Law_Sarhaed_Kinship_and_Honour_in_The_Four_Branches_of_the_Mabinogi.

Hunter, Jerry. "A Feast of Words: Conspicuous Consumption and Praise Poetry in Medieval Wales." *Proceedings of the Harvard Celtic Colloquium* 14 (1994): 38–48.

Huot, Sylvia. *Madness in Medieval French Literature*. New York: Oxford University Press, 2003.

Hutton, Ronald. "Medieval Welsh Literature and Pre-Christian Deities." *CMCS* 61 (Summer 2011): 57–85.

Huws, Daniel. "Descriptions of the Welsh Manuscripts." In *WKC*, 415–24.

———. "The Earliest Version of *Llyfr Iorwerth*: A Description of BL, Cotton Caligula A.iii (fols. 149–98)." In *MWM*, 177–92.

———. "Leges Howelda at Canterbury." *National Library of Wales Journal* 19 (1975–76): 340–44.

———. "ii. The Manuscripts." In *LAL*, 119–36

———. *Medieval Welsh Manuscripts*. 2000. Reprint, Cardiff: University of Wales Press and the National Library of Wales, 2002.

———. *Peniarth 28: Darluniau o Lyfr Cyfraith Hywel Dda*. Aberystwyth: National Library of Wales, 1988.

———. "Peniarth 28: Illustrations from a Welsh Lawbook." Accessed July 13, 2011. http://www.llgc.org.uk/index.php?id=570. I also consulted the print version: *Peniarth 28: Darluniau o Lyfr Cyfraith Hywel Dda*. Aberystwyth: National Library of Wales, 1988.

Hyams, Paul. *Rancor and Reconciliation in Medieval England*. Ithaca, NY: Cornell University Press, 2013.

Insley, Charles. "Fact and Fiction in Thirteenth-Century Gwynedd: The Aberconwy Charters." *Studia Celtica* 33 (1999): 235–50.

Jack, R. Ian. *Medieval Wales*. Ithaca, NY: Cornell University Press, 1972.

Jackson, Kenneth. "Some Popular Motifs in Early Welsh Tradition." *Études Celtiques* 11 (1964–65): 83–99.

Jacobs, Nicholas. "Animadversions on Bastardy in the Red Book of Hergest: Early Welsh Gnomic Poems, IV.6." *CMCS* 55 (Summer 2008): 51–59.

James, Elizabeth Meinir. "*Secretum Secretorum*: Astudiaeth feirniadol o ddetholiadau Cymraeg a

Lladin o'r llythyr ffug-Aristotelaidd at Alecsander Fawr." PhD thesis, University of Wales, Aberystwyth, 1986.

Jenkins, Dafydd. *Celtic Law Papers Introductory to Welsh Medieval Law and Government.* Studies Presented to the International Commission for the History of Representative and Parliamentary Institutions, 42. Brussels: Les Éditions de la Librairie Encyclopédique, 1973.

———. *Conspectus of the Manuscripts of the Cyfnerth Redaction.* Cambridge: Seminar Cyfraith Hywel, 2010.

———. "Crime and Tort and the Three Columns of Law." In *TCC,* 1–25.

———. "The 'Cyfnerth' Text." In *WLW,* 132–45.

———. *Cyfraith Hywel.* Llandysul: Gwasg Gomer, 1970.

———. "*Cynghellor* and Chancellor." *BBCS* 27 (1976–78): 115–18.

———. "Distain." *BBCS* 22 (1966–68): 127–28.

———. "Excursus: The Lawbooks and Their Relation." In *WKC,* 10–14.

———. "A Family of Medieval Welsh Lawyers." In *CLP,* 121–33.

———. "Hawk and Hound: Hunting in the Laws of Court." In *WKC,* 255–80.

———. *Hywel Dda a'r gwŷr cyfraith.* Aberystwyth: Adran y Gyfraith, Coleg Prifysgol Cymru, 1977.

———. "Kings, Lords and Princes: The Nomenclature of Authority in Thirteenth-Century Wales." *BBCS* 26 (1974–76): 451–62.

———, ed. *The Law of Hywel Dda: Law Texts from Medieval Wales Translated and Edited.* Welsh Classics, vol. 2. Llandysul: Gomer Press, 1986.

———. "The Lawbooks of Medieval Wales." In *The Political Context of Law: Proceedings of the Seventh British Legal History Conference, Canterbury 1985,* ed. R. Eales and D. Sullivan, 1–15. London: Hambledon Press, 1987.

———. "A Lawyer Looks at Welsh Land Law." *Transactions of the Honourable Society of Cymmrodorion,* 1967, pt. 2 (1968): 220–47.

———. "Legal and Comparative Aspects of the Welsh Laws." In "The Welsh Laws," special issue, *Welsh History Review* (1963): 51–59.

———. "The Medieval Welsh Idea of Law." *Tijdschrift voor Rechtsgeschiedenis* 49 (1981): 323–48.

———. "Pencerdd a Bardd Teulu." *Ysgrifau Beirniadol* 14 (1988): 19–44.

———. "Prolegomena to the Laws of Court." In *WKC,* 15–28.

———. "Property Interests in the Classical Welsh Law of Women." In *WLW,* 69–92.

———. "The Significance of the Law of Hywel." *Transactions of the Honourable Society of Cymmodorion* (1977): 54–76.

Jenkins, Dafydd, and Morfydd E. Owen, eds. *The Welsh Law of Women: Studies Presented to Professor Daniel A. Binchy on His Eightieth Birthday.* Cardiff: University of Wales Press, 1980.

———. "The Welsh Marginalia in the Lichfield Gospels, Parts I and II." *CMCS* 5 (Summer 1983): 37–66, and 7 (Summer 1984): 91–120, respectively.

Johns, Susan M. *Gender, Nation and Conquest in the High Middle Ages: Nest of Deheubarth.* Manchester: Manchester University Press, 2013.

Johnson Lizabeth. *Kinship and Violence in Wales, 800–1415.* PhD diss., University of Washington, 2008.

———. "Mutilation as Cultural Commerce and Criticism: The Transmission, Practice, and Meaning of Castration and Blinding in Medieval Wales." *Historia: An Online Graduate History Journal* 1.1 (2008). Accessed November 3, 2011. http://depts.washington.edu/cliograd/istoria/Volume_1/contents.html.

Johnston, Dafydd. "Erotica and Satire in Medieval Welsh Poetry." In *Obscenity: Social Control and Artistic Creation in the European Middle Ages*, ed. Jan M. Ziolkowski, 60–72. Leiden: Brill, 1998.

———. *Llên yr Uchelwyr: Hanes Beirniadol Llenyddiaeth Gymraeg 1300–1525* Cardiff: University of Wales Press, 2005.

Johnston, Mark D., ed. *Medieval Conduct Literature: An Anthology of Vernacular Guides to Behaviour for Youths, with English Translations*. Medieval Academy of America Books, no. 111. Toronto: University of Toronto Press, 2009.

Johnstone, Neil. "*Cae Llys Rhosyr*: A Court of the Princes of Gwynedd." *Studia Celtica* 33 (1999): 251–95.

———. "An Investigation into the Location of the Royal Courts of Thirteenth-Century Gwynedd." In *Landscape and Settlement in Medieval Wales*, ed. Nancy Edwards, 55–69. Oxford: Oxbow Books, 1997.

———. *Llys and Maerdref: An Investigation into the Location of the Royal Courts of the Princes of Gwynedd*. Gwynedd Archaeological Trust, Report 167. Bangor: Gwynedd Archaeological Trust, 1995.

———. "*Llys* and *Maerdref*: The Royal Courts of the Princes of Gwynedd: A Study of Their Location and Selective Trial Excavation." *Studia Celtica* 34 (2000): 167–210.

Jones, Owain Wyn Jones. *Historical Writing in Medieval Welsh*. Bangor: Bangor University, 2013.

Jones, R.M. "Narrative Structure in Medieval Welsh Prose Tales." In *Proceedings of the Seventh International Congress of Celtic Studies, held at Oxford, from 10th–15th July, 1983*, ed. D. Ellis Evans, John G. Griffith and E. M. Jope, 171–98. Oxford: Cranham Press, 1986.

Jones, Rhys. "The Formation of the *Cantref* and the Commote in Medieval Gwynedd." *Studia Celtica* 32 (1998): 169–77.

Jones, T. "Historical Writing in Medieval Welsh." *Scottish Studies* 12 (1968): 15–27.

Kahn, Victoria, and Lorna Hutson, eds. *Rhetoric and Law in Early Modern Europe*. New Haven, CT: Yale University Press, 2001.

Kantorowicz, Ernst. *The King's Two Bodies: A Study in Medieval Political Theology*. 1957. Reprinted with a preface by William Chester Jordan. Princeton, NJ: Princeton University Press, 1997.

Karras, Ruth Mazo. *From Boys to Men: Formations of Masculinity in Late Medieval Europe*. Philadelphia: University of Pennsylvania Press, 2002.

———. *Sexuality in Medieval Europe: Doing unto Others*. New York: Routledge, 2005.

Keen, Maurice. *The Outlaws of Medieval Legend*. Rev. ed. London: Routledge, 1977. First published in 1961.

Kelly, Fergus. *Early Irish Farming: A Study Based Mainly on the Law-Texts of the 7th and 8th Centuries AD*. Dublin: Dublin Institute for Advanced Studies, 1998.

———. *A Guide to Early Irish Law*. Dublin: Dublin Institute for Advanced Studies, 1988.

———. "An Old-Irish Text on Court Procedure." *Peritia* 5 (1986): 74–106.

Kendall, Elliott. *Lordship and Literature: John Gower and the Politics of the Great Household*. Oxford: Oxford University Press, 2008.

Kennedy, Ruth, and Simon Meecham-Jones, eds. *Authority and Subjugation in Writing of Medieval Wales*. New York: Palgrave Macmillan, 2008.

Kirby, D. P. "Hywel Dda: Anglophil?" *Welsh History Review* 8 (1976–77): 1–13.

Knight, Stephen. *Robin Hood: A Complete Study of the English Outlaw*. Oxford: Basil Blackwell, 1994.

———. *Robin Hood: A Mythic Biography*. Ithaca, NY: Cornell University Press, 2003.

———. *Robin Hood: An Anthology of Scholarship and Criticism*. Cambridge: D. S. Brewer, 1999.

Koch, John T., ed. *The Gododdin of Aneirin: Text and Context from Dark-Age North Britain*. Cardiff: University of Wales Press, 1997.

———. "Some Suggestions and Etymologies Reflecting upon the Mythology of the Four Branches. *Proceedings of the Harvard Celtic Colloquium* 9 (1989): 1–11.

———. "A Welsh Window on the Iron Age: Manawydan, Mandubracious." *CMCS* 14 (Winter 1987): 17–52.

Kroll, Jerome, and Bernard Bachrach. *The Mystic Mind: The Psychology of Mystics and Ascetics*. New York: Routledge, 2005.

Krynen, Jacques. *L'Idéal du prince et pouvoir royal en France à la fin du Moyen Age (1380–1440): Étude de la littérature politique du temps*. Paris: Picard, 1981.

Labarge, Margaret Wade. *A Baronial Household of the Thirteenth Century*. London: Eyre and Spottiswoode, 1965.

Larson, L. M. *The King's Household in England Before the Norman Conquest. Bulletin of the University of Wisconsin*, History Series, vol. 136. Madison: University of Wisconsin Press, 1904.

Ledwon, Leona, ed. *Law and Literature: Text and Theory*. New York: Garland, 1996.

Le Goff, Jacques. "Head or Heart? The Political Use of Body Metaphors in the Middle Ages." In *Zone 5. Fragments for a History of the Human Body: Part 3*, ed. Michel Feher with Ramona Naddaff and Nadia Tazi, 13–27. New York: Zone Books, 1989.

Lieberman, Max. *The Medieval March of Wales: The Creation and Perception of a Frontier, 1066–1283*. Cambridge: Cambridge University Press, 2010.

Lloyd-Morgan, Ceridwen. "Crossing the Borders: Literary Borrowing in Medieval Wales and England." In *Authority and Subjugation in Writing of Medieval Wales*, ed. Ruth Kennedy and Simon Meecham-Jones, 159–73. New York: Palgrave Macmillan, 2008.

———. "*Gender and Violence* in the Four Branches of the Mabinogi." In *150 Jahre "Mabinogion": Deutsch-Walisische Kulturbeziehungen*, ed. Bernhard Maier and Stefan Zimmer, with Christiane Batke, 67–77. Tübingen: Max Niemeyer Verlag, 2001.

———. "Medieval Welsh Tales or Romance? Problems of Genre and Terminology." *CMCS* 47 (Summer 2004): 41–58.

———. "Narrative Structure in *Peredur*." *ZCP* 38 (1981): 187–231.

Lochrie, Karma, Peggy McCracken, and James A. Schultz, eds. *Constructing Medieval Sexuality*. Minneapolis: University of Minnesota Press, 1997.

Loth, J. "Un genre particulier de compensation pour crimes et offenses chez les Celtes insulaires." *Revue Celtique* 48 (1931): 332–51.

Lovecy, I. C. "The Celtic Sovereignty Theme and the Structure of *Peredur*." *Studia Celtica* 12–13 (1977–78): 133–46.

Lowe, Jeremy. "Contagious Violence and the Spectacle of Death in *Táin Bó Cúailnge*." In *Language and Tradition in Ireland: Continuities and Displacements*, ed. Maria Tymoczko and Colin Ireland, 84–100. Amherst: University of Massachusetts Press, in cooperation with the American Conference for Irish Studies, 2003.

———. "Kicking over the Traces: The Instability of Cú Chulainn." *Studia Celtica* 34 (2000): 119–30.

Lynch, Peredur I. "Court Poetry, Power and Politics." In *WKC*, 167–90.

Mac Cana, Proinsias. "Aspects of the Theme of King and Goddess in Irish Literature." *Études Celtiques* 7 (1955–56): 76–114, 356–413; and 8 (1958–59): 59–65.

———. *Branwen, Daughter of Llŷr: A Study of the Irish Affinities*. Cardiff: University of Wales Press, 1958.

———. "On the Early Development of Written Narrative Prose in Irish and Welsh." *Actes du*

IXème Congrès international d'études celtiques, Paris, 7–12 juillet 1991, deuxième partie: linguistique, literatures. *Études Celtiques* 29 (1992): 51–67.

Maier, Bernhard, and Stefan Zimmer. With Christiane Batke. *150 Jahre "Mabinogion"—Deutsch-Walisische Kulturbeziehungen*. Tübingen: Max Niemeyer Verlag, 2001.

Mallory, J. P. *In Search of the Indo-Europeans*. London: Thames and Hudson, 1989. Pbk. ed., 1991.

Mallory, J. P., and D. Q. Adams. *The Oxford Introduction to Proto-Indo-European and the Proto-Indo-European World*. New York: Oxford University Press, 2006.

Malone, Patricia. *"Entirely Outside the World": Rhetoric, Legitimacy, and Identity in the Biography of Gruffudd ap Cynan*. PhD diss., Harvard University, 2009.

———. " 'There Has Been Treachery from the Beginning': The *Historia Gruffudd ap Cynan* as Narrative Hybrid." In *Proceedings of the Celtic Studies Association of North America Annual Meeting 2008, CSANA Yearbook* 10, ed. Morgan Thomas Davies, 61–74. Hamilton, NY: Colgate University Press, 2011.

Marvin, William Parry. *Hunting Law and Ritual in Medieval English Literature*. Cambridge: D. S. Brewer, 2006.

Matonis, Ann. "Rhetorical Patterns in *Marwnad Llywelyn ap Gruffudd* by Gruffudd ab yr Ynad Coch." *Studia Celtica* 14/15 (1979–80): 188–92.

Maund, K. L. "Fact and Narrative Fiction in the Llandaff Charters." *Studia Celtica* 31 (1997): 173–93.

———, ed. *Gruffudd ap Cynan: A Collaborative Biography*. Woodbridge: Boydell Press, 1997.

McAll, Christopher. "The Normal Paradigms of a Woman's Life in the Irish and Welsh Texts." In *WLW*, 7–22.

McAvoy, Liz Herbert. *Medieval Anchoritisms: Gender, Space and the Solitary Life*. Gender in the Middle Ages, 6. Woodbridge: D. S. Brewer, 2011.

McCone, Kim. "Dubthach maccu Lugair and a Matter of Life and Death in the Pseudo-Historical Prologue to the *Senchas Már*." *Peritia* 5 (1986): 1–35.

McGerr, Rosemarie. *The Lancastrian Mirror for Princes: The Yale Law School New Statutes for England*. Bloomington: University of Indiana Press, 2011.

McKenna, Catherine. "The Colonization of Myth in *Branwen Ferch Lŷr*." In *Myth in Celtic Literatures, CSANA Yearbook* 6, ed. Joseph Falaky Nagy, 105–19. Dublin: Four Courts Press, 2007.

———. "Learning Lordship: The Education of Manawydan." In *Ildánach Ildírech: A Festschrift for Proinsias Mac Cana*, ed. John Carey, John T. Koch, and Pierre-Yves Lambert, 101–20. Andover: Celtic Studies Publications, 1999.

———. "Revising Math: Kingship in the Fourth Branch of the Mabinogi." *CMCS* 46 (Winter 2003): 94–117.

———. "The Theme of Sovereignty in *Pwyll*." Reprinted in *Mabinogi*, 303–30.

———. " 'What Dreams May Come Must Give Us Pause': *Breudwyt Ronabwy* and the Red Book of Hergest." *CMCS* 59 (Winter 2009): 69–99.

McSheffrey, Shannon. *Marriage, Sex, and Civic Culture in Late Medieval London*. Philadelphia: University of Pennsylvania Press, 2006.

Meecham-Jones, Simon. "Where Was Wales? The Erasure of Wales in Medieval English Culture." In *Authority and Subjugation in Writing of Medieval Wales*, ed. Ruth Kennedy and Simon Meecham-Jones, 27–55. New York: Palgrave Macmillan, 2008.

Meens, Rob. "Politics, Mirrors of Princes and the Bible: Sins, Kings and the Well-Being of the Realm." *Early Medieval Europe* 7.3 (1998): 345–57.

Menuge, Noël James. *Medieval English Wardship in Romance and Law*. Cambridge: D. S. Brewer, 2001.

———, ed. *Medieval Women and the Law*. Woodbridge: Boydell Press, 2000.

Mertes, Kate. *The English Noble Household, 1250–1600*. Oxford: Blackwell, 1988.

Miller, Sarah Alison. *Medieval Monstrosity and the Female Body*. New York: Routledge, 2010.

Miller, William Ian. *Bloodtaking and Peacemaking: Feud, Law and Society in Saga Iceland*. Chicago: University of Chicago Press, 1990.

Morse, Ruth. "Medieval Biography: History as a Branch of Literature." *Modern Language Review* 80 (1985): 257–68.

Nagle, D. Brendan. *The Household as the Foundation for Aristotle's Polis*. Cambridge: Cambridge University Press, 2006.

Nagy, Joseph Falaky, ed. *Myth in Celtic Literatures, CSANA Yearbook* 6. Dublin: Four Courts Press, 2007.

Nagy, Joseph Falaky, and Leslie Ellen Jones, eds. *Heroic Poets and Poetic Heroes in Celtic Tradition: A Festschrift for Patrick K. Ford, CSANA Yearbook* 3–4. Dublin: Four Courts Press, 2005.

Nederman, Cary, and Kate Forhan, eds. *Medieval Political Theory—A Reader: The Quest for the Body Politic, 1100–1400*. London: Routledge, 1993.

Nelson, Janet L. "Kingship, Law and Liturgy in the Political Thought of Hincmar of Rheims." In *Politics and Ritual in Early Medieval Europe*, ed. Janet L. Nelson, 133–71. London: Hambledon Press, 1986.

Newman, Martha. "Considerations on Life and Death: Medieval Asceticism and the Dissolution of the Self." *Method and Theory in the Study of Religion* 21.2 (2009): 177–96.

Ní Chonaill, Bronagh. *The Place of the Child in Medieval Irish and Welsh Law*. PhD. diss., Trinity College Dublin, 2011.

O'Brien, Bruce R. "The Becket Conflict and the Invention of *Lex Non Scripta*." In *Learning the Law: Teaching and the Transmission of Law in England, 1150–1900*, ed. Jonathan A. Bush and Alain Wijffels, 1–16. London: Hambledon Press, 1999.

———. *God's Peace and King's Peace: The Laws of Edward the Confessor*. Philadelphia: University of Pennsylvania Press, 1999.

Ó Cathasaigh, Tomás. "The Body in *Táin Bó Cúailnge*." In *Gablánach in Scélaigecht: Celtic Studies in Honour of Ann Dooley*, ed. Sarah Sheehan, Joanne Findon, and Westley Follett, 131–53. Dublin: Four Courts Press, 2013.

O'Connor, M. "The Body in the Bible: Anatomy and Morphology." In *In the Service of the Church: Essays on Theology and Ministry in Honor of Reverend Charles L. Froehle*, ed. Victor Klimoski and Mary Christine Athans, 29–33. St. Paul, MN: University of St. Thomas Press, 1993.

Ó Flaithearta, Liam. "An Chulaith Nua." In *Dúil*, 97–107. 3rd ed. Dublin: Sáirséal Agus Dill, 1966. First published 1953.

Oggins, Robin S. *The Kings and Their Hawks: Falconry in Medieval England*. New Haven, CT: Yale University Press, 2004.

Oliver, Lisi. *The Body Legal in Barbarian Law*. Toronto: University of Toronto Press, 2011.

Over, Kristen. *Kingship, Conquest, and Patria: Literary and Cultural Identities in Medieval French and Welsh Arthurian Romance*. New York: Routledge, 2005.

Owen, Morfydd E. "The Archaism of the Welsh Poetic Tradition." In *Welsh and Breton Studies in Memory of Th. M. Th. Chotzen: Proceedings of a Colloquium Organized by the A. G. van Hamel Foundation for Celtic Studies, Utrecht-Amsterdam, 23–24 April 1993*, 37–63. Utrecht: Celtic Dragon, 1995.

———. "Bwrlwm Llys Dinefwr: Brenin, Bardd a Meddyg." *Carmarthenshire Antiquary* 32 (1996): 5–15.

———. "IV. The 'Cyfnerth' Text." In *LAL*, 179–200.

———. "Y Cyfreithiau—(1) Natur y Testunau," and "Y Cyfraithiau—(2) Ansawdd y Rhyddiaith." In *Y Traddiodiad Rhyddiaith yn yr Oesau Canol*, ed. Geraint Bowen, 194–244. Llandysul: Gomer Press, 1974.

———. "Cynllwyn a Dynyorn." *BBCS 22* (1966–68): 346–50.

———. "The *Excerpta de Libris Romanorum et Francorum* and Welsh Law." In *TCC*, 171–95.

———. "Gwŷr Dysg yr Oesoedd Canol a'u Dulliau Rhyddiaith." *Ysgrifau Beirniadol* 17 (1990): 42–62.

———. "The Laws of Court from Cyfnerth." In *WKC*, 425–77.

———. "Literary Convention and Historical Reality: The Court in the Welsh Poetry of the Twelfth and Thirteenth Centuries." *Actes du IXème Congrès international d'études celtiques*, Paris, 7–12 juillet 1991, Deuxième partie: linguistique, literatures, 69–85. *Études Celtiques* 29 (1992): 69–85.

———. "*Meddygon Myddfai*, a Preliminary Survey of Some Medical Writings in Welsh." *Studia Celtica* 10/11 (1975/76): 210–33.

———. "Royal Propaganda: Stories from the Law-Texts." In *WKC*, 224–54.

———. "Shame and Reparation: Woman's Place in the Kin." In *WLW*, 40–68.

———. "The Three Columns of Law from Cyfnerth X." In *TCC*, 238–57.

Ozment, Steven. *When Fathers Ruled: Family Life in Reformation Europe*. Studies in Cultural History. Cambridge, MA: Harvard University Press, 1985.

Pacaut, Marcel. *Frederick Barbarossa*. London: Collins, 1970.

Page, William. "The Place of Law and Literature." Review Essay. *Vanderbilt Law Review* 39 (1986): 391. Accessed August 7, 2014. http://ssrn.com/abstract=1414446.

Patterson, Nerys. "Honour and Shame in Medieval Welsh Society." *Studia Celtica* 16/17 (1981–82): 73–103.

———. "Wife as Vassal: Gender Symmetry in Medieval Wales." *Proceedings of the Harvard Celtic Colloquium* 8 (1988): 31–45.

Pencak, William. *The Conflict of Law and Justice in the Icelandic Sagas*. Amsterdam: Editions Rodopi B.V., 1995.

Pennington, Kenneth. *The Prince and the Law, 1200–1600: Sovereignty and Rights in the Western Legal Tradition*. Berkeley: University of California Press, 1993.

Peters, Edward. *The Shadow King: Rex Inuitilis in Medieval Law and Literature, 751–1327*. New Haven: Yale University Press, 1970.

Peters, Julie Stone. "Law, Literature, and the Vanishing Real: On the Future of Interdisciplinary Illusion." In *Teaching Law and Literature*, ed. Austin Sarat, Catherine O. Frank, and Matthew Anderson, 71–85. New York: Modern Language Association of America, 2011.

Phillips, Helen, ed. *Robin Hood: Medieval and Post-Medieval*. Dublin: Four Courts Press, 2005.

Phillips, Kim M. "Written on the Body: Reading Rape from the Twelfth to Fifteenth Centuries." In Menuge, *Medieval Women and the Law*, 125–44.

Phillips, Manon. "Defod a Moes y Llys." In *WKC*, 347–61.

Pierce, T. Jones. "The Age of the Princes." In J. Beverley Smith, *Medieval Welsh Society*, 19–38.

———. "The Laws of Wales—the Kindred and the Bloodfeud." In J. Beverley Smith, *Medieval Welsh Society*, 289–308.

———. "Social and Historical Aspects of the Welsh Laws." "The Welsh Laws." Special issue, *Welsh History Review* (1963): 33–49.

Pollard, A. J. *Imagining Robin Hood: The Late-Medieval Stories in Historical Context.* London: Routledge, 2007.

Pomeroy, Sarah B. *Goddesses, Whores, Wives and Slaves.* 1975. Reprint, New York: Schocken Books, 1995.

Porsdam, Helle. "Doing What Comes Naturally?—Fish, Posner, and the Law and Literature Enterprise." *American Quarterly* 44.3 (September 1922): 494–505.

Posner, Richard. *Law and Literature: A Misunderstood Relation.* Cambridge, MA: Harvard University Press, 1988.

Post, Gaines. *Studies in Medieval Legal Thought: Public Law and the State, 1100–1322.* Princeton, NJ: Princeton University Press, 1964.

Powell, J. Enoch. "Floating Sections in the Laws of Hywel." *BBCS* 9 (1937): 27–34.

Pryce, Huw. "British or Welsh? National Identity in Twelfth-Century Wales." *English Historical Review* 116.468 (2001): 775–801.

———. "The Context and Purpose of the Earliest Welsh Lawbooks." *CMCS* 39 (Summer 2000): 39–63.

———. "Duw yn Lle Mach: Briduw yng Nghyfraith Hywel." In *LAL*, 47–71.

———. "Early Irish Canons and Medieval Welsh Law." *Peritia* 5 (1986): 107–27.

———. "Ecclesiastical Sanctuary in Thirteenth-Century Welsh Law." *Journal of Legal History* 5.3 (1984): 1–13. Reprinted in *Custom, Courts and Counsel*, ed. A. Kiralfy et al., 1–13. London: Frank Cass, 1985.

———. "Yr eglwys a'r gyfraith yng Nghymru'r oesoedd canol." In *Cof Cenedl X*, ed. G. H. Jenkins, 1–30. Llandysul: Gomer Press, 1995.

———. "The Household Priest (*Offeiriad Teulu*)." In *WKC*, 82–93.

———. "Lawbooks and Literacy in Medieval Wales." *Speculum* 75 (2000): 29–67.

———, ed. *Literacy in Medieval Celtic Societies.* Cambridge: Cambridge University Press, 1998.

———. *Native Law and the Church in Medieval Wales.* Oxford: Clarendon Press, 1993.

———. "The Origins and the Medieval Period." In *A Nation and Its Books: A History of the Book in Wales*, ed. Philip Henry Jones and Eiluned Rees, 1–23. Aberystwyth: National Library of Wales in Conjunction with the Aberystwyth Centre of the Book, 1998.

———. "The Prologues to the Welsh Lawbooks." *BBCS* 33 (1986): 151–87.

———. "Welsh Custom and Canon Law." In *Proceedings of the Tenth International Congress of Medieval Canon Law*, ed. Kenneth Pennington, Stanley Chodorow, and Keith H. Kendall, 781–89. Vatican City: Biblioteca apostolica vaticana, 2001.

Puhvel, Jaan. *Comparative Mythology.* Baltimore: Johns Hopkins University Press, 1989.

Radner, Joan N. "Interpreting Irony in Medieval Celtic Narrative: The Case of Culhwch ac Olwen." *CMCS* 16 (Winter 1988): 41–59.

Richards, Gwenyth. *Welsh Noblewomen in the Thirteenth Century: An Historical Study of Medieval Welsh Law and Gender Roles.* Lewiston, Queenston, and Lampeter: Edwin Mellen Press, 2009.

Roberts, Brynley F. "*Breuddwyd Maxen Wledig*: Why? When?" In *Heroic Poets and Poetic Heroes in Celtic Tradition: A Festschrift for Patrick K. Ford, CSANA Yearbook* 3–4, ed. Joseph Falaky Nagy and Leslie Ellen Jones, 303–14. Dublin: Four Courts Press, 2005.

———. "Geoffrey of Monmouth and Welsh Historical Tradition." *Nottingham Medieval Studies* 20 (1976): 29–40.

———. "Historical Writing." In *A Guide to Welsh Literature I*, ed. A. O. H. Jarman and G. R. Hughes, 244–47. Swansea: Christopher Davies, 1976.

———. "Oral Tradition and Welsh Literature: A Description and Survey." *Oral Tradition* 3 (1988): 62–77.

———. "Penyd Rhiannon." *BBCS* 23 (1968–70): 325–27.

———. *Studies on Middle Welsh Literature*. Lewiston: Edwin Mellen Press, 1992.

———. "Where Were the Four Branches of the *Mabinogi* Written?" In *The Individual in Celtic Literatures, CSANA Yearbook* 1, ed. Joseph Falaky Nagy, 61–72. Dublin: Four Courts Press, 2001.

Roberts, B. F. and Morfydd E. Owen, eds. *Beirdd a Thywysogion: Barddoniaeth Llys yng Nghymru, Iwerddon a'r Alban*. Cardiff: University of Wales Press, 1996.

Roberts, Helen A. "Court and *Cyuoeth*: Chrétien de Troyes' *Erec et Enide* and the Middle Welsh *Gereint*." In *Celtic Arthurian Material*, ed. Ceridwen Lloyd-Morgan, 53–72. Arthurian Literature, vol. 21. Cambridge: D. S. Brewer, 2004.

Roberts, Michael. "Sickles and Scythes: Women's Work and Men's Work at Harvest Time." *History Workshop* 7 (1979): 3–28.

Roberts, Sara Elin. "Addysg Broffesiynol yng Nghymru yn yr Oesoedd Canol." *Llên Cymru* 26 (2003): 1–17.

———. "Emerging from the Bushes: The Welsh Law of Women in the Legal Triads." In *Law, Literature, and Society. CSANA Yearbook* 7, ed. Joseph Eska, 64–66. Dublin: Four Courts Press, 2008.

———. "The Iorwerth Triads." In Edmonds and Russell, *Tome*, 155–64.

———. "Law Texts and their Sources in Medieval Wales: The Case of *H* and Tails of Other Legal Manuscripts." *Welsh History Review* 24 (2008): 41–43.

———. "Legal Practice in Fifteenth-Century Brycheiniog." *Studia Celtica* 35 (2001): 307–23.

———. "More Plaints in Welsh Medieval Law." *Studia Celtica* 48 (2014): 171–99.

———. "Plaints in Welsh Mediaeval Law." *Journal of Celtic Studies* 4 (2004): 219–61.

———. "*Tri Dygyngoll Cenedl*: The Development of a Triad." *Studia Celtica* 37 (2003): 163–82.

———. *The Welsh Legal Triads*. London: Selden Society, 2015.

Rodway, Simon. "The Where, Who, When and Why of Medieval Welsh Prose Texts: Some Methodological Considerations." *Studia Celtica* 41 (2007): 47–89.

Rollo-Koster, Joëlle. "The Politics of Body Parts: Contested Topographies in Late-Medieval Avignon." *Speculum* 78.1 (January 2003): 66–98.

Roper, Lyndal. *The Holy Household: Women and Morals in Reformation Augsburg*. Oxford Studies in Social History. Oxford: Clarendon Press, 1989.

Rousseau, Philippe. *The Cultural Turn in Late Ancient Studies: Gender, Asceticism, and Historiography*. Durham, NC: Duke University Press, 2005.

Rowlands, E. I. "Bardic Lore and Education." *BBCS* 32 (1985): 143–55.

Russell, Paul. "The Arrangement and Development of the Three Columns Tractate." In *TCC*, 60–85.

———. "Canu i Swyddogion Llys y Brenin." In *WKC*, 552–60.

———. "The Etymology of *Affaith* 'Abetment.'" *BBCS* 38 (1991): 104–10.

———. "From Plates and Rods to Royal Drink-Stands in *Branwen* and Medieval Welsh Law." *North American Journal of Celtic Studies* 1:1 (2017): 1–26.

———. "'Go and Look in the Latin Books': Latin and the Vernacular in Medieval Wales." In *Latin in Medieval Britain*, ed. Richard Ashdowne and Caroline White. Proceedings of the British Academy. London: Oxford University Press, 2017: 213–46.

———. "The Laws of Court from Latin B." In *WKC*, 478–526.

———. "*Y Naw Affaith*: Aiding and Abetting in Welsh Law." In *TCC*, 146–70.

———. "Scribal (In)competence in Thirteenth-Century North-East Wales: The Orthography of the Black Book of Chirk." *National Library of Wales Journal* 23 (1995–96): 76–129.

———. "Scribal (In)consistency in Thirteenth-Century South Wales: The Orthography of the Black Book of Carmarthen." *Studia Celtica* 43 (2009): 135–74.

———. "*Swydd, Swyddog, Swyddwr*: Office, Officer, and Official." In *WKC*, 281–95.

———. "Texts in Contexts: Recent Work on the Medieval Welsh Prose Tales." *CMCS* 45 (Summer 2003): 59–72.

———. *Welsh Law in Medieval Anglesey: British Library Harleian MS 1796 (Latin C)*. Cambridge: Seminar Cyfraith Hywel, 2011.

Saunders, Corinne. "A Matter of Consent: Middle English Romance and the Law of Raptus." In Menuge, *Medieval Women and the Law*, 105–24.

Schäfer, Hans-Bernd, and Alexander J. Wulf. "Jurists, Clerics, and Merchants: The Rise of Learned Law in Medieval Europe and Its Impact on Economic Growth." *Journal of Empirical Legal Studies* 11.2 (June 2014): 266–300.

Scott, Joan Wallach. "Gender: A Useful Category of Historical Analysis." *American Historical Review* 91.5 (December 1986): 1053–75. Reprinted in *Gender and the Politics of History*, ed. Joan Scott, 28–52. Rev. ed. New York: Columbia University Press, 1999.

———. "Gender: Still a Useful Category of Analysis?" *Diogenes* 57 (2010): 7–14.

Sheen, Erica, and Lorna Hutson, eds. *Literature, Politics and Law in Renaissance England*. Basingstoke, Hampshire: Palgrave Macmillan, 2005.

Sheringham, J. G. T. "Bullocks with Horns as Long as Their Ears." *BBCS* 29 (1981–82): 691–708.

Sherman, Claire Richter. *Imagining Aristotle: Verbal and Visual Representation in Fourteenth-Century France*. Berkeley: University of California Press, 1995.

Siewers, Alfred K. *Strange Beauty: Ecocritical Approaches to the Early Medieval Landscape*. New Middle Ages. New York: Palgrave Macmillan, 2009.

———. "Writing an Icon of the Land: The *Mabinogi* as a Mystagogy of Landscape." *Peritia* 19 (2005): 193–228.

Sigston, Alex. "'As Far as His Horn May Be Heard': A Terminological Analysis of *Nawdd* in Early Medieval Welsh Law." Master's thesis, University of Cambridge, 2014.

Sims-Williams, Patrick. "Celtic Civilization: Continuity or Coincidence?" *CMCS* 64 (Winter 2012): 1–45.

———. "Celtomania and Celtoscepticism." *CMCS* 36 (Winter 1998): 1–35.

———. "Clas Beuno and the Four Branches of the *Mabinogi*." In *150 Jahre 'Mabinogion'—Deutsch-Walisische Kulturbeziehungen*, ed. Bernhard Maier and Stefan Zimmer with Christiane Batke, 111–27. Tübingen: Max Niemeyer Verlag, 2001.

———. *Irish Influence on Medieval Welsh Literature*. New York: Oxford University Press, 2011.

———. "Post-Celtoscepticism: A Personal View." In *Saltair Saíochta, Sanasaíochta agus Seanchais: A Festschrift for Gearóid Mac Eoin*, ed. Dónall Ó Baoill, Donncha Ó hAodha, and Nollaig Ó Muraíle, 422–28. Dublin: Four Courts Press, 2013.

———. "The Submission of Irish Kings in Fact and Fiction: Henry II, Bendigeidfran, and the Dating of the Four Branches of the *Mabinogi*." *CMCS* 22 (1991): 31–61.

Smail, Daniel Lord. *The Consumption of Justice: Emotions, Publicity and Legal Culture in Marseille, 1264–1423*. Ithaca, NY: Cornell University Press, 2003.

———. *Imaginary Cartographies: Possession and Identity in Late Medieval Marseille*. Ithaca, NY: Cornell University Press, 1999.

Smith, G. Rex. "The Manor of Aberffraw, 1284–1339." *CMCS* 60 (Winter 2010): 81–91.

Smith, Jennifer. "Women, Land and Law in Occitania." In Menuge, *Medieval Women and the Law*, 19–40. Woodbridge: Boydell Press, 2000.

Smith, J. Beverley. "Dynastic Succession in Medieval Wales." 33 *BBCS* (1986): 199–232.

———. "Judgement under the Law of Wales." *Studia Celtica* 39 (2005): 63–103.

———. *Llywelyn ap Gruffudd, Prince of Wales*. Cardiff: University of Wales Press, 1998.

———, ed. *Medieval Welsh Society: Selected Essays by T. Jones Pierce*. Cardiff: University of Wales Press, 1972.

———. "*Ynad Llys, Brawdwr Llys, Iudex Curie*." In *WKC*, 94–115.

Smith, Llinos Beverley. "A Contribution to the History of 'Galanas' in Late-Medieval Wales." *Studia Celtica* 43 (2009): 87–94.

———. "'Cannwyll Disbwyll a Dosbarth': Gwŷr Cyfraith Ceredigion yn yr Oesoedd Canol Diweddar." *Ceredigion* 10.3 (1986): 229–53.

———. "Disputes and Settlements in Medieval Wales: The Role of Arbitration." *English Historical Review* 106 (1991): 835–60.

———. "The *Gravamina* of the Community of Gwynedd Against Llywelyn ap Gruffudd." *BBCS* 31 (1984): 158–76.

———. "A View from an Ecclesiastical Court: Mobility and Marriage in a Border Society at the End of the Middle Ages." In *From Medieval to Modern Wales: Historical Essays in Honour of Kenneth O. Morgan and Ralph A. Griffiths*, ed. R. R. Davies and G. H. Jenkins, 64–80. Cardiff: University of Wales Press, 2004.

Stacey, Robert. *Politics, Policy and Finance Under Henry III, 1216–1245*. Oxford: Oxford University Press, 1987.

Stacey, Robin Chapman. "Ancient Irish Law Revisited: Rereading the Laws of Status and Franchise." In *Understanding Celtic Religion: Revisiting the Pagan Past*, ed. Katja Ritari and Alexandra Bergholm, 99–119. Cardiff: University of Wales Press, 2015.

———. "Archaic Core." In *LAL*, 14–46.

———. "Clothes Talk from Medieval Wales." In *WKC*, 338–46.

———. *Dark Speech: The Performance of Law in Early Ireland*. Philadelphia: University of Pennsylvania Press, 2007.

———. "Divorce, Medieval Welsh Style." *Speculum* 77 (October 2002): 1107–27.

———. "Further Musings on the 'Celtic' in 'Celtic Law.'" Robert T. Farrell Lecture for the American Society for Irish Medieval Studies. *Eolas: The Journal of the American Society of Irish Medieval Studies* 9 (2016): 55–76.

———. "Hywel in the World." *Haskins Society Journal* 20 (2008): 175–203.

———. "Instructional Riddles in Welsh Law." In *Heroic Poets and Poetic Heroes: A Festschrift for Patrick K. Ford, CSANA Yearbook* 3–4, ed. Joseph Falaky Nagy and Leslie Ellen Jones, 336–43. Dublin: Four Courts Press, 2004.

———. "King, Queen, and *Edling* in the Laws of Court." In *WKC*, 29–62.

———. "Law and Literature in Medieval Ireland and Wales." In *Medieval Celtic Literature and Society*, ed. Helen Fulton, 75–81. Dublin: Four Courts Press, 2005.

———. "Law and Order in the *Very* Old West: England and Ireland in the Early Middle Ages." In *Crossed Paths: Methodological Approaches to the Celtic Aspect of the European Middle Ages*, ed. Benjamin Hudson and Vickie Ziegler, 39–60. Lanham, MD: University Press of America, 1991.

———. "Learning to Plead in Medieval Welsh Law." *Studia Celtica* 38 (2004): 107–23.

———. "Legal Writing in Medieval Wales: *Damweiniau I*." In *Wales and the Wider World: Welsh History in an International Context*, ed. T. M. Charles-Edwards and R. J. W. Evans, 57–85. Donington: Shaun Tyas, 2010.

———. *The Road to Judgment: From Custom to Court in Medieval Ireland and Wales*. Philadelphia: University of Pennsylvania Press, 1994.

Steiner, Emily. *Documentary Culture and the Making of Medieval English Literature.* Cambridge: Cambridge University Press, 2003.

Steiner, Emily, and Candace Barrington, eds. *The Letter of the Law: Legal Practice and Literary Production in Medieval England.* Ithaca, NY: Cornell University Press, 2002.

Stephenson, David. *The Governance of Gwynedd.* Cardiff: University of Wales Press, 1984.

———. "The Laws of Court: Past Reality or Present Ideal?" In *WKC*, 400–414.

———. *Welsh Law Courts*. Aberystwyth: Canolfan Uwchefrydiau Cymreig a Cheltaidd Prifysgol Cymru, 1980.

Stevens, Scott Manning. "Secular Heart and Sacred Brain." In *The Body in Parts: Fantasies of Corporeality in Early Modern Europe*, ed. David Hillman and Carla Mazzio, 262–82. New York: Routledge, 1997.

Strasser, Ulrike. *State of Virginity: Gender, Religion and Politics in an Early Modern Catholic State.* Ann Arbor: University of Michigan Press, 2004.

Sturges, Robert S. *Law and Sovereignty in the Middle Ages and the Renaissance.* Arizona Studies in the Middle Ages and Renaissance. Turnhout: Brepols, 2011.

Sturzer, Ned. "Inconsistencies and Infelicities in the Welsh Tales: Their Implications." *Studia Celtica* 37 (2003): 127–42.

———. "The Purpose of *Culhwch and Olwen*." *Studia Celtica* 39 (2005): 145–67.

Sullivan, C. W., III. "Inheritance and Lordship in *Math*." Reprinted in *Mabinogi*, 347–66.

———. *The Mabinogi: A Book of Essays*. New York: Garland, 1996.

Suppe, Frederick. "The Cultural Significance of Decapitation in High Medieval Wales and the Marches." *BBCS* 36 (1989): 147–60.

———. "Interpreter Families and Anglo-Welsh Relations in the Shropshire-Powys Marches in the Twelfth Century." *Anglo-Norman Studies* 30 (2007): 196–212.

Surridge, Marie. "Words of Romance Origin in the Four Branches of the Mabinogi and Native Welsh Tales.'" *Études Celtiques* 21 (1984): 239–55.

Sweetser, Eve E. "Figurative Harmony: Convergences and Tensions Among Metaphors and Metonyms for the Heroic Society in Early Welsh Poetry." In *Heroic Poets and Poetic Heroes in Celtic Tradition: A Festschrift for Patrick K. Ford, CSANA Yearbook* 3–4, ed. Joseph Falaky Nagy and Leslie Ellen Jones, 344–58. Dublin: Four Courts Press, 2005.

Tardif, Richard. "The 'Mistery' of Robin Hood: A New Social Context for the Texts." In *Robin Hood: An Anthology of Scholarship and Criticism*, ed. Stephen Knight, 345–61. Cambridge: D. S. Brewer, 1999.

Thibodeaux, Jennifer, ed. *Negotiating Clerical Identities: Priests, Monks, and Masculinity in the Middle Ages*. New York: Palgrave Macmillan, 2010.

Thomas, Brook. "Reflections on the Law and Literature Revival." *Critical Inquiry* 17 (1991): 510–39.

Thurneysen, Rudolf. "Celtic Law." In *CLP*, 49–70.

Valente, Roberta L. "Gwydion and Aranrhod: Crossing the Borders of Gender in *Math*." Reprinted in *Mabinogi*, 331–45.

Van Dam, Raymond. *Leadership and Community in Late Antique Gaul.* Berkeley: University of California Press, 1985.

Visconsi, Elliott. *Lines of Equity: Literature and the Origins of Law in Later Stuart England.* Ithaca, NY: Cornell University Press, 2008.

Wahlgren, Erik. "A Swedish-Latin Parallel to the *Joca Monachorum*." *Modern Philology* 36 (1949): 239–45.

Walker, David. *Medieval Wales*. Cambridge: Cambridge University Press, 1990.

Walters, D. B. "Comparative Aspects of the Tractates on the Laws of Court." In *WKC*, 382–99.

———. "Roman and Romano-Canonical Law and Procedure in Wales." In *Recueils de mémoires et travaux publiés par la Société d'histoire du droit et des institutions des anciens pays de droit écrit*." 15 (1991): 67–102.

———. "Société et droit dans la littérature du Pays de Galles au Moyen-Age." *Études Celtiques* 29 (1992): 415–22.

Warren, W. L. *Henry II*. Berkeley: University of California Press, 1973.

Watkins, Calvert. *How to Kill a Dragon: Aspects of Indo-European Poetics*. New York: Oxford University Press, 1995.

Weisberg, Richard, and Jean-Pierre Barricelli. "Literature and the Law." In *Interrelations of Literature*, ed. Joseph Gibaldi and Jean-Pierre Barricelli, 150–75. New York: Modern Language Association, 1982.

Weisberg. Robert. "The Law-Literature Enterprise." *Yale Journal of Law and the Humanities* 1.1 (1989): 1–68. Accessed August 7, 2014. http://digitalcommons.law.yale.edu/yjlh/vol1/iss1/4.

Welsh, Andrew. "*Manawydan fab Llŷr*: Wales, England, and the 'New Man.'" Reprinted in *Mabinogi*, 121–41.

———. "The Traditional Narrative Motifs of *The Four Branches of the Mabinogi*." *CMCS* 15 (Summer 1988): 51–62.

———. "Traditional Tales and the Harmonizing of Story in *Pwyll Pendeuic Dyuet*." *CMCS* 17 (Winter 1989): 15–41.

West, M. L. *Indo-European Poetry and Myth*. New York: Oxford University Press, 2007.

West, Robin. "Economic Man and Literary Woman: One Contrast." In *Law and Literature: Text and Theory*, ed. Leona Ledwon, 127–36. New York: Garland, 1996.

White, James Boyd. *Heracles' Bow: Essays on the Rhetoric and Poetics of the Law* Madison: University of Wisconsin Press, 1985.

———. "The Judicial Opinion and the Poem: Ways of Reading, Ways of Life." In *Law and Literature: Text and Theory*, ed. Leona Ledwon, 5–28. New York: Garland, 1996.

———. *The Legal Imagination*. Abridged ed. Chicago: University of Chicago Press, 1985.

White, Stephen D. "The Ambiguity of Treason in Anglo-Norman-French Law, c. 1150–c. 1250." In *Law and the Illicit in Medieval Europe*, ed. Ruth Mazo Karras, Joel Kaye, and E. Ann Matter, 89–102. Philadelphia: University of Pennsylvania Press, 2008.

———. "Prosecuting and Proving Sexual Infidelity at the Court of King Arthur: The Case of Guinevere v. Lanval." In *Law and Private Life in the Middle Ages: Proceedings of the Sixth Carlsberg Conference on Medieval Legal History 2009*, ed. Per Andersen and Mia Münster-Swendson, 123–48. Copenhagen: Djoef, 2011.

———. "Protection, Warranty, and Vengeance in *La chanson de Roland*." In *Peace and Protection in Medieval Europe*, ed. Tom Lambert and David Rollason, 155–67. Toronto: Pontifical Institute of Medieval Studies and Durham Centre for Medieval and Renaissance Studies, 2009.

Williams, Ifor. "Two Poems from the Book of Taliesin." In *The Beginnings of Welsh Poetry*, ed. Rachel Bromwich, 155–80. Cardiff: University of Wales Press, 1980.

Winward, F. "Some Aspects of the Women in *The Four Branches*." *CMCS* 34 (Winter 1997): 77–107.

Wogan-Browne, Jocelyn. "Chaste Bodies: Frames and Experiences." In *Framing Medieval Bodies*, ed. Sarah Kay and Miri Rubin, 24–42. Manchester: Manchester University Press, 1996.

Wood, Juliette. "The Calumniated Wife in Medieval Welsh Literature." *CMCS* 10 (Winter 1985): 25–38.

Woolgar, C. M. *The Great Household in Late Medieval England*. New Haven, CT: Yale University Press, 1999.

Wormald, Patrick. "*Lex Scripta* and *Verbum Regis*: Legislation and Germanic Kingship from Euric to Cnut." In *Legal Culture in the Early Medieval West: Law as Text, Image, and Experience*, ed. Patrick Wormald, 1–43. London: Hambledon Press, 1999.

———. *The Making of English Law: King Alfred to the Twelfth Century*. Oxford: Blackwell, 1999.

Yeager, R. F. "The Body Politic and the Politics of Bodies in the Poetry of John Gower." In *The Body and the Soul in Medieval Literature*, ed. Piero Boitani and Anna Torti, 145–65. Cambridge: D. S. Brewer, 1999.

Ziolkowski, Jan M., ed. *Obscenity: Social Control and Artistic Creation in the European Middle Ages*. Leiden: Brill, 1998.

INDEX

ACKNOWLEDGMENTS

Somewhat incredibly, my very first papers on the subject that became this project date back nearly two decades, which is a prolonged gestation period indeed. I wish I could say that it had simply taken me that long to do the research, since one might infer from that fact much noble and diligent toiling in the archives. In fact, however, an uncanny amount of that span was spent figuring out what I wanted to argue, which, though necessary, can be a frustrating way to spend time. Happily, a number of much wiser colleagues were willing to help me make my way through the thickets I encountered, and I am very grateful to them for their guidance. Thomas Charles-Edwards, Catherine McKenna, and Paul Russell read and commented on the penultimate draft of this book, and in so doing improved it immensely. All three of them had much more important things to do with their time, and I can only hope that the final product does justice to their generosity in some measure at least. I would also like to thank Emily Steiner, one of the readers for the University of Pennsylvania Press and a specialist in medieval English literature and law whose work I very much admire; her knowledge and perspective were invaluable to me in my revisions. Other notable scholars with whom I have discussed issues arising from this work include Liam Breatnach, Thomas DuBois, Patrick Ford, Elissa R. Henken, Lizabeth Johnson, Charles MacQuarrie, Amy Mulligan, Joseph Falaky Nagy, Huw Pryce, Sara Elin Roberts, Robert Stacey, and Eve Sweetser. Special thanks also go to colleagues who made their research available to me in advance of publication, most notably Thomas Charles-Edwards, Lizabeth Johnson, Patricia Malone, Bronagh Ní Chonaill, Paul Russell, and Alex Sigston. One of the very great pleasures of having worked for so long on a single project is the number of friends one makes along the way, and it is but a small measure of my gratitude to impute to their insights such merits as might accrue to this work and exculpate them from the errors that remain.

Several institutions and programs provided me with the opportunity to share my work with colleagues working in a variety of disciplines over the years, and it is a pleasure to be able to thank them here: the Celtic Studies Association of North America; the Centre for Medieval Studies of the University of Bergen; the Department of English of the University of Georgia; the Department of History and the School of Law of the University of Western Ontario; the Departments of Scandinavian Studies, Folklore, and Comparative Literature of the University of Wisconsin; the Dublin Institute for Advanced Studies; the Finnish Society for Celtic Studies and Societas Celtologica Nordica; the Program in Medieval Studies of Princeton University; and the Walter C. Schnackenberg Memorial Lecture Endowment of Pacific Lutheran University. The Medieval Academy of America and the University of Wales Press graciously permitted me to reprint earlier work for the purposes of this book, and I am grateful to them for their help. As always, Jerry Singerman and Ruth Mazo Karras of the University of Pennsylvania Press have been unfailingly fair and supportive.

Essential financial support for this project was provided by the School of Celtic Studies in the Dublin Institute for Advanced Studies, which generously welcomed me as a Visiting Scholar in September of 2011. I am also very grateful to the University of Washington Department of History and the Lawrence J. Roseman Fund for Excellence for helping to meet costs associated with publication. In these days of shrinking resources for the humanities particularly, it is impossible to overemphasize the importance of funds and institutions like these. Larry Roseman is someone who I know cares intensely about such matters, and I am honored to call him a friend as well as a benefactor.

And finally, on a more personal note. In January of 2012—on my birthday, in fact—my son Will, a Marine Corps sergeant on his fifth combat deployment, was killed in Afghanistan a month before he was scheduled to return home. As those who have lost someone essential to them will already be aware, a dark chasm opens up when one is faced with such a death. For a while, there is nothing but pain and an elemental search for a way to survive. Eventually, however, one has to make a choice: either one succumbs to the darkness and is swept away by it, or one finds the strength to resist it and walk again in the world. No one can do the latter alone, and I would not be here today—let alone have finished this book—had it not been for those who in loving and mourning Will so fiercely propped me up so that I could not fall. His death devastated two families and innumerable friends, and it is a tribute to the person he was that we reached out our hands to one another and became one. Anna, Kimmy, Max, Alex, Kyle, Gina, Lizzy, and Connor: you will carry him into the future, and I stand in awe of your courage. Bob, Dad, Elspeth, Wes, Alison, Jean, Tom, Charlie, Linda, Rosemarie, Amoeba, Squad, the WTF Book Club, Z, Devon, Larry, Bill, Pat, Joan, Darlene, and Denise: thank God tears and laughter go so well together, because otherwise I really haven't any idea where we would all be. My beloved Will: this book is for all the things you started (like your own book) but never got to finish. You mattered hugely to a very large number of people, and I am so very proud to be your mother. To this day, I still wonder whether you are okay.

Shortly after Will's death, my daughter Anna and I went to Charleston on a long-planned trip. While there, we toured an elegant old house, the last owner of which had chosen when he died to have his ashes placed in a hole at the heart of an ancient and stately tree on his property. It was a beautiful old veteran of another age: tall and leafy and gnarled in the way such things are. As we stood looking at it, it came to me then that this is how all of us will now find our way in the future, carrying Will always at the heart of us, being nurtured from within as we ourselves grow old in the world.